WHO'S WHO IN AVIATION HISTORY: 500 Biographies

Who's Who In Aviation History:

500 Biographies

William H. Longyard

Airlife

England

DEDICATION

To Margaret Strom

Whose kind words, and complete trust given to me at the beginning of this project supported me for the fourteen years it took to see it completed.

Copyright © William H. Longyard 1994

This edition published in the UK in 1994
by Airlife Publishing Ltd.

British Library Cataloguing in Publication Data
A catalogue record of this book is available
from the British Library

ISBN 1 85310 272 5

Printed in the U.K. by WBC, Bridgend.

Airlife Publishing Ltd.

101 Longden Road, Shrewsbury SY3 9EB

ACKNOWLEDGEMENTS

Two men in particular helped me to launch this project back in 1979. They are Mr Donald Lopez and Dr Howard Wolko of the National Air and Space Museum. I am indebted to Mr Lopez who spent many hours telling me of his fascinating aviation career which spanned membership in the Flying Tigers to acquaintanceships with Theodore von Karman, Hanna Reitsch, and many more. One of the most selfless acts I've ever witnessed was when Dr Wolko reached behind his desk and handed me his manuscript he had written for the *Who's Who* project on important scientists. That generous act was a crucial building block in this project. Over the years others helped too, including the well-known editor of *World War One Aero*, Leo Opdycke. I am just one more in the very long list of names that he has helped. Not a day goes by in my professional career that I do not make use of advice he has kindly given to me. Additionally, the prize-winning author Tom Foxworth yielded important information, as did the late Sir Thomas Sopwith. Peter Bowers read an early draft of the book and suggested some important changes, all of which I was glad to incorporate.

Additional information and assistance was provided by the following people: Gregory Alegi – Gruppo Amici Velivoli Storici, Italy; Lennart Arjevall – Svensk Flyhistorisk Förening, Sweden; Bill Baker – Antique Aeroplane Assoc. of Australia, Australia; Gilbert Biousse – Musée de l'Air, France; Peter Grosz – USA; Jim Halley – Air-Britain, England; Michael Hundertmark – Museum für Verkehr und Technik, Germany; Walter Bruce Johnson – USA; Lennart Johnsson – Sweden; Gordon Leith – RAF Museum, England; Herlnf Rasmussen – Denmark; Oswald Reeh – Germany; Walter Schroeder – Österreichishe Flugzeug Historiker; Harry Woodman – England.

Finally I would like to thank John Beaton, John Millington, and J. D. Storer, my editors at Airlife, for all of their help.

INTRODUCTION

If you seek to know the true story of aviation you will not find it on a modern day flight line. Nor will you find it lying about in heaps of aluminium stuffed in the back of the Smithsonian's restoration facility at Silver Hill. You will not find it splendidly presented in shiny cases containing the uniforms and medals of Guynemer at Les Invalides, or amongst the last possessions of a VC winner kept forever under halogen lights at the Imperial War Museum in Lambeth. For all its sound and fury, spectacle and expense, even Oshkosh Almighty is not the repository of aviation's true history. You may look a long time, and in every corner of the sky – but it is not to be found. That history is mostly now buried or burned. For the true history of aviation is not in the machines, the wings or engines. Nor in the countries, the companies, or conflicts. The true history of aviation was in the minds of the men who dreamt it — and then did it. If you want to know about aviation, then know about the men and women who gave this world its wings.

The book you are about to read was written out of necessity. The author found that there was not a single source published that comprehensively dealt with the most important aspect of aviation history – the people who lived and died it. I resolved to remedy this by writing this book. My first task was to enumerate those whose lives should be included. As time went by my list grew from a few dozen to a hundred, and then two hundred, and three, and so on until finally I had to set a practical limit, which was about 500. I do not dare suggest that these 500 names alone made aviation what it became. I acknowledge that that list is many times longer. What I present to you here is a list which contains 500 names which are among the most important. I assert no priority. The names rendered here include the daredevils and the killers, the Olympians and the unexpected, and the dreamers, but, mostly, the doers. Aviation history is littered with the names of those who would, but only rarely do we find those who did.

Some worthies that I would like to have included are not in this book. Undoubtedly you, the reader, will be disappointed to find one whose bold life is not chronicled here. Let us hope that the next edition will right that wrong.

William H. Longyard
Winston-Salem, North Carolina

Note on dates

In some instances it has not been possible to establish a subject's dates and these are marked with an asterisk(*). When there is some doubt about a date it is marked(?).

ABRUZZO, BEN L.
1937–1985

Ballooning has often been considered the sport of millionaires. It is not surprising that most of the nineteenth century aerostatic accomplishments were made by wealthy adventurers. Ben Abruzzo was a wealthy man when he began his quest to balloon across the Atlantic in the mid-1970s. He had earned his money the hard way though. Barely twenty years old, he had started a used car business upon discharge from the Air Force. He gave this up however to start a uranium mining business in New Mexico. When this failed, he found himself $40,000 in debt, and out of work. Determined to succeed, he became a door-to-door salesman, peddling encyclopedias, brooms, and pots and pans. He eventually worked himself out of debt completely, and having done so, started a very successful real estate business.

In 1977 Abruzzo joined with Maxie Anderson (qv) in an effort to fly the *Double Eagle* balloon across the Atlantic. This flight ended in near disaster off the northern coast of Iceland. With typical determination, the team tried again the next year and succeeded in the *Double Eagle II*.

Abruzzo and Anderson later became rivals in an attempt to fly across the continental United States in a balloon. Although he failed in this project, Abruzzo triumphed when he and partner 'Rocky' Aoki (qv) crossed the Pacific Ocean in 1981 with two others.

His hard-charging, high-flying career came to a fiery end when, as pilot in command, Abruzzo failed to coax his Cessna 421 back to the airport after a mechanical failure on take-off. The crash also killed his wife and four others.

ADER, CLÉMENT
1841–1925

Ader was born in Muret, France and became a prosperous electrical engineer, successfully experimenting with primitive telephones. In 1873, he became interested in the possibilities of human flight, but it wasn't until nine years later that he began construction of his first airplane. Named the *Éole,* it resembled a large bat on wheels. Ader built and installed a light steam engine in the *Éole,* and on 9 October, 1890, he achieved a powered 'hop' (as opposed to a controlled, sustained flight). This accomplishment, the world's first powered take-off from a level start, encouraged Ader to seek government support. (Du Temple and Mozhaiski (qqv) had begun their flights down ramps.)

He began to build a second craft, the *Avion II* (Avion is now the French word for airplane). Before completing this aircraft, he moved on to the *Avion III* which he tested in front of military observers on 12 and 14 October 1897. A similar design to the *Éole,* it failed too. On its second test run, it was blown off the track by wind. This laid the basis for Ader's claim nine years later, after Santos-Dumont's (qv) success, that he had actually flown in 1897.

The French military observers later stated categorically that Ader had never flown, thus Ader must join Gabriel Voisin (qv) as a man whose pride led him to so inflate his personal achievements that in reality, he cheapened them. Although Ader's hop was an impressive accomplishment, it influenced no subsequent airplane designs.

ALCOCK, SIR JOHN
1892–1919

Born in Manchester, Alcock grew up with engines and loved them. In 1910 he was smitten by the aviation bug and left home to become an aircraft mechanic at Brooklands. He managed to get flying lessons on Farman Longhorns and earned his brevet in 1912, No. 363. At the outbreak of World War I, he joined the RNAS and was posted as an instructor to Eastchurch. His true desire to be a combat pilot was fulfilled when he joined No. 2 wing in the Aegean. There he earned a DSC for gallantry after single-handedly attacking three enemy aircraft. He experimented with aircraft design and created a strange hybrid using salvaged parts from a Camel, Triplane, and other Sopwith odds and ends. He didn't get a chance to fly this airplane because he was shot down in September, 1917 by Turkish 'archie' fire. While in prison, a message was smuggled to him telling that his plane had flown. Luckily, he survived the Turkish imprisonment and returned to England in 1918.

His luck continued after the war when, unlike thousands of other ex-service pilots, he was able to secure a paying job as a pilot, this was for Vickers. On 14-15 June 1919 he and Arthur Whitten Brown completed the first non-stop flight across the Atlantic. Departing Newfoundland, they made a hazardous journey through terrible weather conditions before landing safely in Ireland. Both were knighted.

Six months later Alcock died while trying to land in heavy fog near Rouen, France.

AMUNDSEN, ROALD
1872–1928

Amundsen, a Norwegian, earned world renown as an explorer whose exploits included finding the magnetic North Pole in 1904–05, and reaching the South Pole in 1911, the first to do so. After World War I he turned to aircraft to aid him in exploration and used one to try to reach the North Pole in 1925. Although this failed, a year later he tried again using the airship *Norge* and her crew rented from the Italian government. Because Byrd (qv) had presumably already been the first to overfly the Pole, Amundsen decided to attempt the first trans-Polar flight. The airship left Spitzbergen in May 1926 with Amundsen quarrelling with the ship's captain Umberto Nobile (qv) over command. They successfully crossed the North Pole on a line from Spitzbergen to Teller, Alaska.

Two years later Amundsen disappeared while searching for his former rival Nobile, who had crashed on another Polar exploration.

ANDERSON, MAXIE LEROY
1934–1983

Maxie Anderson was lying in bed one evening in February, 1977 reading the *National Geographic* magazine when it occurred to him that he should be the first to fly across the Atlantic Ocean in a balloon. He had already

led an adventurous life. The son of a prosperous mine owner, he had often stood armed guard over the family's mining property. Boundary disputes were common in the wild early days of uranium prospecting. He routinely made large business deals for his father's company while in college at the University of North Dakota, where he earned a degree in industrial engineering. Seven years after graduating, he became president of the company and increased its value many times over.

After deciding to attempt the Atlantic crossing, he contacted his friend and fellow balloonist Ben Abruzzo (qv), who agreed to join him. Their first flight took place less than a year later in the custom-built, high tech balloon *Double Eagle*. This flight nearly cost them their lives when they entered a severe storm off the north coast of Iceland and were forced into the freezing North Atlantic waters. American rescue helicopters plucked them to safety.

After their initial failure they tried again. This time with better planning and equipment, but more importantly, with much more experience. They decided to take a third crew member to relieve the strain and chose Larry Newman (qv).

They lifted off from Presque Isle, Maine on 11 August 1978 and reached Misery, France in the early evening of the seventeenth. Not since World War II had a group of Americans been so warmly received in France.

Anderson soon separated from his ballooning associates, to pursue flying records with his son. In May 1980 they flew non-stop from San Francisco to Grosses Roches, Quebec. They claimed to be the first to fly across the North American continent non-stop, but the claim was challenged by many, including, ironically, Ben Abruzzo who was at that time preparing a trans-continental flight of his own.

Like his one-time friend Abruzzo, Anderson was killed in a flying accident – piloting a balloon.

ANDRÉE, SALOMON AUGUSTE
1854–1897

Andrée was Sweden's first aeronaut. As head of

the patent office, he was familiar with the many scientific advancements of the late nineteenth century. After meeting John Wise (qv) in 1876, he began to explore the possibilities of long distance flights. In 1894 he began a subscription campaign to raise funds for a flight across the North Pole. Two years later he was ready, but ominous bad weather delayed the launch until 11 July 1897, when he and his two companions set off from Spitzbergen. They never returned alive and weren't heard of again for thirty-three years.

Remarkably, in 1930, the frozen bodies of the unfortunate balloonists were discovered by the crew of the ship *Bratvaag*. Also discovered were their diaries and undeveloped films. The film was processed and the photographs printed as if they had only been taken the day before.

Their balloon had grounded 500 miles from the Pole, and the explorers had begun the long trek south. One by one they died, but they may not have died from the cold. One diary entry says that they shot and then ate a polar bear. Polar bear flesh is well known for carrying trichinosis, and this may have caused their lonely deaths.

Their bodies were returned to Sweden and buried with great honours.

ANTONOV, OLEG K
1906–1984
Antonov, as a youth, belonged to a model airplane club. He graduated from the Leningrad Polytechnic Institute in 1930 and found employment at a glider factory near Moscow. Despite typical political harassment from Stalin, he managed to design the A-7 cargo glider which flew both troops and supplies into combat during World War II. In 1943 he went to work for Yakovlev (qv).

After the war, Antonov was given his own design bureau at Kiev, and a year later, in 1947, appeared the An-2. The An-2 cargo plane was by Western standards an antiquated design. A single-engine biplane, it was stoutly designed and perfectly suited for duty in the harsh Soviet environment. Thousands were built.

The An-10 turbo-prop airliner of 1957 was considered to be the most comfortable of Soviet machines until structural failures caused it to be withdrawn from service. Another Antonov design, the An-22 of 1965 was for a time the largest aircraft in the world. It lost this title in 1968 to the Lockheed Galaxy.

ANZANI, ALESSANDRO
1877–1956
Speed and success were Anzani's two goals. From modest beginnings in Italy, he became a champion bicycle racer and then turned to motorcycles which he manufactured in Milan. Paris was the hub of the racing world during the waning days of La Belle Époque, and Anzani moved there to pursue his first rise to the top. Anzani's personality was said to be much like his engines: crude, but successful.

In 1909 Louis Blériot (qv) recognized the value of the unrefined but reliable Anzani fan engine and used it for his cross-Channel flight. After this, Anzani's success was assured. He opened factories in France and England, where he produced both motorcycles and aero-engines. He retired in Paris.

AOKI, HIROAKI 'ROCKY'
1938–
After moving to the United States from his native Japan, 'Rocky' Aoki opened a small restaurant in New York. From these humble beginnings he built a huge financial empire including the Benihanna restaurant chain. A thrill-seeker by nature, he was a keen powerboat racer until nearly killed in a crash. In 1981 he joined the *Double Eagle V* team which successfully flew the first man-carrying balloon across the Pacific Ocean. The flight from Japan lasted four days and ended in a crash landing near Covelo, California. Aoki was temporarily knocked unconscious but recovered to enjoy the champagne toast to victory.

ARCHDEACON, ERNEST
1863–1957

Practicing law made Archdeacon a rich man and he used his wealth to foster the development of aviation in Europe. As chairman of the Aéro-Club de France, he sponsored many aviation competitions, tapping his personal resources for prize money.

Gabriel Voisin (qv) got his start in aviation through the generosity of Archdeacon who financed Voisin's early gliding experiments and later the Syndicat d'Aviation which later still became Voison Frères. Capt. Ferber (qv) also benefited from Archdeacon's gifts.

European aviation truly benefited from his promotional efforts, the greatest of which was the organisation of the Rheims Week of 1909.

Though prominent for many years in French aviation, Archdeacon holds only one record: that of becoming the first airplane passenger in Europe on 29 May 1908.

ARCHYTUS
428–347 BC

Archytus was in every way a renaissance man, two millenia before the period began. A Greek from Tarentum, his interests included mathematics, philosophy, science and even war. His contemporaries and friends included Plato and Pythagoras.

Perhaps his most intriguing contribution to history was his claim to have invented a wooden bird capable of flight. It is presently believed that his invention was actually a reaction propelled device balanced on a long swing arm. Shaped like a bird, water may have been heated inside the body and the generated steam propelled it around the axis. It is also possible that he experimented with hot air balloons, but no accurate records survive.

ARMSTRONG, NEIL ALDEN
1930–

As the first human being ever to set foot on another heavenly body, Neil Armstrong was fortunate to be chosen to represent the thousands of men and women, beginning with Archytus (qv), who helped make his 'one small step for man, one giant leap for mankind', a reality.

Armstrong's dreams of wings became a reality as a sixteen-year-old Ohio youth, when he soloed. He trained as a naval flight cadet before assignment to Korea where he flew seventy-eight combat missions. Next came test pilot duties with the NACA and this led to acceptance into the astronaut program.

Although Armstrong had been closely associated with military aviation while working for NACA and NASA, he had become a civilian on returning from Korea. This civilian status gave him the edge when NASA made its choice for the first human to set foot on the Moon. Armstrong commanded *Apollo XI* during its historic mission in July 1969. His first footprint on the lunar surface, made on 21 July ranks, in the opinion of some scholars, with the voyage of Columbus or even the first sea creature struggling to dry land – but whatever its importance, Armstrong has always acknowledged that he was just a member of a team.

Armstrong eventually left NASA and went into private industry.

ARNOLD, HENRY HARLEY
1886–1950

'Hap' Arnold attended West Point, from where he graduated in 1907. He then saw a tour of duty in the Philippines, but in 1911 he transferred to the Army's aviation division. Orville Wright (qv) taught him to fly that year. In 1912 he made the first observations from an airplane reporting to the ground via radio. That year he set an altitude record of 6,450 feet (1,967m). During World War I he organized an air command in the Panama Canal Zone.

Following the war, Arnold championed the cause of airpower. He organized Army record-breaking flights, lobbied Congress for more funding, and was one of Billy Mitchell's (qv) few supporters. He had great organizational skills which he used to full capacity during

World War II as a member of the Joint Chiefs of Staff. He helped map out the American strategic bombing offensive which crippled German and Japanese industry.

Arnold's chief asset was his ability to foresee the changes being wrought by the twentieth century. He knew that the US military couldn't return to its conservative nineteenth century methods. He worked successfully to get the Congress to make the Air Force independent from the Army and became its first five star general. Before he died he helped map out the goals for the Air Force for the rest of the century, with emphasis on scientific advancement.

AUDEMARS, EDMOND
1882–1970
Audemar's slight stature allowed him to be one of the few people who could fly a Demoiselle. Of Swiss parentage, he became part of the Paris aviation scene flying mostly the Demoiselle. He participated in the 1910 Bournemouth air meet, the Belmont Park meet on Long Island, and was a member of the Moisant International Aviators troupe. His most famous flight occurred in 1912 when he was the first to fly from Paris to Berlin, which was considered at the time to be a goodwill gesture. At the end of his flying career he entered the aeronautical instrument business.

AURIOL, JACQUELINE MARIE-THÉRÈSE SUZANNE
1917–
Few women have led a more exciting life than Jacqueline Auriol. As a member of the French resistance in World War II, she was often on the run from the Gestapo. Following the war, she became a pilot, but was seriously injured in a plane crash in 1949. Though badly disfigured and against her family's wishes, she returned to aviation and in two years had qualified as a helicopter and jet pilot. She became a test pilot for the French government and set numerous speed records for which she won the Harmon Trophy. In 1955 she became one of the few women to break the sound barrier.

BACON, ROGER
c.1214–1292
Bacon was an Englishman who earned a Master of Arts degree at Oxford. He then moved to Paris where he continued his studies and lectured in Latin. He developed an interest in physical sciences and, ironically, this devoutly religious man invented gunpowder (for the Western world) in 1242. Twenty-six years later he produced the world's first encyclopedia at the request of Pope Clement IV. Later, the Church turned on Bacon, imprisoning him for heresy, claiming his scientific studies were ungodly.

Although da Vinci (qv) usually receives the credit, Bacon actually described the first designs for submarines, automobiles, and flying machines. He proposed a machine which could fly with wings made to flap by a man turning a crank and, five hundred years before the Montgolfier's (qv) first experiments, he correctly reasoned the principles of lighter-than-air flight.

BADEN-POWELL, MAJOR BADEN FLETCHER SMYTH
1860–1937
Baden-Powell was not the first to experiment with man-lifting kites. Credit for this may go to the Chinese, and there were even experimenters in nineteenth century Europe. Baden-Powell did, however, bring practical kites to the attention of British military authorities who made use of them in the Boer War for reconnaissance. Born into a wealthy family, his brother, Robert, was a military hero in the Boer War and founder of the Boy Scouts. After joining the Army, Baden requested transfer to the Military Balloon section at Aldershot where he helped develop military ballooning and began his kite experiments. In 1894 he became the first grown man to be lifted by a kite. (Pocock's (qv) kites raised his children.)

In 1880, he joined the Aeronautical Society of which he remained a member for over fifty years. Although not successful with heavier-than-air experiments other than his kites, which were only moderately so, he became the second Englishman to fly with Wilbur Wright (qv) in 1908. Not long after the flight, he stated prophetically: 'that Wilbur Wright is in possession of a power which controls the fate of nations, is beyond dispute'.

BADER, GROUP CAPTAIN SIR DOUGLAS ROBERT STEWART
1910–1982

Bader was an energetic young man when he received his commission into the RAF in 1930. His enthusiasm led him to take-off in a Bristol Bulldog the following year without permission for a bit of 'crazy flying'. Tragedy ensued when the plane crashed and he lost both legs. He was forced to leave the RAF even though he proved he could fly with two artificial legs. He returned to fighter duties at the outbreak of World War II, soon becoming famous as the leader of a Spitfire Wing, and amassing a score of 22·5 victories. He also pioneered fighter squadron tactics which helped defeat the Luftwaffe during the Battle of Britain. Bader was shot down in 1941 over France and taken prisoner. His celebrity status made him popular with his captors, and they arranged for him to receive a replacement artificial leg from England. Bader promptly returned the hospitality by trying to escape; the first of two unsuccessful bids. In 1946 he joined Shell Petroleum Co. and became managing director of Shell Aircraft Ltd. Bader devoted much of his time to helping the disabled.

BALBO, GENERAL ITALO
1896–1940

Balbo was Italy's best known flier during the inter-war years, and in his native country, his fame was rivalled only by Mussolini's.

Balbo joined Italy's Alpine troops during World War I, earning two medals for bravery and displaying his talents as a born leader. Not well educated, he joined the Fascist movement with the hope that they could restore Italy to it's former glory. In recognition of his support, Mussolini appointed Balbo Secretary of State for Air in 1926. This appointment surprised Balbo who knew nothing of aviation. With characteristic zeal he plunged into his new role, learning to fly and navigate in a short time. He then set about modernizing the Reggia Aeronautica which until then had been rife with corruption and mismanagement. Balbo led by example and was much admired by the ranks.

He managed to put Fascism in a good light, unlike Il Duce. In 1933, he brilliantly led twenty-four Savoia-Marchetti seaplanes across the Atlantic to a perfect landing on Lake Michigan near the Chicago Century of Progress Exposition. The American press hailed him as a twentieth century Columbus. In Italy, national pride swelled as Italian aviation went from triumph to triumph.

Mussolini knew he had a rival in the red-headed, gregarious Balbo and at the outbreak of World War II, when Balbo declared that Italy should side with Britain, Mussolini prepared to murder his enemy. At first, Balbo was appointed Governor of Libya. Not content with his political role, Balbo often led air patrols over the North African war zone. Returning one day from a patrol in 1940, his plane entered the traffic pattern where it was easily identifiable. Suddenly, his own base's anti-aircraft guns opened fire on him and his plane crashed. The Italian government called it a tragic accident.

BALCHEN, BERNT
1899–1973

Balchen was the world's most experienced Polar pilot. Born in Norway, he became an officer in that country's air force in 1924. A year later he was sent to rescue Amundsen's (qv) failed North Pole expedition, a task he accomplished. In 1926 he helped Amundsen in preparation for another Polar flight, but did not join his flight crew due to weight restrictions. He then gave Richard Byrd (qv) helpful advice for his flight which beat Amundsen over the Pole. In appreciation, Byrd took Balchen with him on a promotional tour of the United States and while there, he joined the Fokker company as a test pilot. In 1927 he piloted Byrd's trans-Atlantic Fokker tri-motor, the *Atlantic,* across the ocean, and barely reached Europe, having to land on the French coast. The next year he successfully rescued the stranded *Bremen* crew in Labrador. In 1929 he made perhaps his greatest flight when he flew Richard Byrd over the South Pole in a 1,600-mile (2,574km) display of outstanding navigational skill. He made other Antarctic flights with both Byrd and Ellsworth (qv) prior to joining Royal Norwegian Airlines as their operations manager in 1935

When the Germans invaded Norway in 1940, Balchen was in the United States. He immediately joined the RAF and ferried aircraft between San Diego and Singapore. In 1941 he joined the American Army Air Force and established the Blue West 8 air base in Greenland. There, he continued to rescue downed airmen, and once took part in the destruction of a secret German meteorological station in northern Greenland. In 1944 he organized a clandestine air service from Scotland to Scandinavian countries which rescued airmen, and dropped supplies and agents to resistance forces. He flew on 110 such missions. After the war he returned to Royal Norwegian Airlines, but in 1948 he rejoined the US Air Force and was given command of a rescue squadron in Alaska. He became a US citizen in 1931.

BALDWIN, FREDERICK WALKER
1882(?)–1948
'Casey' Baldwin attended the University of Toronto, where he and his friend J.A.D. McCurdy (qv) studied engineering. It was his friendship with McCurdy which brought Baldwin into contact with Graham Bell (qv) and membership in the AEA. Baldwin was selected to pilot the AEA's first successful machine, the *Red Wing,* and thus on 12 March 1908, became the first British subject to pilot an

airplane. This flight took place at Hammondsport, NY where Curtiss (qv) had his manufacturing facilities.

In 1909, the AEA dissolved with Baldwin, McCurdy, and Bell founding the Canadian Aerodrome Co, Canada's first aircraft company. It folded a year later. Baldwin accepted an offer from Curtiss to manage the Curtiss plant in Toronto which built JN-3 Canucks during World War I. After the war he experimented on hydrofoils with Graham Bell, and set a world water speed record.

BALDWIN, THOMAS SCOTT
1860–1923
Baldwin started his life-long career as a showman while still a young man, out of necessity. During the American Civil War, his parents were murdered in a raid on their Missouri home. At 14, Baldwin ran away from an orphanage and found work on the railroad before joining a circus. He loved the life of a travelling showman and came to prominence when he began flying balloons at local fairs. In 1887, he dropped from a balloon under a parachute of his own design for the first time. This caused a sensation each time he performed it and his usual fee for a drop at a fair was a hefty $2,000.

From balloons he turned to dirigibles, and completed the first successful American dirigible, the *California Arrow*, in 1904. In this machine, he made the first flying circuit in America on 3 August 1904 near Oakland, California. The success of the *Arrow* lay in the fact that it used a Curtiss motorcycle engine. In November 1904, Baldwin went to talk to Curtiss (qv) about future dirigible projects, and can thus be credited with formally bringing Curtiss's attention to aviation. In 1908, Baldwin sold the US Signal Corps America's first powered aircraft, *Army Dirigible No. 1*. It used a Curtiss engine also.

BALL, CAPTAIN ALBERT, VC
1896–1917
Ball was born into a wealthy family in Nottingham, England, and achieved many of

his successes through brilliant marksmanship.

Ball was a mystery to his comrades. A quiet, devoutly religious youngster, he tended to live apart from the rest of the flyers. He kept a neat vegetable garden and rabbit pen at his camp, and when not out on a lone patrol or practising his marksmanship, he could be heard softly playing a violin.

His fighting tactics were well calculated and he greatly admired Nungesser and Fonck (qqv). His combat experiences were sometimes stranger than fiction. On one patrol, while fighting two German Albatroses single-handedly, he ran out of ammunition. Instead of diving for home, he out-manoeuvred both his opponents, chasing them back to their own bases armed only with a pistol!

On 17 May 1917 his string of forty-four victories ended when his plane crashed mysteriously while engaged in combat. Ball won a posthumous VC. The British press had never been allowed to create heroes out of their aces the way other countries had done. The General Staff felt that air aces were no more than soldiers of the sky. Trenchard (qv) changed this policy and Ball became the first well known British air hero.

BANFIELD, LINIENSCHIFFSLEUTNANT GODFREY RICHARD
1890–1986
Banfield was born the son of an Irishman who was an officer in the Austro-Hungarian Navy. Like his father, Banfield entered that navy, changing his nationality from British to Austrian. He saw sea duty from 1910 through 1912. In 1913 he was sent to Paris to study aviation, returning to Pola for flight instruction.

Despite a seriously broken leg from a crash into a naval vessel, Banfield was on active duty when Italy declared war against the Austro-Hungarians in May 1915. He undertook dangerous one-man patrols over the harbour at Venice during which he shot down a number of enemy planes. When the Italians and French attempted to bomb Trieste harbour, Banfield's adept defence brought down more enemy planes. During one epic action he single-handedly defended the harbour against eight intruding planes, of which he shot down three. His war total is variously assigned at nine or more, but was probably around twenty-one. His bravery earned him the title of 'the Eagle of Trieste'.

After the war he became an engineer in England for a short time, but moved to Italy where he became an Italian subject in 1920. For many years he ran a marine salvage company started by his wife's family. He built it up to be one of the most successful in Europe, and it was responsible for clearing the Suez Canal after the war in 1956.

BARACCA, MAGGIORE FRANCESCO
1888–1918
Baracca seemed to personify the chivalric image of the World War I pilot-hero. Handsome and dashing, he came from a well-to-do Italian family. He began his aviation career when he transferred from the cavalry to the air corps in 1912 during the Libyan war. By 1915 he was back in Italy where he achieved ace status in November 1916. Baracca's fame rose steadily in Italy until March, 1918 when he was shot and killed while strafing Austrian ground troops.

Baracca's spirit lives on today though. In the mid-1920s his mother presented her son's personal emblem, the prancing horse, to a young Italian race driver. Enzo Ferrari has placed the emblem on all his cars ever since.

BARBER, HORATIO C.
1875–1964
One of the most unique British aircraft built before World War I was the Valkyrie, a monoplane canard. Its designer, Horatio Barber, formed the Aeronautical Syndicate Ltd in 1909 to market the plane. Safe and reliable, it failed to find a large audience even though

Barber opened a flying school at Hendon in 1910. In 1911 it earned its place in the record books when it became the first plane ever to deliver cargo by air in the British Isles. The payload was a box of lightbulbs which was flown from Shoreham to Hove. For this flight Barber earned £100 which he donated to the Royal Aeronautical Club so that they could establish the Britannia Trophy.

Though the Valkyrie proved to be a very safe aircraft, monoplanes were generally frowned on in Britain at that time, and lack of orders forced the sale of Aeronautical Syndicate Ltd to Handley Page (qv) in 1912. Barber continued his career in aviation as a flight instructor and author.

Ever ebullient Pancho Barnes.

BARKER, MAJOR WILLIAM GEORGE, VC
1894–1930

Barker grew up in Manitoba, Canada. His interests in horse riding and guns led him to join the Canadian Mounted Rifles when World War I began. The Western Front needed no mounted troops in 1915, so Barker found himself ingloriously stuck in the mud with the rest of the 'Tommies'. He requested a transfer to the RFC, which he entered as a mechanic in December. After working his way up to observer he was allowed to train as a pilot. He soloed after only an hour's training and was back in the front line in January 1916.

He quickly proved both his bravery and skill, but more importantly, showed that he could fight as a team member. Barker's most famous battle occurred only two weeks before the end of the war when he *single-handedly* engaged over fifty enemy aircraft. Though wounded three times, he brought down four Germans and then dived for his own lines where he crash-landed.

Barker survived the war, gaining fifty-two victories and the VC. He returned to Canada where he helped found the RCAF and one of Canada's first airlines with his friend Billy Bishop (qv). In 1930, a plane he was test piloting crashed, and he was killed.

BARNES, FLORENCE LEONTINE LOWE
1901–1976

Though she was the granddaughter of Thaddeus Lowe (qv), few people could have guessed that Florence Lowe, daughter of a dignified Californian 'society' family, would choose amongst her many careers, the life of a hobo, sailor, stunt pilot and saloon owner. But she did – and she preferred to be called Pancho.

Pancho started out to lead a 'normal' life. In fact, she married a preacher, C. R. Barnes, not long after ending her formal education that included time at an all-boys school and a convent. Pancho never fitted in as a 'tea party' hostess, maybe it was her rattlesnake mouth, so she ran away from home and joined a circus. Leaving that, she wandered through North and South America often pretending to be a man. She earned her keep working odd jobs, including mate on a cargo boat. In Mexico she made friends with gun-running bandits and picked up the handle 'Pancho'.

Always looking for adventure and something new, she latched onto airplanes, learning to fly at age twenty-seven. Through great ability and a mouth to match, she talked and flew her way into a job with Union Oil. Women pilots were a novelty then and were good publicity. She went into racing next and in the early 1930s became a stunt pilot in Hollywood. Amongst her credits was work in Hughes' (qv) *Hell's Angels*. While in Hollywood she fought to get fair treatment for underpaid movie pilots by helping organize the Motion Pictures Pilots Association.

During World War II she opened Pancho's Fly Inn outside Muroc Field near Los Angeles. As Muroc later had its name officially changed to Edwards Air Force Base, Pancho's Fly Inn unofficially had its name changed to the Happy Bottom Riding Club by the rough and ready military test pilots who made it their after- work watering hole. Anything went at the Riding Club and Pancho was known and loved by all the patrons, some of whom were soon to become heroes as astronauts. The wild atmosphere of the Club caused the government to force its closure, and not even Pancho's verbal hurricane could save it for her boys.

BARNWELL, CAPTAIN FRANK SOWTER
1880–1938
Barnwell apprenticed as an automobile and maritime engineer in Scotland before joining his brother in 1905, to build an airplane powered by a five horsepower motorcycle engine. Though it failed, Barnwell pursued his aeronautical interests and in 1911 he became a draughtsman for the Bristol and Colonial Aeroplane Co. He was soon designing planes including the Scout, and later the monoplane Bullet. The British prejudice against monoplanes caused the excellent Bullet not to be adopted by the air services. Barnwell joined the RFC so that he could better learn the actual needs of combat pilots. From his experiences, he designed the F-2b, the long-lived Bristol Fighter (Brisfit).

Never one to sit and watch others take chances, Barnwell insisted on test flying some of his own designs, and the Bristol company lost several of its valuable prototypes to Barnwell's poor piloting skills. In the 1920s, he created the Bulldog, but his greatest design may

have been an airplane built from private funds because the military wouldn't finance it. This plane, capable of out-flying any RAF plane of the day, became known as the Blenheim. An all metal monoplane, it forced the RAF Marshals to re-examine their preference for biplanes.

Barnwell was killed in 1938 piloting a light plane, and all three of his sons were killed in World War II – two while flying Blenheims.

BATTEN, JEAN
1909–1982
Less well-known than such contemporaries as Amelia Earhart and Amy Johnson (qqv), Jean Batten was nevertheless an equally great flier. A dentist's daughter from Rotorua, New Zealand, she became interested in flying after reading accounts of Bert Hinkler's (qv) flights in 1928. Within a year, she journeyed to London to become a pilot.

Three years later she attempted a flight from Lympne, Kent to Australia. Engine trouble forced her to return to England, but she tried again the next year. This flight also ended in failure. In 1934 she tried for a third time. In a little over two weeks she reached Darwin, thus breaking the existing women's record. Before climbing out of the cockpit to accept the congratulations of the public, she characteristically powdered her nose. It was her style.

After this flight, she went on to make other notable flights, including the first women's UK to Australia and return flight, a thirteen-hour fifteen-minute flight from Britain to Brazil, and a dangerous crossing of the Tasman Sea in 1936.

Though she lived well into the age of the Concorde, she died in obscurity and was laid to rest in a simple grave after having needlessly died because she refused to tell anyone of a dog bite that she had received which became infected.

BEACHEY, LINCOLN
1887–1915
Lincoln Beachey was America's first great stunt pilot and defined the genre for all time. Born in

Ohio, he joined Tom Baldwin's (qv) air circus around 1906. He and Roy Knabenshue (qv) had a team act in which they would 'race' dirigibles in front of the enthralled public, most of whom had never seen a balloon, let alone an aerial 'speed duel'. Aerostation was too tame for Beachey so in 1910 he switched from dirigibles to airplanes – which were faster and more dangerous. He joined the Curtiss team and soon became their 'ace' pilot. No stunt was too dangerous for Beachey, who was the first American to loop the loop and fly upside down. He considered his ex-wife more dangerous than flying 'hands off', as he often did, so he deposited the huge fees he earned at each show in dozens of banks across the country so she couldn't find them.

In 1911 he flew *under* Niagara Falls by diving over the rim of the falls and flying through the swirling clouds. His fame grew steadily and in 1913 he began a series of aircraft versus automobile races. These classic 'races' were in fact staged events between Beachey and legendary racer Barney Oldfield. Oldfield had been temporarily forced out of regular automobile racing when he defied the racing establishment and raced the famous boxer Jack Johnson, a black man. By alternating victories, Beachey and Oldfield held public interest all summer long, and earned large gate fees.

Beachey's flying grew bolder and bolder and in 1914 he set a world record by looping seven consecutive times. Perhaps the expression that there are no old, bold pilots originated with Beachey's death in 1915. In March of that year, while performing his crowd-thrilling 'dip of death' in front of a home town audience in San Francisco, his plane, which he had designed, broke up in the air and crashed into San Francisco Bay where he drowned. It's possible that not all of his bank accounts were ever found.

BÉCHEREAU, LOUIS
1880–1970
Béchereau studied at the École d'Art et Métiers d'Angers before founding his own engineering firm in 1909. Later that year, Armand Deperdussin (qv) asked him to build a mock aeroplane to display in a Paris department store. Deperdussin hoped to draw crowds to displays of his textile goods. Béchereau built the plane which so pleased Deperdussin that the latter proposed the formation of a company to build real aircraft. Société Pour les Appareils Deperdussin (SPAD) was born in 1910. Béchereau's talents made the company an immediate success. He pioneered construction techniques years ahead of the competition, most notably monocoque construction. Béchereau developed the monocoque technique from the suggestion of a Swiss marine engineer named Eugene Ruchonnet.

'Deps' won many races prior to the war, including the 1913 Schneider Trophy. In 1912 a monocoque land plane broke the 100mph 'barrier' for the first time. Louis Blériot (qv) bought the company in 1913, but retained Béchereau as chief designer. By 1916 he had designed the Spad VII, which became a favourite mount of the aces. From this design came better military pursuit planes, which evolved after the war into fine racers.

BEECH, OLIVE ANN
1903–1993
BEECH, WALTER HERSCHEL
1891–1950
Olive and Walter Beech, a wife and husband team, are more responsible than anyone for growth of business general aviation in America.

Walter gained early experience with aircraft when he and a friend rebuilt a Curtiss pusher in 1913. Walter soloed the plane early the next year. During World War I he joined the Signal Corps and served as an aircraft mechanic at Rich Field near Waco, Texas. After the war, he became a salesman for Laird, but was forced to supplement his income by barnstorming. In 1924, he and Lloyd Stearman (qv) quit the company, which by then had become Swallow, feeling that aircraft should be built from steel tubing and not wood as was Swallow's practice. Together with another barnstormer, Clyde Cessna (qv), they formed Travel Air which immediately captured a large share of the commercial aircraft market. Stearman was the chief designer, and Walter had the sales ability. Secretarial duties were handled by Olive Mellor who was hired in 1925.

Stearman quit in 1926 to form his own company, and Cessna left the next year to do the same. Travel Air continued to be successful, but Walter sold it to Curtiss-Wright in 1929. His keen business sense perhaps had warned him of the coming Depression. He spent the next three years working for Curtiss-Wright, although he did take time out in 1930 to marry his secretary who then became Olive Beech. In 1932 they gambled their futures to start the Beech Aircraft Company. Despite the horrible economic conditions, Walter felt there was still a market for large, luxury executive aircraft. In seven months, with a team of less than twenty men, the company built its first aircraft – the Model 17 Staggerwing. The Beechs had scored a direct hit.

With the Model 17, Beech began it's dominance of the business aviation market. With the growth of this market, there was an ever-increasing demand for more sophisticated communications and pilots. This opened the doors for general aviation as it developed after World War II.

The aircraft business has always been competitive, but the Beechs were able to meet all-comers. In 1940, when American aircraft manufacturers were reaping huge war profits, a group of Beech directors tried to gain control of the company from Olive and Walter. Both were in hospital at the time, Walter in a coma, and Olive having just given birth. Outraged, Olive had herself discharged from the hospital, returned to the Beech offices and fired the disloyal directors. In 1953 she faced a similar challenge and triumphed.

The Beechs' success was due to combining excellent engineering with an almost unfailing business sense. When Walter died in 1950, Olive took charge and remained in the captain's seat for over thirty years

BELENKO, VIKTOR IVANOVICH
1947–

Though the Soviet Union had little trouble getting reams of valuable technical data from the West, the reverse was not true. That is why Viktor Belenko's defection in 1976 was such an important intelligence bonanza for the West.

Belenko led a life typical of post-war Russia. Living alternately with divorced parents, he had no shoes until the age of six. Schooling was rudimentary but included a full dose of anti-West propaganda which served to increase his interest in the forbidden hemisphere. Though stocked only with sanctioned books, his school library did contain a book by de Saint-Exupéry (qv) and this fired Belenko's desire to fly. In 1965 he joined the military, and learned to fly from a woman instructor. Belenko shared the thrill of freedom that flying offers to pilots the world over, but for a man raised in Russia, it was a more intense feeling.

Belenko married and became a father, but his domestic happiness was no greater than his parents. He drew assignments at various air bases in the Soviet Union, and in 1976 found himself stationed in the far east.

The complete details of how Belenko planned his flight to Japan may never be known. He may have done it on his own, but some claimed that he was helped by a British agent. On 6 September 1976 he took off in a super secret MiG-25 on a routine training mission, but instead of returning to base, flew straight for Japan. Belenko was liable to be shot down by either Japanese defence forces, or his own country's jets. The harrowing flight was made more difficult through strict radio silence and bad weather. With little fuel left, he made a landing at Hakodate airport. He hoped to trade the plane for asylum in the United States.

Belenko was granted asylum, but didn't have to make a deal for it. He co-operated fully with Western intelligence as they disassembled the MiG to make a detailed inspection. The Soviets made threats against Belenko and his family, but the pilot refused to return. He had earned his freedom.

The West learned much from the MiG-25,

which they later returned to the USSR. They learned that it wasn't a crude copy of an F-15 as some opponents of military funding in Washington had claimed. It turned out to be a high performance fighter which posed a greater military threat than had been anticipated. Belenko provided valuable details about training and the morale of the Soviet Air Force. These details aided greatly in the West's future defence planning against the USSR.

BELL, ALEXANDER GRAHAM
1847–1922
Bell was twenty-three in 1870 when his father brought him to Canada from Edinburgh. Two years later, the young Bell had moved south to Boston where he opened a school for the deaf. His interest in speech and communication led him to wonder if words could be transferred by electrical means. With the help of Thomas Watson, an electrical engineer, Bell tackled the problem and only a few years later, in 1876, received a patent for the telephone. He was not the only scientist working on the problem, but he was the first to realize the vast commercial potential of his work, and this earned him a fortune.

By 1907, Bell had read vague accounts of the Wright brothers' (qv) work and decided to form his own scientific association to build a flying machine. He hired two engineering students, F. W. Baldwin and J. McCurdy (qqv), and an American Army officer T. Selfridge (qv), to assist him. He also contacted Glenn Curtiss (qv) who agreed to provide engine expertise. In less than a year this group, known as the Aerial Experiment Association, and financed largely by Bell's wife, had succeeded in building and flying a bamboo biplane, the *Red Wing*. By the summer of 1908, they had built a truly practical airplane, with ailerons and a wheeled undercarriage, the *June Bug*. Curtiss flew this plane on 4 July 1908 thus making the first official public flight in America. (It had previously flown on 21 June 1908 but that flight was not monitored.)

The AEA was dissolved in March 1909,

though Bell continued to experiment with tetrahedral kites.

As if inventing the telephone and spawning a new family of aeroplanes weren't enough, Bell became interested in hydrodynamics and designed an improved hydrofoil boat. With such a boat, he established the world's water speed record in 1918. Nearing the end of his career, he said that all of his accomplishments, the one he was most proud of was having been able to teach the deaf.

BELL, LAWRENCE DALE
1894–1956
Lawrence Bell began his aviation career at the age of eighteen, as a mechanic for his barnstorming brother Grover, and Lincoln Beachey (qv). Not a true engineer, but nevertheless good with his hands, he converted a Martin biplane into a bomber for the Mexican rebel Pancho Villa. In 1913 he went to work for Glenn Martin (qv) as a shop hand. He soon rose to foreman and one day suggested that Martin hire a proper engineer. He recommended Donald Douglas (qv). In 1917, then only twenty-three years old, he was put in charge of building a new plant in Cleveland. In 1928 Rueben Fleet (qv) hired him as vice-president at Consolidated in Buffalo, New York. He stayed seven years until Consolidated moved to San Diego. In 1935 he formed Bell Aircraft to promote advanced military aircraft concepts. Bell's willingness to pursue original ideas led to the development of the mid-engined Airacobra series, the X-1 rocket plane and a very successful family of helicopters.

BELLANCA, GUISEPPI MARIO
1886–1960
Bellanca was born in Sicily to a working class family. His father noticed his mathematical ability and worked hard to send him to the Technical Institute in Milan. In 1908, he built his first airplane, a two-seat pusher biplane. It wasn't very successful and after building a monoplane, he emigrated to the United States

in 1910 the hope of finding more funds. In 1911 he built a parasol plane, his first successful aircraft, in which he taught himself to fly. He started a flying school at Mineola on Long Island, where he taught hundreds to fly before and during World War I. One of his students was Fiorello La Guardia, who later became a World War I pilot and later still New York city's greatest mayor. During the early 1920s he continued to build aircraft, mostly passenger planes, while serving as a consulting engineer to Wright. In 1927 he formed his own company to build large monoplanes. One of their first aircraft was actually built in 1926 and became known as the *Miss Columbia*. The future of Bellanca's company may have been entirely different had Charles Lindbergh (qv) been allowed to buy the plane. He wasn't, but the aircraft eventually crossed the Atlantic with Clarence Chamberlain and Charles Levine.

Bellanca's aircraft were noted for their aerofoil-shaped cabins and lift struts. Although the struts did provide additional lift, the cabin profile was purely cosmetic. Bellanca retired not long after World War II, but his company was still in business in the 1980s.

BELLONTE, MAURICE
1896(?)–1984

Maurice Bellonte was Dieudonné Costes' (qv) taciturn navigator for several record-setting flights in the 1920s, but is best remembered for perfectly navigating the Atlantic on the first Paris to New York direct flight in 1930. It was due to Bellonte's meticulous planning that Costes was able to fly the Point d'Interrogation through terrible weather from Le Bourget to Curtiss Field, Long Island after failing on a similar attempt a year earlier.

Fifty years after the historic flight, Bellonte again flew from Paris to New York – this time on a Concorde. The 1930 flight took thirty-seven hours, while the Concorde arrived in three.

BENNETT, FLOYD
1890–1928

Bennett was raised in upstate New York. He left school at seventeen to become an automobile mechanic and soon bought part-ownership of a garage. In 1917 he joined the Navy hoping to become a pilot. Flight training was denied as the Navy considered him over-age and under-educated.

He stayed with the Navy after the war and learned to fly independently. In 1925 he was assigned to Byrd's (qv) aviation command in Greenland. Byrd was impressed with Bennett and asked him to pilot the trans-Polar flight of 1926. They accomplished this in the *Josephine Ford* Fokker Tri-motor. In 1927 they planned to make a New York to Paris flight, but Bennett was seriously injured in a test flight of the Fokker Trimotor *America* in April.

Having recovered from his injuries, Bennett set out with Balchen (qv) to rescue the stranded *Bremen* crew. On the way to Labrador, he became ill and died in Quebec.

BENNETT, JAMES GORDON, JR.
1841–1918

Bennett obtained great wealth from his father who founded the *New York Herald* newspaper. When the younger Bennett inherited the family empire at the age of thirty-one he was already a well-known yachtsman, backer of sporting events, and businessman. Bennett increased his fortune by creating the demand for the news which he also supplied. Sending Henry Stanley to Africa to find Dr Livingstone in 1870 was just one of many news-generating devices he developed. Not all of his ideas were made just to benefit himself. He helped to revolutionize the communications industry by organizing a world-wide cable company, and an early storm warning network for ships.

When not on his lavish yacht, Bennett spent most of his time in Paris. He had been ostracised from New York society after fighting a duel with his one-time fiancée's brother. His self-imposed exile was lived in complete luxury, and he was a leader of French society. He began European editions of the *Herald*, from which today's International *Herald Tribune* is descended.

He sponsored many boating and automobile races, but is best remembered for the Gordon Bennett International Balloon races which ran between 1906 and 1938, though cancelled from 1915–1919 due to war, 1931 due to the world depression, and finally dying in 1939 when Germany invaded that year's host country Poland.

His other great trophy contest was the Gordon Bennett Cup, or Coupe Internationale d'Aviation, which started at the Rheims meet in 1909. That year's victor was Glenn Curtiss (qv).

BENSEN, IGOR BASIL

1917–

Bensen was born in Russia, but emigrated while still young with his parents. He earned a degree from the University of Louvain, Belgium before settling in the United States. From 1940 to 1951 he was an experimental engineer and test pilot with General Electric where he gained experience with gyrocopters and helicopters. He helped develop an automatically stable rotor head which made helicopters easier to fly.

In 1951 he went to Kaman as their head of research, but left in 1953 to form Bensen Aircraft, which developed ultra low cost gyrocopters for the homebuilders' market. Bensen earned a patent for the Rotochute, a strap-on gyrocopter blade for use instead of a parachute. Though Bensen is most famous for his inexpensive gyros, he continued to experiment with automatically stable helicopters and formed a company in the mid -1980s to market this advancement.

BERLIN, DONOVAN REESE

1898–1982

After earning an engineering degree from Purdue, Berlin went to work for the Army in the aerodynamics lab at McCook Field. He followed this with several years each at Douglas and Northrop, where he designed the Alpha and Gamma, before joining Curtiss in 1934. Berlin was responsible for designing the famous Hawk series, which culminated in the P-40.

Berlin first laid out plans for the P-40 in 1937 when the Army announced it would fund the Allison V-1710 engine. He hoped to design the world's most advanced aircraft, which the P-40 never became. It was noted for its reliability and ruggedness however.

During the war Berlin went to General Motors where he helped to organize their aircraft production lines, and developed Allison engine installation methods. Later still he served with McDonnell and then became president of Piasecki, which later became Vertol.

BERLINER, HENRY ADLER

1895–*

Emile Berliner came to the US from Germany in 1870. In 1878 he started work as an equipment inspector for Bell Telephone where he began to experiment with improved microphones. After earning patents for his loose contact microphone, he broadened his scope to include experiments with engines, lectures on preventative medicine, and a treatise on religion.

Henry, son of Emile, got his start in aviation when he and his father designed and built one of the first experimental helicopters in the US. Powered by a Bentley engine, it flew for 1·5 minutes in 1924.

In 1926 Henry formed the Berliner Aircraft Company which became Berliner-Joyce in 1929. Henry left the next year to form ERCO, which produced production tools before turning to aircraft. The ERCO Ercoupe became one of America's most loved aircraft.

BIARD, HENRI C.

1892–*

Biard was born into an Anglo-French family and brought up in England. At the age of eighteen he went to the Grahame-White school at Hendon to take flight instruction. After waiting in vain the first day for a pilot to take him up, he became impatient and bluffed his way onto a warmed-up box-kite the next day.

Without any instruction, he managed to take-off and made a safe two mile flight.

After receiving more formal instruction, he taught flying at the school before joining the RFC in 1914. In the RFC, he continued instructing, but also took part in early anti-submarine patrols, and shot down an Albatros over the Western Front.

In 1919 he joined Supermarine and ran a cross-Channel air service for them, while also serving as a test pilot. In 1922 he captured the Schneider Trophy in Naples in the Supermarine Sea Lion, but three years later was injured when the Supermarine S-4 developed wing flutter at full speed and crashed.

BIRKIGT, MARC
1878–1953
Born in Geneva, Birkigt studied engineering and while still in his teens, obtained a job designing mining equipment. In 1898 he moved to Spain where he had been offered a job designing trains. In 1904 he became a partner in Sociedad Hispano-Suiza Fabrica de Automobiles. The engines he designed were soon recognized as innovative and dependable. By 1913 the company opened a second plant in Paris. Hispano-Suiza automobiles were the normal mounts of rich European scions who appreciated their speed and slender lines.

Birkigt turned to aero engine design and in 1915 his first V-8 roared into life. It's high performance and low weight helped turn average aircraft designs into thoroughbreds, such as the S.E.5A

Though the post-war automobile business remained good for Hispano-Suiza, Birkigt expanded the company line to include armaments. He personally designed a 20mm cannon which remained an Allied standard for two decades.

The automobiles are Birkigt's greatest legacy to the world. All his designs are highly prized as they represented the best engineered and perhaps most beautiful cars available in their day. The stork emblem, which became the mascot of all 'Hissos' after World War I, was adopted from the flying stork painted on the side of Georges Guynemer's (qv) Spad. Birkigt had befriended the ace during the war and used the emblem to preserve the memory of the fallen hero.

BISHOP, MAJOR WILLIAM AVERY
1894–1956
'Billy' Bishop's career has led to great dispute amongst aviation historians. To some, he was the most tenacious ace on the Allied side. To others, he was a lying 'miles glorious' who exaggerated his victories, and invented certain combats. That Bishop shot down a great many aircraft is beyond dispute

He was kicked out of the Royal Military College in Ontario in the spring of 1914 for cheating on a test. It was later said that it was due to his being allergic to horses. The advent of the war caused him to be recalled and he was sent to England as part of the Canadian cavalry. While in London, he met a wealthy socialite who helped him to get transferred to the air force. He was a below average pilot and wrecked several aircraft, but, just on the verge of being grounded, he was given one more patrol. He shot down his first aircraft on this flight. His comrades said that though he was brash, and undisciplined, he loved dogfights and knew no fear. During the summer of 1917 Bishop claimed forty-seven aircraft – a staggering amount. In June he claimed to have carried out a solo attack on a German base far behind the lines during which he said he managed to shoot down three planes which rose to defend the base. Some historians have questioned the validity of the account, even though Bishop was awarded the Victoria Cross for the action.

Following the war, he helped organize one of Canada's first airlines, and later rose to the rank of Air Marshal in the RCAF.

BLACK, TOM CAMPBELL
1899–1936
Black was born in England and enlisted in the

RFC in 1917 where he learned to fly. During the 1920s he was a well known air racer, winning the Mansfield Robinson Trophy three times. He also undertook long distance flying and set several records on flights to Africa. While in Kenya he established Wilson Airways, and even taught Beryl Markham (qv) to fly.

Because of his long distance achievements he was asked to be one of the pilots of the DH 88 Comet entered by the hotelier A. O. Edwards in the 1934 MacRobertson Race from England to Australia. Together with C. W. A. Scott (qv), Black won the historic speed contest despite some apparent engine problems. The next year while flying a DH 88 Comet from England to South Africa he and his co-pilot were forced to bale out over the Sudan when a propeller malfunctioned.

In 1936 Black was sliced to death when a Hawker Hart taxied into his Percival Mew Gull on the ground at Speke airport at Liverpool.

BLACKBURN, ROBERT
1885–1955
Blackburn was a talented engineer working in France when Wilbur Wright (qv) took the country by storm in 1908. This started him on an aviation career, and by the next year he had designed a solid-looking monoplane, loosely based on the Demoiselle. A unique feature of the plane was its sliding seat, which enabled the pilot to shift the centre of gravity. Blackburn himself made the first test flight which ended in a minor crash.

In 1911 Blackburn was back with another aircraft. This one looked much like an Antoinette and it flew well. Blackburn won a military contract to licence build BE-2cs, and this started his more than forty-year association with the British military.

In the inter-war years his company produced aircraft for both the RAF and Royal Navy, notably the Skua and Roc. During the war his firm once again licence-built aircraft – Swordfish and Sunderlands.

After the war, in 1949, he merged his company with General Aircraft. Blackburn and General Aircraft Ltd produced the Beverley Freighter and designed the Buccaneer, though Blackburn died of heart failure before the latter aircraft flew.

BLADUD
883–840 BC
Bladud was one of England's more colourful monarchs. Educated in Athens, this powerful king was the father of King Lear. He developed Bath into a flourishing health resort and founded England's first college at Stamford.

His downfall (literally) was due to his belief in the black arts, especially his conviction that, like the gods, he could fly. To prove his ability to commune with the gods Bladud constructed a pair of large wings out of bird feathers and leapt off the Temple of Apollo, which he had built in Tinovantum (London). This verse from John Taylor's *Memorial of English Monarchs*, printed in 1622, tells of Bladud's fate.

> Bathe was by Bladud to perfection brought,
> By Necromanticke Arts, to flye he sought,
> As from a Towre he thought to scale the sky,
> He brake his necke, because he soar'd too high.

BLANCHARD, JEAN-PIERRE
1753–1809
Born into a poor family, Blanchard developed an interest in things mechanical as a youth. Before the Montgolfiers (qv) had achieved their success, Blanchard was experimenting with parachutes and flap-wing models. His parachute designs were tested by throwing sheep off the tops of buildings. The flap-wing design included the novel feature of a French horn player seated behind the pilot to provide soothing music as the pilot vigorously pumped the lever! Undoubtedly the first suggestion for in-flight entertainment.

Blanchard turned to practical flying after the introduction of the balloon, and in 1784 was invited to London to demonstrate his aerostats. There he met Dr Jeffries (qv) who offered the Frenchman the very large sum of £800 to fly him across the English Channel. Blanchard took the money, but when they were about to depart from Dover, on 7 January 1785, he told Jeffries that the balloon was capable of carrying only one man. The outraged doctor suspected trickery and questioned Blanchard as to the bulge around his waist. Forcing him to take-off his outer coat, Jeffries discovered that Blanchard had loaded himself down with a lead weight belt! After the confrontation, they launched in front of a crowd of nearly a quarter of a million. As the wind pushed them out over the Channel, Blanchard accidentally valved too much hydrogen and the balloon plunged. They scrambled to throw out all excess ballast; food, books, sandbags, and even their brandy. The situation became so desperate that they had to discard most of their clothes. Jeffries even recommended that they vomit over the side. They did, in fact, urinate over the side. They finally stabilized the balloon, and after flying for two hours, reached the French coast – too low to clear the cliffs. The difference in coastal temperature caused the balloon to rise and they just managed to get over the cliffs before crashing into some trees.

The crossing was a spectacular triumph and both men became famous. Blanchard was given a pension by Louis XVI. He went on to establish the world's first aeronautical school in Vauxhall, near London, and then embarked on a tour of Europe. The tour ended when the Austrians imprisoned him for spreading 'anarchistic propaganda'. He escaped, but instead of returning to revolutionary France, he went to America where he made the first free flight in the New World on 9 January 1793. George Washington issued the world's first passport when he gave Blanchard a paper requesting anyone who came in contact with the aeronaut to help him in a way 'which may render honour to their country'. Blanchard's flight from Philadelphia ended in rural Gloucester, New Jersey, and the passport aided the non English-speaking Blanchard to deal with the startled locals.

Blanchard's eventful life ended when he suffered a heart attack in 1809. After his death, his wife, Madeleine-Sophie, continued the family trade. She specialized in night flights illuminated by fireworks. She met her end in 1819 when one of the fireworks set her balloon ablaze. She plunged to her death on a Paris rooftop.

BLAND, LILIAN E.
1878–1971
Lilian Bland liked to smoke cigarettes, shoot guns, drive cars, and do just about anything an Edwardian lady didn't do. She was one of England's first female journalists, specialising in sporting events. After Blériot's (qv) cross-Channel flight she decided that if men were meant to fly, so were women. She needed an aeroplane, and the best way to get one was to build it.

Her family estate was in Ireland, where she returned in the spring of 1910 to build first a glider. Few pioneers of the day heeded the Wright brothers' (qv) example to train on gliders before powered craft, but Bland was wise enough to do so. The crudely-built glider was made from a combination of bamboo, ash and elm. With the help of a friend it was ready in just a few months. With a little bit of Irish wit, she christened it *Mayfly*.

Mayfly did fly – though barely, but it was enough for Bland to order an engine from A. V. Roe (qv). The engine finally arrived after delays, but the fuel tank took longer. Impatient, Bland used a whisky bottle feeding into her aunt's ear trumpet for a temporary fuel system. It worked.

In August, 1910, having installed the engine in *Mayfly*, Bland made the first flight in Ireland. She made a half-hearted attempt to start an aircraft company before her father made a deal with her. He said he'd buy her a Model T Ford if she'd get rid of the plane. She accepted the offer.

In 1912 she accepted the offer off another man, to become his wife, and they moved to Canada. Bland returned to England in 1935.

BLÉRIOT, LOUIS CHARLES-JOSEPH
1872–1936
Blériot merits a high position in aviation history.

The honesty and integrity associated with his name equals that afforded only to the Wright brothers.

Born in Cambrai, France and educated as an engineer, Blériot made a small fortune by designing and manufacturing powerful and dependable 'after market' automobile headlamps. These beautiful lamps are prized collector's items today. His first attempt at building a flying machine was a flap-wing rig made in 1901. Four years later, he witnessed Voisin (qv) pilot the Archdeacon (qv) float glider on the Seine river. After the 'flight', Blériot formed a partnership with Voisin which spawned several unsuccessful aircraft before dissolving in 1906.

During the next two years, Blériot built several more aircraft with the help of a small, imaginative staff which included Louis Peyret and Raymond Saulnier (qv). Blériot exhibited immense personal courage as he test flew all his aeroplanes despite continual mishaps. Crash by crash his knowledge increased, but it wasn't until the summer of 1908, after witnessing Wilbur Wright's (qv) masterful demonstration, that Blériot began to understand the elemental functions of a successful aircraft.

In January, 1909 the Blériot XI, designed by Saulnier, flew for the first time. This was the clean, simple design that Blériot had badly needed and had spent nearly all his wealth to get. Blériot knew he had a winner, but that without more money, he would be forced to close his shop. By a strange twist of fate, Alice, his wife, happened to save the life of the son of a wealthy friend. The child had nearly fallen off a balcony. In gratitude, the friend advanced Blériot F25,000 to keep his shop open, and to attempt the first aeroplane crossing of the English Channel, for which a prize of £1,000 had been offered.

On 25 July 1909 Blériot made the thirty-seven minute cross-Channel flight which assured his financial success and honoured place in history. This flight may be considered the third most important flight in history, following only the Wright's first flight, and Lindbergh's (qv) Atlantic flight. For the first time, politicians and military men began to look at the airplane as a device which made borders unenforceable.

Blériot went on to set several speed records in 1909, but ended his active flying career that same year. In four years, he had suffered nearly fifty crashes which resulted in countless cuts, bruises, broken bones and burns. For the sake of Alice, and his six children, he gave up flying to concentrate on business.

BLOCH, MARCEL
1892–1986
Bloch was one of four sons born to a wealthy Parisian doctor. A technically-minded youth, he entered the prestigious L'École Breguet where he studied electrical engineering and upon graduation, at the age of nineteen, received his diploma from Louis Breguet (qv) himself. He then studied aeronautics at L'École Supérieure D'Aéronautique after which he apprenticed at the Panhard automobile factory. In 1914 he was drafted into the Corps of Engineers and assigned to the aeronautical laboratory at Chalais-Meudon where he cleaned-up the Caudron G-3 design for easier mass production. He transferred to the Maurice Farman (qv) factory later, but then decided to open his own aircraft factory.

His first venture into production was with an efficient propeller he had designed. Using the factory of his future father-in-law, Bloch, with his partner, Henri Potez (qv), constructed propellers under the trade name 'Éclair' for the French Air Force. In 1917 the pair formed SEA to build a two-seat scout they had designed. The air force bought over 100 of these aircraft.

Following the war there was a downturn in the aviation business, so Bloch began to produce low-cost homes. While other airplane companies went bankrupt, Bloch's company struggled on until the early 1930s when they returned to aviation. Bloch produced both commercial and military aircraft, and just when his aviation business was becoming profitable, the French government made the disastrous decision to nationalize all the large aviation companies. Bloch's prediction that the government control would ruin production came true as the yearly totals decreased in the late 1930s just before the war.

When the Germans occupied France in 1940, Bloch was pressured to build planes for the Nazis. When he refused, he was arrested as a Jew and sent to Buchenwald concentration camp. Miraculously, he survived and was liberated in 1945.

Witnessing life and death in the prison camp had transformed Bloch. He vowed never to passively watch his country subjugated again. To show his new fighting spirit he changed his last name from Bloch to Dassault. Dassault is French for 'attack' and was the *nom-de-guerre* of his brother Paul, a general in the French resistance.

As Marcel Dassault, he became one of the most controversial and quoted business leaders in post-war France.

BOEING, WILLIAM EDWARD
1881–1956

Though William Boeing's career in aviation lasted less than twenty years, he laid the foundation for aviation's longest-lasting and greatest dynasty.

Born in Detroit, Boeing received an excellent education both in the US and abroad. In 1903, one year short of graduating from Yale, he moved to Washington State when he speculated on some timber land. His investment paid off and soon young Boeing had reaped a fortune. In 1914 he went for his first airplane ride and fell in love with flying. He learned to fly at the Glenn Martin (qv) school, but was unhappy with the quality of the training planes. Deciding to start his own manufacturing company, he persuaded a friend, Conrad Westervelt to join him, and by 1916 the Boeing Company had built its first two airplanes, both float biplanes.

The Boeing company not only built aircraft but owned an airline, Boeing Air Transport, which was formed in 1927. In 1929, he and Frederick Rentschler (qv) masterminded the stock-swapping deal that created the industrial giant known as United Aircraft and Transport

Company. In 1934, when the U.S. government declared that building aircraft and operating an airline violated anti-trust laws, Boeing sold out and retired. His corporate empire split with the airline becoming known as United.

Though he returned to corporate duties briefly during World War II, he left again, having spent only eighteen years with the company that today is synonymous with the high quality aircraft he had originally hoped to build.

BOELCKE, HAUPTMANN OSWALD
1891–1916

Boelcke's great contributions to aviation history were the introduction of the fighter squadron, and the development of fighter tactics. Boelcke earned his pilot's certificate two weeks after the war started and flew numerous reconnaissance missions in Albatros planes with his brother as observer. He earned an Iron Cross in 1915 and was then selected to fly the new Fokker Eindecker with synchronized guns. He quickly began to compile an impressive victory total which he attributed to rules he developed for himself. These rules became known as Boelcke's *Dicta* and were learned by all German airmen.

In 1916 he persuaded the German High Command to organize planes into units according to type. He took command of Jagdstaffel 2 and began to drill its hand-picked members in fighter tactics, marksmanship, and aerodynamics. The unit produced many aces including one awkward ex-cavalry officer whom Boelcke had rescued from inglorious bomber duty in Russia – Manfred von Richthofen (qv).

Boelcke achieved hero status and was awarded the Pour le Mérite. Most of the forty victories he earned were gained by waiting until he was nearly on top of his opponent before firing. He brought down the first American ever killed in aerial combat, Victor Chapman.

Boelcke would have undoubtedly added many more aircraft to his score had he not been accidentally killed when his plane was struck in mid-air by a student's plane. The pupil, Erwin Böhme, had to be restrained from committing suicide. Boelcke's name is honoured today by a German Luftwaffe squadron which bears his name.

BONG, MAJOR RICHARD IRA
1920–1945
In May, 1941, Bong was one month away from getting his teaching certificate when he decided he'd rather be a pilot. He joined the Army Air Corps, and after receiving his wings, spent a few months as a flight instructor. He was then sent to the Pacific theatre where the war was by then in progress. Flying a P-38 with the 5th Air Force, he ran up a score of twenty-eight kills by April, 1944. He volunteered for a second tour of duty, securing twelve more victories before being brought home to become a test pilot. He was thrilled to be given the chance to fly the new P-80 Shooting Star, but may have been safer back in the Pacific. On 6 August 1945, the day Hiroshima was bombed, the P-80 he was flying 'flamed out' and Bong crashed to his death. With a total of forty confirmed kills, he was the highest scoring American of all time.

BOOTHMAN, FLIGHT LIEUTENANT JOHN NELSON
1901–1957
Boothman joined the RAF in the early twenties and proved himself to be a natural pilot. He became a test pilot with an emphasis on float and seaplanes. When the RAF was granted last minute permission in 1931 to try to capture the Schneider Trophy, Boothman was chosen to fly the Supermarine S-6B. As the British were unopposed, Boothman's victory would have been quite hollow had he not set a course record of 340.08 mph (547.31km/hr).

He remained in the RAF and flew photo-reconnaissance missions during the war. Following this, he guided the RAF's technical development as an officer in the Ministry of Supply, before rising to the head of Coastal Command.

BOREL, GABRIEL
–
Borel began his aviation career as a partner with Morane (qv). In 1910 he started his own manufacturing business. The first craft was a two-seater monoplane, immediately followed by a seaplane in 1913. With the latter airplane, he hoped to win the Schneider Cup, but that year Deperdussin deprived him of victory.

The seaplane was developed into a military scout and won contracts from the British and Italian governments for Borel. Subsequent designs saw Borel move towards advanced streamlining, and in the early 1920s when his company became known as SCIM, he produced very fast racing planes.

BOYD, ALBERT
1906–1976
Boyd was born in Tennessee and attended college in North Carolina before joining the Air Corps in 1927. He was sent to the Advance Flying School and Air Technical School where he learned the techniques of being a test pilot. Boyd earned an international reputation as a test pilot, and during his career flew over 300 types of aircraft. During World War II he evaluated captured aircraft and in 1949 helped establish Edwards AFB as the world's most advanced testing centre. For his work, which bridged the gap between pilots and scientists, Boyd became known as the father of modern flight testing.

BOYINGTON, GREGORY
1912–1988
'Pappy' Boyington was born in Idaho and graduated from the University of Washington before joining the Marines in 1936. He became a pilot, and in 1941 joined the Flying Tigers (American Volunteer Group) in China. He shot down six Japanese planes before the Flying Tigers were brought into the US Army Air Corps in mid-1942. In 1943 he organized his own squadron, recruiting not only new replacement pilots, but also veterans, some of

whom had been reprimanded for disciplinary problems.

The legend of the 'Black Sheep' squadron was born from this mixed bag of fliers, and over the years their escapades have been greatly exaggerated. Sometimes lost amongst the myths is that fact that Boyington was a great pilot, and before flying his last mission, had shot down twenty-five enemy planes. On his last flight, he added three more to the total before being brought down himself. He floated alone in the water for two hours and was strafed by Japanese aircraft before one of their submarines picked him up and took him to a POW camp in Japan. Boyington spent twenty months as a prisoner.

Boyington ended his memoirs with what he called the moral of the book: 'Just name a hero and I'll prove he's a bum'. Boyington's fortune sank after the war as he became an alcoholic and bounced from job to job. But like a true hero, he beat the odds and reformed to fit his role as the most successful Marine ace of all time.

BRABAZON OF TARA, LORD
(See J. T. C. Moore-Brabazon)

BRACK-PAPA, FRANCESCO
1891–1973
Brack-Papa became one of Italy's first military pilots after earning his brevet on Farmans in France in 1912. He set several altitude records before the war, but then joined the air fighting. He returned to test flying for FIAT during the war, and kept that position for over a dozen years. In 1922, in a FIAT racer, he set a new world speed record which was never officially recorded. He and his Italian compatriots didn't want to bother with the paperwork which needed to be approved by the FAI in Paris. The French, after all, were rivals.

Avanti! Italian speed demon Francesco Brack-Papa.

BRAHAM, JOHN RANDALL DANIEL
1920–1974
Braham gained the distinction of earning more medals for gallantry than any man in the long history of British military service since 1974. He first flew combat missions in Blenheim night fighters in 1940. After seven months, he had shot down only two enemy planes. In the summer of 1941, he was allowed to fly night interdiction missions over the continent, and it was during these dangerous flights that he proved his lethal qualities. In just three years he brought his score up to twenty-nine kills, and these included some of Germany's top pilots. Amongst them was Heinz Vinke with fifty-four kills. Braham's luck ran out on 25 June 1944 when he was brought down near Denmark. Captured, he spent the rest of the war as a prisoner.

BRANCKER, SIR WILLIAM SEFTON
1877–1930
Brancker was commissioned in the Royal Artillery in 1896, and served gallantly in the South African War where he was wounded. After a tour of duty in India, he returned to England where he learned to fly in 1913. The

next year he became the deputy director of military aeronautics. He moved up the chain of command, but when the war ended in 1918 he had not been able to lead the bombing raid on Berlin which he had planned.

In 1919 he joined the Aircraft Manufacturing Company which inaugurated a regular London to Paris air service. In 1922 he became the director of Civil Aviation, a position he assumed with relish. His vision was to have all of Britain's far-flung colonies united by a vast network of airways. Not only did he promote air races and long distance flights, he took part in them. In 1924 he accompanied Cobham (qv) on a London–Rangoon flight.

After witnessing the first de Havilland Moth flight in 1925, he recommended the formation of government-subsidized flying clubs using Moths. He wanted to create a pool of pilots in case of national emergency. This plan was later implemented, though Brancker didn't live to see the fruit of his hard work. In 1930 he died in the tragic crash of the R101 airship.

von BRAUN, DR WERNHER
1912–1977

As a young man, von Braun had only one dream – to build rockets. He was born into a wealthy, aristocratic family, but instead of indulging in all the pleasures his position could bring, he studied all he could find about rockets and physics. By his twenty-second birthday, he had earned his doctorate in physics at the University of Berlin.

In 1930 Walter Dornberger (qv) met von Braun and was so impressed by the visionary and yet realistic young scientist, that he put him in charge of a secret army rocket research base. Some of the older engineers and technicians there resented the young man directing them, but von Braun's maturity and undeniable genius soon won them over. In 1936 the work at the base was transferred to Peenemünde, and von Braun became one of the leading directors of research for the entire Nazi rocket program. The A-4 rocket was the main goal of the work at Peenemünde with the first example being launched in 1942. Two years later these ballistic missiles commonly known as V2s, began to fall on London.

When the end of the war seemed imminent, von Braun left Peenemünde and surrendered to the American forces. He voluntarily went to the US, where, despite his previous association with the Nazis, he became the technical director at the White Sands missile range. During the fifties he directed the Jupiter, Juno and Pershing rocket programs, and the first launching of a US satellite, *Explorer 1* in 1958.

When President Kennedy declared that America would put a man on the Moon before 1970, von Braun plotted the mission profile. He then took charge of designing the Saturn V booster, the world's most complex, yet successful, launch vehicle. When the *Eagle* landed in July, 1969, von Braun saw it as only the beginning of the possibilities for space flight. Others realized that it was the end, at least temporarily. Bitterly disappointed at the narrow-mindedness of Congress, von Braun remained with NASA for three more years.

Portrait of a rocketeering genius as a young man – Wernher von Braun.

Those who worked with him said he often walked up and down the halls lost in thought, a man with a dream trapped by inactivity. He left NASA and joined Fairchild in 1972. It was his first ever non-government job. He died a youthful sixty-five, having helped bomb London and put a man on the Moon.

French pioneer Louis Breguet.

BREGUET, LOUIS
1880–1955

Breguet was born into a wealthy Parisian family which had become famous as clock makers to the French royal court. He attended the École Supérieure d'Électricité de Paris. After working in the family business, he turned his attention to aviation and in 1907, with his brother Jacques and Professor Charles Richet, built the first helicopter capable of lifting a man. It was completely unstable, which precluded further development.

His first successful airplane flew in June, 1909. It was the first ever to use steel tubing for its main structure. Though the plane had little success at Rheims the following August, he built an improved version the next year and covered it with sheet aluminium which earned it the name 'the Coffee Pot'. In 1911 he developed a successful biplane and formed his

own company. During World War I the solidly-built Breguet 14 earned a reputation as one of the best Allied reconnaissance planes.

In the post-war years Breguet founded Compagnie de Messageries Aériennes, an early airline which became Air France. For this company he developed the Breguet Range equation which is used to this day to formulate the costs of operating air routes.

Today, the Breguet company lives on. In a move to stave off nationalization, it merged with Dassault in 1972. Unlike it's struggling government-run cousin Aérospatiale, it has managed to remain profitable yearly.

BREWER, GRIFFITH
1867–1948

Brewer was a wealthy Englishman who helped to revive ballooning as a sport during the Edwardian era. He never set any great record of note, but was at the social centre of the aeronautical world of those years. He made his first balloon flight in 1891 which set him on a career as a casual barnstormer. He experimented with small balloons as photography platforms and took some of the earliest aerial photos of London. In 1908 he befriended Wilbur Wright (qv) in France, which led to his being the first Englishman to fly as a passenger in a heavier-than-air craft.

His friendship with the Wrights helped the Americans to gain formal recognition in Britain as the first to fly. The kindly attitudes fostered led to Orville loaning the *Flyer* to the London Science Museum.

BROOKINS, WALTER RICHARD
1888–1953

Brookins was an elementary school student of Katherine Wright who brought him into contact with her famous brothers. In 1909, Orville (qv) taught him to fly at a newly established flying field in Montgomery, Alabama. Brookins soloed in only 2·5 hours, and with this scant training, was left to run the Wright's winter school in Montgomery. His first student was Arch Hoxley (qv).

During the pre-war years he earned a national reputation as a daring stunt pilot, part of which he gained in 1910 when, after establishing an altitude record of 6,175 feet (1,882m), his engine cut out. Dead-stick landings were highly unusual in those days, but Brookins descended and landed safely. That year he also made the first night flight in America. He later established the Brookins Aircraft Corporation in Los Angeles. He unwittingly dramatically affected the course of bombing history when he introduced David Davis (qv) to Reuben Fleet (qv) so that Davis might sell Consolidated his special wing design. The B-24 bomber used the Davis wing.

A brave young daredevil, Walter Brookins.

BRUMOWSKI, HAUPTMANN GODWIN
1889–1936
Born in the Polish area of Austro-Hungarian Empire, Brumowski began WWI in the Army. One year of mud on the ground convinced him to transfer to the Air Force, which he did in August 1915. He started as an observer, but became a pilot by teaching himself to fly. In 1916 he took command of Fliegerkampagnie 12, and flew combat missions over the Italian front. His score rose steadily, and he was selected to study German fighter tactics under von Richthofen (qv). From the German master, he learned the need for proper organization and fighter groups instead of solo missions. With this in mind, he returned to Austria, but repeated efforts to convince his superiors of the need to reform the air force failed. He returned to combat as commander of an Albatros squadron and finished the war with forty kills.

Having survived three years of aerial combat, Brumowski lost his life in a commercial airline accident at Schiphol airport in Holland in 1937.

BRYAN, GEORGE HARTLEY
1864–1928
Bryan came from an intellectual background. His father was a professor at Clare College, Cambridge. He became a mathematician and applied his knowledge to exposing the dynamic forces which act upon an aeroplane. In 1903 he read a paper before the Aeronautical Society in London entitled *The Longitudinal Stability of Aeroplane Gliders.* He had performed research for the paper with model gliders. The paper was politely received, but few saw how it could really help bring about an actual flying machine. By 1911, when Bryan published *Stability in Aviation*, there were many aeroplanes flying, and his work began to be appreciated. In 1915 he was awarded the Gold Medal of the Royal Aeronautical Society and the same year presented the Wright Memorial Lecture *The Rigid Dynamics of Circling Flight.*

Bryan's studies of forces acting on moving bodies proved invaluable to manufacturers who wanted to build strong yet light airframes. His work inspired empirical research into aerodynamics.

BULLARD, EUGENE JACQUES
1894–1961
Bullard was the grandson of slaves, and though slavery had been abolished for over thirty years

when he was born, his life in Georgia was little different from his grandmother's. He had ambitions however and was told that blacks were treated fairly in France. He stowed away on a ship and made his way to Paris. In 1914 he joined the Foreign Legion. He was wounded at Verdun, but by then his fighting spirit had earned him the *nom-de-guerre* 'the Black Swallow'.

He transferred to the Air Force and earned his pilot's wings, but flew very few missions. Perhaps it was the Americans, who had just joined the fight, who pressured the French into forcing Bullard back to the trenches. In any case, Ballard was charged with insubordination and returned to the infantry.

After the war, he stayed in Paris, a city in tune with Bullard's love of life and broad personality. He became a bandleader and club owner, and married a French countess. During World War II he was a resistance fighter and was again wounded. After the war, he returned to America which had little changed in his absence, and worked at numerous odd jobs until his unheralded death.

Eugene Bullard who overcame enormous obstacles to serve the cause of freedom.

BULMAN, PAUL WARD SPENCER
1896–1963
Forever linked to the story of the Hurricane fighter will be its first pilot, 'George' Bulman. He served a year in the Royal Artillery before transferring to the RFC in 1915. A fine pilot, he earned the Military Cross by the war's end. He went to Farnborough as a test pilot until 1925, and ironically, one of the last planes he tested there was a light plane called the Hurricane. He joined Hawker and exemplified the new breed of test pilot. No longer were seat-of-the-pants flyers needed – it was the dawn of the engineer-pilot. The first fighter he tested was the Woodcock. Several years later that radial-engined biplane gave way to Sydney Camm's (qv) in-line monoplane Hurricane, which Bulman first flew on 6 November 1935 at Brooklands. Upon landing he knew he had a winner.

He stayed at Hawker through the war, but in 1945 left to go into private business.

BURNELLI, VINCENT JUSTUS
1895–1964
Burnelli deserves a special note in the history of aviation. He was a man who spent his entire career pursuing one dream, and although he often came close to realizing it, he never quite succeeded. Burnelli's dream was to produce fleets of flying-wing aircraft. His designs were not true flying-wings however; they had very thick wing sections into which were installed the pilot's compartment, the engines, and cargo or passenger cabin, but in the rear there were normal empennages. Between 1922 and 1950 he was able to find backers to build several of his designs, both biplane and monoplane. When he couldn't raise money in the US he went to England.

Burnelli got into aviation in 1915 by designing the Burnelli-Carisi biplane. When the government refused to purchase it, it became the first aircraft owned by the New York City Police Department! Though Burnelli was a clear-sighted, if single-minded, man, some of his difficulties may have stemmed from his early association, in 1917–18, with the Continental Aircraft Company run by an eccentric named Dr William Whitney Christmas. Christmas' great contribution to the US war effort was to build a wholly impractical flexible wing aircraft which killed its incautious test pilot on the first flight. Burnelli was unable to persuade Dr Christmas to abandon the idea. In 1919 Burnelli worked for Alfred Lawson (qv) as an engineer on the Lawson Airliner.

Despite the death of his brother Lawrence in a racing aircraft accident in 1925, Burnelli pursued his dream almost to the end of his life.

Vincent Burnelli who dreamed of a world of flying wings.

BUSEMANN, ADOLF
1901–1986
Almost by accident, Adolf Busemann helped to change the course of aviation history. Busemann was born in Lübeck, Germany, and earned an engineering degree in 1924. While conducting high-speed wind experiments at the Kaiser Wilhelm Institute during the early 1930s, it occurred to him that supersonic airflow might be analogous to a ship's wake. He wondered if

swept wings might not be the key to breaking the sound barrier. In the early thirties his aerodynamic theories were ahead of engine technology and so his theories were purely academic. Fate intervened in 1935 when he was invited to give a lecture at the Fifth Volta Congress of High Speed Flight in Rome. Caught unaware at short notice, he decided to present his idea for a swept wing.

The scientists attending knew that supersonic speed was not yet attainable, but several years later when transonic aircraft were under development in Germany, Busemann's idea was re-examined and applied successfully to the Me-262 and Me-163. These aircraft set the style for high-speed jets of the future.

Busemann left Germany following the war, going first to England for two years, and then to the US where he worked for NASA. He died in Boulder, Colorado.

BUTLER, FRANK HEDGES
1856–1928
Butler was born into the lap of luxury as a descendent of one of the founders of the Hedges and Butler company. Like Griffith Brewer (qv), he never made any great contribution to aviation, but he helped to further the cause in Britain by co-founding the Aero Club, which served as a gathering place for aspiring aviators in Edwardian England. Butler was active in anything to do with automobiles, ships or balloons. He made over 100 ascents and even set some long distance records.

BYRD, RICHARD EVELYN
1888–1957
Byrd began his career as an explorer at the age of twelve when he travelled around the globe by himself. In 1912 he graduated from the Naval Academy, but leg injuries suffered during a football game forced him into administrative duties until World War I when he talked his way into the pilot training program.

A natural leader and a gifted navigator, Byrd had helped to plan the NC flying-boats trans-

Atlantic flight in 1919, and was bitterly disappointed when he wasn't chosen to lead it. In 1926 he and Floyd Bennett (qv) made, they claimed, the first aeroplane flight over the North Pole, which earned them both the Congressional Medal of Honour. The next year Byrd attempted to beat Lindbergh (qv) to Paris, but was unable to start on time because his plane crashed on a test flight. During the 1930s he extensively explored the South Pole and pioneered Arctic survival techniques.

Byrd's alleged flight over the Pole became the centre of a controversy because his plane theoretically didn't have enough range for the flight. The dispute may never be accurately settled.

CABRAL, SACADURA
1892–1924

Cabral, a naval pilot, left Portugal with his commanding officer, Vice-Admiral Gago Coutinho, in March, 1922, attempting to be the first to fly across the south Atlantic to Brazil via the Canary and Cape Verde Islands. Everything went well until they reached St. Paul's Rock, off Brazil, where their Fairey biplane crashed and was destroyed. A local pilot lent them a plane which proved incapable of reaching the mainland, so Cabral had to wire to Portugal for another plane. This plane was damaged en route, so yet another had to be sent for. More than ten weeks after their start, the undaunted Portuguese took off and made their way to Pernambuco, Brazil where they landed to a hero's welcome. For the first ever crossing of the southern route, though it was a qualified success, they won a $50,000 prize.

CALDERARA, MARIO
1879–1944

Mario Calderara, an engineer in the Italian Navy, was Italy's first pilot. He first tried to fly in an aircraft he had designed in association with Ambroise Goupy (qv) in Paris. The aircraft, the Goupy II, barely flew in March, 1909, so Calderara returned to Italy where he was taught to fly by Wilbur Wright (qv) in April, 1909 at

Centocelle, near Rome. Wilbur's puritan style didn't completely mesh with his student's. In fact, after the lessons, he wrote about Calderara: 'I left him with greater misgivings than my other pupils, because he was a cigarette fiend, and was being very badly spoiled by the attention and flattery he was receiving.'

Maybe smoking and flying didn't mix, because shortly after the lessons Calderara did crash. He recovered from the accident and entered several European air contests. He later became the air attaché at the Italian embassy in Washington.

Italian aviator Mario Calderara.

CALDWELL, GROUP CAPTAIN CLIVE ROBERTSON
1910–

Born in Sydney, Australia, Caldwell joined the Air Force at the outbreak of World War II and was posted to England. He was sent to Palestine in the summer of 1941, where he joined No 250 Squadron flying Tomahawks. He began to average three kills per month, from June to

December, and on 5 December 1941, he single-handedly shot down five Stukas over the Western Desert. The next month he received his first command, No 112 Squadron. He spent the summer of 1942 flying against the Germans from Kenley, England, but in September was sent back to Australia where he assumed command of No 1 Fighter Wing. By the war's end, he had scored 28·5 victories, eight against the Japanese, and thus was Australia's top war ace.

CAMM, SIR SYDNEY
1893–1966

One of the greatest aircraft designers of all time, Camm was born in Windsor, and began building model airplanes at the age of eighteen. In 1914, after having built a man-carrying glider, he became a shop apprentice for the Martinsyde company, where he made friends with its chief designer G. H. Handasyde (qv). Handasyde spotted Camm's talents and promoted him into the design department as a draughtsman. Camm left in 1923 to become the head draughtsman at Hawkers. That year he was assigned to design a light plane entry for the Lympne competition. This, his first powered aircraft, was the delicate Cygnet which received high praise for its efficiency. In 1925, at the age of thirty-two, Camm became Hawker's chief designer. From then on, Hawker rose to the forefront in Britain's aviation industry. In 1928 the Hart biplane was produced. This design and its derivatives kept much of the British aviation industry in business during the lean years of the Depression.

In 1933 Camm proposed building a low wing monoplane fighter. Such a radical departure from the *status quo* didn't interest the Air Ministry, but T. O. M. Sopwith (qv), the head of Hawker, believed in Camm's vision and agreed to finance the prototype. Once again, it was private industry in Britain which laid the foundation for victory in World War II. The result of Camm's work was the immortal Hurricane.

Camm followed this masterpiece with many other great designs like the Typhoon, Tempest, Sea Fury and Hunter. In the later fifties he broke new ground with vectored thrust aircraft. This work developed into the Harrier.

For forty-one years Camm remained Hawker's chief designer. Like R. J. Mitchell (qv), he will never be forgotten in the annals of aviation history.

Douglas Campbell, American ace.

CAMPBELL, LIEUTENANT DOUGLAS
1896–1990

Most of the US Air Service pilots of World War I were college graduates, and many of them were Ivy Leaguers. Douglas Campbell was educated at Harvard, and joined the Air Service in 1917. He only received ground training in the US before being rushed to France late that year. He taught himself to fly, for the most part, on a clipped wing Nieuport, and in March, 1918, became one of the original members of the famous 94th Pursuit Squadron. On 19 March he joined Eddie Rickenbacker and Raoul Lufbery (qqv) to fly the first American patrol over enemy lines in *unarmed* Nieuport 28s! On 14 April he shot down an Albatros scout plane near Toul, thus becoming the first American pilot in an American unit to shoot down an enemy plane. Six weeks later, on 31 May, he scored his fifth victory, making him the first US Air Service ace. A week later he was shot and seriously wounded which forced his return to the US. After the war he went to work with W. R. Grace, whose air operations were eventually absorbed by Pan Am.

CAPPER, COLONEL JOHN EDWARD
1861–1955

Capper was a key figure in bringing modern aviation to Britain. Trained as a Royal Engineer, he saw more fighting in the Boer War than he did construction projects. His good service in the war earned him the command of the Balloon Section in 1903. He had gained practical balloon experience in 1883 when he helped with the construction of the first military balloon in England, the *Sapper.*

The respect which his fellow officers bestowed on Capper helped legitimize the suspect cause of military aviation. In 1904 he went to the US where he met Chanute, Langley, and the Wright brothers (qqv). He became especially well acquainted with the Wrights, and was their staunchest European supporter prior to 1908. In 1907 he won support for the construction of Britain's first airship, the *Nulli Secundus.* Having met S. F. Cody (qv) in 1904 when he assisted him in demonstrating man-carrying kites, Capper further encouraged Cody to develop an aeroplane and lent him equipment to help with the effort. Capper's open mind and resourcefulness were uncharacteristic of military officialdom of the period, and it was due to these great traits that Britain's first aircraft was flown. Cody rewarded his benefactor on 14 August 1909 when he took Capper for a flight as passenger. It was the first passenger flight in Britain.

Though Capper almost single-handedly brought his hesitant country into the aerial age, he chose to return to an infantry command during World War I and was again noted for his success as a general.

CAPRONI, DR GIANNI (CONTE DI TALIEDO)
1886–1957

Caprioni was born into a wealthy family in Arco, Italy. He was studying to be an electrical engineer when Wilbur Wright (qv) came to Europe in 1908. He immediately turned his attention to aviation and had soon designed several aeronautical appliances, including a variable pitch propeller, double gas bag dirigible, and a glider based heavily on the Wright machine. In 1910 he produced his first powered plane, an Avro-looking biplane. It was noted for using metal tubular spars.

Year by year the Caproni planes improved, although they were heavily influenced by foreign designs. By World War I Caproni was pioneering on his own with large triplane bombers. These set the tone for his large flying-boat project following the war. With nine wings and eight engines, the Ca-60 gave new meaning to the term 'ugly duckling'. The impractical, half-conceived extravagance crashed on its first flight from sixty feet. A half-hearted attempt to rebuild it was ended with a mysterious fire. Though this failure proved a temporary embarrassment to him, it didn't prevent Caproni from building a huge, successful manufacturing empire prior to World War II.

CASTOLDI, DR ING MARIO
1888–1968

Castoldi studied engineering before going to work at a government airplane factory in Turin during World War I. In 1922 he became the technical director at Macchi, a position he held for twenty-two years. His best known designs were the fabulous Schneider Trophy racing planes of the twenties and thirties. Developed under incredible secrecy, due to Castoldi's almost psychotic paranoia, these Italian racing thoroughbreds established Italy as a leader in aeronautical advancement. Castoldi numbered all of his race planes in multiples of thirteen, and it was MC-72 which earned the record for the fastest piston-engined seaplane of all time in

1934 – 440 mph (708km/hr). Castoldi went on to produce equally sleek fighters.

CAUDRON, GASTON
*–1915

CAUDRON, RENÉ
1884–1959

The Caudrons were another French brother team which started by building biplanes. They began to build in 1908, and had soon produced a very simple and relatively inexpensive airplane. Training schools purchased Caudron airplanes because they were easy to maintain, and less likely to crash than their larger counterparts. In 1913, René travelled to China and took aerial photos over the city of Peking. The Chinese government then placed an order for twelve aircraft which were used for reconnaissance over feuding warlords. Occidental governments also appreciated the value of the Caudrons which had fast rates of climb, if slow overall speed.

René and Gaston designed each model independently from each other. René's designs started with the letter 'R', and Gaston's with 'G', i.e. the Caudron G. 3, the Caudron R. 11, etc. Gaston was killed in a crash during World War I, but René carried on the business until World War II. Following the war, the remnants of the Caudron establishments were absorbed by nationalization.

CAVENDISH, HENRY
1731–1810

Cavendish was born to English parents in Nice, France. In 1766 he discovered that hydrogen, which he called 'inflammable air', is seven times lighter than ordinary air. He isolated the gas by pouring oil of vitriol (sulphuric acid), on hot iron filings.

He realized the importance of his discovery, but was unable to find a means to exploit hydrogen's properties. He didn't have a light enough container within which he could capture the gas and thus float the container.

When his father died, his inheritance made him one of the world's wealthiest men. He poured his money into scientific research and, fortunately, lived well past Charles's (qv) introduction of the hydrogen balloon. Having devoted his life to science, he never married.

CAYLEY, GEORGE
1773–1857

George Cayley was, unquestionably, the father of heavier-than-air flight. His work led directly, and traceably, to the first flight in 1903. That his name is not well-known outside of aviation circles is an injustice, as Cayley's work encompassed many other fields.

The son of landed gentry from Yorkshire, England, he was encouraged by his mother to have an open mind, and this quality he later showed in both scientific and social causes.

In 1796 he built his first flying device, a contra-rotating model helicopter which he based on scientific calculations. Three years later he reached his greatest scientific conclusions: 1. Defining the forces acting on an aerodyne; lift, gravity, thrust, and drag. 2. Establishing that the mechanism for lift should be separate from that of thrust. In this latter theory he was proved correct until the advent of the helicopter.

Cayley managed to produce an abundance of far-sighted inventions. He invented the adjustable tension wheel (bicycle type), empennages for aircraft, mechanical hands, seat belts, and many other devices for aviation, railroads, public safety, and agriculture. In 1804 he built and flew the first successful model glider. Forty-five years later he designed a boy-carrying glider which lifted a ten-year-old pilot off the ground on a short flight. The world's first pilot's name is lost to history, as is the name of the first adult to fly four years later, in 1853, in another Cayley glider. Upon landing, the man, in fact Cayley's coachman, resigned, telling his employer that he had been hired to drive coaches, not flying machines! These two great flights were as unheralded in Cayley's lifetime as they are today.

Cayley's humble brilliance inspired Henson, Stringfellow, and, through them, others. The world has certainly benefited from the open-mindedness his mother fostered.

CESSNA, CLYDE
1880–1954

Cessna grew up on a small farm on the dusty plains of Kansas. As a boy, he earned a reputation for being an excellent mechanic by fixing local farm equipment. His aptitude brought him a job with the local Overland automobile distributor, and through hard work he eventually opened his own dealership.

In February, 1911 he witnessed a flying exhibit put on by the Moisant International Aviators. The first time he saw their handsome Blériots he knew he would have to have an airplane for himself. He ordered a Blériot fuselage from a catalogue house, and set about building a set of wings which he designed himself. Two months later the first Cessna was ready to fly, but it's builder wasn't. It took Cessna one summer and thirteen crashes to learn to fly. He left the automobile business and became a barnstormer. He was the first pilot to fly over Wichita, Kansas, a town which would later hear a lot more from Cessna.

In 1916, he began to manufacture aircraft, though his company didn't survive World War I. In 1924 he joined Walter Beech (qv) to form Travel Air, but Cessna left in 1927 over design disputes. He wanted to build fully-cantilevered monoplanes.

He started his own company again and his timing couldn't have been better. A month later Lindbergh (qv) soloed the Atlantic and the aviation industry exploded with sales until the Depression.

In 1937 Cessna retired and turned over the presidency of the company to his nephew Dwane Wallace. His trust was well placed, as is attested to by any airport flight line in the US.

CHADWICK, ROY
1893–1947

Like many choirboys before him, when Roy Chadwick went to church on Sundays he always brought paper and a pencil. These were not to take notes of the sermon, but rather to sketch out grand aeroplanes of the imagination. Chadwick's zeal for aeroplanes was so strong that he introduced himself to A. V. Roe (qv) and begged the pioneer aviator to hire him as a trainee draughtsman. Roe accepted the offer and thus in 1911 began Chadwick's long association with AVRO.

One of his earliest assignments was to help with the design of what would become the 504. Chadwick's attention to ergonomic details, even before this was widely considered important, has been credited with making the 504 such a success for nearly two decades.

During World War I he helped design the 530 fighter though it did not go into production. An attempt to create a market for light planes caused him to design the AVRO Baby, a delightful little biplane, but he was nearly killed in one of these when he crashed one into Roe's brother's garden.

Progressively larger aircraft flowed from Chadwick's pen in the 1920s and 30s including the Aldershot bomber, the Bison, the all-metal Ava and others. His ultimate contribution to Britain's military strength was the mighty Lancaster four-engined bomber, of which 7,366 were built.

Chadwick was killed in the crash of a Tudor II airliner in 1947.

CHANUTE, OCTAVE
1832–1910

Chanute played a major role in bringing about heavier-than-air flight. Born in Paris, he moved to New York at the age of six where he became a prosperous civil engineer. His bridge designs helped to expand America's railway system.

After collecting information on the history of flight, he published in 1894 *Progress in Flying Machines*, the world's first accurate compilation of aeronautical experiments and their results. Next, in 1896, he began building man-carrying gliders. These gliders were an advancement over Lilienthal's (qv) type, because they employed a Pratt truss structure instead of 'bat' wings.

Chanute could not fly due to his advanced age, so he hired William Avery and Augustus Herring (qv) as pilots. Most of their flights took place on the shores of Lake Michigan, but later flights were made at the Wrights' (qv) camp at Kill Devil Hill.

In 1900 the Wrights contacted Chanute, having become acquainted with his book, and through correspondence and personal visits, they became friends and associates. Chanute persuaded the Wrights to use the Pratt truss wing structure. Europe heard of the Wright's experiments through Chanute, and it was he who announced their success to a disbelieving French Aéro-Club.

Though he was a scrupulously honest man, Chanute angered the Wright brothers when he perhaps exaggerated his influence on them and stated that they were his 'disciples'. Before his death, the Wrights had softened their feelings towards the man who had helped to put them on the right track. European flight would have been delayed even longer without Chanute's reports.

The Wright's French connection and mentor Octave Chanute.

CHARLES, PROFESSOR JACQUES ALEXANDRE CÉSAR
1746–1823

When the French Academy of Sciences learned of the Montgolfier's (qv) experiments, they decided to sponsor a balloon design of their own. Bartholemy Faujas de Saint Fond, a geologist, raised a subscription for the academy and offered Charles, then a noted physicist, a grant to develop the rival balloon. Charles knew of the work of Cavendish (qv), Black and Cavallo, and realized that hydrogen would make a suitable lifting agent. The problem was finding a light, air-tight container. Charles learned that the Robert brothers had recently discovered how to dissolve rubber in turpentine, so he asked them to build him a four-metre (13ft) balloon of rubberized silk. This was filled with hydrogen in Paris, and flew for the first time on 27 August 1783. After a forty-five minute flight, it landed in the village of Gonesse, about sixteen miles (26km) from Paris, where the frightened villagers attacked it thinking it was a demon!

A larger balloon was constructed and on 1 December 1783 Charles and Marie-Noel Robert took off on the first piloted hydrogen balloon flight. Their flight covered 17 miles (43km), from Paris to Nesle. Delighted at this success, Charles decided to launch again from Nesle that day. In the cool evening air, and with only one man aboard, the balloon shot up to 9,000 feet (2,743m). The combination of the rapid climb, and seeing the sun set for a second time in one day, so frightened Charles that he never flew again.

The balloons Charles and the Robert brothers designed set the standard for most gas balloons up to the present day. They incorporated a net to surround the bag, a light, wicker basket, a safety valve, and ballast.

CHAVEZ, GEORGES
1887–1910

Chavez was born in Paris to Peruvian emigrés. He combined his talent for engineering and his love of sport by learning to fly in 1909 at the

Henry Farman (qv) school. He immediately entered many of the European flying contests, setting several altitude records including one of 8,487 feet (2,587m) on 8 September 8 1910.

Two weeks later, the twenty-three-year-old pilot attempted the first crossing of the Alps, from Brigue, Switzerland to Dommodossola, Italy. Fighting strong winds and freezing temperatures, he forced his Blériot through the Simplon Pass, reaching his objective after forty-two gruelling minutes. Triumph turned to tragedy when the Blériot suddenly nose-dived from only thirty feet (9m). Witnesses said Chavez had probably become too numbed by the cold air to control the plane, though a stall is more likely. They pulled him from the wreckage and took him to a local hospital where he died two days later. Before he died, legend has it that he murmured 'Arriba, mas arriba'. These words, 'Higher, ever higher', became the motto of the Peruvian Air Force.

CHENNAULT, COLONEL CLAIRE LEE
1890–1958

Chennault was a grammar school teacher at the outbreak of World War I, but quit to join the Army. His initial application for flight training was rejected, and he didn't become a pilot until the early 20s. He wasn't satisfied just to fly however. Perhaps it was his background as a teacher which led him to develop his own tactical methods which he hoped to teach others. One of his ideas was that future pilots should fly in pairs. He outlined this and other ideas in *The Role of Defensive Pursuit,* another one of military history's great manuals which no one paid any attention to at the time it was published. Chennault formed a precision aerobatic team called 'Three Men on a Flying Trapeze' which he used to prove that close formation flying and team work in the air were possible.

Friction with his superiors through the years, in particular over the Mitchell (qv) case, was a persistent theme of Chennault's military career. In 1937 he retired, citing deafness, though, in fact, he had quite clearly heard the offer by

Madame Chiang Kai-Shek who asked him to organize China's air defence against the Japanese. After a tour of China to survey the situation, Chennault returned to the U.S. in 1940 to assemble a 300-man volunteer air force. He took this small army, which he had formed with the help of President Roosevelt, along with 100 out-moded P-40Bs to China in 1941. There he drilled his men in the 'Chennault Doctrine' of fighter tactics. Despite facing an enemy with many more men, airplanes and support, Chennault's *Flying Tigers* time and again bested their foe. Their advantage was Channault's ability to make average pilots better.

In July, 1942, The *Flying Tigers* became part of the regular air force and Chennault was given command of the 14th Air Force the next year. He held that post until the end of the war.

In October, 1945 he resigned from the Army in protest over the US government's weak support of Nationalist China. He stayed in China to re-organize their air force and set up an airline to fly-in relief supplies.

CHESHIRE, LORD, VC (GEOFFREY LEONARD)
1917–1992

To describe Cheshire's life as a law student at Oxford in the 1930s as 'mercurial' would be unfair – he was simply one of the most immature, irresponsible undergraduates ever to pretend to be engaged in scholastic exercise there. His pranks ranged from the usual gambling and drinking to the bizarre of darting in front of oncoming automobiles and trains.

For diversion from his serious fooling around he learned to fly with the Oxford University Air Squadron and later transferred to the RAFVR convinced that war was very unlikely. When it came time for his final exams at Oxford he made a Herculean effort to cram for them, but nevertheless did poorly, much to his parents' perennial disappointment. When war seemed imminent he took a permanent RAF commission and was assigned to a bomber squadron.

His first operational sortie was with Whitleys of No 102 Squadron. Still known for his erratic behaviour outside of the cockpit, he managed to show an astuteness behind the stick that was to bring him the respect of his colleagues. He was the first junior officer to receive a DSO after he pressed on to attack the Cologne railway yards, despite a gaping twelve-foot hole having been ripped in the side of his Whitley by an anti-aircraft shell.

He next moved to Halifaxes with No 35 Squadron, but as these aircraft were beset with teething problems, he volunteered to do a quick trip to Canada to ferry back a bomber. In Canada his callow side again manifested itself when he took a raucous side trip to New York. There he had a whirlwind love affair with an actress. They were hurriedly married before Cheshire's return to England as a co-pilot of a Hudson.

He began operational duties in the Halifax though he found this bomber to be overweight and said so to his superiors. Even so, he worked to make each bomb run a success. By early 1942 he had become war weary and was posted to instructional duties. At this time he wrote a successful book called *Bomber Pilot*. With its publication, and with the medals he had already won, he was recognized as a public figure. Fame did not get in his way when he returned to combat duty. By the end of 1942 he had earned another bar to his DSO.

The next year he was given the heavy responsibility of revitalizing Guy Gibson's (qv) former squadron No 617. He plunged into this task and devised new methods to increase the precision of bombing. He insisted that the squadron have its own pathfinders for better co-ordination. His tactical insights worked as did his personal leadership. His bravery in leading attacks earned him a VC.

His stature as a war hero caused him to be withdrawn from combat duties, except for one noteworthy occasion. He served as one of two British observers to the Nagasaki atomic bomb raid.

After the war Cheshire founded a network of homes for the ill and dying. A foundation was created which, under its founder's guidance, grew until it comprised over 250 homes in nearly 50 countries. He earned even more fame for his charitable work than he had as a warrior.

CHICHESTER, SIR FRANCIS CHARLES
1901–1972

Though Chichester has never gained the recognition that other golden age pathfinders, like Lindbergh or Hinkler (qqv), received, he nevertheless made some equally challenging voyages, both by air and sea, and what is more, wrote eloquently of them.

As the black sheep of a noted family from North Devon, England, he set off on his own, aged eighteen, to find his fortune. Few people thought much of his plan to find wealth in New Zealand, but Chichester settled there anyway, earning some money as a semi-professional, lightweight boxer, a lumberjack, a gold miner, and an insurance salesman. None of these got him much money, but then at the age of twenty-six, he entered a real-estate partnership. Business boomed, and within a year, he was earning £10,000 per annum – in those days a remarkable sum. In 1929, he returned to England a moderately wealthy man, and purchased a Gipsy Moth. After only four months training, he embarked on a solo flight to Australia, the second ever, and landed there in triumph. Other record flights followed – Australia to New Zealand, New Zealand to Japan, and one from New Zealand to Australia across the Tasman Sea which he vividly recounted in *Alone Over the Tasman Sea*.

His talents weren't limited to flying and writing. He also invented his own simplified system of navigation which he used successfully on some of his flights, and which was later taught to RAF pilots in World War II. In addition, he became a gifted ship's skipper, and in 1960 completed a solo crossing of the Atlantic. To celebrate his sixty-fifth birthday, he undertook a *solo* round-the-world voyage which ended in triumph as he sailed into an English port. It had been many years and many miles since Chichester had been considered the black sheep of the family.

de la CIERVA, JUAN
1895–1936

Cierva was born in Murcia, Spain, the son of a lawyer. He demonstrated a talent for mathematics and became interested in aviation in 1909. With some school friends, he built two gliders of his own design, after which he built a powered plane. In 1919 a three-engined bomber he designed crashed, which caused Cierva to consider the possibilities of a safer form of flight. He conceived the idea of autogyration the next year, but it took two more years for him to develop a practical machine. He was delayed by the tendency of his machines to flip over on one side. He discovered the problem to be the differing amounts of lift generated by advancing and retreating blades. When he cured the fault by hinging each blade, the autogyro was born.

Autogyros offered extremely short take-off runs, often only fifteen yards. Landings could be made vertically. Cierva autogyros were licensed-built in several factories around the world. Though Cierva pioneered a safer form of transportation than the aeroplane, he still relied on aeroplanes for travel around Europe. He was killed in one at Croydon on 9 December 1936.

CLARK, VIRGINIUS
1886–1948

Clark graduated from the US Naval Academy where he distinguished himself as a brilliant engineer. A few years before World War I, he learned to fly and this led him to a further study of aerodynamics. In 1917 he was posted to the newly formed NACA and initiated an exhaustive study of aerofoil sections. He consequently developed his own series of which the Clark Y is the most famous. Dozens of aircraft utilized this simple-to-construct aerofoil shape with its flat underside, most notably the *Spirit of St. Louis*. Many homebuilders also took advantage of the high lift, low drag qualities of the Clark Y.

Late in his career, Clark entered private business and introduced duramould construction. This method of building aircraft utilizes plastic-impregnated wood. The largest aircraft ever made, the Hughes HK-1 flying-boat *Spruce Goose*, was fabricated by duramould.

CLOSTERMANN, PIERRE H.
1921–

When World War II started, Clostermann wasn't even old enough to join the armed services of France, but by 1945 he had become its top scoring ace. He was in Brazil when France fell in 1940, therefore, when he came of age, he was free to go to Britain to join the RAF. He first flew with No 341 (Free French) Alsace Squadron out of Biggin Hill in 1943. Two years of combat later, he had risen to command of No 3 Squadron flying Tempests. He officially scored thirty-three kills, though only about fourteen of those were verified properly. Most of his fights were against Germany's best pilots while flying over France and Germany.

After the war he became head of the Cessna operations in Rheims, France.

COANDA, HENRI
1885–1972

Coanda was the son of a Romanian general, and planned to follow in his father's footsteps. Military life disagreed with him though, and so he turned to engineering and art. In 1905, he built a model of a rocket-powered airplane which set him on an aviation career. The next year he happened to meet Gabriel Voisin and Louis Blériot (qqv) while on a train trip in France, and they convinced him to move to Paris, then the supposed capital of aviation. Coanda agreed and enrolled in the École Supérieur de L'Aérostation from which he graduated in 1909. He hadn't completely given up on art and was praised by Rodin for his sculpture work.

In 1910, he exhibited his first full size airplane at the Paris Salon. A clean sesquiplane with a cruciform tail, it reflected Coanda's artistic flair. The most striking aspect of the plane was not its airframe, but rather its novel form of propulsion.

It was the first airplane to employ a jet-like engine. The engine consisted of a centrifugal compressor driven by a fifty horsepower Clerget engine all wrapped inside a neat, metal cowling. Most historians now agree that the propulsion unit was more like a ducted fan than a true turbo-jet.

Coanda later claimed that the plane was capable of flight, though this seems unlikely as it crashed on its maiden flight. His talents as a designer continued to manifest themselves when he moved to England and designed excellent military aircraft for the Bristol & Colonial Aeroplane Company.

COBHAM, SIR ALAN JOHN
1894–1973

To many Britons, Cobham's globe-spanning flights of the twenties and thirties were nothing more than typical aviation news screamed on the headlines of a newspaper. In fact, they helped lay the foundation for Imperial Airways' air routes.

Cobham came from a poor London family. Hating dull routine, he joined the Royal Artillery just before World War I. A year before the war's end he transferred into the RFC where he learned to fly. He joined a barnstorming act after the war called Berkshire Aviation Tours Ltd. Two years later, de Havilland hired him as a test pilot. He delivered the first Moth to a flying club.

Survey and route testing flights came next and his most important were from London to Capetown; London to Rangoon; and London to Australia. While flying between Baghdad and Basra on this last flight, his mechanic was killed by the chance rifle shot of a Bedouin tribesman from the desert below.

Cobham's later work included charting a trans-African course for Imperial Airways, and promoting air-mindedness in Britain. To this end, he formed with Sir Sefton Brancker (qv) a Municipal Aerodromes campaign. Other than his record flights, he is noted for pioneering work with in-flight refueling.

Jackie Cochran, a truly inspiring heroine.

COCHRAN, JACQUELINE
1906(?)–1980

One of the most poignant stories in aviation history is of Jacqueline Cochran's rise to fame and fortune. Born in Pensacola, Florida, she was given up to a foster home when still an infant. Her foster parents were migrant farm workers who earned barely enough money to feed themselves. Jacqueline's earliest memories were of scrounging for food. At the age of six she took her first job – that of a midwife, whose duties she performed often on her own. Two years later she made her first upward career move by taking a job in a textile mill where she earned six cents an hour. After several weeks of careful saving, she purchased a pair of shoes – the first she ever owned. Her fashion sense dictated that these be high heels.

Despite acute poverty, she had one priceless asset – the love of life. At twelve she talked her way into a job as a hair stylist and moved from salon to salon until she got to New York city. There, she became a well-known beautician and soon had opened up her own establishment and introduced a line of beauty cosmetics.

In 1932 she learned to fly. Her first solo flight ended with a forced landing due to engine failure. Within a year, she had made sufficient progress to become a competitive pilot. Her first race was an all-woman event at Roosevelt Field, Long Island. In 1934 she entered the MacRobertson England to Australia race, fielding a two-seat Gee Bee racer. Control problems forced her out of the race in Romania, and she sold the dangerous, yet fast, airplane to Francisco Sarabia (qv) who was later killed in it.

In 1938 she won the Bendix Trophy in spite of being only the second woman ever allowed to compete in the race. The next year she made the first blind landing by a woman. During World War II she fought the Army brass to establish the Women's Airforce Service Pilots. She won this fight and the WASPs proved invaluable in ferrying aircraft. In 1953 she was the first woman to break the sound barrier.

A devoted patriot, she attempted to win a congressional seat after the war, but failed. She was instrumental in urging General Eisenhower to run for President.

A woman of immense ability both in science and business, Jacqueline also had a spiritual side. She claimed that she and Amelia Earhart (qv) could psychically communicate with each other and that after Earhart's disappearance, the location of the downed airplane was revealed to her mystically. A pilot of great prowess, Cochran's courage was not confined to the cockpit.

COCKING, ROBERT
1777–1837
The son of an Irish cleric, Cocking was a water-colourist by profession. In 1802, he witnessed Garnerin's (qv) first parachute descent in Britain. After the display, he asked the Frenchman why his parachute had shaken so violently. Garnerin didn't know why, but said the action made him ill. Cocking promised to design a better parachute. Thirty-five years later, and twelve after Garnerin's death, Cocking appeared with his new parachute. It was the inverted 'dihedral' type first proposed by Cayley (qv).

On 24 July 1837, Cocking ascended in Green's (qv) *Royal Nassau* balloon. At 5,000 feet (1,525m), he released the parachute which immediately folded up in the air. The horrified spectators ran to Cocking who was still breathing after plummeting to earth. He died minutes later, leaving his would-be rescuers to wonder why he waited until the age of sixty to parachute for the first time, and why he never thoroughly tested his device.

CODY, COLONEL SAMUEL FRANKLIN
c.1861–1913
Cody was born in Forth Worth, Texas and joined a 'Wild West' show as a young man. Although no relation to 'Buffalo Bill' Cody, he too displayed an outgoing, hearty personality that endeared him to people. In the early 1890s, he took his own 'wild west' theatrical troupe to Europe, where they performed feats which would have amazed even real cowboys. In Italy they staged chariot races! Cody's home base became England, and around 1900 he began to experiment with kites. Early attempts to interest the British Army were unsuccessful, but his experiments continued until he had developed practical meteorological kites, and man-lifters. The military's reluctance to consider Cody seriously was only natural. One of their own officers, Captain B. F. S. Baden-Powell (qv), with all his financial resources and scientific backing, had been unable to develop a practical kite. To them Cody was only a mere showman who, during much of the initial correspondence, was touring with a show called 'The Klondyke Nugget', whose special effects included live horses and gun fights on stage! Finally, in 1904, the Army consented to review Cody's improved kites and, to their surprise, found them worth developing.

Cody's association with the military led to the success of Britain's first military dirigible, the *Nulli Secundus*. He then built the first aeroplane to fly in England. A Gothic-looking machine based on the Wright brother's (qv) latest model, it flew on 16 October 1908 on Laffan's Plain, Farnborough. In 1909 he became a naturalized

British citizen in order to enter the *Daily Mail* £1,000 prize contest for the first mile flight in Britain. The prize was then won by J. T. C. Moore-Brabazon (qv).

Cody died in 1913 when his plane broke up in mid-air. His son, Frank Cody, was killed in aerial combat in World War I.

COFFYN, FRANK TRENHOLM
1878–1960

Coffyn's father was a banker who had dealings with the Wrights (qv) and this is how the young Coffyn was introduced to aviation. Orville taught him to fly in 1910, whereupon he joined the Wright's exhibition team. He had not yet soloed when he was sent to his first show in Indianapolis, and so he made his first flight alone in front of 120,000 spectators. He later became a test pilot for the Burgess-Curtiss company, after having built the first aluminium pontoons in 1911. He joined the Air Service in World War I. His last achievement of note was earning FAI helicopter pilot's licence No. 2 in 1944.

COLDING, JOHAN PETER
_

Colding, a Dane, made his first balloon ascent on 10 November 1811. His contributions to aviation history include being the first to send mail, unchaperoned, by air. He did this by making small balloons in which, when the wind was favourable, he sent packets to Denmark's out-lying islands. He was also the first to drop propaganda pamphlets by air when he launched his mail balloons with political pamphlets in the direction of Sweden.

COLI, FRANCOIS
*–1927

Coli was born into a French maritime family and attended the naval academy at Marseille. He became an expert navigator while in the French Navy and later joined the merchant marine. In 1912 he entered into his family's business and was in Argentina when war began two years later. He returned to France and requested assignment to the infantry where he found all the action he desired. His bravery cost him two wounds, but earned him a battlefield commission. In late 1917 he developed frost-bite in his toes, and was granted his request to transfer to the air force. His bravery again won him promotion and he took over command of the 62nd Squadron.

After the war he made several noted flights, flying sometimes as pilot-in-command and sometimes as navigator. In late 1926 he joined with Nungesser (qv) in an attempt to win the Orteig prize by flying from Paris to New York. Their efforts led to the construction of the *L'Oiseau Blanc* aircraft in which they hoped to make an East–West Atlantic crossing. On 8 May 1927 they took off from Paris in very bad weather with a twelve per cent fuel reserve which many experts considered inadequate. They were last seen off the coast of France and many hours later false reports said that they had landed in New York. In fact, the *L'Oiseau Blanc* disappeared with its brave crew and was never found.

In the mid-1980s a group in the US was formed to use modern aerial surveillance methods to try to find the missing aircraft. They believed it may have gone down in the rugged hills of Maine.

COLLISHAW, SQUADRON COMMANDER RAYMOND
1893–1976

Collishaw was a native of British Columbia and a merchant mariner before joining the RNAS. During 1917 he commanded the famous 'Black Flight' Squadron and his personal Sopwith Triplane was known as the *Black Maria*. He was a keen marksman, and this skill enabled him to earn sixty victories, including one over the German ace Karl Allmenröder.

When Winston Churchill sent troops to support the White Russians in southern Russia during 1919, Collishaw went as commander of a fighter squadron. There he earned two more victories by downing Bolshevik planes. During the early stages of World War II he commanded the RAF forces in Egypt which thoroughly defeated the Reggia Aeronautica.

CONGREVE, WILLIAM
1771–1828

Congreve was the son of a British army officer. At a relatively young age he began to experiment with pyrotechnic displays, and these led him to wonder if rockets could be used for military purposes. After trying various gunpowder formulations and packing methods, he developed a rocket that was powerful, accurate and reliable – thus suited for war.

He then convinced the Admiralty to use only rockets for their attack on the French fleet at Boulogne harbour in 1805. The Royal Navy, armed with thousands of Congreve's rockets, attempted such an attack, but bad weather foiled the scheme. In late 1806 a similar raid was mounted, but this time it was a great success. Subsequently, Congreve rockets took part in British military operations all over the world, including battles in Denmark, India, Canada and the US. Their participation in the bombardment of Fort McHenry near Baltimore inspired one observer, Francis Scott Key, to write about 'the rocket's red glare'.

Congreve's work was the link between the rocketry of the middle-ages and that of the twentieth century.

CONNEAU, JEAN
1880–1937

During the summer of 1911 one of aviation history's greatest rivalries was fought by two very brave, and very different men. They were Jules Vedrines (qv) and Jean Conneau. Conneau was a French naval officer and expert navigator. He learned to fly in 1910, and took a leave of absence during the summer of 1911 to participate in several European air races. The Navy couldn't allow one of their officers to officially race, so they stipulated that Conneau use an alias. He chose André Beaumont.

Conneau was a well-mannered, carefully dressed man whose pride in doing things right was reflected in his approach to aviation. He adapted his navigation skills to aviation, and was the first pilot to fly by what became known as 'dead reckoning'. This method allowed him to fly, usually, point-to-point, while other racing pilots were forced to follow railway lines and winding roads. Such a pilot was Conneau's arch-rival in sport, and temperamental opposite, Jules Vedrines. During the summer of 1911 they competed against each other in four major races. Conneau won three of them.

COPPENS de HOUTHULST, WILLY
1892–1987

Born at Watermael, near Brussels, Coppens was an infantryman when the war started in 1914. In 1915 when he requested that he be transferred to the air force, his superiors approved on the condition that he went to England and took lessons at his own expense! He did, returning in 1916 as a fighter pilot. It took him until April, 1918 to gain his first victory, but then he quickly added to his tally, rising to become Belgium's leading ace. His final score was thirty-seven – twenty-six of which were against the extremely hard-to-down observation balloons. On his last mission of the war, he crash landed and lost a leg. He remained in the Belgian military after the war and only retired after his country had fallen in 1940.

CORNU, PAUL
1881–1944

In 1905 Cornu began to experiment with model helicopters. Using a modified two horsepower (1.5kW) Buchet engine, he achieved a few flights with a large model, and this encouraged him to build a full-size machine.

Cornu designed his machine carefully, testing several sets of rotor blades before choosing the set which generated the most lift. When he had got the blades he wanted, he attached two sets of them to a lightweight steel tube airframe on which was mounted a twenty-four horsepower

(18kW) Antoinette engine. On 13 November 1907, near Lisieux, France, Cornu climbed into his helicopter and started the engine. In it he was lifted about one foot (0.3m). This flight earned him the credit of having been the first true helicopter pilot, despite that fact that two months earlier the Brequet-Richet machine had flown. That vehicle needed four men to hold it steady.

Cornu never progressed beyond this tentative success because he lacked money.

CORRIGAN, DOUGLAS

1907–

Clyde Corrigan, Jr. was born in Galveston, Texas to an Irish father and English mother. About a dozen years later when his parents divorced, his mother told him she didn't want anything in the house to remind her of his father, so she changed his name to Douglas. When Corrigan was fifteen, his mother died leaving him to take care of his younger brother and sister. He worked various jobs, including bottle washer and truck driver, until one day he saw two barnstormers flying near Los Angeles. He talked them into teaching him to fly in exchange for helping them around the flying field. At the age of seventeen he became a pilot.

He next got a job with Ryan in San Diego. He taught flying and maintained the aircraft at their flying school. When Lindbergh's (qv) aircraft was under construction in 1927, Corrigan was involved as a mechanic. When Ryan moved to St Louis, Corrigan decided to strike out on his own, and took several jobs before barnstorming around the south-east. In 1938, he made a most unusual flight which he later swore was by complete accident. On 17 July he took off from Floyd Bennet Field in New York, alleging that he intended to fly to California. Instead, his nine-year-old Curtiss Robin landed near Dublin, Ireland. He claimed he had read his compass backwards!

Corrigan became a world hero, not because his flight was significant, it had been done many times since 1927, but because Corrigan was a modest, common man. His airplane was already a near antique, which he bought for $325; the engine was new but because of a lack of funds Corrigan had installed it himself; the plane had no radio nor did it have a fuel gauge. The 'mix-up' was probably due to Corrigan's need to avoid bureaucracy which had already decreed before the flight that they wouldn't allow him to fly across the Atlantic because his aircraft wasn't up to a suitable standard.

Not even bureaucrats can keep a good man down, and Corrigan succeeded in the end. His success brought him another name change however. After his flight he became known as 'Wrong-way' Corrigan.

In subsequent years he flew as a civilian in the war-time Ferry Command, worked as an airplane salesman and even ran for the US Senate on an anti-liquor platform.

COSTES, DIEUDONNÉ

1896–1973

Costes was France's most celebrated inter-war flier. A scout plane pilot with eight victories in World War I, he turned to commercial aviation in the 1920s and pioneered several Europe-to-North Africa air routes. During the late twenties he made notable flights from Paris to Persia, Senegal to Brazil, and Paris to Buenos Aires.

Flying was a science to Costes who planned each flight meticulously. After his most famous flight, the first Paris to New York direct flight in 1930, he brushed aside his hero's welcome and gave credit for his triumph to his radioman and navigator, Bellonte (qv).

COURTNEY, FRANK T.

1894(?)–1982

Frank Courtney, an Irishman, was known as 'The Man with the Magic hands'. He earned this reputation not because he could count money quickly, although that would have been an attribute in his first chosen field, that of a bank clerk, but rather it came from the skill he demonstrated in his second career – that of one of the world's top test pilots.

Courtney did not look the role of a dashing test pilot. He was tall, but awkward, and he wore pince nez spectacles. He was working as a humble bank clerk in Paris when the aviation craze swept Europe in the early years of this century. He left his job and went to England where he worked in Claude Grahame-White's (qv) Hendon facility as an unpaid trainee. There he learned to fly and thus started the career of perhaps the world's most unlikely great pilot.

Though initially rejected as an RFC pilot at the outbreak of World War I because he wore glasses, Courtney's superior flying skill eventually brought him to the front lines, and it was while flying a Morane Parasol that he was wounded during a patrol both by shrapnel and bullets. After convalescing he became a test pilot at Farnborough.

The next two decades saw him take over one hundred different aircraft up on their initial flights. He made in excess of 10,000 test flights. There wasn't any type of machine he wouldn't put through its paces, though he became a specialist and leading authority on flying-boats. Juan de la Cierva (qv) hired him to test his early autogyros because the Spanish pilots were proceeding too slowly. Courtney helped Cierva fix the vibration-prone machine when he suggested adding hinges to allow horizontal blade movement in addition to those already installed that allowed vertical movement. Cierva at first balked at this idea, but after a crash that injured Courtney seriously, the inventor relented and instantly had an airworthy machine.

The series of crashes, mishaps, and firsts that highlight Courtney's career seems almost too fantastic to be true. He raced planes in the twenties, winning the English Aerial Derby in 1920 and the King's Cup in 1923. In 1928 he attempted for the second time to fly across the Atlantic but ditched in mid-ocean due to an engine fire. He spent twenty-four hours adrift before being rescued.

Courtney left England after some minor legal wranglings and because that country's aviation firms were employing more 'in house' test pilots. Because of his eyesight, he couldn't get a commercial pilot's licence so he moved to America. There, he continued to fly but also started a writing and lecturing career. Later he became associated with Convair and had some input into the design of the Atlas missile – not bad for a former bank clerk.

Beaming Frank Courtney about to attempt a trans-Atlantic flight.

COUTELLE, JEAN-MARIE JOSEPH
1748–1835

In 1794 Napoleon established the world's first air force – four balloons with an experimental station at Chalais-Meudon. The station still exists. He placed in charge of La Première Compagnie d'Aérostiers Jean-Marie Coutelle. In May, Coutelle took one of the balloons, *L'Entreprenant*, north to Maubeuge where the French were resisting Austrian attempts to cross the Sambre river. On 2 June he ascended in the balloon with an engineering officer and together they observed the enemy troop movements. This flight was of little tactical value, except that it helped to fortify the French morale.

Three weeks later, on 26 June Coutelle again launched his balloon, this time at Fleurus. Accompanying him was General Jean-Baptiste

Jourdan who, after surveying the battle from aloft, dropped notes and battle orders to his commanders below. Whether these orders, or just Austrian confusion generated by being observed from above for the first time, helped the French to win is a matter of debate. The balloon, no doubt, aided in the defeat.

In 1798 Coutelle's air force followed Napoleon's army to Egypt. During the naval battle at Aboukir Bay the force's cargo ship was sunk, and Napoleon declined to resupply them. It would be a half a century before military ballooning returned to France.

COUTINHO, GAGAL
(see CABRAL)

COXWELL, HENRY TRACEY
1819–1900

Coxwell's accomplishments identify him as perhaps the world's greatest aeronaut. The son of a British Royal Navy commander, he originally trained to be a dentist. For a young man who had witnessed Green's (qv) early flights, and Cocking's (qv) fatal parachute descent, the dentistry trade held little promise of excitement. Instead, Coxwell learned how to build and fly balloons. At the age of twenty-six in 1845, he founded and published Britain's first aeronautical journal *The Balloon or Aerostatic Magazine*. When the magazine went out of business several months later Coxwell was glad that he had published under the pseudonym Henry Wells, Esq.

His flying career was more successful, though not without incident. In 1847, while on a flight with several friends, his balloon passed through a thunderstorm and somehow its gas was released. The balloon plunged earthwards, but Coxwell, with great presence of mind, climbed the rigging and cut off the bottom of the gas bag which caused the top to inflate like a parachute. The lucky balloonists landed safely.

During the next few years Coxwell began development of the balloon as an offensive weapon. He demonstrated, in Germany, the

practicality of flying over a target and dropping 'aerial torpedoes', but it wasn't until 1870 that the Germans asked him to build two attack balloons for their siege on Paris.

His greatest contributions to aeronautics were the flights he made with James Glaisher (qv) the noted scientist. During these high altitude flights he gathered useful information on the nature of the upper atmosphere. These historic flights occurred between 1862 and 1865, though the most astonishing one was made on 5 September 1862. On this flight, loaded with scientific instruments, Coxwell and Glaisher began a long ascent which soon brought them to over five miles (8km) high. Though they began to feel faint, they let the balloon continue to rise. At six miles (9.7km), Glaisher lost consciousness and Coxwell had trouble staying alert. When he tried to scrape ice off the gas bag his fingers froze, and when he tried to pull the gas release rope he found his limbs had become almost unmovable. In a last desperate attempt to arrest the ascension, he grabbed the rope in his teeth and pulled. The valve opened and the balloon reversed its course.

When the aeronauts landed they were amazed to find that the barometer indicated that they had reached 37,000 feet (11,280m). Later, scientists recalculated the voyage and estimated that 34,000 feet (10,360m) was more accurate. That is approximately the altitude at which commercial jets fly!

Coxwell was always a strong proponent of the balloon and held little hope for dirigibles or heavier-than-air craft. He recounted his remarkable experiences in *My Life and Balloon Experiences*, a classic in aerostatic literature.

CUNNINGHAM, JOHN
1917–

During World War II the British public became well aware of 'Cat's Eyes' Cunningham's exploits. He was the first Briton of the war to shoot down an enemy bomber at night. Flying a radar equipped Beaufighter, he intercepted and destroyed a Ju-88 on the night of 19/20 November, 1940. This victory proved the concept of airborne radar. Cunningham continued to excel in this difficult work and by the war's end had shot down twenty planes, nineteen at night. After the war, he went to de Havilland as a test pilot, and flew the Comet 3 around the world in 1955, making a 30,000 mile (48,270km) journey in fifty-six hours.

CUNNINGHAM, LIEUTENANT RANDALL H.

1941-

Cunningham was born in Los Angeles the day after the Pearl Harbor attack, and later attended the University of Missouri. In 1967 he received a commission in the Navy, receiving his pilot's wings the next year. During the Vietnam conflict he was assigned to the USS *Constellation* from which he flew two tours of duty. On his second tour, he flew with William Driscoll as his Weapon Systems Officer, and together they succeeded in downing five MiGs.

On 6 May 1972 Cunningham received a 'Dear John' letter from his girlfriend. Perhaps it was the frustration of receiving this letter which he took out on his North Vietnamese opponents two days later, for on 8 May he shot down three enemy jets, including Hanoi's top ace, the mysterious Colonel Toon. After the epic battle, Cunningham's Phantom was hit by SAM shrapnel, and began to veer out of control. He later recounted that when the jet was hit, he immediately began to believe in God. Suddenly the plane righted itself, and Cunningham chuckled at his sudden conversion, deciding it was akin to superstition. Just then, the plane went out of control again! He mentally apologised and decided to believe. Just as suddenly, the plane righted itself just long enough for him to eject. He was rescued by American helicopters off the North Vietnamese coast. He ended the war with five victories and a new faith.

CURTISS, GLENN HAMMOND

1878-1930

Next to the Wrights (qv), Glenn Curtiss was the greatest of America's early aviators.

Glenn Curtiss, arch-rival to the Wrights.

He grew up in Hammondsport, NY, a town named after an ancestor, and after finishing school took work at George Eastman's Kodak plant in Rochester. He showed a flair for mechanical things and combined this with his love of bicycle-racing to start a bicycle manufacturing business. He soon added motorcycles to his product list, and in 1907 he set a World Land Speed record of 136.3mph (219km/hr) on an eight-cylinder motorcycle of his own design. The success of his engines brought him to the attention of Alexander Graham Bell (qv) who made him a member of the AEA team. His job was to provide the engines for the group's airframes. The AEA's third aircraft, the *June Bug*, was designed in 1908 by Curtiss and became their first truly successful design. On 4 July 1908, Curtiss made the first official public flight in the US in this airplane and won the Scientific American trophy. Curtiss later retired the trophy after winning the 1909 Gordon-Bennett Cup at Rheims, and making the first Albany to New York city flight in 1910.

In 1909 Curtiss founded America's first aircraft manufacturing company in partnership with A.

Herring (qv), Chanute's (qv) former partner. On 26 January 1911 he made the world's first flight in a *practical* hydroplane. In 1914 his company produced an excellent multi-engined flying-boat named the *America*. This was intended to fly across the Atlantic non-stop, but World War I thwarted the plan.

Although Curtiss gained great popularity and wealth, his business dealings caused him much worry. Herring had gained control of the company and claimed that Curtiss was little more than a 'driver'. Herring may have been lacking in talent himself, if not ambition. At any rate, Curtiss forced the bankruptcy of the company and started again. His new company was soon bought out by financiers of the auto industry, including J. N. Willys.

Curtiss continued to do engineering work, but later moved to Florida where he became one of that state's first real estate developers. Bad business dealings and lengthy patent litigation with Herring sapped his strength.

D'ANNUNZIO, GABRIELE
1863–1938
Gabriele D'Annunzio was born Gaetano Rapagnetta, but adopted the name D'Annunzio from his father's uncle. When Italy entered World War I he became a fifty-three-year-old cavalry officer in the White Lancers. He left them to join an aviation squadron, and it was in the air that he gained his greatest fame during the war.

D'Annunzio had first flown in 1911 with Glenn Curtiss (qv) at the Brescia Air Meet. After joining the Italian Air Force, he became a major in the Lion of St. Mark Squadron where he won approval for his plans to lead long distance bombing and reconnaissance raids against the Germans and Austrians. His most remarkable deep penetration raid occurred on 9 August 9, 1918 when he guided a flight of seven SVA fighters from Brescia across the Alps and on to Vienna, where they dropped propaganda leaflets. Until then, Vienna's airspace had been considered impenetrable. This flight lasted nearly seven hours and foreshadowed the long-range fighter escort missions of World War II.

Italian poet-aviator Gabriele D'Annunzio.

D'ARLANDES, MARQUIS
(see FRANCOIS LAURENT*)*

DASSAULT, MARCEL
(see MARCEL BLOCH*)*

DAVIS, DAVID R.
1894(?)–1972
Davis was a sickly child who was advised to spend as much time outdoors as possible. He was sent on an educational camping trip with a tutor while a young man, during which they retraced the route of Lewis and Clark. When he was fifteen he moved to California with his mother. Their home was near where Glenn Martin (qv) was experimenting and Davis would often help Martin ground-handle his plane. In 1911 Davis made his first flight and four years later he bought his first aeroplane. During World War I, he served in the Army. Following hostilities, he became a barnstormer before joining with Donald Douglas (qv) in 1920 to start the Davis-Douglas Airplane Company. This

venture failed and Davis was completely wiped out with the Stock Market crash in 1929.

Davis took an everyday job to support his family but he never gave up his penchant for airplanes. He tried to develop a variable pitch propeller, but lack of funds hampered this effort. By the late 1930s, he had developed a theory of aerofoils that he thought could greatly increase the efficiency of wings. He tested model sections mounted on a borrowed car. Through Walter Brookins (qv), he was able to convince Reuben Fleet (qv) of the possibilities inherent in his new wing. Fleet had a wing section tested at the California Institute of Technology where the scientists said the wing was an impossible 102 per cent efficient. They disassembled their wind tunnel to see what was wrong! Fleet ordered that his next seaplane be built with a 'Davis Wing' – a million dollar gamble. In 1939 this plane was flown by an amazed test pilot who said that it handled like a fighter.

Davis and his partner Brookins received royalties for every plane built using a Davis wing. They accrued well over $250,000. The Navy later investigated Davis's original patent application and found that the aerofoil ordinates were 'doctored'. They insisted that Davis return all his royalties. He confessed that in his patent application he had knowingly falsified the data so that others would not steal his idea. The Navy compromised, allowing Davis to receive reduced future royalties. The most significant airplane to employ the Davis wing was the B-24.

DEERE, SQUADRON LEADER ALAN CHRISTOPHER
1917–

A sheep farmer from New Zealand, Deere went to Britain in 1937 to join the RAF. During the Battle of Britain he flew with No 54 Squadron, and brought down the first Messerschmitt Bf-109 of the war. The rest of the war proved equally eventful, as Deere was shot down three times, once during the evacuation of Dunkirk. He rose to take command of the Biggin Hill Wing in 1943 and after the war remained with the RAF. His final tally was 21·5 enemy planes.

de HAVILLAND, SIR GEOFFREY
1882–1965

The most successful of all British aviation pioneers, de Havilland was born the son of a clergyman. Before his twentieth birthday he designed a motorcycle and after graduating from the Crystal Palace Engineering School began a short-lived career in the automotive industry. By 1908, when flying was just beginning to be noticed in Britain, he persuaded his grandfather to loan him £1,000 from which he could fund the construction of an airplane. Along with his assistant Frank Herle, an engine and a biplane were built and ready for test flying in 1909. This aircraft managed to hop a few times before crashing, and so a second machine was built in 1910. This machine was a typical box-kite of the period and in no way revolutionary, but in 1910 it was one of Britain's few domestically-produced flyable aircraft. Of it, one newspaper reported: 'Its speed is great, possibly thirty miles an hour !' The success of this machine, in which de Havilland taught himself to fly, brought him to the attention of the British military which bought his plane for £400 and offered him a job at HM Balloon Factory.

At the government factory he produced such aircraft as the FE-2, the SE-1 canard, the BE-1 and BS-2. In 1914 he joined the Aircraft Manufacturing Company as chief designer and test pilot. Interestingly, he test flew all of his own designs until 1918.

His most notable achievements at Airco were the DH-4, DH-9, and DH-10. These aircraft were all considerably larger than the average fighter of the day and gave de Havilland important experience in designing aircraft with high payload ability. At the war's end he put this knowledge to use.

Airco folded in 1920 and that same year, in September, de Havilland founded his own company. De Havilland decided to target the commercial market and reject, for the most part, the military one. His factory, first at Stag Lane, Edgware and later at Hatfield, produced a steady stream of well-designed, though perhaps not spectacular, biplanes for the civil and commercial markets.

De Havilland's long-time interest in engines led to the creation of the Cirrus 60hp engine using cheap parts from war-surplus Renault engines. The successful mating of this unit to a simple biplane led to the wide-spread ownership of private aircraft. This plane was the classic DH-60 Moth.

Moths and their progeny garnered for Britain innumerable aviation awards. De Havilland aircraft grew larger and larger with the approach of war until in 1937 the DH-91 Albatross with its 104-foot span, gracefully took to the air. Like many de Havilland aircraft the Albatross was as much noted for its aesthetic lines as its technical achievement.

To conserve vital war metals, de Havilland's company designed the Mosquito fighter, using less important wood for its structure. The 'Mossie' is considered by some to have been the best all-round aircraft of the war. Even before the war's end de Havilland had produced both airframes and engines for early Allied jets. After 50 years some DH Vampires are still flying

Not all of de Havilland's aviation life was happy though. Two of his three sons were killed in test flying crashes, and in 1966 his company was forced to merge into the Hawker Siddeley Group.

De Havilland was not the only member of his family to achieve fame and fortune. His cousin, Olivia de Havilland established herself as a lasting star of the silver screen.

DELAGE, PAUL-ARISTIDE GUSTAVE
1883–*

Delage was born in Limoges, and graduated from L'École Navale before receiving a commission in the French Navy. Hearing of the success of others with aircraft in France, he began experimenting with gliders and in 1910 earned his pilot's licence. The next year he was flying a Nieuport Scout, and met Edouard Nieuport (qv). In early 1914, after the deaths of both the Nieuport brothers, Delage was asked to become the firm's chief designer. He left the Navy to take the job and soon the Nieuport Scouts he designed became the fabled mounts of aces.

Delage continued the Nieuport tradition of lightly-built, small aircraft. Though his early designs were somewhat under-strength for combat duties, he eventually improved them and by the early twenties Nieuport was building advanced plywood monocoque racers.

Gustave Delage was not related to Louis Delage, the French automobile mogul.

DELAGRANGE, LÉON
1873–1910

Born in Orleans, the son of a wealthy industrialist, Delagrange led a colourful life as a popular Parisian sculptor. His works received critical praise and were often exhibited at the Paris Salon. In 1905 he became interested in Voisin's (qv) glider experiments and commissioned him to build an aeroplane. Delagrange designed an aeroplane, which, despite it's artistic merit, would have been impossible to build, so Voisin persuaded him to buy a 'standard' Voisin-type biplane with a few modifications. Delagrange took delivery in 1907, but wasn't able to achieve a true flight until March, 1908.

After teaching himself to fly, Delagrange embarked on a tour of Europe. He became the first person ever to fly in Italy, and also the first to carry a female passenger. She was his sculptress friend Mme Thérèse Peltier. Though he managed to set several early speed and distance records, he is not remembered as one of Europe's premier pilots. He was the sixth man ever to pilot an aeroplane, and became the sixth man to be killed in one. This occurred on 4 January 1910 at Bordeaux, when he overstressed his Blériot in a tight turn which caused the wings to break off. He plunged about seventy feet to the ground and was crushed to death by the engine.

DE LESSEPS, JACQUES
1883–1924

De Lesseps was the grandson of Ferdinand De Lesseps, the builder of the Suez Canal. He came to prominence as a sportsman pilot after the

Rheims meet, and managed a minor coup in May, 1910 when he won the Ruinart Prize, a French prize offered for the first Channel crossing. Through an oversight, Blériot (qv) had improperly filed for it the previous year. He continued to build his reputation that year in Europe, but even more so in North America where he participated in the Belmont Park meet, and made the first flights over Toronto and Montreal.

During World War I he was decorated for bravery and commanded an aviation squadron. He met his death in Canada when his survey plane disappeared in the sea near Gaspe.

DEMOZAY, JEAN
1916–1945

Demozay was serving as an interpreter for the RAF in France in the summer of 1940 when the German advance prompted him to escape to England. In England, he formally joined the RAF and became a fighter pilot, flying first Hurricanes and then Spitfires. His kill tally rose steadily as he became noted for his solo attack style. He also undertook dangerous low-level raids into France and even sank a minelayer. By 1943 he had shot down twenty-one aircraft.

Following this success, he was posted to a training squadron and later a bombing group. After the war he helped rebuild the Armée de l'Air but was killed in a flight from England to France.

DEPERDUSSIN, ARMAND
*–1924

Deperdussin was a salesman extraordinaire, whether he was coaxing people into a make-shift theatre to see the first Lumière films, or selling silk to department stores all over France. His silver tongue and suave manners brought him a fortune, but he always wanted more. In 1909, aeroplanes were on everyone's mind in France, and Deperdussin came up with a plan to capitalize on this interest by displaying a mock aeroplane near his textile merchandise in a Parisian department store. He hired a young engineer, L. Béchereau (qv) to build a fake, but instead of putting together a cheap imitation, Bechereau created a nearly flyable machine. Deperdussin was so impressed that he founded an aircraft company and hired his young engineer as chief designer. Almost immediately the 'Deps' earned a reputation for advanced engineering and high speed. In 1913, at the height of his career and power, Deperdussin was arrested for defrauding investors of millions of francs. Imprisoned, he was forced to sell his company to L. Blériot (qv). After four years of legal battles, he was finally convicted but given a suspended sentence. In 1924, penniless, he shot himself.

DEUTSCH de la MEURTHE, HENRI
1845(?)–1919

Deutsch de la Meurthe was born to a wealthy Parisian family that held major engineering and oil concerns. Deutsch studied engineering and became an avid patron of anything containing a gasoline engine or that flew. He also had a soft spot for poor musicians and wrote an opera himself which was performed in 1911.

As an organizer of the L'Automobile-Club de France, he recognized the need to provide a support group for struggling aeronautical experimenters in France. To this end he founded L'Aéro-Club and sponsored major prizes which tempted aviators. Santos-Dumont (qv) won one of these prizes when he flew around the Eiffel Tower, and Farman (qv) won one with the first European circular kilometre. These incentives and the club proved crucial in fostering a camaraderie and understanding amongst French experimenters that was to be found in no other country. Not even Chanute's (qv) efforts in America brought together the divergent groups to such an extent.

Deutsch later founded the L'Institut Aérotechnique at St-Cyr which did much to place aeronautics in France on a scientific footing.

DOLLFUS, CHARLES
1893–1981

Dollfus was France's greatest aviation historian. He was born in Paris to a natural scientist with fashionable family connections. He was often taken to the balloon establishment at Saint Cloud, a Paris neighbourhood, where he met the Belle Époque aeronauts. He went for his first balloon ride in 1911.

Though he maintained a life-long love of aviation and taught its history as a professor, he was also actively involved in French social causes such as prison reform. A tireless author, he championed the cause of the Wright brothers against doubters from his own country and abroad. It is due to his scientific enquiry for the truth behind aviation history, rather than for evidence to support preconceived notions, that Dollfus will be remembered.

The man who could fly anything well – Jimmy Doolittle.

DOOLITTLE, LIEUTENANT-GENERAL JAMES HAROLD
1896–1993

Doolittle was born in Alameda, California and attended the University of California where he studied engineering. He joined the Army in 1917. In 1920 he was posted to the air corps where his engineering background helped him to rise quickly. In 1922 he made the first air crossing of the United States in under twenty-four hours. He was next assigned to various governmental aviation advisory boards. Sponsored by the Guggenheim Fund, he made the world's first totally blind flight on 24 September 1929. Much of the instrumentation for this flight had been developed by Doolittle himself.

He retired from the Army and joined Shell Oil in the early 1930s. His duties included promotional sales tours of North and South America and also aiding in the development of new aviation fuels. During this time, he set many speed records and won many important races. His most notable wins were the Schneider in 1925, the Bendix in 1931 and the Thompson in 1932.

Doolittle returned to military aviation in 1940. Perhaps his greatest accomplishment was the conception and organization of the B-25 Tokyo raid in April 1942. Seemingly against the laws of physics, Doolittle led a flight of bombers off the aircraft carrier *Hornet* in a sneak attack against mainland Japan that helped to swing the course of the war. This brilliant raid caused the shocked Japanese to pull back front line air squadrons to protect the homeland, which weakened their offensive capabilities when they could least afford to. It also served as a huge moral boost for America, which was still reeling from the embarrassment of Pearl Harbor.

The success of this raid earned Doolittle his general's star and the command of the 12th Air Force in North Africa. He later commanded the mighty Eighth Air Force in England from 1944 – 45.

DORNBERGER, WALTER
1895–1980

Dornberger volunteered for military duty in 1914 and joined the German Army. His career there was to last for thirty-three years. He studied engineering and became an expert on advanced ordnance. In 1930 he became the Chief For Rockets on the Army Board of Ordnance. In this role, he led development work on Germany's most advanced war weapons, including the V-2 rocket and the V-1 flying bomb. To Dornberger goes the credit of spotting the talent in young Wernher von Braun (qv) whom he hired to work at Peenemünde on the rocket projects. Dornberger's work was full of intrigues with the Gestapo who sought to wrench control of the Peenemünde establishment away from the army. Only Dornberger's willingness to risk his own career and life kept the SS from arresting several of the rocket team's most important scientists, including von Braun.

He spent two years, in a British POW camp after the war. Set free, he moved to America where he developed missiles at Wright-Patterson AFB. In 1950 he became a consultant for Bell.

The stable hand behind Germany's wartime rocket programme, Walter Dornberger.

DORNIER, PROFESSOR CLAUDIUS
1884–1969
A native of Bavaria, Dornier received a thorough

engineering education in Munich before being hired by Count Zeppelin (qv) to calculate stresses on his airships. With the Zeppelin company, Dornier undertook the design of floatplane scouts. The speed and manoeuvrability of these scouts were unusually good for floatplanes and to add to their reputation they featured such advanced construction details as metal cantilever wings.

Following the war Dornier set up his own manufacturing company, but the Versailles treaty restrictions forced him to locate outside Germany in Switzerland and Italy. From these plants emerged a fine series of all-metal large flying-boats, notably the Wal twin-engine transport and the gargantuan Do-X, a twelve-engined seaplane. The Do-X is best described as one of the three most impressive flying-boats ever built, behind the Saro *Princess* and the Hughes *Spruce Goose*. It was the first aeroplane ever to fly with one hundred passengers and once even managed to carry 169 – all this in 1929!

Dornier's company produced outstanding aircraft during World War II including the Pfeil, a push-pull fighter that included an ejector seat. In the after-war years, Dornier returned to civil aircraft. The leadership of the company passed to his son who helped to steer the company back to its roots by launching the design of a modern turbo-prop seaplane.

DOUGLAS, DONALD WILLS
1892–1981
Douglas was once praised by Theodore von Karman (qv) as the 'dour Scot who will go down in history as having made aviation great without a government subsidy.' Von Karman was right.

Douglas was born in Brooklyn and had attended the Naval Academy for several years when he witnessed Orville Wright (qv) demonstrate the Army's first biplane at Fort Myer. He left the Academy and transferred to MIT where he worked with Jerome Hunsaker (qv). Upon graduation he briefly worked for the little known Connecticut Aircraft Co. before joining Glenn Martin (qv) in California as chief engineer. Martin moved the firm to Cleveland at the end of World War I. Douglas found the climate too cold and decided to move back to California and establish his own company. His assets totalled $600. In 1920, David Davis (qv) put up $40,000 and the Davis-Douglas Co. was formed to build an aircraft capable of flying across the US non-stop. Davis crashed this aeroplane, the *Cloudster,* in Texas and the company was dissolved.

Douglas struck out on his own and landed a contract to build torpedo aircraft for the Navy. In 1924, two Douglas aircraft became the first to circle the world in a voyage that lasted 175 days!

The company grew slowly until 1935 when it introduced the immortal DC-3, a plane that Douglas was reluctant to produce, considering the DC-2 already being built. C. R. Smith (qv), president of American Airlines, swayed him during a long telephone conversation with the promise of an order for twenty planes. The success of his company was assured by the DC-3, thousands of which are still flying over fifty years after they were first produced.

In 1967 the company merged with McDonnell.

DOUGLAS OF KIRTLESIDE, LORD (WILLIAM SHOLTO)

1893–1970

Born in Oxford, the son of a colourful Scottish historian, Douglas grew up amid aristocratic surroundings. He learned to fly in France before the war and in August, 1914 joined the RFC. Posted to No 2 Squadron (reconnaissance), he made most of his early flights in unarmed BE-2a's.

He later transferred into a fighter unit and eventually rose to command Nos 43 and 84 Squadrons. During one air battle he tangled with Hermann Goering (qv) but without result. Nevertheless, by the end of the war Douglas was an ace with five victories.

In the inter-war years, he was Handley Page's chief test pilot from 1919–20, and commanded forces in the Sudan. During World War II, he

was given large responsibilities, the most important as head of Fighter Command upon Dowding's (qv) transfer. He commanded the RAF in the Middle East in 1943, then took charge of Coastal Command from 1944–45. After the war, he became Military Governor of the British Zone in Germany. Later he directed BOAC. His last position was as Chairman of British European Airways, a post he held for fifteen years.

DOUHET, GIULIO

1869–1930

Arrogant, precocious, and tactless are the words best used to describe Douhet, the most controversial, considered and defamed of all air strategists. Although in general his theory that airpower was the key to future wars proved correct, many of his theories were practically impossible and during World War II they were proved to be so, until the unexpected invention of the atom bomb.

Douhet was born into a family of Neopolitan military officers. Joining the service himself, he tried to apply modern technology to military affairs. In 1909 he published his first paper on military aviation and this earned him a position in Italy's budding air force. Douhet commanded the air squadron that conducted the world's first aerial bombing. This unit bombed Turkish positions in Libya in 1911.

Prior to the First World War he pushed for an Italian strategic bombing capability, but overstepped his authority when he asked Count Caproni (qv) to begin construction of three-engined bombers. For this typically presumptuous act, his superiors court-martialled him and he spent a year in jail.

In 1921 he published a book that brought him to world-wide attention. *Il Dominio Dell'Aria* (The Command of the Air) expounded Douhet's philosophy that large air forces and bombing fleets, would be able to fly unopposed anywhere in the world and strike at defenceless cities causing such terror and panic that the victims would be forced to surrender. This grandiose theory started a debate that continues even into these days of ICBMs, ABMs and AABMs. Perhaps it was the very pomposity of the idea that appealed to Mussolini, but for whatever reason, the dictator appointed Douhet as Commissioner of Aviation.

Douhet held the position for several years, but his personality so conflicted with that of Italy's truly great air hero, Balbo (qv) that Douhet was forced to retire.

DOWDING, LORD (HUGH CASWALL TREMENHEERE)
1882–1970

An enigmatic, misunderstood career officer, Dowding, without question, was the one man most responsible for establishing and co-ordinating Britain's defences in the late summer of 1940.

He joined the Army in 1900, during the Boer War, as an artillery officer. After trooping to remote British outposts around the world for fourteen years, he returned to England in 1914 just before the war, and took flying lessons. When war started he transferred to the RFC where he served as a combat pilot. By the war's end he had risen to Brigadier-General and his future seemed bright.

Further promotion came slowly after the war. Dowding (nicknamed 'Stuffy' by his critics) couldn't seem to make friends with his fellow officers, many of whom were put off by his all too precise manners, his pensiveness and mostly perhaps his conviction that he could communicate with dead soldiers! His only passion was skiing and he headed Britain's Ski Club.

In 1930 Dowding became the Air Member for Supply and Research; this was where he was to begin to show his tactical and strategic genius. It was under his guidance that radar research was begun; that the aircraft industry in Britain switched from wood to metal; and that the Hurricane and Spitfire were built. Dowding very slowly dragged Britain's lax air defences out of the 1914–18 days. In 1936 he was appointed head of Fighter Command. During the four years he held this post, he re-organized Britain's defence systems,

established a well-rehearsed chain of command, and formed a workable air warning network. In August, 1940, when Goering (qv) unleashed his Luftwaffe against the British Isles, Dowding's fighters were in top form and waiting. The proof of the quality of Dowding's far-sighted work was the survival of Britain.

When the Battle of Britain had been won in November of 1940, he left Fighter Command, retiring altogether in 1942, a mistrusted, yet great military leader.

DOWTY, SIR GEORGE HERBERT
1901–1975

Born in Worcestershire, Dowty attended the Worcester Royal Grammar School. He went to work in the aviation industry in 1918 with Heenan and Froude. Later he moved to A. V. Roe then Gloster.

In 1931 he founded his own company to specialize in undercarriages. Dowty products, like alloy wheels, hydraulic controls, and retractable undercarriages helped make many British aircraft winners during the war.

DREXEL, J. ARMSTRONG
1891–*

Drexel was the son of Anthony Drexel, a member of the vastly wealthy Philadelphia family of financiers. Young 'Chips' Drexel lived in Europe with his father. In early 1910, he travelled to Pau in southern France where he was taught to fly by Claude Grahame-White (qv). Immediately he embarked on a career as a competition pilot which saw him set several altitude records. He also was involved in air racing and flew in the 1910 meet at Belmont Park.

DUFAUX, HENRI
1879–*

DUFAUX, ARMAND
1883–*

The Dufaux brothers were multi-talented Swiss designers who in 1905 introduced an after-market gasoline engine that could be attached to ordinary bicycles to turn them into motorcycles. Their 'Motosacoche' company was laughed at by larger firms but the buying public made it a success. For the first time, a person of very ordinary income could afford a motor vehicle.

That year also saw the brothers in Paris where they demonstrated a model twin-bladed helicopter powered by a small three horsepower gasoline engine. It took off under its own power, though it was attached to guide cables.

In 1907 they attempted to fly an aeroplane powered by a large 120 horsepower engine of their own design. It crashed. By 1910 they were sufficiently skilled to build a workmanlike biplane which Armand flew the length of Lake Geneva.

DUNNE, JOHN WILLIAM
1875–1949

Dunne stumbled into the world of aviation by accident. The son of a general, Dunne campaigned in the Boer War where he was wounded twice. Returning to England, he took up the study of aerodynamics to occupy his free time. In 1902 he met H. G. Wells. The two men had common interests in science, chess and mathematics. Wells encouraged Dunne to experiment with aircraft. Dunne met Colonel Capper (qv) of Farnborough who gave him a job as the chief designer of military kites. Dunne's goal was to design a completely stable aircraft though, so when official support for this project was not forthcoming he left Farnborough and established a company to build the aircraft he designed.

His first powered plane flew in Scotland in 1908. It was a swept-wing, tail-less biplane. By 1910 Dunne had a successful version of this type of plane, built for him by the Short brothers (qv) that could lift a 600-pound payload. Two years later Dunne's D. 8 stable aircraft amazed the world when its sole pilot left the cockpit and climbed in and out of the rigging on the wing. Its design kept it flying straight and level.

Dunne licenced his design to Nieuport of France and Burgess in the US. The latter developed it into a successful floatplane.

Poor health ended Dunne's aviation career and he became a well-known, but controversial, writer who dabbled in pseudo-science. A methodical, somewhat mysterious man, Dunne was the inventor of the powered flying-wing.

DUPUY de LOME, HENRI
1816–1885

Dupuy de Lome was already a well-known naval architect when the French government commissioned him to design and build an airship capable of reaching besieged Paris during the Franco-Prussian war. Dupuy de Lome's design called for a steerable and powered machine with a length well over 100 feet (30.5m). The 'engine' consisted of eight strong sailors turning a single crankshaft with a thirty foot (9m) propeller on the end. The machine was built and the crew could actually develop enough power to propel the dirigible. As a reward, these men were given an extra ration of rum.

The first flight of Dupuy de Lome's airship wasn't until February 1872 after the war ended. The ship proved to be of little value and was dismantled, except for the nacelle which still exists in the Musée de l'Air.

DURANT, CHARLES FERSON
1805–1873

Durant was born into a wealthy family and exhibited an early interest in science. In 1823 he travelled to Paris and studied ballooning with a prominent French aeronaut Eugene Robertson. During one ascent with the Frenchman, Durant saved the balloon from bursting due to a stuck pressure relief valve when he climbed the rigging, knife in teeth, and was able to unstick the valve.

Returning to America, Durant became the first American (*see* Edward Warren) to effect a cross-country balloon flight in the United States when on 9 September 1830 he launched a balloon of his own construction from Castle Garden, New York. He went on to make eleven other flights which helped to popularize flying in America.

Ballooning occupied only one segment of Durant's fertile mind. He was one of America's first naturalists. He experimented with explosives, wrote poetry, and even developed his own theory on sub-atomic particles.

DU TEMPLE, FÉLIX
1823–1890

Du Temple was a naval officer who, with the assistance of his brother, almost succeeded in inventing a practical aeroplane. In fact, in 1857 or 58, he had built and flown a small steam-powered model that could take-off and fly. Encouraged, he proceeded to the next step which was to build a full-size machine. This machine was a *tour de force* in rational thinking. It had plenty of wingspan, an adequate tail group, a wheeled undercarriage, and a steam-driven tractor propeller – not only was it the first tractor monoplane, it almost flew.

In 1874 this brilliant machine, piloted by a sailor, was released, under power, down an inclined ramp. It hopped off the end of the ramp and landed. It is considered the world's first powered take-off.

Hélène Dutrieu confidently prepares to earn her brevet.

DUTRIEU, HÉLÈNE
1877(?)–1961

Dutrieu was a daredevil bicyclist from Belgium who became the second woman to learn to fly. In 1909 she took lessons at Issy-les-Moulineux on Demoiselles, and even survived a crash in one. She went on to make the first flight by a woman lasting one hour and she became the first woman pilot to carry a passenger.

EAKER, IRA CLARENCE
1896–1987

Born in Texas, Eaker had already received a teaching degree when America entered World War I. He joined the infantry but transferred to the Signal Corps and by late 1918 had earned his wings. In the 1920s he engaged in a series of publicity flights for the US Army; the 1926–27 Pan-American goodwill tour, the first dawn to dusk flight to Panama from the US, and the record flight over California in 1929, during which he and Carl Spaatz kept a Fokker monoplane *The Question Mark* aloft for over 150 hours.

Shortly before World War II he took command of the Twentieth Pursuit Group. In January 1942 he was promoted to the rank of general and took command of the bomber element of the Eighth Air Force. On 17 August 1942 he personally led the first American heavy-bomber raid on enemy territory in Europe – a B-17 mission against the Rouen marshalling yards. In 1944 he headed the Mediterranean Allied Air Forces during which time he organized shuttle bombing raids that terminated in Russia. The next year he became the Chief of the US Air Staff, a position he held until 1947 when he retired from the military.

EARHART, AMELIA
1898–1937

Earhart was born in Atchison, Kansas to liberal-minded parents. Few girls in those days wore gym suits as everyday clothes and fewer still made a hobby of shooting rats, but Amelia was allowed to indulge her rather tomboy tastes. During World War I she was a nurse at the

Spadina Military Hospital in Toronto, Canada. In 1919 she entered Columbia University as a pre-med student. Being a 'proper girl' in a prim, pressed uniform didn't appeal to Amelia though, so she moved to California where her parents had resettled.

In 1920 Frank Hawks took her for her first plane ride and she immediately decided that she would get her pilot's licence. By working for a telephone company, she barely earned enough money to pay for her flying lessons. Her mother helped her to buy a small aeroplane with which Amelia performed at several airshows. At that point she didn't think she could make a career at flying, so she tried her hand at professional photography. Failing in this, she re-enrolled at Columbia, but again found that a medical career was not to her liking. She moved to Boston to live with her sister and eventually became a social worker, though she was active in local flying circles.

In 1928 Mrs Frederick Guest, a wealthy Englishwoman, organized a trans-Atlantic flight from which she hoped to be the first woman to fly across the Atlantic in an aeroplane. She had purchased a Fokker tri-motor and hired a pilot and co-pilot for the flight, but family pressure forced her to withdraw from making the flight personally. Mrs Guest decided to find another woman to take her place. The flight was organized from Boston, so a search was conducted for a local woman.

There weren't many female pilots in staid Boston, and so Amelia was approached. She agreed, although she was somewhat dis-appointed that she would not do the actual flying. The Fokker and its crew of three left Newfoundland on 17 June 1927 and landed in Wales almost twenty-one hours later. Amelia instantly became a world-wide celebrity and reaped a rich reward from endorsements, something that Lindbergh (qv) declined to do.

But she was a pilot at heart, not a passenger, so after the flight she began to set aviation records on her own. Some of her successes included being the first woman to fly from the east to west coast and return again; the world's autogyro altitude record in 1931 – 18,415 feet (5,613m); the first person to fly from Mexico City to New Jersey; and the first to fly from Hawaii to California. Her biggest success came in 1932 when she was the first woman to pilot an aircraft across the Atlantic, which she did in a bright red Lockheed Vega.

In 1937 the mysterious legend of Amelia Earhart was born when she evidently crashed and disappeared in mid-ocean during an around-the-world attempt. The flight originated in Miami, but trouble with the navigator's chronometer hampered progress. The most difficult leg of the flight was from New Guinea to Howland Island, a tiny speck in the Pacific. The distance was 2,556 miles (4,113km) and it would take more than just a good navigator to find the way. Although advised to wait to have the chronometer fixed, Earhart and her navigator, Fred Noonan, decided to make the attempt. They departed New Guinea on 1 July 1937 and were never seen again. Their last radio message was 'Position doubtful. . .'

According to some, Earhart and Noonan were actually on a spy flight to chart Japanese positions in the Pacific. These speculators say that the plane was forced down and the two Americans were secretly captured by the Japanese. Though the Japanese at that time did mistrust any foreign pilot overflying their territory, this account has only slim evidence to support it. One investigator, though, claimed that there were witnesses on Saipan to Earhart's execution by the Japanese and after interviewing them, found a blindfold at the alleged spot of execution buried in the sand over 40 years after the supposed event. It was said that she was shot during the war and that Noonan was beheaded.

Fifty years after the flight, her disappearance is still a much talked about enigma. Jacqueline Cochrane (qv) claimed to be able to speak to Earhart after her death.

ECKENER, HUGO
1868–1954
Eckener was an unknown, struggling journalist when he witnessed the first Zeppelin flight in 1900. He viciously attacked the ship as ridiculous and its designer as a quack. By 1906

Eckener had completely reversed his opinion and Count Zeppelin (qv) invited him to join the company. Eckener quickly proved his talents as a practical innovator. He learned to pilot the huge ships and, most importantly for the future success of the company, he proved to be a shrewd publicity agent.

Eckener rose to become the managing head of the Zeppelin Company, which also owned the world's first airline, Delag. During World War I he trained almost every Zeppelin pilot and designed improved military dirigibles.

After the war, he raised public support around the world for airships and designed the *Los Angeles* for the US Navy. When the Nazis came to power in the 1930s, Goering (qv) succeeded in buying out the Zeppelin Company. He ordered the *Graf Zeppelin*, then under Eckener's command, to display the swastika on its tail at the Chicago World's Fair. Eckener was an ardent anti-Nazi who frequently lectured his airship passengers about the impending danger of Naziism. He outwitted Goering by painting a swastika on the upper-left side of the tail and circling Chicago in a clockwise rotation. This kept the symbol hidden from the Chicagoans! This defiant gesture cost him his job and only the fact that he was a national hero saved his life.

During his career he made over 2,000 successful airship flights including one around the world. When he died in 1954, this former cynical journalist was, without doubt, the world's foremost authority on airships.

EGG, DURS
1748–1831
(see PAULY, S. J.*)*

ELLEHAMMER, JACOB CHRISTIAN HANSEN
1871–1946
Jacob Ellehammer came very close to making the first aeroplane flight in Europe, and for years, some said he had. Ellehammer was a rule-of-thumb Danish inventor whose interests ranged

from clock-making to combustion engines. In 1896 he founded his own company which manufactured, among other things, telephones, motorcycles and X-ray machines!

Around 1905 he began to experiment with heavier-than-air machines, and on 24 September 1906 he achieved a short powered 'hop' in a crudely built 'delta' biplane. This hop cannot be considered a flight because it was for only a few feet, and the machine was tethered to a pole at the centre of a circular 'runway'. To his credit though, Ellehammer personally constructed the light, efficient engine for this machine. Other projects included later, more conventional biplanes and from 1912–16 he even experimented with a helicopter.

ELLSWORTH, LINCOLN
1880–1951
Ellsworth was an American multi-millionaire explorer who didn't mind risking his life for adventure. In 1902 he helped survey a transcontinental route for the Canadian Pacific Railway. He explored the Rockies on a biological expedition and made a topological survey of the Andes.

In 1925 he sponsored a joint flight with Roald Amundsen (qv) to the North Pole. This flight, consisting of two Dornier Wals, landed short of its goal and the crews barely managed to repair one of their aeroplanes, hack out a runway in the snow, and fly back to safety. In 1930 Ellsworth accompanied Nobile on a trans-Polar flight from Spitsbergen to Alaska in the dirigible *Norge*.

During the 1930s Ellsworth made four privately funded flights over Antarctica on which he claimed 300,000 square miles (78 million hectares) of territory for the US.

ELY, EUGENE
1886–1911
Ely was one of the original rough'n'tumble pilots in the Curtiss Exhibition Company. He became the first man ever to take-off from a ship when on 14 November 1910 he flew a Curtiss pusher

off a wooden platform built on the forward deck of the USS *Birmingham* which was anchored at Hampton Roads, Virginia. Two months later, on 19 January 1911, he became the first ever to land on a ship. For this landing, a series of ropes weighted with sandbags had been stretched across the deck of the battleship USS *Pennsylvania*. As Ely lowered his plane onto the deck, an arrester hook snagged the ropes and slowed the plane down enough to make a safe landing. Even today the principle hasn't changed.

Ely did not enjoy his success for long. He was killed in October, 1911 during an exhibition at Macon, Georgia. His wife publicly blamed his friend Lincoln Beachey (qv) for tempting Ely to perform dangerous stunts and in fact Beachey gave up stunt flying temporarily in remorse.

ESNAULT-PELTERIE, ROBERT ALBERT CHARLES

1881–1957

Esnault-Pelterie deserves a high place among the ranks of French aviators. Besides being a pilot, inventor and manufacturer, he was one of the first ever to rationally theorize about the possibilities of space flight – and all this before World War I!

The son of a rich cotton magnate, he, like Coanda (qv) studied engineering and sculpture while at college. In 1904 he began to experiment with crude copies of Wright-type gliders, but achieved only meagre success. In 1907 he constructed his first powered plane, the *R.E.P. 1* which could stagger into the air for brief flights.

Improving this design step by step over the next two years, he introduced some very important design features, many of which are still in use today; stress tests, brakes, oleo landing struts, 'cloche' controls, seat belts, steel tube construction, radial engines with odd numbers of cylinders for smoother running, and, on his 1904 glider, ailerons for roll control.

Esnault-Pelterie never achieved any great success with his airplanes, although some were sold to the French military. His fame rests on his innovations and inventions, especially his theories on space flight. During the 1920s and 30s he was a much sought-after lecturer on space flight, about which he published several volumes. In the late 1920s, he established with his own funds an annual award to be given to the author of the best manuscript on astronautics.

ETRICH, IGO

1879–1967

Around 1904, Etrich, an Austrian engineer and naturalist, noticed how gently a certain seed leaf floated to earth after breaking off its mother plant. The leaf, the Zanonia Macrocarpa, was the product of a cucumber plant native to the South Pacific. Etrich carefully studied the leaf's shape, coming to the conclusion that it might be the ideal planform for an aeroplane wing. He hoped that such a wing would prove extremely stable, thus making the aircraft easier to fly.

He first tested a few small models of his proposed all-wing aircraft. Encouraged, he built a full-size machine which he tested in powered and unpowered form between 1907 and 1908. The plane unfortunately lacked the anticipated stability, so in 1909 Etrich added an empennage. The resulting aircraft became the classic Taube (Dove). The plane proved very stable, easy to fly and unusually reliable. These good qualities led several companies to apply for licenses to build the type. Etrich sold the rights to the Rumpler company. It was a German Taube which played the first significant part by an aeroplane in a battle when it reported on Russian troop strengths before the Battle of Tannenberg.

FABRE, HENRI

1882–1984

Fabre first became interested in flight in 1905 when he read accounts of the Blériot-Voisin floatplane experiments. Living in Marseille, Fabre had access to a large body of water, the Mediterranean, so he decided to build his own floatplane. In 1909 the plane was completed, but could not take-off. The next year, he tried a different, and very unusual, design. This floatplane had an exposed girder spar, with a 'canard' planform. Launched at La Mède, near Marseille, on 28 March 1910, it rose gracefully into the air and flew well. Its pilot, Fabre himself, had never flown before!

This plane, named the *Hydravion,* performed the world's first water take-off, but after that was of no practical use. Fabre continued in aviation by undertaking the manufacture of well-made floats, while the *Hydravion* ended its career as a star attraction in the Musée de l'Air.

FAIREY, SIR (CHARLES) RICHARD

1887–1957

Fairey was born at Hendon, North London. He managed to put himself through engineering school after his father died and in 1910 won a model airplane contest. His model infringed on the patents of John Dunne (qv) who demanded to see young Fairey. Dunne was impressed with Fairey's knowledge of aerodynamics and gave him the job of shop manager for the Blair-Atholl syndicate which was building Dunne's stable airplanes. Fairey next worked at Short Bros supervising the construction and design of seaplanes.

By 1915 Fairey had enough experience to form his own company. The first products of his firm were licence-built Sopwith aircraft. Fairey developed trailing edge flaps and tested them for the first time on the *Hamble Baby*, a floatplane based on the Sopwith Baby.

Fairey, through ceaseless effort, rose to the top of the British aviation industry, and became postwar Chairman of the Society of British Aircraft Constructors. His dominating, aggressive style aided the industry during difficult inter-war years. He imported from America the Curtiss D-12 engine (which his company planned to build under licence, and the threat of which prompted Rolls-Royce to begin to design a new engine which eventually became the Kestrel) and the Reed metal propeller. Importing foreign equipment angered the British government during the Depression years. This led to

somewhat 'anti-Fairey' feelings in Britain's aviation circles. Perhaps piqued by this, and also with Belgian contracts in hand, Fairey opened a factory in Belgium – Avion Fairey, in 1931.

One of his company's greatest contributions to Britain was the immortal Swordfish torpedo bomber. Antiquated by the 1940s when it was still being used, the trusty 'Stringbag' sunk one million tons of enemy shipping.

Fairey suffered from poor health most of his life and found relaxation in yachting, a sport at which he became a champion racer. In 1960, several years after his death, the British government nationalized his company and merged it with Westland. Avion Fairey returned to Britain when they purchased the Britten-Norman company in 1972 which built the successful Islander series.

FARMAN, HENRY

1874–1958

Born to English parents living in France, Farman, who grew up in Paris, usually spelled his name 'Henri'. He spoke little English and eventually became a naturalized French citizen. During 1908 he was France's premier flyer.

He and his brother Maurice (qv) caught the bicycling craze in the 1890s and became championship racers. Henry continued to race motorcycles and then cars. He and a different brother, Dick, opened an agency for Panhard-Levassor, Renault, and Delauney-Belleville automobiles in Paris, but a near fatal accident soured Henry's interest in cars. Like so many others, he became enthused with Voisin's (qv) float glider experiments on the Seine and in 1907 ordered his first plane. In less than a year, he became France's leading aviator by flying the first European circular flight at Issy on 13 January 1908. Later that year, he overshadowed his friend and rival Delagrange (qv) with a seventeen mile (27.4km) cross country flight. He improved his plane by adding ailerons and modifying the tail. In 1909 he ordered a second plane from Voisin, but just as he was about to take delivery, Voisin sold the plane to J. T. C.

Moore-Brabazon (qv). This underhand act so infuriated Farman that he set up his own factory at Billancourt. He was soon producing successful biplanes which were copied the world over.

At the Rheims meet that year, he was the top prize winner with 63,000 francs. He later joined his brother in building military planes and after World War I they introduced the famed Farman Goliath airliner. The post-war years were difficult for the company so they diversified and attempted to build luxury cars. The automobiles turned out to be mediocre compared to other quality cars of the era and this venture failed after a few years. The company was nationalized in the 1930s.

FARMAN, MAURICE ALAIN
1877–1964
Less precocious than his brother Henry (qv), Maurice was in fact the first of the two to fly. He started as a balloonist and took Henry along once for his first flight. He became acquainted with Captain Ferber (qv) and in 1909 helped design the Kellner-Neubauer airplane. Maurice opened his own factory in friendly competition with his brother and in 1912 introduced the safe, if unspectacular, M. F. Longhorn, the world's first great training plane. He produced bombers during World War I and eventually merged his firm with his brother's.

FARRE, HENRI
1871–1934
Farre was a French artist living in Buenos Aires when World War I started. He returned to France and volunteered for flight duty. On combat missions as an observer and bombardier, he carried a sketch pad on which he used to jot down quick drawings. Later, he turned these first-hand sketches into oil paintings which today are considered the best paintings depicting the air war. Farre's paintings were realistic, though in the impressionist style.

He avoided the contemporary trend of psychoanalytical, representational art that was so much in vogue during the war years. By painting actual scenes with recognizable people and machines, Farre was able to depict his subjects and evoke feelings of compassion that could not have been created with another style. Farre didn't avoid the horror of the war in his paintings, but he was uniquely able to bring that horror down to a human scale, a feat which eluded most war artists. Not all of his paintings during the war dealt with combat. Some were simply colourful essays on the beauty of flight, a subject he was eminently qualified to paint.

FEDDEN, SIR (ALFRED HUBERT) ROY
1885–1973
Fedden was the main force behind the development of powerful radial engines in Britain between the wars.

A native of Bristol, he started as an automobile engineer for the Brazil-Straker Co. in 1906. He persuaded his employers to build engines, and when they agreed he became the chief engineer. During the war Brazil-Straker built licensed versions of Rolls-Royce and Renault engines, but in 1918 they instructed Fedden to begin the design of a new radial engine. His efforts resulted in the Jupiter, the first of Britain's great radial engines.

In 1920 the Brazil-Straker company became part of the Bristol Airplane Co. From then until 1942 Fedden headed Bristol engines and was responsible for producing such fine engines as the Mercury, Hercules and Centaurus. In later years, Fedden was a consultant for the British government and NATO.

FERBER, CAPTAIN FERDINAND
1862–1909
Perhaps best described as an important failure, Ferber was born in Lyon and entered the École Polytechnique in 1882. He joined the Army and rose through the military ranks as an artillery officer, eventually commanding the Alpine Artillery Battery at Nice.

Ferber began emulating Lilienthal's (qv) experiments in 1899. His approach was often haphazard and his machines were poorly made. In 1901 Ferber wrote to Octave Chanute (qv) who replied in early 1902 with descriptions and illustrations of the Wright brothers' (qv) gliders and their wing-warping technique. Ferber immediately replaced the Lilienthal wing with a biplane type, but due to poor construction, the new glider achieved little success.

Ferber's importance is due to the example he set for other Europeans, particularly the French experimenters. He continued to experiment when most others had given up. He introduced Chanute to French aviation circles and Chanute made them familiar with the Wright brothers' work. Ferber influenced Archdeacon (qv), Voisin (qv) and thus the entire French aviation community. Although he never built a successful plane by himself, he did aid somewhat in the design of the Antoinette. During 1909 he competed at Rheims under the pseudonym 'de Rue'. He won several minor competitions but on 19 September 1909 lost his life in a crash at Boulogne.

FERGUSON, HARRY GEORGE
1884–1960

Ferguson was an automobile mechanic and motorcycle racer from Ireland who, in 1909, witnessed the Rheims Meet in France. He predicted that aeroplanes would soon be a lucrative industry and so he set out to learn all he could about them. He determined that he would build and fly an aeroplane before the end of 1909. His machine turned out to be a monoplane which borrowed heavily from the Antoinette. He began testing it in November of that year but suffered one setback after another. He went through a series of twelve propellers trying to achieve success. On the last day of the year, in severe wind conditions, he threw caution away and attempted a flight. He succeeded in staggering into the air for about 400 feet (122m), just enough to meet his goal.

Ferguson realized he didn't have a practical aircraft so over the next several years he modified the aeroplane trying different engines, wings, landing gear, etc. Though his designs

never sold, he could still enjoy the distinction of having been the first Briton to design, build, and fly a monoplane. He gave up his aeronautical interests around 1912 and his greatest fame arises from his career as a farm implement innovator and manufacturer.

Light plane builder Gerhard Fieseler.

FIESELER, GERHARD
1886–1987

Fieseler was born near Cologne. He was a combat pilot during World War I, gaining fame in the Middle East theatre as the 'Tiger of Macedonia'. By the war's end he had amassed twenty-two victories. Following the war, he entered into a career as a stunt pilot. His routine was more than just a showy display of crowd-pleasing antics; he worked hard for aerobatic perfection and helped to introduce advanced flying techniques to European air forces. He demonstrated the outside loop in France and Britain in 1928. In 1930 he purchased an established sailplane manufacturer, but it wasn't until 1932 that he renamed the company Fieseler-Flugzeugbau. In 1932 he built and flew a radical push-pull delta aircraft designed by Lippisch (qv) called the *Vespe*.

Fieseler's company built some of the most unusual aircraft of World War II, including the Storch utility plane, the V1 flying-bomb, and the V2 ballistic missile.

FLACK, GROUP CAPTAIN MARTIN
1882–1931

Flack was born in Borden, Kent and educated at Oxford University, where he received degrees in chemistry and medicine in 1908. After studying physiology at London Hospital and in Europe, he took a commission in the army at the outbreak of World War I. He began studying the special medical problems related to flying, such as the effects of high altitude flight, gravitational strains on the heart and motor reflexes at low temperatures. When the RAF Medical Service was formed, he became its first director of research, laying down the foundations of modern aero-medical research.

FLEET, REUBEN HOLLIS
1887–1975

Fleet was not an engineer but a determined businessman whose stamina and determination led him to found one of the United States' great aviation companies.

He was born in the state of Washington and attended the Culver Military Academy. There, he developed the self-confidence that was to serve him well all his life. After graduating, he returned to Washington where he became a school teacher. Leaving that profession, he sold real estate and showed an early flair for putting together profitable business deals. He joined the National Guard and gained a reputation for good organizational skills and so during World War I he was assigned the task of organizing pilot training for the Signal Corps. He also organized the first US airmail flight from Washington, DC to New York.

From his involvement with pilot training, Fleet learned that the ubiquitous Jenny, so often the object of admiration by pilots who never flew it,

was in fact a lumbering, inefficient death trap. He set a goal to re-equip the flying services with modern, safe trainers. To this end, he established his own aircraft company in 1923 calling it Consolidated Aircraft Corporation.

Consolidated grew to be a giant in the aviation industry, building everything from trainers to seaplanes, and bombers to missiles. Fleet, disgruntled by high taxes and union troubles, agreed to sell his shares in his company ten days before the Pearl Harbor attack.

FLETTNER, ANTON
1885–1961

Flettner had just completed his studies in 1905 when he was asked to develop an improved control system for Zeppelins. He invented the Flettner tab, a remote-control device that allows a light 'stick' force to move a large control surface. Jet aircraft today use a similar system.

During the 1920s he taught at a technical institute in Amsterdam. It was during this time that he developed the remarkable Flettner rotor for ships. Instead of sails, a boat could be equipped with a large rotating tube, perhaps the size of a silo. The wind blowing against this tube, due to the Magnus effect, would cause a force against the rotor which in turn propelled the ship. Two ships were tested at the time with this system and it worked! In modern times, Jacques Cousteau, the famous sailor/environmentalist, has built a ship which also uses the Flettner rotor.

Flettner started an aircraft company in Berlin in 1926 and by 1933 was testing helicopters. In 1938 he introduced the FL-265, the first helicopter with intermeshing blades. The subsequent model FL-282 was a very practical machine which the Luftwaffe ordered in quantity. Stationed on warships in the Mediterranean, it became the world's first operational military helicopter.

Following the war, Flettner emigrated to the United States where he at first worked for the Navy before founding his own company in New York in 1949.

FLYNN, JOHN
1880–1951

Prior to the work of Reverend Flynn, the aeroplane had alternately been an object of sport or warfare. It found a more noble role in 1925.

Since 1911, Flynn had been a wandering missionary and doctor, travelling around the Great Outback of Australia either by camel or dilapidated Dodge. Stopping at each isolated ranch or miner's hut, Flynn would prelude his sermons with medical assistance. The vast distances between each farm or town were Flynn's greatest impediment, along with the lack of instant communications. Often people who required only slight medical attention would die because their wounds became infected before a doctor could reach them. To remedy this tragic situation, Flynn founded the Australian Inland Mission (AIM), whose purpose was to organize a communications network in the Outback and to purchase an aeroplane to transport a doctor to any seriously injured patient in the region. With the help of Qantas Airlines, such a service was initiated in 1925, and has grown steadily since then. Presently known as the Royal Flying Doctor Service, it has saved thousands of lives.

Flynn became a Moderator of the Presbyterian church in Australia and received the Order of the British Empire.

FOCKE, HEINRICH KARL JOHANN
1890–1979

Focke built his first aircraft, a glider, in 1908. During World War I he joined the Aviation Corps but after suffering a crash in 1917, returned to aircraft design. When the war ended, he obtained an engineering degree in Hanover and began to collaborate with a friend on the construction of several light planes. The success of these craft prompted Focke and his associate, Georg Wulf (qv) to found their own company in 1924. Focke-Wulf began by producing small commercial transports along with training planes. Flying a Focke-designed trainer, the Ente, Wulf lost his life in 1927.

When Focke hired Kurt Tank (qv) in 1931, the company's future was assured. Focke then began to indulge his own interests in helicopter design, producing in 1933 a licensed version of the Cierva autogyro. Differences with the Nazi régime caused Focke to lose control of his company. He was invited, however, to start another company to continue his promising work on helicopters. That company was known as Focke Achgelis. That year, the Fa-61 prototype appeared, flying to world attention two years later when Hanna Reitsch (qv) demonstrated it before an impressed audience in the Deutschland-Halle, Berlin. Although Focke designed several excellent early helicopters, none saw wide-scale use in World War II.

FOKKER, ANTHONY HERMAN GERARD
1890–1939

Aviation history's enfant terrible, Anthony Fokker is among the most controversial of all aeronautical figures. Born in Kediri, Java to a wealthy Dutch plantation owner, Fokker had just reached school age when, upon the retirement of his father, his family returned to Holland. Young Tony was an accomplished tinkerer, experimenter, and troublemaker. One time he built an electric train set, powering it by splicing into the main power lines in front of his home! Among his other self-professed hobbies he included cheating at school – for the sheer fun of it.

This was the character of the young man who in 1910 talked his father into sending him to 'engineering' school. Unbeknown to the elder Fokker, the school was really a vocational mechanic's school in Germany that Fokker wanted to attend because he knew that it had plans to build an aeroplane.

The school was perfect for a young man of his ambition. The instructors were almost totally ignorant of the new sciences of internal combustion engines and aeronautics. Fokker's fast mouth and ready wit brought him to the forefront. Soon he had everyone involved in the construction of an aeroplane. The plane crashed on its first flight but Fokker had seen enough to think he could start his own manufacturing business.

This he did in 1911 with his father's financial backing. His first plane was the Spin, a robust yet awkward looking monoplane that was built in several versions. To everyone's surprise it flew well, due in part to Fokker's uncanny flying skill. The Spin won him recognition as the most gifted aircraft constructor in Germany. Military orders for the plane trickled in and his company grew.

With the outbreak of World War I, Fokker stayed in Germany to build planes for the Imperial Air Service. In later years, Fokker would claim that he offered his services to the Allies, who rejected him, but, like many of his statements, this doesn't seem to be entirely true.

Fokker was fortunate in hiring Reinhold Platz (qv) as a company welder. Platz proved himself to be a brilliant designer and soon took over that post from Fokker, although this too is a fact that the Dutchman would later play down. Fokker's main contribution to his company was his incredible ability to sell planes. Whether as one of the world's truly great test and demonstration pilots, or as a profferer of 'un pot-de-vin' to the right government minister, Fokker was able to market many aeroplanes in the competitive, corruption-plagued world of 1914–18 Berlin.

When the war ended and a Communist insurrection seemed imminent in Germany, Fokker sought to move his factory to Holland. Government restrictions prevented him from exporting his machines and material, but such regulations had never stopped Fokker before. Hiring several long trains of box cars in 1919, Fokker had a large part of his factory loaded during the night hours, and, after bribing the border guards, happily escaped to Holland with his booty.

In a time when few aircraft manufacturers were able to sell any planes, Fokker continued to reap large orders. Platz had developed the steel tube fuselage and cantilever wooden wing into a very efficient and strong structural combination. Fokker transports, using this combination, proved to be safe, reliable and very economical. Fokker established a factory at Schipol Airport near Amsterdam and began to produce his famous transports. The factory exists to this day.

In the late 1920s he established a manufacturing company in America to build and market his planes. These aircraft charted many new air routes, and helped make the world's budding airlines profitable. The planes continued to be popular everywhere in the world until 1931 when the famous American football coach Knute Rockne was killed in the crash of a Fokker. Overnight the Fokker factory lost all its orders and people refused to ride in Fokker aircraft. Even before this accident, which caused a nationwide sensation in America, Fokker in the US had been taken over by G.M. which soon renamed the company General Aviation Corporation. This eventually became North American Aviation and later still Rockwell International, the maker of the Space Shuttles. The Amsterdam plant continued to produce original designs, and at one point assembled DC-2s.

The great days of Fokker were over. Fokker, an habitual traveller, was in New York in 1939 when he contracted a throat infection and died.

FOLLAND, HENRY PHILLIP
1889–1954

When Geoffrey de Havilland (qv) went to join Airco, Folland, still in his 20s became the chief designer at the Royal Aircraft Factory. His first design was the S.E.-4, a very advanced biplane. It was followed by the S.E.-5 in 1916 and then his masterpiece, the S.E. 5a, which established Folland as a superior designer. After the political storm that broke-up government-owned design teams during the war, he joined British Nieuport where he designed the Nighthawk. Later still he went to Gloster for whom he designed the Gauntlet and the Gladiator. He was a firm proponent of the biplane over the monoplane even in the 1930s, though he did design the Gloster F. 5/34 to compete with the Hurricane and Spitfire.

In 1937 he founded his own company which did sub-contracting work during World War II. Though he retired in 1951, the company went on to produce the Gnat trainer.

FONCK, CAPTAIN RENÉ PAUL
1894–1953

A native of Alsace, Fonck's early heroes were Blériot and Latham (qqv). Though trained as an engineer, he was assigned to dig ditches at the outset of World War I. He longed to fly and got his chance when, in February, 1915, he was posted to Le Crotoy for flight training. He proved to be a natural pilot and displayed his talents early by downing several enemy reconnaissance planes despite flying a lumbering Caudron G 3. His unflinching bravery once led him to successfully 'corner' and capture an enemy plane by simply circling and out-manoeuvring it until it landed.

Fonck graduated to single-seaters in May, 1917 and thus began his brilliant career as a fighter pilot. Fonck was not an aerial showman, but neither would he turn down a mission. His victories rose by twos and threes and twice he brought down six enemy aircraft in one day. His marksmanship surpassed that of even Ball's (qv) and he usually expended less than six shots per kill. An equally great defensive flyer, he rarely returned with a bullet hole in his plane, much to his mechanic's delight. He became the top scoring French ace in late July, 1918 after passing Guynemer's (qv) score. He finished the war with seventy-five confirmed kills. His true score is probably around 125, which would have made him the war's greatest ace even counting all of von Ritchthofen's (qv) unconfirmed victories.

Fonck barnstormed after the war and attempted a few record flights. During an attempt to be the first to fly from New York to Paris, he crashed a hastily built Sikorsky, killing two crew members. He returned to military aviation in 1937 as Inspector of Fighter Aviation. He worked to reorganize the French Air Force but retired in 1939.

Enrico Forlanini, helicopter pioneer.

FORLANINI, ENRICO
1848–1930

Forlanini was an Italian civil engineer who built in 1877 a steam-powered model helicopter that flew well. It weighed 7.7 pounds (3.5kg), but its engine generated $1/4$ horsepower. This was enough to lift it forty-two feet (12.8m) and sustain it for about twenty seconds.

In 1909 he launched his first dirigible, a semi-rigid craft powered by a forty horsepower engine. Later he developed hydrofoil speedboats.

FOSS, MAJOR JOSEPH JACOB
1915–

Foss had already earned a degree from the University of South Dakota before joining the Marines after Pearl Harbor. He became a fighter pilot and was assigned to the South Pacific with Fighting Squadron 121. He participated in the battle of Guadalcanal and quickly ran up a tally of twenty-three kills by the end of 1942. By war's end he had gained a total of twenty-six, losing much time to state-side morale boosting tours.

His post-war activities were equally energetic. He started a flying service business while helping to organize the South Dakota Air National Guard. He won the gubernatorial election in South Dakota twice, in 1954 and 1956. In 1960 he became the commissioner of the American Football League. Later still he became an officer for KLM of Holland.

FOULOIS, MAJOR-GENERAL BENJAMIN D.
1879–1967

Foulois enlisted in the Army at the age of nineteen. He earned a commission three years later and was posted to the Army Aero Section in 1908. He learned to pilot the Army's first dirigible, a former Baldwin (qv) mount. The next year he flew with Orville Wright, soloing in 1910 at Fort Sam Houston in the Army's first airplane.

After learning to fly, he set about making the aeroplane a practical military weapon. He pioneered air-to-ground radio and artillery observation techniques. He commanded the Air Service troops along the Mexican border shortly before America entered the war. Foulois went to Europe to lead the Air Service there but a personality clash with Billy Mitchell (qv) caused General Pershing to divide the command, with orders for Foulois to guide the training and support structure while Mitchell commanded the front-line squadrons. Later Foulois took his revenge on Mitchell during the latter's famous court-martial.

Foulois constantly strove to prove the value of a large air force. In 1931 he organized an air display at Mineola, Long Island which saw 600 planes in the air at one time. He overreached himself however when he told President Roosevelt that the Army could fly the airmail in 1934. The resulting fatalities severely embarrassed the service. However, that same year he pressed to initiate a program to build a four-engined long range bomber, the program that ultimately led to the B-17.

Foulois retired in 1935 from the military but continued to lecture about aeronautics for the rest of his life.

FOWLER, HARLAN DAVEY
1895–*

Fowler was an aeronautical engineer who, despite having a correspondence school education, went on to be involved in an incredible variety of aircraft design. From 1922–25 he worked for the Naval Aircraft Factory on the *Shenandoah* dirigible. He moved on to the nearby Pitcairn company and designed the Mailwing. He was associated with the Fokker, Glenn Martin, and Consolidated companies but gained his greatest fame as the inventor of the Fowler Flap, that allows high lift to be developed by a small wing.

FRANTISEK, JOSEF
1914(?)–1940

In two years Frantisek belonged to no less than four air forces! A fighter pilot in the Czech Air force in 1938, he disobeyed the 'no resistance' order of his superiors and strafed German columns entering his country that year. After this gesture, he was forced to land in Poland to avoid arrest. There he joined that country's air force. When the Germans attacked in 1939, he was one of the few Polish pilots able to shoot down any Luftwaffe planes. When Poland fell, he escaped to Romania but was interned. He escaped from prison and made his way to Syria ending up in France just as the Germans attacked in May 1940. He joined the Armée de l'Air and flew as a fighter pilot until that country fell. He again escaped, this time to England where he joined the RAF as a member of No 303 (Polish) Squadron, flying Hurricanes. In five weeks, during September and October, he shot down seventeen enemy planes, giving him a total of twenty-eight kills.

This brave pilot lost his life not to enemy guns, but to a landing accident on 8 October 1940. He was the war's highest scoring Czech pilot.

FRANTZ, SERGEANT JOSEPH
1890–1979

Frantz was the first French pilot to shoot down an enemy aircraft in World War I. He had learned to fly in 1911 and soon set an endurance record for flight in a two-passenger plane of four hours and twenty-seven minutes. He joined the air service in 1912 and at the beginning of the war was assigned to a Voisin squadron on a reserve basis. On 5 October 1914 he and his mechanic, Quénault were out on a bombing mission when they spotted an Aviatik over French territory. Frantz guided the Voisin into position so that Quénault could have a clear shot. The gun jammed after firing a few shots but moments later the German went into a spin and fell.

Frantz and Quénault received numerous honours including the Légion d'Honneur. After the war, Frantz worked in the French aviation industry.

FRISE, LESLIE GEORGE
1897–*

Frise had just graduated from Bristol University and was about to enter active service with the RNAS when Frank Barnwell (qv) convinced him to resign from the military and join Bristol as an engineer. Thus began an association that was to see the creation of some of the world's greatest military planes. Frise was to be a key designer of such planes as the Bristol Fighter, the Bulldog, the Blenheim, the Beaufighter and Beaufort, and many, many more.

In 1920 Frise had designed a balance control for the ailerons of the Badger II, but the AVRO company complained that these infringed on one of their patents. Frise revised the design and in the process invented an entirely new type of aileron. The Frise aileron allows for continued airflow despite high angles of attack. Frise reaped fifteen years' royalties on his design, which helped in spin prevention.

Towards the end of his career he moved to Hunting Percival and participated in the design of the Pembroke, Provost and others.

FULLARD, CAPTAIN PHILIP FLETCHER
1897–1984

Fullard was one of the lesser known aces of World War I but he achieved a remarkable total of between forty-two and fifty-three victories in the space of only eight months! From May to November of 1917 while flying either a Nieuport or an S.E.-5, Fullard was able to bring his great marksmanship to bear against the German Air Force, to deadly effect. His promising career came to a premature end when he broke a leg during a soccer game at his flying field. He spent the remainder of the war in England. Following the war, he went on a publicity tour of the United States and worked in Germany for the occupying army. During World War II he held staff positions with the RAF.

GABRESKI, FRANCIS
1919–*

Born in Oil City, Pennsylvania to Polish immigrants, Gabreski was pursuing a pre-med education at Notre Dame in 1940 when he left to join the Air Corps. Sent with a P-40 squadron to Hawaii, he was one of the few Americans to get airborne during the Pearl Harbor attack. In 1942 he went to England where he studied RAF fighter tactics with No 315 (Polish) Squadron. Later that year he took command of the US 61st Squadron flying Thunderbolts. Gabreski admired the 'Jug' and used it to shoot down thirty-one German planes. On 20 July 1944 he was shot down during a strafing raid over Germany and became a POW for the remainder of the war.

During the Korean War he again saw combat, this time flying F-86 Sabres. He shot down 6·5 MiG-15 fighters to become America's seventh jet ace.

At the end of his military career he worked as a transportation consultant in New York.

GABRIELLI, PROFESSOR GIUSEPPE
1903–1987

Born in Sicily, Gabrielli was educated at Turin and Aachen. In Aachen he studied under von

Karman (qv) who was to remain a life-long friend. He worked initially for the Piaggio company from 1929–30, but in 1931 switched to FIAT. He helped make that firm an important fixture in European aviation, personally taking a hand in designing over 125 airplanes of which about sixty were actually built. He also led the design of Italy's first jet fighter, the 1951 G-80. He was a prolific author and professor, and received at least twenty-five patents.

The first to slip the surly bonds of earth completely, Yuri Gagarin.

GAGARIN, YURI A.

1934–1968

Rarely has the name of a Soviet military figure become well-known in the United States. An exception is that of Yuri Gagarin whose launch into orbit around the Earth on 12 April 1961 alarmed every American and began the Space Race.

Rocketed into orbit in a Vostok I spacecraft, he was the first man to enter outer space and experience total weightlessness. Gagarin was billed by some newspapers as the new Columbus or Magellan but in fact was nothing more than a passenger in a relatively simple metal ball. As with American space flights, the true credit belonged completely to the scientists and technicians on the ground. Nevertheless, it was Gagarin's life on the line.

When Gagarin returned to Earth after one orbit in 108 minutes he became an instant Soviet 'pop' idol, one of the few that country has ever had. He was sent on a goodwill tour of the world spreading the message that the Soviet Union was no longer a country technically inferior to the United States. They had become a technologically advanced force to be reckoned with. Unfortunately, the popular young Russian was killed in a jet crash in 1968, one year before America landed a man on the Moon.

GALLAND, GENERAL ADOLF

1912–

Chosen in 1932 by Lufthansa to train as a pilot, Galland began his career as a commercial pilot. During the Spanish Civil War he was recruited by the Luftwaffe and flew over 300 ground attack missions with the Condor Legion. He returned to Germany to instruct fighter pilots on ground attack techniques.

Galland finally became an air fighter pilot in the spring of 1940 when he became adjutant to JG 27. He gained his first aerial victory on 12 May against a Belgian Hurricane. In June he took control of Gruppe III of JG 26, a squadron he was soon to lead through the Battle of Britain. Upon Moelders' (qv) death in 1941, Galland was made General of Fighters at 29 years old. He had become Germany's youngest general in modern warfare. For the rest of the war he pleaded with Hitler and Goering to change the role of fighters from ground attack to air superiority. Hitler refused and demoted him in January, 1944. Spared from probable execution for past service, Galland was allowed to form an elite squadron of jet fighters, personally leading them against the overwhelming Allied air assault.

When the war ended, Galland had 104 victories. During the 1950s he revitalized the Lutwaffe, later becoming the director of Air

Lloyd. A frequent lecturer at international aviation gatherings, he became living proof that enemies in war can become valued friends in peace.

GARNERIN, ANDRÉ JACQUES
1770–1825
Like many young men, Garnerin found his college studies boring and pointless. As an escape, he began to study the principles of ballooning. He launched hand-made paper balloons from the college grounds despite being threatened with expulsion. When Napoleon rose to power Garnerin joined the Committee for Public Safety and was sent on a secret mission. He was captured by the Austrians and shipped off to a prison in Budapest in 1795. Garnerin formulated a plan to escape from his prison tower by means of a parachute, but before he could act he was returned to France as part of a prisoner exchange.

Two years had passed since his capture and few people in the capital remembered him. He turned from politics back to his first love, aeronautics. After building a hot air balloon and testing several parachute designs, he attempted the world's first descent from a balloon on 22 October 1797. His parachute was a twenty-four-foot (7.3m) ribbed parasol attached beneath a balloon. Garnerin stood in a bucket under the canopy. When he reached 3,000 feet (914m), the courageous Frenchman released his apparatus, the canopy unfurled and he dropped slowly earthwards. The amazed audience cheered as Garnerin's bucket smashed onto the pavement. The force of the crash injured a leg, but otherwise he was safe.

In 1802 he made the first parachute drop in England. Two years later he was appointed the official aeronaut to Napoleon's government. He organized an aerial display for the Emperor's coronation.

Garnerin's wife, Jeanne, became the first woman to pilot a balloon and also the first to make a parachute jump – in 1798. His niece, Elisa Garnerin, became the first professional woman parachutist.

GARROS, ROLAND
1888–1918
The Rheims Meet of 1909 inspired a second generation of world flyers. One such young man was Garros. He had gone to Paris to study to become a concert pianist, but the Rheims week changed his life. He heard music in the air.

He gave up his musical ambitions and an automobile repair shop he had started, to train full-time as an aviator. He purchased a Clement-Bayard Demoiselle and learned to fly it at Issy. He embarked on a career as an exhibition pilot which took him to America as part of the Moisant International Aviators in 1910. In 1913 he made one of the pre-war year's most significant flights when he flew from France to Tunisia across the Mediterranean Sea, a distance of 453 miles (729km)!

When World War I broke out in August, 1914, Garros was ironically in Germany giving the military advice on the use of airplanes in warfare! The night the conflict began, he quietly slipped out of his room, entered the hanger where his airplane was stored, started the engine himself and flew in darkness to Switzerland. This, in fact, was one of the most dangerous flights of his career. Back in France, he joined Escadrille M.S. 23 as a scout pilot. In late March, 1915 he had metal plates attached to his propeller blades, behind which he rigged a machine-gun. The plates would deflect any bullet that didn't go between the blades. On April Fools Day, he surprised an Albatros two-seater and brought it down in flames. He made four more kills in the next sixteen days and became France's greatest hero. An American journalist heard Parisians call Garros an 'ace', a term used to describe a great sportsman. The journalist took this to be an official term for flyers with five victories and the term stuck.

Fate surprised Garros on 18 April when his engine failed due to enemy gunfire which severed his fuel line and he force-landed behind German lines. He might have escaped except that he tried to set fire to his machine so that the enemy wouldn't discover his secret. He was captured before destroying the plane and the

Germans found the deflector plates. They introduced a greatly improved system to achieve the same results after bringing Garros' device to Fokker (qv).

For three years, Garros sat in a POW camp until he managed to escape in early 1918. He retrained as a combat pilot and returned to action six months later. Military flying had changed dramatically in those years and the old Morane-Saulniers had given way to faster Spads and Nieuports. Flying a Spad, Garros was shot down and killed one month before the war ended.

GASTAMBIDE, JULES
*–1944

Gastambide was a civil engineer and owner of an electrical power plant in Algeria. While on vacation in France in 1902 he agreed to back Levavasseur's (qv) proposed design for a new engine. The engine would be named after Gastambide's daughter, Antoinette. Within a few years the engine had proved itself a champion by powering several racing motorboats to the winner's circle. In 1906 a company to market the engines was formed with Gastambide, Levavasseur, and Blériot (qv) as directors. In 1907 the company decided to build aeroplanes, at which point Blériot dropped out. The first machine was a canard pusher that was not completed. The next was a tractor monoplane named the *Gastambide-Mengin I* (Mengin was another director). It was first tested in early 1908 at Bagatelle in the Bois de Boulogne. It was soon modified and renamed the *Antoinette II*. In this form, it became the first monoplane to carry a passenger, Robert Gastambide, Jules' brother, in August, 1908.

After World War I, Gastambide and Levavasseur designed a remarkable airplane which featured a variable camber wing. It had front and rear flaps which slid into position, thus greatly expanding the lifting capacity of the wing. This little-known machine was built for them by Jean Latham, the cousin of Hubert Latham (qv).

GÉNET, DR EDMOND-CHARLES
1763–1834

Génet was the head of the translating department in the French Ministry of Foreign Affairs at the time of the French Revolution. He later settled in America and married the daughter of the Governor of New York State and became a gentleman farmer. His active mind struck upon the idea of using balloons to lower and raise canal boats instead of time-consuming water locks. He applied for a patent which was granted in 1825, signed by President John Quincy Adams. It was the first aeronautical patent issued in the United States.

GIBBS-SMITH, CHARLES HARVARD
1909–1982

For many years of this century, Aviation History as a subject has been fraught with controversy. It has been an emotional topic often discussed with a strong bias of nationalism. It has been packed with half-truths, superstitions, publicity gloss, political lies, and other difficulties which made its study a difficult undertaking. Into this quagmire of confusion waded a gentle, unassuming historian who, with the publication of several books, almost single-handedly brought truth and the scholarly method back to aviation history.

Gibbs-Smith was this historian. After receiving his degree, he began work at the Victoria and Albert Museum in London in 1932. During World War II he worked for the Ministry of Information. It was for his investigative work into the early history of aviation that he earned his great reputation. He searched for the precise truth in everything, rather than a convenient generalization. He tracked down all leads though one might destroy a previously held 'fact'. He firmly established the priority of early flights, proving beyond any doubt that the Wright brothers (qv) were the first to fly a controlled aeroplane in sustained flight. His international approach to history brought a credence to his work that won over any lingering doubters.

Required reading for anyone interested in

aviation history are his classic books: *Aviation,* and *The Invention of the Aeroplane (1799–1909).*

GIBSON, WING COMMANDER GUY PENROSE, VC
1918–1944

Gibson was born in India. He became an RAF officer in 1937 and was assigned to No 83 Squadron. At the war's outbreak he was a Hampden pilot, though he soon transferred to the night-fighting Beaufighter. With No 106 Squadron he gained experience with the mighty Lancaster. Bravery exhibited during bombing runs earned him a DSO and DFC.

In 1943 he was selected to organize a new squadron for 'special duties'. This became No 617 Squadron later known as the 'Dambusters'.

On the night of 16/17 May, 1943 he led the unit on a raid against the Eder, Möhne, Schwelme and Sorps dams in Germany. This mission featured Barnes Wallis' (qv) 9,250lb (4,200kg) 'skip' bombs. Gibson's plane dropped first bomb against the Möhne dam. It took four more bombs to finish the job and so give the other attacking bombers a better chance, Gibson distracting enemy ground defences by flying low. The Lancasters headed next to the Eder dam where only three bombs sufficed. The other two dams were not destroyed.

For his part in leading the raid, Gibson won the Victoria Cross. He became famous immediately and was taken by Winston Churchill to America to drum up Allied confidence in British ability. Despite an invitation from the Prime Minister to enter politics, Gibson refused. Nor did he want a staff position, he wanted to go back to combat duty. He got his wish.

On 19 September, 1944 he was killed when his plane was shot down during a raid on Rheydt and München-Gladbach.

GIFFARD, HENRI
1825–1882

Inspired by Jullien's (qv) small model dirigible,

the successful French engineer Giffard turned his attention to aerial navigation. Giffard built a three horsepower engine which weighed ninety-nine pounds (45kg) not including accessories, relatively light given the standards of the day. He attached the engine to a cat-walk suspended beneath a 144-foot (44m) long tapered gas bag and on 24 September 1852 flew 'under steam' from Paris to Trappes at a speed of six miles per hour (9.6km/hr). He could effect minor course adjustments but not proper full turns. Still, this was a notable achievement.

Giffard continued to experiment but was stricken with an eye infection that blinded him. Depressed, he committed suicide by taking chloroform.

GLAISHER, JAMES
1809–1903

Glaisher was born at Rotherhithe, England and studied to be a scientist. He earned a position at the Royal Observatory, Greenwich where he headed the magnetic and meteorological departments. An enlightened scientist, he tried to develop principles for weather forecasting. He recognized the potential of hydrogen balloons and was able to experiment with balloons when he formed an historic partnership with Coxwell (qv).

Glaisher and his partner began to explore the upper atmosphere by hydrogen balloon, taking scientific instruments up with them on their flights. They were carried so high on one flight, above five miles, that Glaisher blacked out and was only saved by Coxwell's bravery.

In 1866 Glaisher helped found the Aeronautical Society. He was also a founding member of the Meteorological Society.

GLENN, JOHN HERSCHEL, JR.
1921–

An Ohio native, Glenn joined the Marine Corps in 1942 after spending three years at college. He earned his wings in March, 1943 and was sent to the Pacific theatre. After fifty-nine missions he had earned two DFCs. During the Korean War he flew ninety missions and earned two more DFCs. Later in the 1950s he flew as a test pilot for the Naval Air Test Center. He subsequently advised industry on fighter plane design.

In 1959 he was one of seven chosen for the prestigious astronaut program. On 20 February 1962 he became the first American to orbit the earth when he piloted the *Friendship 7* around the globe three times. His safe return to earth brought a great sigh of national relief to America which had been worried that the Soviets held the lead in space technology. Glenn's flight temporarily allayed that fear and he was hailed across the country as a national hero, receiving a ticker-tape parade in New York that rivalled Lindbergh's (qv).

In 1974, after two defeats, Glenn was elected to the Senate and pursued a successful political career.

GODDARD, DR ROBERT HUTCHINGS
1882–1945
Goddard was the most successful early experimenter with liquid fuel rockets though his experiments weren't wholly successful.

His early life was that of an invalid, forced to remain in his bed for months at a time due to a weak constitution. While bed-bound, he read all of Jules Verne's (qv) adventure stories and became convinced that space flight would one day become a reality. After studying physics at the Worcester Massachusetts Polytechnic Institute, he went to Clark University where he obtained his Ph.D. in 1911.

During his years at Clark, Goddard began to speculate on the advantages of liquefied fuel rocket propulsion. Efficiency and the ability to control the motor made the liquid fuel rocket a better device than solid fuel rockets.

Goddard was an ordnance expert during World War I but returned to rocket flight in 1919 when he published *A Method of Reaching Extreme Altitude*. In this classic paper he theoretically demonstrated that a liquid fuel rocket could be launched into outer space. Furthermore, he proposed building an eight to ten tonne rocket large enough to reach the

Moon. When this proposed rocket struck the lunar surface, it was to ignite a magnesium flare visible on Earth to prove it had reached its destination. More than just a Vernian vision, this proposal received serious consideration. The Smithsonian Institution presented Goddard with a grant to begin experimenting with rockets. By 1926, he had built a small rocket and on 26 March 1926 launched it from Auburn, Massachusetts. It reached a modest 184 feet (56m) but became the first liquid fuel rocket to fly. Goddard launched a second rocket from this site, but was forced to relocate to New Mexico when his neighbours complained about the noise.

The Guggenheim Foundation, following the advice of Lindbergh (qv), bestowed a grant on Goddard. This money enabled him to develop his rockets and incorporate such sophisticated devices as gyroscopic controls, gimbal and jet vane steering, and pressurized fuel tanks. By 1935 his rockets were flying as high as 8,000 feet (2,440m) at supersonic speeds.

The value of Goddard's work has been the subject of much debate. Since he worked in self-imposed secrecy he influenced few other engineers in the United States. However, Wernher von Braun (qv) stated that his early interest in rockets was spurred by Goddard's work, so perhaps Goddard had profound significance after all.

GOERING, REICHSMARSCHALL HERMANN WILHELM
1893–1946
The son of a minor German diplomat, Goering applied for aviation school at the outbreak of World War I but was rejected due to a low score on the entrance exam. He had been an infantryman since 1912 and during the war gained distinction for bravery. He suffered from arthritis which made life in the trenches unbearable but had a stroke of luck when a friend, Bruno Loerzer, helped him to enter the air service.

Goering was a very good pilot who was known for flying all-white aircraft. By the end of the war he had shot down twenty-two planes and was in command of von Richthofen's (qv) squadron.

As the social turmoil increased in Germany after the war, Goering became an ardent anti-communist, gravitating to the Nazi party. He made friends with Hitler and was involved in the 1923 'Beer Hall Putsch'. When Hitler came to power in 1933, Goering received broad political powers. He set about establishing a new air force and at the same time formed the Gestapo and had concentration camps built. He became drunk with power, seeking every chance to appropriate huge estates, hunting lodges, castles, art collections and more. As his aesthetic greed grew, his attention to military duties waned, with the result that the Luftwaffe had no cohesive leadership when it needed it in 1940.

As head of the Luftwaffe, Goering was personally responsible for switching the objectives of the Battle of Britain in September 1940, thereby losing the battle if not the war.

Blunder followed disastrous blunder as Goering made his way through the war, never bothering to listen to battlefield commanders but always ready to pontificate. One declaration of his became the rallying call of the Allied bomber pilots. In 1940 he had announced: 'No enemy plane will fly over the Reich territory, or my name is Meyer!' By the end of the war much of Germany had been bombed into a wasteland.

Goering was captured in 1945 and tried as a war criminal. He was sentenced to death but escaped the gallows by taking cyanide.

GOUPY, AMBROISE
1876–1951
Goupy is one of the least known of the early pioneers. In 1908 he had Voisin (qv) build him a triplane which Goupy test-hopped in September and December of that year. His next aeroplane the *Goupy II*, was built in collaboration with Calderara (qv) in Blériot's (qv) shop and was simply a Blériot fuselage with biplane main and tail surfaces. This was the first tractor biplane and influenced aeroplane design for the next twenty-five years. The plane was modified and renamed the *Goupy III*. It flew well enough that several examples were built which were used at a flying school.

GRADE, HANS
1879–1946
For a country that produced the likes of Lilienthal (qv) and Zeppelin (qv), surprisingly, Germany had very few aeronautical experimenters during the first eight years of this century. One of those few was Hans Grade. Grade had studied engineering in Berlin before opening a motorcycle factory while still in his early twenties. He read accounts of Ellehammer (qv) and Santos-Dumont (qv) which whetted his appetite to try something more exciting than motorcycles.

His first aeroplane was a clumsy triplane built in 1908. The next year he built a wonderfully simple tractor monoplane which looked remarkably like many of today's ultralights. He flew this in August, 1909 and it marked the first flight in Germany of a German machine. Grade went on to build other planes, including a two-seater, but was not a force in the development of German aviation.

GRAHAME-WHITE, CLAUDE
1879–1959
Grahame-White's enthusiastic, self-confident personality was one reason for his tremendous success. He was born into a wealthy family and while a teenager disposed of all the horse-drawn lorries in his uncle's wool factory, replacing them with gasoline types. He toured Europe and Africa, took an engineering degree at Bedford and then opened a Renault dealership in London where he also sold Blériot (qv) headlamps. It was natural then that while attending the 1909 Rheims Meet he would look up the French manufacturer. He marvelled at Blériot's machine and purchased one, insisting that 'le patron' personally teach him to fly, though Bleriot deferred. Impatient, Grahame-White trained himself and after several crack-ups earned British certificate No. 6.

In 1910 he became one of Britain's premier aviators, participating in flying meets in the United States and Europe. His most exciting race was the London to Manchester contest during which he made a thrilling night flight in an unsuccessful bid to defeat Paulhan (qv). His business interests sprouted that year when he opened flying schools at Pau, Brooklands, and most notably, Hendon.

Grahame-White was an earnest patriot who undertook a campaign in 1912 to heighten the British public's awareness of the future importance of aviation. During this campaign he flew across England in a Farman biplane painted with the legend 'Wake up England' which was outlined in lightbulbs. His development of Hendon served to bring aviation closer to Edwardian Londoners who could travel there by 'tube' to see weekend flying displays.

During World War I he joined the RNAS and participated in a raid on German bases in Belgium. He resigned shortly thereafter to concentrate on warplane production.

After the war he formed a company to build lightweight cars but achieved little success. He lost his Hendon holdings through government intrigue, though he was successful in a suit to get payment for the property. His most successful dealings were in real estate in London. He was married to the former Ethel Levey, ex-wife of the famous American musician George M. Cohan but he too divorced her shortly before World War II.

GRANVILLE, ZANTFORD D.
1901(?)–1934

The 'Golden Age' of aviation certainly boasted an unusual cast of characters but one of the most unexpected geniuses of those years was a young man named 'Granny' who, though he had no engineering training and had been fired from his only job with an aviation company, went on to design and build aeroplanes that were faster than any military aeroplane in the world – and all before he was thirty years old!

Granville was born in Madison, New Hampshire and received an average education.

He expressed an early interest in inventing things. At the age of twenty he went for his first aeroplane ride in a Curtiss flying-boat. Soon after this he opened an auto repair garage but gave that up in 1925 to join the Boston Airport Corporation. There he got into an argument with his boss and was fired. He decided to start a mobile aeroplane repair service and to this end fitted out a large old passenger car with a covered body to hold his tools and supplies. In the course of the next four years he learned much about aircraft design from simply repairing aeroplanes. By 1929 he felt well enough informed to design his own aeroplane.

He designed a small, side-by-side biplane with such unique features as four flaps and an overhead control stick. He built this craft with help from his four brothers. In typically eccentric fashion, he decided to test his aeroplane in darkness without previously informing his brothers. It was after 3 a.m. on the morning of 3 May 1929 that he opened the throttle and took off. The sky was pitch black and his flight took place between two fierce thunderstorms.

With the success of this machine, the Granville brothers received financial backing and formed the historic Gee-Bee Company. In just three short years, Granny's aeroplanes, which seemed to be all engine and little else, completely outclassed all competition in the major races in America. They won many races including the Thompson Trophy twice. In the hands of skilled pilots the stubby, brutish Gee-Bee racers were winners, if temperamental and sensitive ones.

Flushed with success, Granny began to experiment with canard aircraft and even designed a futuristic but thoroughly practical Indy 500 race car. But as suddenly as it all started, the magic of the Gee-Bee Company vanished in a succession of unfortunate crashes that were only partially the fault of the airplanes' designs. In late 1933 these crashes wiped out many of the fastest Gee-Bees. The orders for the planes stopped and the company folded.

Granny opened up a design office in New York and seemed set for a full recovery when he was killed while attempting to land a Gee-Bee on a delivery flight. He stalled at low level trying to avoid some construction workers who were standing in the middle of a runway. He was thirty-two. His brothers, Thomas, Edward, Mark and Robert drifted into other jobs, mostly related to the aircraft industry.

GREEN, CHARLES
1785–1870

Green's career ran the gamut from his great contributions to ballooning as a scientist to his ridiculous stunt exhibitions.

Green was a native Londoner and on 19 July 1821 he commemorated George IV's coronation with the world's first balloon ascent using coal gas. He had discovered that by tapping into London's newly installed street lamp gas lines, he could obtain a buoyant gas cheaper than conventional hydrogen. Seven years later he performed the silly stunt of riding a pony into the air. The trained animal, with Green astride, stood on a small platform slung beneath a balloon. This flight on 29 July 1828 was the first of its type in England. Green returned to serious aeronautics in 1836 with a thrilling 480 mile (772km) night flight from London to Weilburg, in the duchy of Nassau, Germany. The flight introduced overnight voyages and, more importantly, the first use of the guide rope as an automatic ballast. Green's expert handling of the balloon during the trip placed him as the world's greatest aeronaut until Coxwell's (qv) flights in the 1860s.

He continued to perform trivial but popular stunts such as lighting fireworks beneath his balloon, throwing monkeys overboard harnessed to parachutes, and more. He lived a long life making over 500 ascents and deserves to be remembered as a great aeronaut.

GREY, CHARLES GREY
1875–1953

It is not surprising that the land which produced Shakespeare, Swift, Shaw and Wilde should also produce the world's best editorial writers.

Britain has always had that distinction which continues to this day. In the early days of powered flight, far and away the best writer on aeronautical subjects was C. G. Grey.

Grey was educated in Dublin which may account for the genesis of his future caustic wit. He studied engineering at the Crystal Palace School of Engineering before joining the staff of *Autocar*. Aeroplanes were initially reported in automobile magazines, so in 1908 Grey was sent to cover the 1908 Paris Aeronautical Salon at the Grand Palais. He sensed the importance of aeroplanes in the future and convinced the Iliffe publishing company to launch a magazine, *Aero*. Grey edited this magazine until 1911 when he founded his own, *Aeroplane*. For the next twenty-eight years this famous journal became Grey's personal platform from which he launched the most incisive, perceptive, sardonic barbs and edicts about the state of aviation in Britain and elsewhere ever to emanate from a single source. Grey was either loved or hated by his audience, but all listened. He was occasionally condemned as anti-British when he criticized his nation's sometime lack of progress, but unlike many editors and journalists Grey always sought to improve the aircraft industry in Britain, not to harm it.

In addition to his magazine, he also edited *Jane's* from 1916–41.

GRIFFITH, DR ALAN ARNOLD
1893–1963

Griffith began his aviation career in the Royal Aircraft Factory. After several years working on fracture mechanics at the University of Liverpool, he turned to turbine engine research, publishing in 1926 a farsighted paper entitled *An Aerodynamic Theory of Turbine Design*. In this paper he laid the foundations for the axial flow turbojet.

In 1939 he was able to put his theories into practice when he joined Rolls-Royce as chief scientist on their jet engine project. His work at Rolls eventually led to the Avon and Conway engines. In 1954 he directed a project in which two Nene engines were used to vertically launch a test rig platform. The launch of the *Flying Bedstead* marked the first use of reaction propulsion for a manned vertical, controlled take-off craft.

Griffith continued his work and helped to develop VTOL control features. These were first used on the Short SCI.

GRUMMAN, LeROY RANDLE
1895–1982

Grumman attended Cornell University where he studied engineering. Upon graduation, he went to work for the New York Telephone Company. He left when America entered World War I and joined the Navy hoping to become a pilot. After taking various non-aviation training programmes, he was able to sneak into the pilot programme having been initially denied because of mis-diagnosed flat fleet.

He became a flight instructor and was assigned to test-fly Loening fighters built at the Navy's Philadelphia factory. After the war, Loening (qv) hired Grumman as an engineer. Grumman stayed with this employer until late 1929 when Loening was sold. Grumman and several associates did not relish the prospect of leaving their Long Island location however, so they formed their own company under Grumman's name. Their financial backers, interestingly, included Loening himself.

Starting a new enterprise right at the beginning of the Depression may have seemed foolhardy, but because Grumman and his selected staff remained flexible to all marketing possibilities, they survived. Initially they built aluminium floats, aluminium canoes, and even introduced aluminium truck trailers. Their skill with working this light metal earned them Navy contracts and within a few years the Grumman name was to become synonymous with Naval aviation. Grumman himself managed his company with what today would be called enlightened management techniques. His human skills as well as his engineering foresight helped to create one of the country's greatest aviation firms.

Though Grumman died in 1982, his company received its largest contract ever a few years later worth over one billion dollars. This contract was not for its Navy jets, but rather for ultra-modern mail delivery trucks whose ancestry can be traced back to the Grumman aluminium truck trailers of the 1930s.

GUGGENHEIM, DANIEL
1856–1930

Many countries have had patrons of aeronautical development. France had Deutsch de la Meurthe and Archdeacon (qqv). England had Lord Northcliffe (qv) and Lady Houston. In America the greatest sponsor of aeronautical progress was Daniel Guggenheim who, at a critical moment, stepped in and rescued a sick industry.

Guggenheim was born in Philadelphia, the son of an immigrant businessman. Together with his father, they built up a marketing enterprise that brought them moderate wealth. Around 1880 the Guggenheims became rich when a silver mine they had purchased in California Gulch, Colorado struck ore – and a lot of it. They received $50,000 *a month* from this mine and went on to purchase many more.

In 1923 Daniel Guggenheim retired and began to pursue what he considered to be the duty of the wealthy – philanthropy. He had always been conscious of workers' needs and considered donating his money to their benefit. He rejected this finally because he felt the government was sufficiently supporting workers' rights. His son, Harry, had become interested in aviation prior to World War I and had learned to fly. Subsequently he became a naval aviator, though his wartime duties were mostly logistical. Through Alexander Klemin (qv) the younger Guggenheim heard of the need to fund an aerodynamics program at New York University. He persuaded his father to endow this programme with a gift of $500,000. In 1926 the Daniel Guggenheim Fund for the Promotion of Aeronautics was established and eventually funded with $3,000,000. This fund promoted the development of blind flying, rocketry, and safety devices for aircraft.

At a time when America seemed more interested in air heroes, than air research, the Guggenheim funds provided the seed money to help the unsung heroes – the engineers and scientists – develop aeroplanes that were safe enough to make flying almost routine for the rest of the population.

GUREVICH, MIKHAIL I.
1882(?)–1976
Born in the Kursk region of Russia, Gurevich studied engineering in Paris at L'École Supérieure de l'Aéronatique as a classmate of Marcel Bloch's (qv) before returning to his homeland. He then studied aircraft design at the Kharkov Technical Institute, leaving there in 1925. He went to work designing various machines until 1929 when he joined the Russian team assisting the French aircraft designer Paul Richard who had gone to work for the Soviet government. That group broke up after only a year, but in 1937 Gurevich became the head of design at Aircraft Factory No. 1 in Moscow, a job which required as much political skill as engineering skill. Three years later he began his work with Mikoyan (qv) which led to a string of world class combat planes beginning with the World War II MiG 1.

de GUSMAO, BARTOLOMEO LAURENCO
1686–1724
De Gusmao built the first lighter-than-air balloon in history, seventy-four years before the Montgolfiers (qv) had ever begun their experiments.

Born in Brazil, de Gusmao sailed as a young man to Portugal to study for the priesthood. In Lisbon, he quickly proved his intellectual capabilities, both spiritually and scientifically. In 1709, he was allowed to demonstrate a small hot air balloon before King John V at the royal court. This was an impressive accomplishment for a young person not yet twenty-five. He called his small balloon the *Passarola* and it flew for a few minutes but then fell in flames. So

impressed was the King that he immediately granted the young cleric all patent rights to all flying machines and forbade anyone else from experimenting with them under pain of death.

Why de Gusmao didn't further develop his balloon is unknown. A famous, inaccurate sketch of the *Passarola* circulated for many years. This sketch depicted an open boat with a cloth billowed over it as a sort of horizontal sail. Because of this sketch, it wasn't until the middle of this century that de Gusmao received full credit for his accomplishment, which initially had been passed off by aviation historians as impossible.

GUYNEMER, CAPITAINE GEORGES MARIE LUDOVIC JULES
1894–1917
Born on Christmas Eve in 1894, Guynemer was a frail child who was over-protected by his family. He was a poor student in school but hoped to enter a technical school. World War I provided the youth with a chance to do something noteworthy so he attempted to join the Air Force but was turned down twice. His father's political influence finally won him a chance to be a mechanic. Early in 1915 after pulling more strings, Guynemer wangled his way into pilot training.

When he became a fighter pilot, his flying style was noted for its reckless but aggressive character. He frequently made bad landings, but that was more or less commonplace for new pilots. Guynemer persevered until on 19 July 1915, he scored his first victory. His unit eventually became known as the *N. 3 Cigones* (Storks), a breeding ground for fine pilots. Guynemer's score rose steadily, but was punctuated by being shot down himself seven times, including once when his plane was hit in mid-air by an artillery shell!

Guynemer's boyish looks proved very popular with the French press which helped to make him a national idol. Often interviewed, decorated, and lauded, Guynemer grew more aloof and moody as the months wore on. The aerial action shifted north into the British sector in the autumn of 1917 and Guynemer found it harder to score victories to the point that in attempting his fifty-fifth victory, he imprudently flew into a cloud while attacking a German two-seater. He was never seen again, and though the Germans claimed they had brought him down, they could never prove it.

HAENLEIN, PAUL
1835–1905

Haenlein was a German engineer from Mainz who received a patent in 1865 for a semi-rigid airship. He built this ship and flew it in 1872 at Brunn, in the Austro-Hungarian Empire. This dirigible is notable as being the first to be powered by an internal combustion engine. In this case, Haenlein's 3.6 horsepower engine used coal gas directly from his gas bag as fuel. The dirigible was tethered during its flight but its handling qualities were said to be good.

HAFNER, RAOUL
1905–*

Hafner was born and educated in Vienna where he began to experiment with single-seat helicopters in the very early 1930s in partnership with Bruno Nagler. In 1933 Hafner went to England to demonstrate his machine. He decided to stay there establishing his own company in 1935. That year he introduced a greatly improved autogyro which included what would later become staple features of the helicopter – collective and cyclic pitch control in the hub. This landmark machine firmly established Hafner's reputation as a serious designer. During the war he developed novel, unpowered autogyro units which could support, while towed, individual infantrymen, jeeps, and even tanks. In 1944 he was invited to direct Bristol's new helicopter department. In that role, he laid the foundation for Britain's future helicopter industry. His first machine for that company was the 171 Sycamore.

HALL, ROBERT LEICESTER
1905–1991

When 'Granny' Granville (qv) found financial backing to start a manufacturing company in 1929, he immediately sought the help of engineers who could properly stress an airplane. One of the three he hired was Robert Hall who was seeking to rise quickly with a small firm.

Hall's first year and a half at Gee-Bee was slow because the Great Depression had struck and few planes were sold. In 1931 Hall convinced Granville and his financial backers to form the Springfield Air Racing Associates. It was this organization which started Gee-Bee on its road to victory at the Cleveland Air Races. Though a Gee-Bee designed by Hall won the 1931 race, the Gee-Bee which he piloted finished fourth.

Hall became dissatisfied with the Granvilles and left in the winter of 1931–32 to design his own planes. He found financial backing from Marion Guggenheim and with it had his racer, the *Bulldog*, built. It was a beautiful failure, mainly due to engine problems. Nevertheless, he finished sixth in the 1932 Thompson Trophy.

After helping to design the Stinson SR series, Hall moved on to Grumman (qv) where he worked as a designer and test pilot. He retired from that firm in 1970.

HAMEL, GUSTAV
1889–1914

Hamel was the son of a German doctor who attended to the cream of London society. Hamel enjoyed all the privileges of the day and received an education at Westminster and Cambridge. He learned to fly in 1910 and soon became a darling of the British public. He was the first English pilot to loop, and in 1911 carried the first official airmail. This he did on the event of King George V's coronation when he flew from Hendon to Windsor. He won a roguish but polite reputation for frequently flying lady passengers, and astounded Europe in 1913 when he announced a plan to fly the Atlantic. For this, he intended to use a purpose-built Martin-Handasyde monoplane. Before he could effect his plan, he disappeared while flying over the English Channel. War-spooked people in England said that he had really disappeared in order to join the German Air Force and direct Zeppelin raids against London. However, fishermen later found a mangled body in the Channel that, though lost due to foul seas before it could be positively identified, was probably that of Hamel.

HAMILTON, CHARLES KEENEY
1881–1914

Hamilton was a two-fisted stuntman who thrilled audiences around the world with his bravery prior to World War I. He was born in Connecticut, where he conducted his first flying experiment by jumping out of a window holding on to an umbrella. He left home at eighteen to find adventure. In 1905 Hamilton approached Israel Ludlow, the misunderstood New York lawyer turned heavier-than-air experimenter, and offered to 'pilot' the latter's kite/gliders. Ludlow quickly accepted. Hamilton experienced crash after crash while in Ludlow's gliders which were towed behind automobiles and later power boats.

That same year, Hamilton talked his way into flying Baldwin's (qv) *California Arrow* dirigible which was giving a demonstration on Long Island. After this taste of controlled flight, he spent the next four years as a dirigible and parachute showman, even travelling to Japan where he was jeered by Shinto fundamentalists who believed that flying was an intrusion into the sacred realms of ancestors.

While in Japan, Hamilton read of the Rheims Meet and hastily returned to America where he met Glenn Curtiss (qv) in Chicago. Curtiss couldn't avoid the persistent Hamilton, and showed him how the controls of his aeroplane worked, inviting him to visit the factory in Hammondsport. Hamilton rushed to Hammondsport where Curtiss gave him a few lessons. Hamilton took advantage of an absence by Curtiss who was away on business, to take an aeroplane up for a lengthy flight though he had not been approved for solo flying. When Curtiss returned, though he was furious at

Hamilton's brashness, he nevertheless admired the natural skill he had exhibited and contracted him as an exhibition pilot.

Hamilton flew with reckless daring in any weather, at any time of day, on any sudden challenge. He flew as if there were no tomorrow even though he was married. He chain-smoked, drank heavily, quarrelled with associates, but when he refused to pay an agreed share of his profits to Curtiss, Curtiss ended his contract and won a judgement against him.

Hamilton continued to fly until 1912 when, evidently, the physical pressures exhausted him. He died of a lung haemorrhage in 1914.

HAMPTON, JOHN
1799–1851

Hampton came from a naval background but his true interests were aeronautical. He made his first balloon flight on 8 June 1838, nearly losing his life when the balloon smashed into the side of a house on landing. Hampton suffered serious injuries from this mishap but recovered and by autumn of the same year had laid plans to make a parachute descent.

The only other Englishman to attempt such a descent was Cocking (qv) who had been killed in the effort. Hampton's friends tried to dissuade him but he went ahead and constructed a relatively small umbrella-shaped parachute using whalebone ribs and bamboo stretchers. He rigged it under a balloon which he had also designed. It was named the *Albion*. His friends then attempted to have the local authorities ban the flight but they had no legal grounds for an injunction. Hampton asked his friends to assist him in launching it for a tethered test flight which they agreed to do, but when Hampton was thirty feet up, he cut the restraining ropes. He rose swiftly to nearly two miles (3.2km).

Whether it was faith or foolhardiness which led Hampton to release his parachute without properly testing it is a matter of conjecture. Anyway, he did descend and his parachute functioned perfectly. He drifted earthwards for thirteen minutes and made a safe landing, the first of its kind by an Englishman.

HANDASYDE, GEORGE HARRIS
1877–1958

Handasyde formed a company in 1908 with H. P. Martin to produce airplanes. Handasyde designed the planes. Their early aircraft were along the lines of the Antoinette, though 'cleaner' and consequently faster. Their third machine was built for Sopwith (qv) in 1911. A two-seater, powered by a fifty horsepower Gnome, performed well. In 1912 the company branched into military production and sold two aircraft to the War Office. During the war they built biplane fighters and the Elephant bomber.

In 1920 Handasyde left the company to found his own. This company folded four years later. In 1928 he came out of retirement to work for the Desoutter company, where he modified the Koolhoven Coupe to meet British airworthiness standards.

HANRIOT, RENÉ
1872(?)–1925

Hanriot developed an interest for engines when he was still a young man. His family's personal fortune allowed him to purchase some of the earliest automobiles ever made, and he entered many of the early continental races. He earned a good reputation as a Darracq driver.

In 1907 a growing interest in aviation compelled him to build a monoplane which he completed in 1909. That year he exhibited the machine at the Salon de l'Aéronautique where it received notice for its clean, efficient lines. In early spring, 1910, Hanriot opened a flight school at Bethaney. Oddly enough, he didn't earn his own brevet until the next year!

Hanriot switched from monoplanes to biplanes around the beginning of the war. The French government did not consider his planes to be as good as the Nieuports and others, so he was forced to find foreign markets. Belgium and Italy gladly purchased his fighters and for these countries they became ace-makers.

Following hostilities, Hanriot pioneered all-metal aircraft, but died suddenly. His son Marcel took control of the firm.

HARGRAVE, LAWRENCE
1850–1915

Hargrave is usually remembered as the man who invented the box-kite, but this pays too little tribute to a great mind.

He was born in Greenwich, England, but as a teenager sailed with his family to a new life in Australia. He became an engineer-draughtsman, also spending some time exploring New Guinea. In 1877 he became an assistant astronomer at the Sydney Observatory, but after receiving an inheritance he was financially free to pursue his true interest, flight. He left the observatory in 1883 and dedicated the rest of his life to aeronautical experiments.

As early as 1884 he predicted that the centre of pressure for an efficient wing should be located at around twenty-five per cent of its chord. He realized the importance of aluminium, the need for ailerons, the benefit of dihedral, and the power of curved wings as opposed to flat ones, and more. He invented the rotary engine, according to some, and built one that worked. Kite experiments led to his greatest discovery – the box-kite. In 1893 he flew his first box-kite, and it was this kite that so greatly influenced European and American aircraft experimenters. The advantage of the box-kite is its strength and stability versus weight. Hargrave once launched himself sixteen feet (4.8m) into the air with a train of four box-kites.

Hargrave published his findings at home and in Europe. He was a frequent correspondent with American scientific magazines, thus any notion that he was an isolated figure is unfounded. In 1899 he visited England and lectured on his experiments but returned home after six months. How would aviation history have changed had he stayed in Europe for the coming critical years?

HARMON, CLIFFORD BURKE
1868–1944(?)

Harmon became a millionaire from developing real estate around New York city. Looking for a gentleman's hobby, he became a balloonist entering many races around the turn of the century. In 1909 he set a balloon endurance record by staying aloft for 48 hours 26.5 minutes. That same year he turned away from ballooning and bought a Curtiss aeroplane. Harmon was older than the average exhibition pilot by about fifteen years and he certainly didn't need the prize money. Nevertheless, the sport and the crowds were ample reward and he set out to earn victories and set records. He participated in the Dominquez Meet in Los Angeles in 1910 and later the Harvard-Boston meet. For the second meet, he switched to a Farman. That year he made the first flight across Long Island Sound.

In 1926 he established the Harmon International Trophy to recognize achievement in aeronautics.

HARMSWORTH, ALFRED CHARLES WILLIAM (LORD NORTHCLIFFE)
1865–1922

The new science of aviation did not immediately catch-on in Britain in the early years of this century. Someone had to awaken that country to the aeroplane's enormous possibilities and Alfred Harmsworth was just the man to do it.

He came from an impoverished background, but grew up with the desire to be rich. After several failed business ventures, he became a journalist and discovered that there was a great untapped market for a new type of newspaper. Social reforms in Victorian England had created a great mass of readers who, though not well educated, still had an interest in world and national affairs, as long as what they were told wasn't overly complicated. Harmsworth set out to cater to this class of citizen. He started several small news magazines that told short, high interest stories. These were so successful that in 1894 he purchased the financially troubled London *Evening News*. He turned this paper into an expansion of his magazine concept. Short, to-the-point news coverage, a serial story, articles of interest to women – these were the staples of the *Evening News* that reaped huge profits for him. In 1896 he started the *Daily*

Mail, a newspaper which sold itself with blaring headlines. His publishing empire grew steadily until it became the largest in British history, incorporating many of the country's leading papers.

Harmsworth was made Baron Northcliffe in 1905 for his publishing prowess. Much of his success was due to his ability to predict trends. He knew that automobiles and aviation would be part of the future and used his papers to promote them. In 1906 he hired the first full-time aerial correspondent, Harry Harper (qv). During the pre-war years the *Daily Mail* was the trumpet which sounded Northcliffe's call for Britain to get airborne. He sponsored races and events including: the model airplane contest which gave A. V. Roe (qv) his start; the cross-Channel flight won by Blériot (qv); the first circular flight of one mile in Britain contest won by Moore-Brabazon (qv); the great London to Manchester race won by Paulhan (qv); the first non-stop trans-Atlantic flight won by Alcock and Brown (qqv), and many more.

A disease robbed Northcliffe of his mental judgement in 1921 and he died the next year.

HARPER, HARRY
1880–1960

Harper's father was a magazine editor, who provided his family with a comfortable living. At the age of eleven, Harper received his first bicycle which started his love of machinery. Six years later, he became a reporter for a small regional newspaper, a job which he found too boring. He worked his way up, though, and became an entertainment critic for a London publication which reported on news of the blossoming West End theatre world. Though successful at this work, Harper had developed an interest in aviation after reading books by Wise and Glaisher (qqv).

In early 1906 he wrote to several wealthy men whom he hoped would sponsor the construction of a glider he had designed. One of these men was Lord Northcliffe (A. Harmsworth) (qv) who decided to interview him. Northcliffe listened carefully to Harper, but after having the design reviewed by specialists, he declined to fund it. However, two months later he recalled Harper and offered him the job as the world's first permanent aviation correspondent. He would work for the *Daily Mail*. The position was joyously accepted.

Harper already knew several members of the small British aviation world including the balloonist Spencer, and Samuel Cody (qv) whom he had met when he covered the American's Wild West show. In early 1907 Harper proposed to Northcliffe that the *Daily Mail* should sponsor a prize for model-making which might encourage British heavier-than-air experimentation. The 'Chief' agreed and this prize was won by Roe (qv).

In addition to his newspaper work, Harper wrote a series of forward-thinking aviation books with Grahame-White (qv). His prolific writing career lasted well into the jet age.

HARRIS, SIR ARTHUR TRAVERS
1892–1984
Born in England, Harris emigrated to Rhodesia as a young man. He joined the infantry in 1914 and saw combat in German West Africa. The next year, he returned to England, joined the RFC and became a fighter pilot. Following the war he served the RAF at various posts worldwide including tours in the US and Palestine. After commanding Group 5 in Bomber Command from 1939-40 and serving as the deputy chief of air staff from 1940-41, he became the commander-in-chief of Bomber Command in February 1942.

As head of Bomber Command, with all the destructive powers of the RAF bombers in his hands, Harris initiated indiscriminate area bombing. His bombers nightly inflicted catastrophic damage to German cities which ultimately killed 50,000 civilians. Post-war analysts have questioned the strategic value of this policy, some of these critics going so far as to call him 'Butcher' Harris. Others have lauded the bombing policy as the only way to have effectively stopped the German war machine. Harris retired in 1946 and received a baronetcy.

HARTMANN, KOMMODORE ERICH ALFRED
1922–1993
Though he became the highest scoring fighter pilot of all time, Hartmann had originally hoped to be a doctor. Upon completion of his secondary education in 1940, he joined the Luftwaffe. His fighter career didn't start until October of 1942, but from then on he amassed a total number of kills that would have made him an ace seventy times over! His first combat assignment was with JG 52 in Russia and he remained with that unit for the rest of the war.

He flew 1,405 combat missions, engaged in 825 dogfights and scored 352 confirmed kills, mostly against fighters. Hartmann was such a deadly adversary that the Russians, against all rules of war, put a price on his head. At the war's end, the Russians captured him and sentenced him to hard labour. He served 10 years in a Soviet prison camp before international pressure forced his release in 1955.

Hartmann rejoined the Luftwaffe that year and became an inspirational figure to future pilots who flew with a now democratic Iron Cross on their wings.

HAVENS, BECKWITH
1890–1969
Havens was born into a prosperous family in New York. In 1910 he journeyed to Hammondsport to talk Curtiss (qv) into appointing him as a company aeroplane salesman and providing free flying lessons. Curtiss told Havens that he must pay $500 for lessons and then he could try to sell the planes. Havens managed to borrow the money and took his lessons with Curtiss himself. He never sold a Curtiss plane because he found it too profitable to be an exhibition pilot. He flew in Cuba, and made the first flight from Chicago to New York in a hydroplane.

After serving as a naval aviator during the war, he tried various promotional efforts until 1928 when he finally began to sell airplanes – for Loening (qv). Successful with this, he moved on to Fairchild in the 1930s.

HAWKER, HARRY GEORGE
1889–1921

Hawker was born in Australia to a poor blacksmith. He bounced from school to school but left at twelve. He found work in a factory and was able to save enough money to travel to England where he hoped to enter the aviation industry. At first he could only find employment in the automobile industry, but in 1912 he landed a job at Sopwith. He worked over 100 hours a week so that he could save enough money to take flying lessons. By September, 1912 he had saved the required £40 and took the lessons. Only a month later he entered and won the British Michelin Cup with a flight that lasted eight hours and twenty-three minutes. The next year he set an altitude record and won the Mortimer Singer Amphibious prize while flying a Sopwith Bat Boat.

Hawker became one of Sopwith's (qv) most important advisers. He had the ability to 'feel' a prototype's strengths and flaws. He helped design every World War I Sopwith scout plane and flew each one on its maiden flight. He awed spectators when on the first flight of the Sopwith Triplane he looped it three times to show his confidence in it.

Hawker piloted the Sopwith trans-Atlantic plane in the *Daily Mail* contest in 1919 but it crashed in mid-ocean when the radiator malfunctioned. For a week, no news was heard of Hawker and MacKenzie-Grieve, the navigator. They were presumed dead. The King and Queen sent their condolences to Hawker's wife Muriel, who, in addition, had received the promise of a pension from Lord Northcliffe (qv).

Suddenly, Hawker and MacKenzie-Grieve reappeared. They had been rescued by a Danish tramp steamer, the *Mary*, which had no radio. Britain went wild with excitement and the two pilots were fêted and bemedalled. Their smashed airplane had even been saved and was put on display at London's famous department store, Selfridge's.

In 1920 the Sopwith company went into voluntary liquidation because of the lack of aircraft orders. It was reformed under the name Hawker so as not to confuse future shareholders about the solvency of the company. Hawker himself returned to race flying and race car driving, the latter at also Brooklands. On 21 July 1921, while practising for the Aerial Derby at Hendon, his plane pitched in at low level and smashed into the earth. The precise cause of the crash could not be determined, though some claimed that Hawker had suffered a sudden haemorrhage, while others said that the carburettor float had come loose and caused a fire. Whatever the cause, reports of Hawker's death this time were not false.

HAWKER, MAJOR LANOE GEORGE, VC
1890–1916

Hawker was the son of a Hampshire naval officer and had gone to Dartmouth College hoping to pursue a similar career. Poor health forced him into joining the Royal Engineers. In 1913 he paid for private flying lessons and joined the newly organized RFC.

Two months after the war started he was in Belgium flying reconnaissance missions. On 31 October Hawker met his first enemy plane while flying solo and immediately attacked, armed only with a service revolver. Hawker then proceeded to devise small bombs fashioned from grenades. His desire always to attack led him, on 18 April 1915, to set out on a solo sortie against the Zeppelin shed at Gontrode. This heroic flight, although only partially successful, earned him a DSO.

The next phase of his armament evolution was to rig a Lewis gun outside his cockpit angled off at forty-five degrees so that the bullets would pass outside the propeller arc. With this primitive rig mounted on his Bristol Scout, he shot down a record three enemy planes in one day on 25 July 1916. This feat astounded the entire RFC and he won not only the Victoria Cross, but also the command of his own Squadron, No. 24, which flew DH-2s. Hawker, like Boelke (qv), exhibited exceptional organizational and training skills and soon his squadron was the most successful in the British service. With his DH-2, he swept Fokker Eindeckers out of the sky, thus dispelling the myth that British planes were 'Fokker Fodder'. He realized that the main mission of any scout plane was to protect the reconnaissance planes and this endeared him to many Army commanders, who relied on aerial photographs.

During the summer of 1916 Hawker was forbidden to fly over enemy lines yet he did so by not filing reports. On 23 November knowing that he was about to be posted home, he led a patrol to bomb the Bapaume area. His flight attacked two German observation planes but were then attacked by Albatros scouts. One was painted red – the colour of von Richthofen (qv).

The German ace later described the thirty-five minute battle as the toughest he had ever flown. Hawker was killed by a bullet to the head just as he reached British lines, across which he had been ordered not to fly.

HAWLEY, ALAN RAMSAY
1869–1938
Hawley was born in New Jersey and became a rich stockbroker. He helped to found the Automobile Club of America but by 1905 had turned his ambitions skyward. In 1906 he travelled to France where he received an aeronaut's licence. He highlighted his European visit by flying a balloon from Paris to England. In 1907 he took Wilbur Wright (qv) for a balloon flight.

Hawley's greatest balloon voyage was in 1910 when he won the Gordon Bennett Balloon Trophy by flying 1,171.13 miles (1,884km) from St. Louis to Chilogoma in the northern reaches of Quebec. He and his assistant, A. Post (qv) crashed in the wilderness and were forced to hike out. In the attempt, Hawley injured a knee which slowed their progress. It was October with winter closing in. By a stroke of luck they stumbled into an isolated trapper's camp and were rescued.

The rumblings of a coming war in Europe alerted Hawley to the need for an American air response. He led the organization of an aerial national guard, and then started the unit which became the 'Escadrille Lafayette', the American volunteers who flew for France.

HEATH, EDWARD BAYARD
1888–1931
Heath was born in Brooklyn, New York. He attended no less than thirty-three schools as a child. After his father died, his mother remarried and the family moved to Chicago. Little is known about his early life except that he may have raced motorcycles and may have worked for a time at the Curtiss' (qv) factory in Hammondsport. By 1910 he was back in New York experimenting with a Blériot-type monoplane. It fell apart repeatedly on taxi rolls which proves that Heath had little notion of sound engineering techniques.

He returned to Chicago and at least as early as 1912 had established himself in the aeroplane parts business. From his catalogues, aviators could order anything from fabric to unassembled flying-boats. During the war, he evidently continued to experiment with aircraft design and by 1918 was marketing a simple biplane called the Feather.

The myth that aeroplanes were available after the war for a song is just that – a myth. Lindbergh's (qv) surplus Jenny cost $500. That money at the time was nearly the average yearly salary in America. Heath wanted to introduce something really inexpensive. In 1925 he mated a wing from a Thomas-Morse scout to a very light fuselage he had designed and thus was born the Heath Parasol. This super-simple aeroplane only required about twenty-five horsepower to fly and that, more than anything else, made it affordable to a dedicated enthusiast of modest means.

Heath sold the Parasol as a factory-built aeroplane but in 1927 began to offer it as a kit. It is not known how many of these were sold, but evidently hundreds. Heath designed another light plane called the Bullet, really a smaller mid-wing Parasol, which he used to win the 300 cubic inch (4.92 litres) class race at the 1928 National Air Races in Los Angeles. Several original Parasols still fly.

In 1931, while developing a low-wing single seater, Heath miscalculated. He failed to add a jury strut to a wing strut, which resulted in a compression failure while in flight. Heath died in the crash. His company later expanded to sell build-at-home radios under the name *Heathkit*.

HEINEMANN, EDWARD HENRY
1908–1991

Born in Michigan to emigrant parents, Heinemann received only a vocational education. In 1926 the Douglas World Cruiser's flight around the world inspired him to become an aeronautical draughtsman and he found a position with Douglas. In 1930 he left to work for Northrop but six years later Douglas bought a large share of Northrop stock and Heinemann returned to his previous employer.

One of his first tasks after rejoining Douglas was to improve a Northrop-designed bomber. His work led to the Dauntless. He went on to design the A-20 and the B-26. Later still he designed the Skyrocket which became the first aircraft to achieve Mach 2.

HEINKEL, ERNST
1888–1958

Heinkel said that his life really began in 1908 when he first saw a Zeppelin. Then an engineering student, he decided to be an aircraft designer. In 1911 he built a box-kite type plane which he flew in July. He made several flights but within two weeks was seriously injured when it crashed. Recovered, he joined LVG as a designer, followed by Albatros, until he joined Hansa-Brandenburg. The wealthy Austrian financier Camillo Castiglioni asked Heinkel to work for him at this time. When Heinkel refused, Castiglioni purchased Hansa-Brandenburg just to get Heinkel's contract!

For this company he designed a series of successful seaplanes that helped Germany to secure their coastal air space during World War I. In 1922 he started his own company under his name. The early products were innovative military planes such as the He-25 which was the first aeroplane to take-off from a launching rail. Heinkel's designs were noted for their clean lines which made them fast.

His company survived the turmoil of World War II and was still in business in the 1980s.

HENSON, WILLIAM SAMUEL
1812–1888

During the first half of the nineteenth century, Britain alone advanced the cause of heavier-than-air flight. One of Cayley's (qv) disciples was Henson. Henson was born in Nottingham and trained to be an engineer. He became a successful inventor, experimenting with everything from electricity to air conditioning. While working at Chard, Somerset in the lace trade, he began to discuss Cayley's treatise on flying with a friend, John Stringfellow (qv). Henson had been experimenting with model gliders and believed a full-sized aircraft was possible. He designed an amazingly advanced model monoplane and light steam engine which Stringfellow built. In 1842 Henson patented his design and the next year he, Stringfellow and two others formed the world's first airline, The Aerial Transit Company. They hoped to sell shares and build a full-scale version of Henson's aircraft. One overly zealous partner claimed that the plane, named the *Aerial Steam Carriage*, would be able to fly to China from London in twenty-four hours. Instantly all the European newspapers and journals carried satirical engravings of the proposed plane flying over exotic locations such as Egypt or India. One Glasgow paper invented a story which said that the plane had already flown over the River Clyde. Public ridicule rose to a crescendo when the Aerial Transit Company petitioned Parliament for development funds. Henson continued to test his models, but now only under the cover of darkness.

Henson and Stringfellow believed in their project so much that they bought-out their two partners. They continued to experiment on large models powered by light engines, but to no avail. In 1848, Henson married and fled his taunting critics by emigrating to the United States. Forty years later he died in Newark, New Jersey.

His *Aerial Steam Carriage* was a clear cut, simple, yet inspired design which incorporated the first use of propellers solely for forward thrust. It had double cambered wings, tricycle landing gear, a scientifically calculated wing area, and a fuselage-mounted engine. The wing design itself would have earned Henson a place in aviation history. It was to be built of wooden spars and ribs, covered in fabric, and braced to a king post with wires. Without doubt it influenced many designs well into World War I.

HERON, SAM D.
1891–1963
Heron was a leading air-cooled engine designer. During World War I he worked at the Royal Aircraft Factory trying to find a way to lighten air-cooled cylinders. With his associates, he developed to a practical stage the use of steel liners placed in aluminium cylinders. When political pressure forced the RAF to cease its production capacity and concentrate on pure research, Heron transferred to Armstrong-Siddeley and took with him an engine he had been developing. It became the Jaguar under that company's name. In the early 1920s he was persuaded to work for the US Army at McCook Field. Within a few years, he tired of his work for the American government. He found the same lethargy plaguing American military development that he had seen back in Britain, and he was known for snapping out at anyone or anything that delayed his work.

In 1926, he joined the Wright engine company where he put to use all the knowledge he had learned while at McCook to design the J-5 Whirlwind, the engine that safely pulled Lindbergh (qv) to Paris. In fact, Heron personally checked all the parts that went into Lindbergh's engine.

Heron was a mechanical engineer but he knew a great deal about chemistry. He invented the sodium cooled valve, which was an improvement on his earlier salt cooled valve. He pioneered the coating of valve seats with stellite, and helped to perfect the use of high octane leaded fuels.

HERRING, AUGUSTUS MOORE
1867–1927
One of the most shadowy figures in all of aviation history was Augustus Herring. Oddly enough, his career started out with much promise.

Herring was born in Georgia to a well-off family that moved to New York when he was a teenager. He received part of his secondary education in European boarding schools where he learned to speak French and German. Returning to America, he entered the Stevens Institute of Technology in New Jersey where he studied to be an engineer. His interest even then, in the late 1880s, was aeronautics. He built two unsuccessful gliders and left Stevens when they rejected his graduating treatise on flying machines.

Herring received an inheritance when his father died and he used part of this to purchase a Lilienthal (qv) glider from Germany. In 1894 he experimented with this glider, and several copies he had made, near New York city. That year, he was introduced to Chanute (qv) who hired him as a quasi-draughtsman/constructor. Langley (qv) also heard of Chanute's experiments and hired Herring as an assistant. He worked for Langley from May until December 1895 but they disagreed on wing design and Herring resigned.

He went back to Chanute and together they went to the Indiana Dunes, east of Chicago, to experiment on actual flying machines. Herring's suggestions were evidently more pragmatic than Chanute's and he had some success as a glider pilot. His strongheadedness irritated his employer and they parted. Herring found backing from a New York enthusiast who provided the funds for him to build a powered version of his glider. This machine, so close in concept to what could have worked, managed only a few extended glides that even Herring admitted weren't as much as hoped for.

By 1902 Herring had expended his talents and came to an intellectual dead end. Re-acquainted with Chanute, the latter took him to Kitty Hawk to visit the Wrights (qv) who immediately distrusted him. Herring knew that the Wrights were close to a solution of powered flight and at the end of 1903, probably aware of their success via Chanute, offered them a partnership. They refused this gall.

What sad thoughts drifted through Herring's brain at the time cannot be known. He realized that the work he had been conducting for the past fifteen years had been brought to nothingness by the two newcomers, the Wrights. He was beaten and nearly broke. For a few years he continued to seek the solution, but achieved nothing. In 1909 he struck on the idea of persuading Glenn Curtiss (qv) that he held a number of valuable patents that he would use to force all aviation companies in the United States to pay royalties to him on aeroplanes that they built. He proposed that if Curtiss would join forces with him, they could shut down the Wrights and have the aerial market to themselves. Curtiss agreed and the Herring-Curtiss Company was formed.

Curtiss had been deceived. Herring had no patents, no expertise and to Curtiss's large investment in the new company, including signing over the entire factory, he contributed less than $1,000. Later, when Curtiss realized his mistake he managed to break-up the company and force Herring out. Herring sued and after many years of courtroom testimony, won a judgement against Curtiss. He died before he collected the damages however.

HILL, GEOFFREY TERENCE ROWLAND
1895–1956

Hill was involved in a number of unusual engineering projects during his career. After serving for a year in France during World War I, he returned to England where he obtained a job as a test pilot for the Royal Aircraft Factory. Following the war, he joined Handley Page as a test pilot, but also assisted in the development of leading edge slots.

The leading edge slots whetted Hill's appetite to further improve aircraft safety. He decided to experiment with tailless, swept-wing aircraft. In 1926 he flew his first such plane. Its safe handling characteristics prompted Westland to build aircraft to Hill's plans. He designed three

similar aircraft for Westland but the designs never progressed beyond prototypes.

Following World War II, Hill developed the aero-isoclinic wing for Short Bros. This unusual wing used tip controls, like his early tailless planes, but for a different reason. This time they were used to control wing tip distortion which was a problem with early thin-wing high speed aircraft. One aircraft, the Sherpa, was built using this novel type of wing, but the design progressed no further.

HILLER, STANLEY, JR.
1924–

Hiller's father was a wealthy aviation enthusiast who encouraged his son's projects. When young Stanley was only fifteen, he formed a company to produce gas-engine powered model cars. By 1942, his interests had shifted to helicopters. One of his employees in the model company engineered Hiller's ideas and by 1944 the 'Hiller-Copter' was ready to fly. It was a very simple design which used contra-rotating co-axial blades. At only nineteen, Hiller was one of the world's handful of helicopter designers.

Hiller united with the Kaiser Company in order to have proper financing to expand. This union lasted less than two years and in 1945 he incorporated as United Helicopters. This company produced the Commuter co-axial helicopter and introduced many advanced features such as jet torque compensation and Rotor-Matic controls.

In the later 1950s the company reorganized as the Hiller Aircraft Company before being bought by Fairchild in 1964.

HILLMAN, EDWARD HENRY
1889–1934

Hillman's life was a story of rags to riches made more notable because it was accomplished at a time when Britain was increasingly socialist.

From a poor family, Hillman had little education. His first job was binding brushes. He worked his way up to be a band boy in a military regiment. He served as a cavalry sergeant during World War I, after which he became a cycle repairman. Ten years of hard work brought him enough money to purchase a bus. With this, he began a scheduled service between Romford and Chelmsford. A shrewd businessman, Hillman edged out several rivals and by 1930 had a fleet of 200 buses plying the roads between England's east coast and London.

Hillman knew that the public was ready for air transport by the early 1930s so he founded Hillman Airways which linked coastal towns with Romford, just north of London. By 1933 he had started international operations with twice-daily flights to Paris. The next year he captured a valuable Royal Mail contract for postal air delivery between London, Belfast and Glasgow. It was Hillman's need for an economical six passenger plane that prompted de Havilland to design the Dragon.

Hillman died suddenly in 1934. His company amalgamated with several other small carriers which eventually became BOAC.

HINKLER, HERBERT JOHN LOUIS
1892–1933
Hinkler grew up in Queensland, Australia and began building gliders before his twentieth birthday. He went to England where, during the early phases of World War I he served as a mechanic and armaments petty officer. He later received pilot training and flew missions in France and Italy.

After the war, Hinkler became a test pilot for Avro. In 1920 he flew non-stop 650 miles from London to Turin in an Avro Baby powered by the same thirty-five horsepower Green engine that Roe (qv) himself had used in his 1910 triplane! This flight earned Hinkler the Britannia Trophy. A month later he won the 1920 Aerial Derby.

Like his fellow countryman, Hawker (qv), Hinkler was physically short, which perhaps accounts for his preference for and mastery of light planes. He flew his Avro light planes all over the world not only safely, but in elapsed times which beat much larger aeroplanes. His greatest flight was his solo 11,000 mile

(17,700km) journey from England to Australia. It lowered the record from twenty-eight to 15½ days and brought Hinkler an honorary commission in the RAAF.

Hinkler made another great flight in 1931 when he flew from Toronto to South America, across the South Atlantic to West Africa and north to England. In 1933 he tried to lower the England to Australia record but was killed when he crashed in the Alps. His death has subsequently raised questions that his aeroplane had been tampered with.

HORIKOSHI, JIRO
1905(?)–1982
Horikoshi was an aircraft designer for Mitsubishi. He helped pioneer advanced features in his country such as retractable gear, flush riveting, and the use of new high-grade alloys. In early 1938 he began the design of what would become the Zero fighter. The Zero was a successful plane early in the war but soon lost its advantage.

Horikoshi's next design was the J2M Raiden which was never competitive.

HORTEN, REIMAR
1915–1993

HORTEN, WALTER
1913–
The Horten brothers were inspired to build tailless aircraft after witnessing the flight of a Lippisch (qv) aircraft in 1931. They built a glider in their home which became known as the *Horten I*. In 1936 they joined the Luftwaffe but left two years later to devote themselves fulltime to design work. Their gliders were beautifully made of plywood and had characteristically long wings. In all, five aircraft were built.

During the war they designed a futuristic flying wing fighter that was to have been powered by two jet engines. In the post-war years, Reimar emigrated to Argentina and Walter helped to re-establish the Luftwaffe.

HOXSEY, ARCH
1884–1910

A native of Illinois, Hoxsey was working as a mechanic in California when he first saw an aeroplane in early 1910. He rushed east to learn to fly at the Wright school, receiving his training from Orville Wright and Walter Brookins (qqv). He then entered the booming air show circuit as a member of the Wright team along with R. Johnstone (qv). The newspapers fabricated a rivalry between the two that helped to generate news and served to make the flying displays more thrilling. Hoxsey and Johnstone, billed as the 'Heavenly Twins', were in fact friends but they did try to best each other's performances.

During the last half of 1910 they performed their aerial *pas de deux* across the United States with such daring that Hoxsey was once grounded by Wilbur Wright (qv) for reckless flying. Undeterred, in November he flew above the clouds during a snow fall in Denver. A month earlier he had taken Theodore Roosevelt for a flight in St. Louis thus making his portly passenger the first President, though not in office at the time, to fly.

Hoxsey's meteoric career ended in December at the Dominquez Meet in California. In attempting to set an altitude record, either he entered a stall/spin or experienced structural failure because his plane came down spinning quickly, apparently out of control. Hoxsey was smashed into the earth.

HUFFAKER, EDWARD CHALMERS
1856–1936

Huffaker was born near Nashville. He was an outstanding student in college at Emery and Henry College, later receiving an M.Sc. in physics at the University of Virginia. He later taught and became a civil engineer. In 1892 he wrote to Chanute (qv) describing his theory of soaring flight, also telling of model gliders he had constructed. Chanute was impressed enough to refer him to Langley (qv), who hired him in 1894 as an engineer for his aerodrome experiments. His work there improved Langley's crude ideas but he chafed under the yoke of Langley's interference so he resigned in 1898.

Chanute hired him immediately and had him construct full-scale gliders which ultimately achieved nothing. In 1901 he visited the Wright's (qv) camp at Kitty Hawk with his boss but proved such an irritation to the Wrights that they were glad when he left.

Huffaker's role in early aviation history might have been much greater had either Langley or Chanute simply provided him with funds to experiment on his own. He understood more about aerodynamics than did his employers. As it was, he was a figure who knew all the players but not how to win the game.

HUGHES, HOWARD ROBARD
1905–1976

Hundreds of stories have been told about Hughes by people who claim to have known him. Some of these stories are true, but many more are false. Hughes was not the carefree *bon vivant* as many have depicted him. Instead, he was a meticulous, gifted airman who devoted himself to advancing the art of aviation.

He was born in Texas to an extraordinarily wealthy oil drilling tool manufacturer. His parents died when he was nineteen and he inherited their fortune. After completing college where he studied engineering, Hughes began his aviation career by making a movie about flying. Entitled *Hells Angels*, it was a multi-million dollar spectacular that many predicted would flop. They claimed that Hughes had begun to squander his family fortune. As he was to do so frequently in later years, Hughes confounded his critics. The movie turned out to be a masterpiece and brought in a large box office, though it probably never broke even. Hughes continued to produce movies and some of these earned Oscars.

During the 1930s he turned to air racing, using his mighty resources to buy or build the world's fastest aeroplanes. The most dazzling example of his aeronautical talent was the H-1 racer. It was probably the most meticulously built aeroplane in history besides being years ahead of its time technically. With this silver and blue jewel Hughes set a world land-plane speed record of 352.322 mph (566.9km) on 13 September 1935. This exquisite monoplane set the standard for future fighter planes and crowned its glory by setting a trans-continental speed record in 1937. It streaked from Los Angeles to Newark, New Jersey, in only 7:28:28 hours, only about two hours longer than a similar jet flight today! The next year Hughes toppled the round-the-world record when he flew a Lockheed 14 around the globe in just ninety-one hours.

During World War II he launched the design of the beautiful Constellation airliner and began work on the 150-ton HK-1 *Hercules*, popularly known as the *Spruce Goose*. With Hughes at the controls, this leviathan troop transport flew only once, in 1947, satisfying its owner but not critics.

The only combat plane he ever designed nearly cost Hughes his life. In 1946 he crashed in the XF-11 high-speed reconnaissance plane, another sleek hot-rod. Hughes was critically injured. After his physical recovery he was never emotionally the same. He became a recluse and this is when legends first appeared. His final years were full of Congressional investigations dealing with his ties to the CIA, the Mafia, and charges of drug addiction. Hughes seemingly vanished from the face of the earth for twenty years.

In 1976 he died while being transported from Mexico to the US in an air ambulance.

HUNSAKER, JEROME CLARKE

1886–1984

Hunsaker was a brilliant man who did more than anyone to put American aviation on a scientific footing in the early part of this century.

He was born in Iowa and attended Annapolis, graduating at the head of his class in 1908. In 1909 he was sent by the Navy to study at MIT. From there, he travelled to France to work with the well-known engineer Eiffel on wind tunnel projects. In 1914 he returned to MIT and set up a wind tunnel. By the end of the year he had established the first university course in

aeronautics in the country at MIT. This was to have a profoundly beneficial effect on American aviation.

In 1916 he was assigned to lead the Navy Bureau of Construction and Repair. In this role, he helped design the NC-4, the first trans-Atlantic aeroplane, and later the *Shenandoah* dirigible. The latter was the first of its type to fly on helium instead of hydrogen.

After the war he worked on the design of launching catapults, carrier aircraft, and engines. In 1926 he turned his fertile mind to aircraft communications when he resigned from the Navy and joined Bell Laboratories. Still later he joined the NACA and became its chairman in 1941.

ILYUSHIN, SERGEI VLADIMIROVICH

1894–1977

Born to peasants at Didyalevo, Vologda, Ilyushin served as a mechanic in the Imperial Russian Air Service. His skill brought him into contact with Sikorsky and he was soon the chief mechanic for all the Ilya Mourometz bombers. When the Revolution began in 1917, he sided with the Bolsheviks and was rewarded with a scholarship to the Zhukovsky Air Academy, from which he graduated in 1924.

In 1929 he built Russia's first high performance glider and was rewarded with his own design bureau. His success was immediate starting with a huge long-range transport plane that on one flight flew from Moscow to New Brunswick, Canada. In World War II he introduced the classic Il-2 Shturmovik ground attack plane that did so much to secure the Soviet victory over German armoured units.

After the war, Ilyushin concentrated on large transports and bombers. During his long career he participated in the design of over fifty aircraft.

IMMELMANN, OBERLEUTNANT MAX FRANZ

1890–1916

Born in Dresden, Immelmann was a moody, vegetarian tee-totaller. He joined the Air Force in 1914 and by early 1915 was flying at the front in the same unit as Oswald Boelcke (qv). Immelmann and Boelcke received two early Fokkers fitted with machine-guns and on 1 August Immelmann attacked a French bomber which he downed. This was the first confirmed German scout victory of the war.

Together, Boelcke and Immelmann evolved some of the world's first fighter tactics. These included unit flying, lead man/wing man teams, and of course the Immelmann turn. When Boelcke transferred to another Front, Immelmann became the most important flying figure in northern France. Based at Douai, his continual success against the enemy caused him to be known as the 'Eagle of Lille'. The British reaction to the success of Fokker Eindeckers, particularly in Immelmann's sector, was to dub their own planes 'Fokker Fodder'. Immelmann became world famous and in 1916 won the 'Blue Max'. He had just finished destroying his sixteenth victim on 18 June 1916 when his own plane disintegrated in the air. An RFC pilot was credited with Immelmann's death but it is possible the German shot off his own propeller accidentally when his synchronizer mal-functioned.

JABARA, CAPTAIN JAMES
1923–1966
Born in Kansas, Jabara was a USAAF veteran of World War II with 3·5 victories to his credit. His previous combat experience paid off when he was sent to Korea to fly Sabres with the 4th Interception Wing. He destroyed fifteen enemy aircraft during his tours of duty. His fifth MiG was shot down on 20 May 1951, making him the first American all-jet ace.

JACOBS, EASTMAN N.
1902–*
Jacobs was from Colorado and studied at the University of California at Berkeley. After a short stint with the Pacific Telephone and Telegraph Company, he joined NACA at Langley Field in 1925 where he worked under Dr George Lewis.

He played a lead role in wind tunnel research which led to high performance aerofoils. He made a major breakthrough when he discovered how to gradually lower the pressure across the chord. This technique allowed the development of laminar flow aerofoils.

JEFFRIES, DR JOHN
1744–1819
A native Bostonian, Jeffries mixed conservative loyalist politics with bold, progressive medical practices. He graduated from Harvard in 1763 and went to Britain where he studied medicine in London and Aberdeen. Returning to Boston in 1769, he established a lucrative medical practice but when the revolution broke out, he chose to follow the British troops, rising eventually to become their Surgeon-General. As the British cause took a turn for the worse in 1779, he returned to London where he became involved in the scientific community. In 1785 he sponsored a flight across the English Channel which he successfully undertook with Blanchard (qv). The perilous flight cost Jeffries a total of £800–£700 for equipment and £100 for the honour of accompanying Blanchard. Jeffries carried with him a letter from Benjamin Franklin's son in London to his famous father then in Paris. It was the first piece of air mail in history.

In 1789 Jeffries returned to Boston where he attempted to present the first lectures in New England on human anatomy. An angry mob stormed the classroom during the second lecture forcing Jeffries to halt his dissection – the mob thought the practice was barbaric. Jeffries lived comfortably in Boston for the next thirty years until his death.

JOHNSON, AMY
1903–1941
So the story goes – when Amy Johnson saw the first Academy Award-winning movie *Wings* in 1927, she decided to emulate, not the hero's

girlfriend, but rather the hero himself, a brave pilot. Employed at the time as a London stenographer, Johnson saved her money shilling by shilling until she could join the London Aeroplane Club. In the club she learned how to fly, navigate, and repair aeroplanes. When the expense of advanced instruction became too great, she left her office job and became England's first licenced female ground mechanic. This allowed her to barter for cheaper lessons.

Shortly after earning her pilot's licence she began to search for a way to make her name known. She decided on a rather ambitious scheme – a solo flight from England to Australia. In 1930 few people had undertaken such a dangerous flight, let alone a woman who had only a few flying hours of navigational training.

With almost no press coverage, Johnson's take- off from Croydon on 5 May 1930 attracted little attention. The few people who had heard of the attempt thought she wouldn't get past southern Europe. Day by day she flew on until after ten days she had reached India. Suddenly the press took notice, led as usual by the *Daily Mail*. Nine days later Johnson reached Port Darwin and met a heroine's welcome. She had been the first woman to link the countries by air. Her reputation grew as she went on to set more flying records. Her flights took her from London to Moscow, Cape Town and even Tokyo.

In 1932 she married another record-breaking flyer, Captain J. A. Mollison (qv), and together they began to undertake record-making flights. In 1933 they attempted a Wales to New York flight. Low on fuel, they were forced to land near Bridgeport, Connecticut. Captain Mollison had piloted the whole trip and had grown very tired. Mrs Mollison offered to take the controls but was rebuffed. Evidently a family spat erupted to the point that no one was in command and the plane crashed injuring the married couple. They were divorced in 1937.

Johnson continued in aviation during World War II, taking an active part in the Air Transport Auxiliary Service. In January, 1941 her Airspeed Oxford was over the Thames estuary when she probably ran low on fuel. She baled out but upon splashing down her flying gear became water-logged and she went under and was not seen again. A crewman from a naval vessel who tried to rescue her died from hypothermia.

JOHNSON, CLARENCE LEONARD ('KELLY')

1910–1990

Johnson ranks as one of America's most diverse and brilliant aircraft designers. In forty separate aircraft, he demonstrated a unique ability to bring together all the right factors that go into building a successful aircraft – and he could do it in a hurry.

He received a degree in aeronautical engineering from the University of Michigan in 1932. At only twenty-two-years-old he became the aeronautical consultant to Studebaker. In 1933 while studying for an M.Sc., he was working in the University's wind tunnel which was being used by the Lockheed Company to investigate stability problems on a new design. Johnson recommended adding a twin tail and thus the Lockheed 10 design was saved. His recommendation earned him a job at Lockheed and he moved to California. By 1938 he had risen to chief research engineer.

Johnson had the rare talent to choose the right man for every design job. His leadership ability first manifested itself with the P-38 Lightning. He then went on to design the P-80 jet fighter and the Constellation airliner at the same time! The fighter was designed in only five months.

1956 was another landmark year for him. That year he unveiled the F-104 Starfighter and the U-2 spyplane. The U-2 was a top secret project from the 'Skunk Works', a separate Lockheed facility. In 1960 the U-2 spawned a mighty successor, the YF-12A, or SR-71. The treacherous-looking delta-wing spyplane was capable of Mach 3. It was made from titanium because Johnson felt he 'wasn't smart enough' to build it from the then exotic new fibre honeycomb materials.

After forty years and forty designs, the man 'who wasn't smart enough' retired in 1975.

JOHNSON, WING COMMANDER JAMES EDGAR ('JOHNNIE')

1915–

Johnson was posted to No. 616 squadron when he completed his training. His first kill was in the summer of 1941. From then until the end of the war he steadily raised his totally flying at every available opportunity. By the war's end he was a wing commander and Britain's top scoring ace with thirty-eight victories. He remained with the RAF until 1965 retiring as an Air Vice-Marshal.

JOHNSON, ROBERT S.

1920–

Johnson joined the USAAF in 1941 and was sent to England in early 1943. His unit, the 56th Fighter Group, flew Thunderbolts and he was given six months of additional training before facing what were considered to be the more manoeuvrable German fighters. Johnson shot down his first enemy in June. During the course of the next year he gained a total of twenty-eight victories, all while flying the 'Jug'. Johnson contributed to fighter tactics by convincing his superiors that close bomber escorts were impractical. He favoured allowing pilots to break formation when they spotted enemy aircraft and to give chase. This concept worked with the result that bombers were better protected. After the war Johnson pursued interests in the aviation industry.

JOHNSTONE, RALPH

1886–1910

Johnstone was from Kansas City, Missouri and as a child learned to perform bicycle tricks. He ran away from home as a teenager to become a vaudeville trick cyclist and was so successful that after a few years he toured Europe. There he married a German girl and returned home.

He knew Knabenshue (qv) and was directed by him to Orville Wright (qv) who in early 1910 was setting up a flying school near Dayton. Orville taught Johnstone to fly and signed him on as an exhibition pilot. Johnstone was more cautious than many of the early exhibition pilots and was satisfied to fight for altitude records. With Hoxsey (qv), he was one of the 'Heavenly Twins' who hopped across the country initiating the opened-mouthed populace into the wonders of flight. He competed in the Boston meet in September, 1910 and later set an altitude record of 9,741 feet (2,969m) at the Belmont Park Meet.

He met his death in November when his Wright biplane broke up at 800 feet (244m) during an air show in Denver. He fought to regain control but was pitched out of his seat. By desperately swinging out an arm, he managed to grab hold of a strut but was mangled when the aeroplane struck the ground. The stunned audience recovered sufficiently to snatch bloody souvenirs including his flying gloves.

JOUKOVSKY, NIKOLAI YEGEROVITCH

1847–1921

Joukovsky (also Zhukovsky) was born in a small village in central Russia. His father's engineering trade provided the funds for him to go to Moscow where he studied mathematics and physics. An adept scholar, he began to teach physics after his graduation.

Around the turn of the century, Joukovsky became interested in aeronautics. To study aerodynamics he built a wind tunnel in 1902 – Russia's first. With this tunnel Joukovsky made several significant discoveries about lift and aerofoil sections. These discoveries reflected Kutta's (qv) earlier work but were developed independently. After the Bolshevik revolution he founded the Central Institute for Aerodynamics (TsAGI). From this institute have graduated many of Russia's leading aircraft designers.

JULLIEN, PIERRE

1814–1877

Through hard work Jullien worked his way up from a factory worker to become a successful clock repairer in a town near Paris. In 1850 he built a model dirigible that used watch springs for power. This flew well when launched at the Hippodrome. In 1858 he demonstrated to the French Society of Encouragement for Aviation a model airplane with a wing span of one metre. Powered by rubber bands, it flew twelve metres. Encouraged by this success, he tried to raise capital to build a full-size machine to be powered by an electric motor. His efforts to secure funds were fruitless and he died penniless.

JULLIOT, HENRI
1856–1923

Julliot was born in Fontainebleau and studied engineering in Paris. In 1901 he received a rather unusual assignment from his employers, the Lebaudy brothers (qv), wealthy sugar refiners, who instructed him to design an airship. They had recognized the commercial possibilities of dirigible flight.

Julliot designed and had built in the shops of the Lebaudy plant a nacelle fitted with a forty horsepower Daimler Benz engine. This was attached to a 187-foot (57m) long envelope built at the Surcouf balloon works.

Named the *Lebaudy I,* but nick-named 'Jaune' after its yellow anti-actinic paint, this was the first successful semi-rigid dirigible. Its speed was about twenty-five miles per hour (40km/hr) and it made numerous cross-country flights. So impressed were the French military that they purchased it in 1905.

Julliot continued to design airships and during the opening months of World War I worked for the French government as an advisor for aeronautics. In 1915 he emigrated to the United States where he worked in private industry as an airship designer.

JUNKERS, HUGO
1859–1935

Born in Rheydt, Prussia, Junkers studied thermodynamics at Berlin, Karlsruhe and Aachen. In 1889 he established his first factory to produce experimental engines, and later thermal heating devices. In 1897 he began to teach thermodynamics at Aachen – where Prandtl (qv) later performed most of his experiments. Junkers' knowledge of thermodynamics provided a solid foundation for his study of aeronautics. In 1910 he patented a design for an all-metal, fully cantilevered flying wing – an idea which wasn't to be realized until the 1940s. In 1915 he shook the aeronautical community with the J.1 – the world's first all-metal plane, made primarily of corrugated sheet steel, not aluminium, because at the time the latter metal was difficult to join. The J.1 was ten years ahead of its time.

In 1919 Junkers introduced the F.13, the world's first all-metal commercial plane. Some of these advanced planes flew for over twenty years. In 1921 he started a commercially successful airline which became one of the founding divisions of Lufthansa, in 1925. In 1927 he began to produce diesel engines for aircraft, becoming the only manufacturer to do this on a large scale successfully. He strongly believed in the future of commercial aviation and in 1929 built the mammoth G.38, a thirty passenger aircraft at a time when most struggled to carry a dozen.

Hugo Junkers who was 20 years ahead of his rivals.

Junkers retired in 1932 to pursue scientific research but lost control of his company in 1934, when it was the largest aviation company in the world, because he refused to co-operate with Hitler.

KAMAN, CHARLES H.
1919–*
Kaman was born in Washington, DC and attended the Catholic University there where he earned a degree in aeronautical engineering. His first job was with United Technologies in Connecticut as an aerodynamicist working with helicopter blades. He thought that this company was wrong to develop Sikorsky's (qv) single rotor helicopter because he had calculated that contra-rotating, intermeshing blades operated by servo tabs provided a more stable hover. He proceeded to develop his idea using a derelict automobile chassis and engine as a test stand. Convinced that he had a better machine and realizing that his employers wouldn't back him, he left in 1945 to start his own company.

In 1947 he completed his first machine, the K-125. It flew and confirmed Kaman's theories about stability. Military orders followed which made his company a success. In 1951 the K-225 was the world's first turbine-powered helicopter.

von KARMAN, THEODORE
1881–1963
Von Karman had one of the greatest scientific minds of the twentieth century. Born in Hungary, he studied engineering in Budapest and Göttingen. He was assigned to the Austro-Hungarian Air Force in World War I for which he designed primitive observation helicopters. These machines were of no military value but foretold the future.

After the war he returned to Gottingen to teach aerodynamics. He discovered several new aerodynamic laws including the von Karman Vortex Street. During the 1920s he travelled to Japan as an aeronautical consultant, advised Junkers and Zeppelin, and lectured in the United States at the invitation of the Guggenheim Foundation.

During the 1930s he made the United States his home and was involved in numerous consultative ventures including balancing the Palomar telescope, fixing turbulence problems on the DC-3, airship design and much more. So important was his wind tunnel advice on developing aircraft that he became known as the 'Airplane Doctor'.

In the 1940s he joined colleagues from Cal Tech, where he had become a professor, and founded Aerojet Engineering Corporation, an important producer of early rockets. He was the head of General Arnold's (qv) Scientific Advisory Group and assessed the value of captured German aircraft.

A brilliant abstract theoretician whose patience and kind wit endeared him to his friends and students, von Karman left a legacy of aeronautical insight that few can match.

KARTVELI, ALEXANDER
1896–1974
Kartveli was born in Russia and studied engineering at L'École Supérieure d'Aéronautique in Paris. After the Revolution he fled to the West, spending time with Blériot and Fokker before joining Seversky (qv) in the United States in 1934. He was in charge of designing the Seversky P-35 and the later P-43. Neither of these planes were a great success but led to the Kartveli-designed P-47, built as a Republic plane after Seversky reorganized in 1939.

Kartveli went on to design a series of jet fighters after the war, starting with the Thunderjet.

KAZAKOV, ALEXANDER ALEXANDROVICH
1891–1919
Kazakov was a Russian cavalry officer before transferring to the Air Force in late 1914. He attempted to make his first aerial victory with a rather unusual weapon. He mounted a long steel cable onto his aircraft at the end of which

he attached a grappling iron. On 18 March 1915 he set out to 'snag' a German Albatros, but failed to hook the plane. Still eager to bring down his adversary he flew above the Albatros and dropped down on its top wing so hard that he smashed it. He lost his undercarriage but gained a victory.

Kazakov was a religious man who not only flew wearing a St. Nicholas icon, but tried to attend the funeral of every enemy airman he brought down. By the war's end he had been credited with seventeen victories. He continued to fight as a pilot for the White Russians, probably bringing down three Bolshevik machines. He was killed on 3 August, 1919 when his plane crashed on take-off. Some considered the crash to be a suicide, stating that Kazakov had become depressed over the continuing success of the Bolsheviks.

KERWOOD, CHARLES W.

1897–1976

Kerwood was a veteran of four wars. In World War I he flew for the Escadrille Lafayette and was twice wounded in combat. He was captured after being shot down and wounded yet again when he tried to escape.

In 1922 he commanded the Greek Air Force during the Greek-Turkish War. He left this command and went to Paris where he picked up the job of organizing American volunteers for a French-Spanish expedition against Berber tribesmen in Morocco.

During World War II he rejoined the American military.

KESSELRING, GENERAL ALBERT

1885–1960

Kesselring was born in Bavaria and served as an artillery officer under Prince Rupprecht during World War I. In 1933 he transferred from the Army to the Luftwaffe and commanded the air fleets during the invasions of Poland and France. In 1941 he went to Africa where he and Rommel directed the Axis forces for two years. In 1943 he became the overall commander in

Italy, including ground forces, and fought a brilliant campaign up the spine of that country delaying the Allied advance for over a year.

After the war he was tried and convicted of war atrocities against Italian hostages. An original death sentence was reduced to five years' imprisonment and he was released in 1952.

KINDELBERGER, JAMES HOWARD

1895–1962

'Dutch' Kindelberger was born into a steel worker's family in West Virginia. He left school at seventeen and worked for a foundry but took a correspondence course to become an Army Corps of Engineers' draughtsman. During World War I he was a pilot. After the war, he joined Glenn Martin (qv) for whom he was a draughtsman and designer. In 1924 he moved to Douglas as the chief engineer and designed the DC-1 and DC-2.

In 1934 he accepted a position as President of the General Aviation Manufacturing Corporation which later became North American. With this company he designed some of the greatest aircraft ever. His designs included the BT-9 and T-6 trainers, the B-25 medium bomber and the classic P-51 Mustang. The Mustang was designed and built in only 127 days!

After the war, Kindelberger had the foresight to diversify the company's product line to include missiles, atomic devices and rocket engines. He continued to design aeroplanes though, and the B-45 Tornado bomber, FJ-1 naval fighter and F-86 Sabre numbered among these. Two of the last of Kindelberger's aircraft were the XB-70 Mach 3 bomber and the X-15 rocket plane.

KINGSFORD-SMITH, SIR CHARLES (EDWARD)

1897–1935

A native of Brisbane, Kingsford-Smith served as a motorcycle dispatch rider at Gallipoli and in Egypt before joining the RFC in 1917. There he worked his way up from mechanic to pilot, winning the Military Cross for bravery.

After the war he went to Hollywood where he flew as a stunt pilot. While there, he began to contemplate a trans-Pacific flight though lack of funds prevented him from ever developing the plan. During the mid-1920s he was back in Australia setting several national records. He met Charles Ulm at this time, another spirited aviator with whom he joined forces to raise funds for a trans-Pacific flight. They found a wealthy American backer who helped them to buy Sir Hubert Wilkin's Fokker F.VII. With this plane they made their planned flight in 1928.

Riding a crest of national popularity, Kingsford-Smith and Ulm set up Australian National Airways. They continued to make record-breaking flights, hoping to show the public the safety and convenience of air travel. However, whatever their beliefs, aviation was still a hazardous business in the 1930s. Ulm lost his life in a flying accident in 1934 and Kingsford-Smith died the next year when his aircraft disappeared in the Gulf of Martaban, off Burma.

KLEMIN, ALEXANDER
1888–1950

Klemin was born in London where he earned a degree in science at London University. He travelled to the United States in 1914 to study at MIT and took up taking charge of its aeronautics program in 1916. Klemin went to McCook Field shortly after America entered the war, where he directed research and pioneered the use of plywood monocoque structures in the US.

For a brief period following the war Klemin operated his own aircraft company, but this failed. He then went to New York University and established an aeronautics programme there. This position allowed him time to write, he was the aviation correspondent for *Scientific American* magazine, and also devoted time to rotary-wing research. This research helped NYU students to establish America as the leader in helicopters following World War II.

KNABENSHUE, A. ROY
1876–1960

Knabenshue was from Bryan, Ohio and became interested in aeronautics around 1900. He built gliders that he tried to fly but had scant success with them. He switched to dirigibles and succeeded in getting airborne. In 1904 he flew his dirigibles at the St. Louis World's Fair where he met the Wrights (qv) and Capt. Baldwin (qv). Baldwin immediately hired him to fly his *California Arrow* dirigible. Knabenshue flew this advanced machine for a few months until resigning to continue on his own in the lucrative exhibition circuit.

During this time, he had a subscription to a news-clipping service which sent him articles on aeronautics. From these, he learned that the Wright's had succeeded in making practical aircraft. He proposed to the brothers that they hire him to book exhibitions around the country to display their aircraft. They accepted the offer and this aspect of their business became highly profitable.

In 1913 Knabenshue built the first passenger dirigible in America calling it *White City*.

KNIGHT, JAMES H.
1893–1945

'Jack' Knight was born in Lincoln, Kansas and became an Army pilot in World War I. In 1918 he became a government mail pilot and in that role made one of the most dramatic airmail flights in history. In the early morning hours of 22 February 1921 an attempt was made by the Post Office to fly mail across country continuously day and night as a way to drum-up enthusiasm, and public funds, in order to continue airmail operations. It was the dead of winter and this last ditch effort seemed doomed to failure. Knight flew the North Platte to Omaha, Nebraska leg but found in Omaha that the pilot for the next leg wasn't available. He had never before flown the Omaha-Chicago leg but took the dangerous job anyway. The future of airmail was at stake and he knew it. Through snow and thick fog he drove his DH-4 on to Des Moines. Fog engulfed the city so, by using his emergency reserve tank, he flew on to Iowa City. By luck, the sleepy watchman at the hidden airfield heard his engine and lit a flare. Knight landed, refuelled and pushed on to Chicago. He made it and received a deserved hero's welcome.

His airmail adventures continued for seven more years until he hung up his goggles and went to work in the public relations department of United Airlines.

KOLLSMAN, PAUL
1900(?)–1982

Kollsman was a German emigrant to the United States who, with his brother Otto, established in 1928 the Kollsman Instrument Company in New York. He believed that existing instruments were too crudely made so he designed an altimeter that used Swiss watch gears to drive the indicator hands. In 1929 Doolittle (qv) tested the device hoping to use it for his blind flight work. It proved a full twenty times more accurate than anything then in existence.

The Kollsman company went on to produce many other precision flying instruments that made bad weather and night flying possible.

KOOLHOVEN, FREDERICK
1886(?)–1946

Koolhoven learned to fly in 1910 on Farmans. He then went to work for the Deperdussin (qv) company as an assistant to Béchereau (qv). He was sent to England to advise the British Deperdussin concern, but when they folded he went to Armstrong-Whitworth. With this company, he rose from works manager to aircraft designer. His first design was the prosaic FK.1 which won no military orders. Later designs for the company were successful and Koolhoven became known as an innovative designer. In 1917 he became the chief designer at BAT where his work led to a superlative fighter, the BAT Bantam. The war's end precluded any orders for this plane and soon Koolhoven returned to his native Holland.

In Holland he designed aircraft for the Nationale

Vliegtuigindustrie which later reorganized under Koolhoven's leadership. This company produced his designs until World War II.

KOROLYOV, SERGEI PABLOVICH
1907–1966

Korolyov was the outstanding figure in Soviet rocketry for over thirty years.

Born in the Ukraine, he studied at Kiev and Moscow. After earning an aeronautical degree in 1929 at the Moscow Technical School he entered the aviation industry, participating in the design of several light aircraft. In the early 1930s he investigated two advanced forms of propulsion, rockets and jet engines. In 1933 he organized the Moscow Group for the Study of Reactive Motion which pioneered Soviet guided missiles and rockets.

During the Stalin purges Korolyov was arrested on trumped-up charges. One of his accusers claimed his rockets might be used in an attempt to assassinate Stalin! Eventually he was released after spending some time in a work camp. Following the war he examined and launched German V-2s gaining valuable experience. With this knowledge, he began to design his country's first launch vehicles. His greatest accomplishments were the designs of the Voskhod and Vostok rocket boosters. These boosters lifted most of the Soyuz spacecraft into orbit.

KOZHEDUB, MAJOR IVAN NIKITAEVICH
1920–*

Kozhedub was such an excellent pilot that the Russian Air Force originally decided to use him as a flight instructor. Constant pleading on his part finally won him a combat posting and he transferred into the 16th Air Army. He arrived there just in time for the monumental tank battle at Kursk in 1943. By autumn of that year he had proven his combat abilities and was chosen to act as a 'fireman', which meant that he was sent wherever the action was hottest.

By the war's end, he had flown 520 combat

missions, shot down sixty-two enemy aircraft, and won the Gold Star among other awards. During the Korean War he commanded Soviet pilots fighting secretly for the North.

KREBS, ARTHUR-CONSTANTIN
1850–1918

Krebs was a captain in the Engineers Corps when Charles Renard (qv) asked him to build a light electric motor to power the dirigible *La France* . Krebs designed and built a 211-pound (96kg), eight horsepower motor. Its reliability and relative lightness made possible the first completely navigable flight of an aircraft on 9 August 1884. That day *La France*, crewed by Renard and Krebs, took-off from Chalais-Meudon, travelled 2·5 miles (4km), to Villacoublay, and returned to its point of origin.

KUTTA, MARTIN WILHELM
1867–1944

Kutta was a German mathematician who conducted his initial aerodynamic research at the University of Munich. There he mathematically studied the forces acting on an aerofoil, discovering the theoretical formulae which allowed improved aerofoils to be created. He published his theories of aerodynamic lift in 1902 and they played a large part in influencing wing design during and after World War I.

LAHM, LIEUTENANT FRANK PURDY
1877–1963

Lahm was born in Ohio and attended West Point. His father was a balloon enthusiast who sponsored his son's entry in the 1906 Gordon Bennett balloon race. Lahm won this with a 402 mile (647km) flight from Paris to Yorkshire, England. He stayed in France to attend the cavalry school at Samur. He was also required to survey the aeronautical scene in Europe. On 9 September 1908 he went for a flight with Orville Wright (qv) who was demonstrating an aeroplane at Fort Myer, Virginia. This flight earned Lahm the distinction as the first

American Army officer to fly in an aeroplane. In October of the next year he became one of the first two officers taught to fly by Wilbur Wright.

Lahm spent most of his career establishing air training stations across the United States and even in the Phillipines. During World War I he organized the lighter-than-air service of the AEF, later assuming broader command of Air Service units.

LAIRD, EMIL MATTHEW
1896(?)–1982

Laird was in his teens and working in an upper floor of a Chicago hotel when he saw Walter Brookins (qv) fly past the window. The young bellhop was stunned. He decided he had to get involved in aviation, but because of his humble family circumstances this seemed impossible. Plunging ahead, he started to build models and joined a local aeroplane model club. From working on models and attending the Gordon Bennett race in Chicago in 1912, he learned enough about aircraft design to initiate his own project. It took until 1913 to finish his monoplane, with help coming from an acquaintance who sold him an engine on credit. This plane crashed on its first flight but Laird had seen the promised land!

By 1916 Laird had built two more planes and become a highly paid exhibition pilot who often flew at night with lights attached to his wings.

Because of a crash while flying another pilot's aircraft, Laird spent most of World War I in a hospital. When he recovered he started his own aircraft company in Chicago, but gave it up when he received an offer for proper financial backing if he moved to Kansas. He jumped at the chance.

The Laird Airplane Company built three-place OX-5 powered biplanes. These were good aeroplanes but there wasn't much interest in aircraft in the post-war economy. Laird and his principal backer disagreed about policy with the result that Laird returned to Chicago in 1923 to start his own company. In the 1930s he gained his greatest fame by designing the Laird Solution and Super Solution, racing planes that achieved victories in the Thompson and Bendix Trophy races.

de LAMBERT, COMTE CHARLES
1865–1944

De Lambert was of French ancestry but was actually a Russian aristocrat. During the latter part of the nineteenth century he became interested in internal combustion-driven vehicles such as speedboats and experimental flying machines. His wealth allowed him to indulge his hobbies which he did in a serious manner. In the 1890s he experimented with early hydroplane speed-boats in England, continuing to build new types when he moved to Paris.

When Wilbur Wright (qv) went back to France in 1909 to establish a flying school, he taught several Europeans to fly, including de Lambert, his first pupil. De Lambert bought two Wright aircraft which he used in an attempt to cross the English Channel during the summer of 1909. This effort ended when he crashed one of the planes. In August he competed at Rheims where he came in fourth in the Grand Prix distance event.

On 9 October 1909 he made his most notable flight when, in a borrowed Wright, he made a flight that most aviators dream about. That day he took off from the Port-Aviation in Paris, flew around the Eiffel Tower, and returned to his starting point.

LAMBERT, WILLIAM CARPENTER
1896(?)–1982

The second highest-scoring American ace of World War I was not Frank Luke (qv) as is so often reported. William Lambert held that distinction, though few knew it because of an historical anomaly.

Lambert was born in Ohio and during the war was seconded to the RFC. In No. 24 Squadron flying SE-5s, Lambert earned twenty-two victories including one each over a Siemens-Schukkert D III and a balloon. Because he was American, he is not normally recorded on lists of British aces, and because he gained all his victories while with the RFC, he is not normally recorded on lists of American aces. For a man who heroically risked his life time and again, this is thankless treatment.

Francesco de Lana-Terzi who correctly theorized aerostatic science, and believed God would never allow flying machines to be used for war.

de LANA-TERZI, FRANCESCO
1631–1687

A Jesuit priest from Brescia, de Lana turned his attentions more towards science than religion – which might have proved to be fatal considering the Church's attitude towards scientists at the time. They had nearly burned Galileo.

In 1670 de Lana published *Prodromo Overo Saggio de Alcune* in which he described a plan for making a lighter-than-air craft. The remarkable priest suggested constructing four twenty-five foot (7.62m) diameter copper spheres, connecting them by rope to an open boat, and then evacuating the air from them. De Lana realized that air has weight, and he correctly reasoned that if an object could be made to weigh less than the volume of air it occupies, it would rise. This was a sublimely simple, yet prophetic, piece of deductive reasoning. The one flaw in his plan was that spheres constructed as he advised would have caved inwards upon evacuation. A lightweight gas was needed to keep the pressure up inside the thin globes, but de Lana didn't have this.

Nevertheless, he predicted that when objects were created that actually did fly, they would certainly change the face of warfare. This grim possibility led him to wonder, though, if God would ever allow such weapons to exist. He thought not.

LANCHESTER, FREDERICK WILLIAM
1868–1946
Born in Lewisham, Lanchester became one of England's greatest engineers. After working as an industrial engineer specializing in internal combustion engines he decided to start manufacturing his own automobiles. In 1895 he built Britain's first all-British automobile (see note) which bristled with innovations. Four years later he and his brother, George, founded the Lanchester Engine Company. The cars they produced were of high quality although of somewhat unusual configuration. Long, low and quiet, they were twenty years ahead of their time. So advanced were they that King George V preferred them to Rolls-Royce.

Amazing as it may seem in retrospect, Lanchester's interest in aviation was only a hobby. Around 1890 he began experimenting with model airplanes. By 1894 he had discovered several principles of aerodynamics, and had applied them to theoretical aircraft flight – all this nine years before an airplane had been flown! In 1897 he submitted a research paper to the Physical Society of London. The paper expounded the circulation theory of sustenation – or how a wing derives lift. This farsighted work was ridiculed at the time because Lanchester's language and style of writing were too amateurish for the society's trained scientists. Lanchester liked to make up his own scientific terms, which tended to confuse his learned readers. A dozen years later

when Prandtl (qv) came to the same theoretical conclusions, the aeronautical world realized the brilliance of Lanchester's work and sought to make amends. An interesting fact is that Lanchester went to visit Prandtl at Göttingen in 1908 and there the two discussed aeronautical theory. How much Prandtl was influenced by Lanchester remains an intriguing question. Note: Herbert Austin has also received credit for this, but his vehicle was almost an exact duplicate of a French machine, the Léon Bollée tri-car. Bollée, coincidentally, was the man who put his factory at the disposal of Wilbur Wright (qv) in August, 1908. There Wright assembled his airplane and repaired some damaged engine parts.

LANGLEY, SAMUEL PIERPONT
1834–1906
Born in Roxbury, Massachusetts, Langley was largely self-educated. His early years were spent as an engineer and architect. After a trip to Europe, he turned to astronomy, making several important discoveries including calculating the solar constant, and inventing the bolometer. The United States government commissioned him to undertake several scientific investigations and finally appointed him to head the Smithsonian Institution.

During the late 1880s, he became interested in heavier-than-air flight and started a serious study of aerodynamics. In 1896 he flew the first of his large model aircraft. During the next seven years he tested six models, one making an excellent flight of 3,000 feet (914m). Langley was on the verge of retiring when the War Department asked him to try to build a full-scale aircraft. Congress appropriated a huge grant of $50,000 and Langley set to work.

The craft he and his assistants built was a tandem wing monoplane named the *Aerodrome*. Its best feature was its engine, designed by Stephen Balzer but later improved by Charles Manly (qv). Two attempts were made to launch the *Aerodrome* off the top of a house boat floating on the Potomac River, the first in November, and next in December, 1903. Both times the machine broke-up and fell into the water nearly drowning its 'pilot', Manly.

The national press lost no time in roasting the *Aerodrome*, which they dubbed 'Langley's Folly'. During the next few weeks most newspapers took a swing at the aging professor. Column followed column on the impossibility of flight – most papers had its own expert. So busy were the newsmen in December of 1903 with Langley that they failed to notice the accomplishments of two brothers who had taken a train to Kitty Hawk.

LATÉCOÈRE, PIERRE
1883–1943
Pierre Latécoère was a munitions and aircraft manufacturer during World War I, but after the conflict decided to begin his own airline. On Christmas Day in 1918 the 'Compagnie Latécoère', based in Toulouse, began flights to Barcelona, Spain with the ultimate goal of laying a trans-South Atlantic air route. The next year the route extended to Morocco and six years later to Dakar, Senegal. In 1927 the company was sold and renamed 'Aéropostale' to reflect its desire to carry bulk airmail.

On 12 May 1930 Latécoère's dream came true when pilot, Jean Mermoz (qv), crossed the South Atlantic from Senegal to Brazil with a plane-load of mail. By 1934 a regular trans-Atlantic route had been established.

In 1932 the airline company was sold to Air France. Latécoère continued to manufacture aircraft even into World War II for the Vichy government.

LATHAM, HUBERT
1883–1912
Hubert Latham was a cultivated, urbane, but thrill-seeking Englishman who lived most of his life in France. Forewarned of an early death by tuberculosis, he plunged into life as if every day was his last. He chain-smoked, raced motor boats, and hunted big game in Africa. After witnessing Wilbur Wright's (qv) flights at Le Mans, he asked Levavasseur (qv) to teach him to fly Antoinettes. He had become acquainted with

Levavasseur during his speedboat days because the engineer's marine engines were amongst the most powerful.

Latham purchased stock in the Antoinette company and became its chief pilot. With an Antoinette monoplane he hoped to beat Blériot (qv) across the English Channel in the summer of 1909. Engine problems forced him into 'La Manche' twice, one time only a few miles from the English coast. Disappointed at his failure, Latham went to the Rheims Meet in August of that year where he won 42,000 francs in prize money, second only to Henry Farman (qv). He went on a tour of European cities with the Antoinette, but soon faded into the back ranks of aviators. On 16 July 1912, while on safari in French Equatorial Africa, Latham was charged by a wild buffalo and gored to death.

LAURENT, FRANCOIS,
The Marquis d'Arlandes
1742–1809
The Marquis d'Arlandes was a French courtier with the rank of major in the infantry. The record is unclear, but he was probably a quasi-official liaison between the royal court of Louis XVI and the Montgolfier brothers (qv). At any rate, on 19 October 19, 1783 he ascended with de Rozier (qv) in a tethered balloon. Sometime after this ascension, he informed Étienne Montgolfier that it would seal his place in history (and beat the Charles (qv)) if a free voyage was made in the balloon with human passengers. Étienne consented and promised d'Arlandes the role of pilot.

The oft-told story that d'Arlandes dissuaded the king from sending up condemned prisoners on the first flight has no evidence to support it. d'Arlandes brought de Rozier with him on the first flight probably because the latter had more experience with the balloon as he had been assisting in its construction. The choice proved wise.

On 21 November 1783 the two launched from the grounds of La Muette. The novelty of drifting through the air so intrigued d'Arlandes that de Rozier became the *de facto* pilot. His level-headed commands saved the ship from burning up. Upon landing, d'Arlandes rushed back to court to receive the accolades, leaving behind his fellow aeronaut.

There is no record to show that d'Arlandes ever flew again. His military career ended during the Revolution when he was drummed-out of the service for cowardice.

de La VAULX, COMTE HENRI
1870–1930
De la Vaulx was a Parisian financier who took up the gentleman's sport of ballooning in 1900. In October of that year he broke John Wise's (qv) long-held distance record with a flight of 1,193 miles (1,920km) from France to Russia. Upon landing in Russia he was arrested as a spy and thrown into jail!

His next important flight came on 13 October 1901 when he and three others became the first to fly a balloon across the Mediterranean, from Marseille to Algeria. In the course of de La Vaulx's aerostatic adventures he made over 250 flights and from 1909-10 owned a Zodiac dirigible.

For many years he was the vice-president of the Aéro-Club of France, and in 1905 he founded the Fédération Aéronautique Internationale, the international record sanctioning body. In 1907 he sponsored Tatin's (qv) failed monoplane project but was otherwise uninvolved in heavier-than-air projects. Unfortunately this fine champion of flight was killed in an aeroplane crash en route to New York from Montreal.

LAVOCHKIN, SYEMYON ALEXANDER
1900–1965
Born in Smolensk, Lavochkin was educated at the Joukowsky Air Academy where he was a contemporary of Ilyushin (qv). In 1938 he began to design fighters with Gorbunov and Gudov, (hence the LaGG-1, etc.). In 1943 he opened his own design bureau which produced the LA-5 and LA-7 fighters. These were among the Soviet's best in World War II.

LAWSON, ALFRED W.
1869(?)–1954
Perhaps the only person in aviation history other than Swedenborg (qv) to design an aeroplane, and found a religion, was Alfred Lawson.

Lawson, who as a child emigrated from England with his parents, exuded enthusiasm and optimism for everything with which he was associated. Whether it was as a player on one of America's first professional baseball teams, or as the founder of America's first aviation magazine, Lawson felt that he could lead the cause to victory. Though poorly educated, he had become a writer and in November, 1908 he published the first issue of *Fly* magazine, just a few months after Curtiss (qv) made the first public flying demonstration in America. The magazine sounded a trumpet blast for Americans to get airborne. Most of the early article's concerned airships and balloons, but a monthly section was devoted to aviation in Europe and told of aeroplane activities there. One issue carried detailed plans for building a Chanute-type glider.

Lawson, it is claimed, first coined the term 'aircraft' in 1908 and in 1910 founded a magazine under that name. He became a pilot himself and flew Blériots and Deperdussins. On America's entry into the war in 1917, he started a manufacturing company in Green Bay, Wisconsin that built training aircraft, the M.T. 2, though only a few were built. Vincent Burnelli (qv) was one of his engineers on the trainer project and after the war Lawson assigned to him the task of designing an airliner.

The C-2 airliner, the first in America, very much resembled a Handley Page 0/400. In August and September, 1919 it flew from Milwaukee to Washington via New York, a wonderful achievement. Lawson was justly hailed as a great pioneer and he predicted that his planes would soon make passenger travel by air commonplace. The next year he received the first Post Office contract to haul airmail.

Flushed with success, Lawson sold shares in his company to raise funds to build an even better aircraft. The L-4 'Midnight Liner' was a remarkable tri-motor biplane that could carry twenty-four passengers. It featured such luxuries as sleeping berths, a toilet, and even a shower! Lawson's stock-holders became impatient for a return on their investments and they rushed the plane towards its first flight. Forced to fly before it was truly ready, the plane crashed on its first take-off in March, 1921. Lawson was nearly ruined and left the aviation business.

Down, but never out, Lawson received a patent in 1926 for two-tier passenger cabins that could be used on aircraft, trains, or boats. The 747 is an example of a modern aircraft that uses the system. During the 1930s he propounded a new theory of economics and developed his own quasi-religion – Lawsonomy. The precepts of this philosophy are best described as a 'can-do', populist approach towards life and society. In 1943 he purchased Des Moines University and changed its name to the Des Moines University of Lawsonomy. In the 1980s students were still graduating from the University of Lawsonomy, then located on farmland not far down the highway from the location of the famous Oshkosh Airshow.

LEAR, WILLIAM POWELL
1902–1978
Though Bill Lear was born in Hannibal, Missouri, the childhood home of Mark Twain, his favourite author was Horatio Alger. Like many of Alger's young heroes, Lear was a poor child with a bleak future – but also like these characters, Lear wasn't about to stay that way.

At the age of ten he decided that radio was the up and coming science of the future and that he would learn the basics. Before he dropped out of high school to join the Navy at sixteen, he had taught himself how to build radios from scratch and had become an expert at Morse code. In the Navy during World War I, he was a radio operator at the Great Lakes Naval Air Training Station.

When he left the service he began to invent and sell improved electronics components. With the profits from these sales, he and a friend set up a small electronics laboratory. One of their first inventions was a practical car radio. This product was very successful and marketed under the name Motorola (Motor + Victrola). He soon branched out into aviation equipment, inventing direction finders, lightweight air radios, and autopilots.

By the 1950s Lear could look back on a long, successful career whose plot even Alger couldn't match. But Lear wasn't finished. In the early sixties he introduced the eight-track cassette player which revolutionized the popular music industry. His greatest moment was the unveiling of the Learjet business jet in 1963. The experts had doubted that a business jet would sell, but Lear's faith in the concept spawned a new industry.

In the last years of his life, he tried unsuccessfully to develop the steam powered car. Its failure was one of his few.

LEBAUDY, PAUL
1858–1937
LEBAUDY, PIERRE
1861–1924
The Lebaudy brothers sponsored the construction of the world's first practical dirigible the Lebaudy I *Jaune*. They were wealthy owners of a sugar refinery near Mantes, France and commissioned their chief engineer Julliot (qv) to design the craft. Completed in 1902, it made well over 100 flights before November, 1905 when it was purchased by the French military.

The Lebaudys continued to build dirigibles as a commercial venture.

LEBLANC, ALFRED
1869–1921
Leblanc was a wealthy French ballooning enthusiast at the turn of the century. In 1907 he set a balloon endurance record of forty-four hours two minutes during the Gordon Bennett race. He was a friend of Blériot's (qv) and awoke that aviator on the morning of his cross-Channel flight telling him that the weather had cleared during the night. When the Type XI had proved itself a great monoplane, Leblanc bought the

first production model and entered a career as an exhibition pilot. In this profession, he won the gruelling Circuit L'Est long distance race in 1910 by flying an astonishing 490 miles (788km). He was one of only two pilots to finish the race. That year also brought him to America where he nearly won the Statue of Liberty race, but his engine cut out near the finish due to fuel starvation and Leblanc crashed. Outraged by the accident which left him injured, though miraculously alive, his sometimes violent temper flared forth and he accused various people of sabotage.

Le BRIS, JEAN-MARIE
1808–1872

Le Bris was one of the greatest glider experimenters of the nineteenth century though his accomplishments are little recognized even today. He was born at Douarnenez, a town in northwestern France. He became a professional sailor, then a sea captain who sailed around both the Cape of Good Hope and Cape Horn. On these voyages he studied the flight of albatrosses and even dissected one to more closely study its wing construction.

He settled down in Douarnenez, and earned his living as the captain of a coastal vessel. With more time on land, Le Bris was able to test his theories of flight. In 1857 he built a full-size glider fashioned to loosely resemble an albatross. This machine represented a *tour de force* of aeronautical insight and was built very much like aeroplanes would be built 50 years later. It was mostly of wood with a fabric-covered wing and fuselage. A fifty-foot (15m) wing span accorded it about 215 square feet (20sq m) of area. This was more than enough to get airborne as the machine weighed a mere ninety-two pounds (42kg). It had at least two axis control as the tail could pivot up and down and sideways, and the main wing had a type of variable incidence control which probably could also adjust camber. All this by a crusty seaman in 1857!

Le Bris test-flew this machine on two occasions. The first time it was mounted on a cart which was

pulled by a horse. With Le Bris on board and with forward speed of probably less than 15mph (24km/hr), the glider lifted off the cart. Claims have been made that the machine rose to 300 feet (91m) and this is not entirely impossible. Le Bris' controls were effective enough for him to bring down the machine in a gentle descent. The first flight voluntarily ended when the cart driver became entangled in the tow rope and Le Bris set down.

The last flight of this machine came when Le Bris attempted to drop-launch it from a mast erected over a quarry. According to witnesses, the plane oscillated downwards before crashing. Le Bris received a broken leg in the accident. The crash may have been due to not gaining enough forward speed to maintain flight and the oscillations were probably a series of semi-stalls.

By now Le Bris was financially in need and he returned to earning a living. In 1867 a public subscription was raised to help him resume his flying activities. With this money, he built another glider much like the first. This glider could actually lift-off by itself in a mild wind. Friends begged Le Bris not to fly in the glider as he was advancing in age, and he consented. The glider was tested without a pilot and launched by a tow rope. It crashed because, Le Bris explained, he was not in it to control it. He clearly understood the need for a pilot and didn't believe in inherent stability, an opinion that would later be proved correct by the Wrights (qv).

During the Franco-Prussian war Le Bris earned distinction as a war hero but was murdered in 1872 during a dispute.

LECOINTE, SADI-JOSEPH
1891–1944

Born at St-Germaine-sur-Bresles, Lecointe learned to fly on Blériots a few years before World War I. During the conflict, he spent eighteen months at the front in the air service before being posted to a training squadron. For the rest of the war, he helped instruct 1,500 student pilots and became involved in test flying.

After the war he became a race pilot first for Spad, then in late 1919 for Nieuport-Astra. Among his many racing victories were the 1920 Gordon Bennett Cup, and the 1924 and 1925 Beaumont Cups.

In 1924 he ran for the Chamber of Deputies as a Radical Socialist, but lost. The next year he led a group of volunteers to North Africa to bomb revolting Berber tribesmen. Charles Kerwood's (qv) group of Americans was under his command in this effort. During the remainder of the post-war years Lecointe flew as a test pilot. He briefly served as the inspector general of civil aviation in France before World War II started. Ater the defeat of France, he commanded an air base in North Africa until being relieved of duty by a Vichy government that felt he was too pro-Allies.

LEDUC, RENÉ-HENRI
1898–1968

Leduc first began to learn about engines as an apprentice in an automobile garage. Serving in the French infantry in World War I, his mechanical abilities were recognized and he was sent to an army engineering school. After the war he continued to study engineering at the École Supérieure d'Électricité. By 1924 he had been hired by the Breguet Company where he began to design ramjet engines.

In 1937 he began construction of a full size aircraft powered by a ramjet. The work was interrupted by the war and the unfinished aircraft was hidden. At the war's end, the plane was completed and flown piggyback fashion on a transport plane in 1947. Two years later it flew under its own tremendous power, achieving 450 mph (724km/hr) on only fifty per cent throttle! This marked the first manned flight of a ramjet aircraft.

Progress continued slowly as the first aircraft, the Leduc 010, was developed into the 021. This second aircraft first flew in 1953. The ultimate goal was to develop an interceptor version, but Leduc himself may have been the cause for the slow pace of development. He became sidetracked on other projects including ejector seats. Eventually, interest was lost in the project and the French government withdrew support in 1957.

LEFEBURE, EUGÈNE
1878–1909

Lefebure was a French engineer who assembled a Wright biplane in Holland at the Hague. There, he taught himself to fly in July, 1909 thus making the first flight in that country. The next month he took part in the Rheims Meet where he shocked crowds with his ground-level high banked turns. As a pilot for the French Wright Company, on 7 September he was testing several newly-built planes when one of them broke in flight. He became France's first aeroplane fatality.

LeMAY, GENERAL CURTIS EMERSON
1906–1990

When LeMay's candidacy for West Point was rejected in 1924, he decided to earn his way to the 'top' the hard way. He joined an ROTC unit and received a commission in the Air Corps in 1930. From then until World War II, he carefully studied all aspects of military aviation, becoming an expert pilot and navigator. In 1942 he led the 305th Bombardment Group to England and drilled it into a model combat unit. Promoted several times for excellent service, LeMay was instructed in July, 1945 to plan the nuclear bombing of Hiroshima and Nagasaki. By 1948 he had risen to Lieutenant-General and was assigned to organize the Berlin Airlift. The success of this historic operation earned him the post of Chief of the Strategic Air Command. LeMay formed SAC into the world's first truly effective strategic air force. SAC's existence, more than anything else, prevented a world war during the turbulent 1950s.

He retired from the Air Force in 1965 and unsuccessfully ran for Vice-President on George Wallace's third party-ticket in 1968.

LENORMAND, LOUIS-SEBASTIEN

1757–1839

Lenormand was a French physicist who made the first parachute jump that can be historically verified. Another claimant to the first jump is a sixteenth century Hungarian who lived in Italy named Fauste Veranzio. Veranzio's claim is possibly true because he left detailed drawings of his device along with a narrative of his jumps.

Lenormand's jumps, the first may have been from a tall tree, were witnessed. In December, 1783 he jumped safely from the tower of the Montpellier Observatory in southern France. His hope was to invent a means of escaping fires in tall buildings!

LEVAVASSEUR, LÉON

1863–1922

The success of European aviation from 1906-1909 is due less to the design ability of such pioneers as Santos-Dumont, Voisin or Blériot than to the brilliant engine designed by Levavasseur.

Levavasseur was seventeen when he left his home in Cherbourg to study art in Paris. Belle Époque Paris offered as many technical wonders as artistic ones, so the young student switched to engineering. His initial business career was as an arc lamp designer with Ferranti-Patin. By 1903 he had received government sponsorship to build an aeroplane. He built this machine in secrecy at Puteaux and when it was complete, under cover of darkness, he wheeled it out for a test. The machine was a failure, but few people knew about it. He built another machine subsequently but never tested it.

1903 wasn't a total loss for the inventor. That year saw the first running of an engine he had designed at the behest of Jules Gastambide (qv). The Antoinette engine, named after Gastambide's daughter, was remarkably advanced for its time. It used aluminum alloys for weight reduction, had evaporative cooling, and most notably, was fuel injected. The engine was built initially in two sizes, twenty-four horsepower and fifty horsepower. Its first success came in motorboat races at Monaco in 1904 and 1905. In 1905 an Antoinette-powered motorboat was used on the Seine to tow the Voisin (qv) gliders. The next year, Blériot (qv), Gastambide, and Levavasseur formed a company to build and market the engines. Santos-Dumont's (qv) first aeroplane flight was powered by an Antoinette.

In 1907 Levavasseur wanted to return to aircraft design but Blériot didn't want the company to compete with his own. Blériot resigned and Levavasseur proceeded. His first design, the Gastambide-Mengin monoplane was a failure. He developed the design until 1909 when he introduced the Antoinette IV. This monoplane with its boat-like fuselage and long, slender wings reflected its designer's artistic origins. It is still considered one of the most beautiful aeroplanes ever to fly. In its day, it was a successful racer, though the Antoinette engines that powered it were susceptible to clogged injectors.

Levavasseur went on to design several other planes, including the carefully streamlined Monobloc of 1911, but none achieved the popularity of the elegant Antoinette IV. As aeroplanes became faster and more manoeuvrable, the Antoinette company's fortunes faded and bankruptcy ensued. By the time Levavasseur died, he was nearly a pauper.

LILIENTHAL, OTTO

1848–1896

Lilienthal was not a genius but rather a practical experimenter whose work directly led to the development of the first successful aeroplane.

Prussian by birth, after studying mechanical engineering and spending several years in a machine shop as an apprentice, he founded his own business. There he designed and marketed light steam engines and marine signal lamps. He had been interested in flight since youth when he and his brother, Gustavus, built strap-on wings. When his business became a success, Lilienthal had the time and resources to devote to flying experiments. He believed most of his life that an ornithopter would be the first type of powered craft to fly, yet he felt that fixed wing gliders were the first step. He built his first glider in 1891. It employed what would become his classic ovoid planform. By 1893 he had made flights of up to 750 feet (230m). These were the first controlled, sustained flights in history. Photographs and accounts of Lilienthal's work spread all over the world. Reports reached the Wright brothers (qv) and they were inspired by the German's work to build their own glider. They originally used Lilienthal's aerodynamic tables, only to find by independent experimentation that the data was incorrect.

Lilienthal was a 'doer' at a time when most were content to postulate. He did not live to see powered flight become a reality however. After over 2,000 successful glides, he was killed in August, 1896 when his glider stalled in mid-air. It slid backwards, smashing into the ground. Lilienthal died the next day of a broken back.

A quiet hero from a frivolous age Charles Lindbergh.

LINDBERGH, CHARLES AUGUSTUS
1902–1974
Much has been written about Lindbergh, a man who spent forty-seven years trying to downplay the adulation he received for a thirty-three hour flight.

He was the son of a prominent Minnesota congressman. After leaving engineering college, claiming it wasn't exciting enough, Lindbergh learned to fly in Nebraska in 1922 and then joined a flying circus. He performed mostly as a wing-walker and parachutist. Tiring of show business, he joined the Air Corps in 1924. Two years later he became an airmail pilot and was forced on several occasions to jump from his plane in bad weather. Within a year he had had enough of this dangerous work and put together a plan to win the Orteig prize for the first New York to Paris non-stop flight.

On his own, Lindbergh persuaded several St. Louis businessmen into sponsoring his entry. He then went to Ryan where he helped them to build the aeroplane that he would use. The plane was designed and built in less than two months! The preparations for the flight were made almost entirely by Lindbergh. In flying the plane, *The Spirit of St. Louis*, from its birthplace in San Diego to New York, he set a trans-continental speed record of twenty-one hours twenty minutes (flying time).

On 20 May 1927, having had only a few hours sleep during the past few days, he took off from Roosevelt Field on Long Island. With a loaded plane, he barely managed to clear telephone lines at the end of the runway. For 33·5 hours the plane droned eastwards. Lindbergh's biggest problem was fatigue. Once, while dozing, he almost crashed into the sea. Finally, he saw the coast of Ireland and navigated his plane southeast towards Paris where he landed at Le Bourget a welcome that he found embarrassing and unbelievable.

As a hero, he was flooded with lucrative endorsement offers, but he turned them all down. He wanted to be a testament to the safety of flying, not to cigarettes or automobiles.

He received the Congressional Medal of Honour and embarked on a goodwill tour of North and South America. While in Mexico City he met the American ambassador's daughter, who became his wife. Together he and Anne Morrow pioneered air routes that would one day be flown by commercial airliners. Tragedy struck the young couple in 1932 when their son was kidnapped and murdered. A German emigrant carpenter was convicted and executed. As late as 1988 the carpenter's wife was still petitioning the court to overturn the conviction, but to no avail. The evidence against him, despite persistent arguments, seemed ironclad.

The Lindbergh's fled to Europe to escape the withering barrage of the press. While there, Lindbergh collaborated on inventing the artificial heart. Herman Goering (qv) invited him to inspect the new Luftwaffe shortly before the war. Impressed by what he was shown, Lindbergh warned the US during 1940-41 to stay out of a European conflict. For this he incurred Roosevelt's wrath and resigned his Air Corps reserve commission.

After Pearl Harbor he jumped back into uniform to help establish B-24 production lines, teach fuel economy techniques to new pilots, and even participate in combat missions in the South Pacific where he destroyed at least one enemy plane.

Since 1927 he had been a technical advisor to Pan Am and he continued in that role after the war. One of his most insightful decisions was to advise against the building of an American SST which he felt would never be profitable. In later years, he championed conservationist causes speaking publicly on the need to preserve wilderness areas. He also distinguished himself as a fine author and won the 1953 Pulitzer Prize for his autobiographical history *The Spirit of St. Louis.*

Lindbergh was more than a temporary, media-generated hero. There were hundreds of those during the 1920s and 30s. He was rather a mythic symbol of what great deeds could be accomplished by a young person in a free, progressive society. What he did seemed like a gift to humanity rather than an event for one. His modesty made him seem more like the classic western hero than a technician of a mechanized era.

LINK, EDWIN ALBERT
1904–1981
In the late 1920s Link started to take flying lessons. The lessons were expensive and he was angered by the condescending attitude of his instructor. Link wondered if he couldn't devise an aeroplane simulator in which a person could teach himself to fly. Within a year Link had built a simulator and had taught his brother to fly in it. He took the machine to several companies but none thought it had any potential. Discouraged, he embarked on a tour of the country, stopping to sell rides in the simulator for twenty-five cents. Then, in the early 1930s the Army noticed the potential training cost-savings the device offered and Link's prospects took a turn for the better.

Over the years his company grew from a one-man operation to a multi-million dollar industry. Link left the business in the 1950s to devote himself to oceanography. For that science, he designed and built several advanced underwater vehicles. Perhaps the most surprising aspect of Link's terrific success was that he was a high school dropout!

LIPPISCH, PROFESSOR ALEXANDER MARTIN
1894–1976
Lippisch studied engineering in Berlin and at Heidelberg University. During World War I he fought in the Army and then the Air Corps. Following the war he developed several aerofoil sections and began to investigate the problem of high speed, low powered flight. In 1931 he demonstrated the Delta I, an efficient flying wing. When he attempted to sell his ideas of delta wing aircraft to German industry, he was laughed out of all their offices as a crank.

Finally, in 1939, after demonstrating a rocket powered, swept wing aircraft to the military, he was sent to Messerschmitt (qv) with whom he was told to develop the concept. The result of this uneasy alliance was the Me-163 Komet rocket fighter, perhaps the most terrifying aeroplane of World War II. At 600mph (965km/hr), it was virtually untouchable but its volatile fuel tended to spontaneously explode killing the pilot.

After the Komet project had been successfully

launched, Lippisch returned to theoretical research and began to develop theories of supersonic delta wing aircraft. Following the war, he travelled to America where his ideas were readily accepted and incorporated in the new generations of jet aircraft. At the very end of his career, he experimented with model vectored thrust aircraft.

LITVAK, JUNIOR LIEUTENANT LYDIA (variously LILYA)

1921–1943

Russia was the only country to use women as regular combat personnel during World War II, and Litvak was their highest scoring female fighter pilot. A member of the 73rd Polk Regiment, she shot down twelve German planes while flying a Yak-1 during the battle of Stalingrad. After less than a year's combat flying, the twenty-one-year-old pilot was killed in an air battle over Orel.

LOCKHEED, ALLAN HAINES

1889–1969

Allan Loughead and his brother Malcolm were born in Niles, California where both had become auto mechanics. Allan became the mechanic for a businessman in Chicago named James Plew, who was starting an aircraft business in conjuction with an automobile distributorship he owned. Allan, after teaching himself to fly on one of Plew's Curtiss pushers, began to build aeroplanes himself. Shortly after he was married he crashed a Curtiss and his wife asked that he at least temporarily give up flying. The couple moved back to California. There, he and his brother joined forces to build aeroplanes under the name Alco Hydro-Aeroplane Company, and their first product was the Model G hydroplane. They had named it 'G' to dupe prospective buyers into thinking they had built half a dozen previous models! The 'G' flew for the first time on 15 June 1913 but received no orders. It was put into storage and Loughead returned to auto repair.

With the advent of World War I, he and his brother decided to try to sell seaplanes to the Navy. In 1916 they formed Loughead Aircraft with a plant in Santa Barbara. They hired John Northrop (qv) as an engineer. Their company built several designs but sold only two flying-boats to the Navy. Though they struggled on and introduced an advanced plywood monocoque sport biplane, the company finally folded in 1921 because of a lack of orders. Malcolm left at this time and successfully developed hydraulic brakes for automobiles, Northrop transferred to Douglas, and Allan went into real estate sales.

In 1926 Loughead and Northrop restarted the company, this time naming it Lockheed. With Northrop as chief designer, the company produced the magnificent Vega monoplane built with a plywood monocoque fuselage. The next year the Vega flew, but orders were too scanty to keep the company solvent. In 1929 it merged with the Detroit Aircraft Company. Even then, its finances were shaky so in 1932 it was sold to an investment group. Under this management, it went on to become an industrial giant.

Loughead left his company when it was sold and started another firm in 1930. This company, Loughead Brothers Aircraft Corporation, lasted four years and built only one plane. In 1937 he again formed a company, Alcor, but it too failed. Loughead legally changed his name to Lockheed in 1934.

LOCKLEAR, ORMER LESLIE

1891–1920

Locklear was born in Greenville, Texas, near Fort Worth. His early life was marked by daredevil episodes that included stunts on motorcycles and horse racing. After witnessing Calbraith Rodgers' (qv) stop-over in Fort Worth during the aviator's trans-continental flight, Locklear built a glider which he flew with some success. It was natural then that with America's entry into World War I he would join the Air Service. He learned to fly at Barron Field in Texas but because of the large surplus of American pilots was not sent overseas. For months he lingered at the air base and restlessness drove him to attempt stunts. Even before joining the service he had performed aero stunts; when in his home town he transferred from a racing motorcycle to the undercarriage of an airplane. But now his stunts would be mostly executed thousands of feet up. Initially, he would get out of a Jenny's forward cockpit, while another pilot controlled the plane, and wander among the wing's rigging. Soon he progressed to climbing on the top wing and standing balanced into the wind. He also learned to crawl under the plane and slide to its tail. Oddly enough, his base commander, when learning of these stunts, ordered him to perform them in the presence of rookie pilots. He felt the demonstrations would boost their confidence.

On 18 November 1918 Locklear transferred from one aeroplane in flight to another. It was an aerial first. Newspapers reported the stunt and by May he had resigned his commission and signed on with a professional promoter. He went on a barnstorming tour of the country that was enormously successful. By August, 1919 he signed a contract to star in Hollywood films. The films he made there over the next year were box office smashes, but even so, the public began to tire of the same routines. In August, 1920 Locklear had just learned that his film contract had not been renewed even though he was filming the final shots of one of his movies. On 2 August he flew up with another pilot to film a night-time spin during which he was to stand on the wing tip. Evidently, blinded by the spotlights, the pilot misjudged his height and never levelled off. The resulting crash drove the engine five feet (1.5m) into the ground and ended Locklear's meteoric sixteen-month career.

LOENING, GROVER CLEVELAND
1888–1976

Loening's aviation career began in 1910 when he graduated from Columbia University with the first ever degree in aeronautical science. He went to work for the Queen (Blériot) Company before joining the Wright Company in 1913 as the factory manager. Moving quickly, he worked in 1914 for the aviation section of the

Signal Corps then in 1915 became vice-president of Sturtevant. In 1917 he founded the first of his several companies. This one, the Loening Aeronautical Engineering Corporation, was formed to compete for a Navy scout plane contract. In addition to the scout, the company also built several amphibious types.

In 1928 Loening sold the company for a hefty $3,000,000 to an investment firm that merged it with Curtiss-Wright. Loening invested in the newly-formed Grumman (qv) company but spent the rest of his career in mostly consultative roles. One of his last jobs was advising on the construction of a heli-pad on top of New York's Pan Am building.

LORIN, RENÉ
1877–1933

Lorin, a French artillery officer, proposed in 1908 a novel scheme for aeroplane propulsion. He suggested that the exhaust manifolds of inline engines should have special nozzles on them so that the exhaust gases could be used as a propelling force. He even thought that variable angle plates should be fitted behind the nozzles to direct the gases thus facilitating vertical take-offs. This rather extreme proposal never saw fruition but when Lorin further developed the idea, he came up with the ramjet engine.

During his lifetime, airspeeds were too slow to allow ramjets to work properly, but after his death the German scientists at Peenemünde showed the practicality of Lorin's idea.

LOWE, THADDEUS SOBIESKI CONSTANTINE
1832–1913

Lowe was born in New Hampshire but despaired of farm life. He left home at fifteen to live in Boston where he hoped to gain an education. His stay in Boston was short due to ill health but he had learned a bit about chemistry. After regaining his health, he embarked on a career as a travelling showman – 'Professor' Lowe.

He had long been interested in balloons and

Yankee aeronaut Thaddeus Lowe.

had met in his wanderings several notable balloonists. By 1858 he had become an aeronaut and the next year began a subscription campaign to build a trans-Atlantic balloon. When built, *The City of New York* spanned a massive 104 feet (32m) diameter. Lowe suffered a setback when it was damaged in a storm though he was able to repair it. On its next inflation, because of the poor repairs, the bag exploded and the project was halted.

Lowe was practising cross-country flying and had landed in Southern territory after the Civil War had started. He was imprisoned as a Union spy, but later released and allowed to return to the North. He immediately offered his services to President Lincoln who referred him to the Army. There, Lowe faced a wall of indifference from the generals who couldn't grasp the potential of a surveillance platform. Despite their resistance, Lowe proceeded to make observations from balloons, telegraphing his observations to the ground. During the war, five Lowe balloons saw service, making their greatest contribution at the first battle of Bull Run, the Peninsula campaign and

Chancellorsville. In 1863, due to lack of support, he gave up military flying.

His post-war career proved very profitable as he marketed improved refrigeration devices and smelting ovens that he had invented. He even proposed a submarine to the Navy during the Spanish-American War, but was brushed aside.

One of his granddaughters, 'Pancho' Barnes (qv) also made a name for herself in aviation.

World traveller and crack pilot Raoul Lufbery.

LUFBERY, MAJOR RAOUL GERVAIS VICTOR
1885–1918
Born in France, Lufbery moved with his father to America in 1891, five years after his mother's death. When seventeen, he left home to become a world traveller, spending time in many countries working at odd jobs to pay his way. In 1908, by now an American citizen, he joined the US Army and served in the Phillipines. After two years he was discharged and travelled the Orient, winding up in Saigon in 1912. He met a French barnstorming pilot there and became his mechanic. The pair were back in France in

1914 when the war started. Lufbery, as an American, could only join the Foreign Legion but was later able to join the squadron of his barnstorming friend as a mechanic. In May, 1915 he received flight training and became a bomber plot. Later still, he trained as a fighter pilot. In May, 1916 he transferred to the Escadrille Americaine which in December became the Escadrille Lafayette.

Lufbery was a relaxed, cunning killer who soon became the best pilot of the outfit, and one of its first aces. In February, 1918 the Escadrille was incorporated into the Signal Corps and Lufbery was made a major. He was given command of the famous 94th Aero Squadron because his commanders prized his leadership skills. On 19 May 1918 his plane was hit with an incendiary bullet and burst into flames. Lufbery jumped out, preferring a quick death to an agonizing one. His final score stood at seventeen kills, though he probably had many more.

LUKE, LIEUTENANT FRANK, JR.

1897–1918

Born in Arizona, Luke joined the Signal Corps in 1917. He received combat training and was sent to France in March, 1918. A superb airman and deadly sharpshooter, he constantly let his fellow pilots know it, making himself unpopular in the process. He often strayed from organized patrols, going off to fight his own private war. His score quickly rose though and he became known as America's most daring 'Sausage Buster' by shooting down fourteen enemy balloons. Having been warned that he was about to be court-martialled for insubordination, Luke defiantly took-off on a lone patrol on 29 September 1918. What happened next became the stuff of legend.

Near Toul he encountered three observation balloons and shot them all down. The Germans had put up a withering 'archie' barrage that finally hit Luke's plane. He crash-landed his machine and, although injured, continued to fire at German infantry troops who were attempting to capture him. One pistol against many rifles

was no match and Luke was killed.

Because his last fight occurred behind enemy lines, the truth about it wasn't learned until after the war.

LUNARDI, VINCENZO

1759–1806

Lunardi was the secretary to the Neapolitan Ambassador in London in 1783 when the Montgolfiers (qv) launched their first balloon. Inspired by what he had heard, Lunardi designed and built a balloon of his own which he successfully launched on 15 September 1784 from London. It was the first balloon flight in England.

He switched from a diplomatic career to an aeronautical one and toured Britain. When an accident killed an English citizen, he was forced to leave the country. He continued his exhibition flights on the continent, dying in Portugal at the age of only forty-seven.

MacCREADY, PAUL B., JR

1925–

MacCready was already a successful aeronautical engineer running his own consultancy business in 1976 when he decided to try for the Kremer Prize. This prize was established by a British industrialist for the first man-powered flying vehicle to fly over an officially observed course.

More than a year's dedicated effort by MacCready and volunteers from the California Institute of Technology paid off on 23 August 1977 when Bryan Allen piloted MacCready's machine, the *Gossamer Condor*, over a figure-of-eight course to win the prize.

Two years later, the MacCready team scored an even more spectacular success when they built and flew a man-powered aircraft, the *Gossamer Albatross*, twenty-one miles across the English Channel.

In the mid-eighties MacCready built a flying replica of a prehistoric bird.

MACH, ERNST

1838–1916

Mach was born in the Moravian section of the Austro-Hungarian Empire. His family later moved to Vienna where he was able to obtain an excellent technical education. While studying ballistics, Mach noted the change in airflow as an object reached the speed of sound. He wrote many papers dealing with this phenomenon, but they received little attention until the 1930s when aircraft began to approach sonic speeds.

In commemoration of his pioneering research, the speed of sound at any given altitude has become known as Mach 1. Mach also investigated psychological phenomena and was elected to the Austrian House of Peers.

MALAN, GROUP CAPTAIN ADOLPH GYSBERT

1910–1963

Born in Wellington, South Africa, 'Sailor' Malan was a merchant Navy Officer before joining the RAF in 1935. He proved himself an excellent pilot and took command of No. 74 Squadron flying Spitfires during the Battle of Britain. His personal claim during the two months of that battle was eighteen.

Promoted to command the Biggin Hill fighter base in 1942, Malan raised his score by war's end to thirty-two victories, making him third on the list of RAF pilots. Among his peers he was considered the greatest fighter pilot in the entire service. After the war he returned to South Africa and became a farmer.

MANLY, CHARLES MATTHEW

1876–1927

In 1898 Samuel Langley (qv) asked his friend, the Dean of Engineering at Cornell University, to recommend a good student who could assist him in developing his flying machines. Charles Manly was singled out and sent to Washington. Arriving there, he was assigned the job of supervising the work of Stephen Balzer who was building an engine for Langley in New York.

Manly made numerous suggestions and took complete control of the project in 1900, moving the engine to Washington. In a little over a year, Manly had redesigned the engine, changing it from a rotary to a radial design. Other important improvements were incorporated with the result that the power jumped from eight horsepower (6kw) to at least forty-two horsepower (31kw)! By contemporary standards it was feather-light at only 208 pounds (94kg).

Langley used this engine in two attempts to fly the *Aerodrome* in 1903 with Manly aboard as pilot, but both times the craft failed.

MANNOCK, MAJOR EDWARD, VC

1887–1918

Mannock was born the son of a professional soldier. When the war started he was working in Turkey as a telephone line inspector and was interned. Because of perceived ill health, he was generously released by the Turks and returned to Britain. Though he suffered a defect in one eye, he managed to sneak into the RFC. On 1 April 1917 he arrived in France where he joined No. 40 squadron flying Nieuports. After a year of steady victories, he took command of No. 74 Squadron on the last day of March, 1918.

His great leadership qualities, combining discipline with personal example, endeared him to many of his comrades who were later responsible for vindicating his record.

Mannock was killed on 26 July 1918 when a chance bullet from a German infantryman pierced his gasoline tank, causing him to crash in flames. His score at the end of the war officially stood at fifty. Loyal friends in the RAF pressed to have him credited with victories that he had made for others, usually rookie pilots, and unclaimed ones of his own. The RAF, in an unusual gesture, agreed to bend the rules and allowed Mannock seventy-three victories, one more than the Canadian 'Billy' Bishop (qv). Will it forever remain a mystery why they did something that could have easily upset ally relations? Could it be that they knew Bishop's scores were exaggerated but couldn't, in the charged post-war political atmosphere, afford a scandal by discrediting the Canadian? Was Mannock's promotion a compromise or an attempt to reach some type of historical justice?

Whatever the case, Mannock's courage and self-sacrifice were never in question and he was awarded a postumous VC.

MANTZ, ALBERT PAUL
1903–1965
Mantz went to Hollywood in the early 1930s to try to break into films as a stunt pilot. All doors were closed to him until 'Pancho' Barnes (qv) got him a chance. Mantz brought a professionalism to stunt flying that the industry had never seen before. Within a few years he dominated the industry, and his business, United Air Services, brought in huge profits. During this time he was a friend and personal adviser to Amelia Earhart.

During World War II he headed the First Motion Picture Unit of the Army which produced high-quality training shorts in addition to the famous documentary *Memphis Belle*. Ronald Reagan was a member of this unit.

Mantz became the only flier to win the Bendix trophy three times in a row. From 1946 to 1948 he captured this prize in a modified Mustang. He had competed for it before the war in a Lockheed Orion but was unsuccessful. At the end of the war he purchased a staggering 475 former military aircraft destined for the scrapyard. He paid $55,000 dollars for the lot but recouped his investment by selling the aviation fuel still in their tanks!

He was tragically killed during the filming of *The Flight of the Phoenix* when the much modified Vultee training plane he was piloting crashed. The camera crew had radioed that they had the right footage, but Mantz said he wanted to make one more pass to make sure.

MAREY, ÉTIENNE-JULES
1830–1904
In the middle of the nineteenth century aviation experimentation was still divided into two camps – those who believed in fixed-wing flight and those who believed in flapping wings. Among the problems of the latter faction was the obscurity of how a bird's wings actually flapped. To penetrate this ancient riddle Étienne Marey, a French physician, took a series of photographs using the new technology of multi-exposure which revealed the complicated motion.

Marey continued his research and developed a wind tunnel with steam injection nozzles so that airflow around various shapes could be observed. His pioneering work led to the development of practical aeronautical theory.

MARKHAM, BERYL
1902–1986
Markham, née Clutterbuck, was born in England but taken to Africa by her divorced father in 1906. Her father's love of horses and farming passed to her as she grew up in the wilds of Kenya. Because she was expelled from school for unruly behaviour, she received very little formal education though her father made her read on a variety of topics.

She was said to be the most beautiful woman in Kenya and eventually she attracted the attention of Denys Finch Hatton, formerly the companion of the Danish authoress Karen Blixen. Blixen became well known for her autobiography *Out of Africa*.

Her carefree lifestyle led her to become a pilot and it was Tom Campbell Black (qv) who taught her to fly in a Moth. From 1931 to 1936 she flew cargo and passengers to different locations throughout East Africa but then decided to make a record flight. On 4 September 1936 she lifted off from an RAF airfield in Abingdon, England in a Percival Gull bound for New York. Having crossed the Atlantic in terrible weather, she force-landed in Nova Scotia with low fuel. Despite landing short of New York, she had completed the first solo east-west crossing of the Atlantic by a woman.

In the US she received a heroine's welcome and a huge ticker-tape parade in New York. She went to California where she married for the third time. Her husband this time was Raoul Schumacher, a writer and editor. In 1942 her autobiography appeared entitled *West with the Night*, considered by many to be one of the best of this century. It is a haunting, lyrical, almost mystical recollection of her life in Africa and her flying experiences. It received a glowing tribute from Ernest Hemingway who said it was one of the best books he had ever read. Later, experts questioned whether she wrote the book by herself or if her husband had contributed to it in a significant way. She but later returned to Africa.

In Kenya, she returned to horse breeding and racing, a sport where she was an acknowledged champion. She died nearly impoverished, after surgery to mend a broken leg sustained after tripping over her dog.

MARS, JAMES C.
1876(?)–1944
'Bud' Mars entered show business at the age of thirteen. Over the years, he was a parachute jumper, a dirigible pilot working for Baldwin (qv), and finally an exhibition pilot for Curtiss (qv).

He joined the Curtiss team in 1910 and soon became the boss's favourite. That year he barnstormed across the country. When in San Francisco, he met Lincoln Beachey (qv) and taught him to fly.

The next year he toured the Orient and became the first foreigner to fly in Japan. In that country he had the unique opportunity of taking Crown Prince Hirohito for his first aeroplane ride. On the same tour he made the first flights in Korea and the Phillipines.

When he gave up exhibition flying, he built airports, trained pilots, and developed real estate.

MARSEILLE, HAUPTMANN HANS-JOACHIM
1919–1942
Marseille was born in Berlin, the son of a military officer. He didn't particularly care for the disciplined life of a serviceman but when war seemed imminent, he joined the Luftwaffe.

Exhibiting individualistic style during the Battle of Britain he often flew on lone patrols. He managed to bag seven planes before being transferred to Africa.

It was in Africa that his talent as a fighter pilot came to life. His most famous combat took place on 1 September 1942 when he shot down an unprecedented seventeen planes in one day. Fellow Luftwaffe pilots cited his uncanny ability to dive upon unsuspecting victims and in one high-speed pass score direct hits. He used a thrifty fifteen rounds on average per kill. He was the top scoring pilot against the Western Allies with 158 victories.

Marseille naturally became a popular hero in Germany. He was awarded the Knight's Cross with Swords for his gallantry, but on 30 September 1942 was killed when he was struck by the tail plane on baling out of a burning Me-109, .

Brash, fun-loving fighter ace Hans-Joachim Marseille.

MARTIN, GLENN LUTHER
1886–1955
Born in Iowa, Martin lived and studied in Kansas before moving with his family to California in

1905. He owned a garage that sold Fords and Maxwells but all the while he was trying to learn about aircraft. In 1907 he built a glider which wasn't very successful. Despite this, he decided to build a powered plane. A rented, unused church became his first factory and it was here that he, with his mother's help, built a pusher biplane. When completed in mid-1909, the plane flew well enough to allow Martin to become a barnstormer. He was noted for his willingness to do anything for publicity and amongst his stunts were: delivering newspapers by air; shooting, allegedly, the first motion pictures from an airplane; aerial coyote hunting, and conducting mock bombings using oranges for ordnance. He also claimed to be the first flyer to take his mother flying!

The first Martin company, founded in 1911, merged with Wright in 1917. That year he moved to Cleveland and founded another company again using his name. In 1929 he transferred his factory to Maryland. For over forty years he built planes that found a ready military market. One of his most notable planes was the Martin 130 trans-oceanic China Clipper. Martin retired from his company in 1952.

MARTIN, SIR JAMES
1893–1981
Born in Ulster, Martin trained as an engineer before starting his own firm in 1929. He specialized in building fighter planes with parts and systems almost completely designed in-house. In 1934 Martin received some much needed capital assistance from Captain Valentine H. Baker, and thus was formed Martin-Baker Ltd.

The company built only about half a dozen fighter planes, all prototypes. The most noteworthy of these was the MB-5. It reputedly could fly faster than any piston-engined fighter of World War II, (460mph at 20,000 feet) (740km/hr at 6,096m). In 1944 the Air Ministry asked Martin to develop an ejector seat because as aircraft speeds increased, the 'baling out' method became unsafe. The first successful 'live' ejection was made on 24 July 1946 from the rear seat of a Meteor. Since then, about 200 lives per year have been saved by the ejector seat.

For his work with this important safety device, Martin was knighted.

MAXIM, SIR HIRAM STEVENS
1840–1916
Maxim was born at Brockway's Mills, Maine where he received a modest one-room schoolhouse education. He spent his spare time studying science books, and took his first job in 1854 with a carriage maker. His technical talents quickly showed themselves and over the years he rose to become an engineer, instrument maker, and a ship's draughtsman. In the early 1870s he invented several electrical devices that secured for him a comfortable income.

Now, as a professional inventor, he travelled to Europe and settled in England in 1881. Two years later he produced and patented his most important invention – the Maxim machine-gun. The enormous profits from this deadly creation gave him the time and money to indulge one of his most consuming interests – powered flight. Maxim first studied airfoil shapes on a swing-arm, and then built two light but powerful steam engines that produced 180 horsepower (134kw) each. With a team of carefully chosen specialists, he constructed a large, ungainly biplane. Powered by the steam engines, this machine with three men aboard managed to rise on its test track in July, 1894. It couldn't execute a true flight, yet it did lift itself, which at the time was a remarkable achievement. Maxim took the success in his stride, glad that he had advanced aeronautical science somewhat. Not long after, though, the machine was scrapped. Maxim's only other venture into aviation was in 1910 with an aeroplane that refused to take-off. He became a British subject in 1900, and the next year was knighted by Queen Victoria. Among his other inventions were a woman's hair curling iron, an automatic fire sprinkler, and, the classic patent itself – an improved mousetrap.

MAYBACH, WILHELM

1846–1929

Born in Heilbronn, Germany, Maybach was orphaned at ten and sent to a children's home. He managed to become a draughtsman and eventually went to work for Nikolaus Otto (the Otto cycle) in Deutz. His friend Gottlieb Daimler also worked for Otto but disagreed with their employer as to the future of the internal combustion engine. Daimler believed its future was to be as a motive power for vehicles. In 1882 Daimler and Maybach left and moved to Bad Canstatt. There, they pursued the vehicle concept and in 1885 ran the world's first four-stroke motorcycle. By the next year they had built a motor carriage and were launched as automobile manufacturers.

Maybach's most important contribution was in making a practical carburettor. His carburettor design was widely copied throughout Europe and led to a series of patent suits. Though Daimler died in 1900, Maybach stayed with the firm and designed the first Mercedes car in 1901. In 1907 he founded his own company as a subsidiary of Zeppelin. Located at Friedrichshafen, it built engines for Zeppelin dirigibles initially but in 1922 turned to automobile production. It stayed in this business until 1939.

McCONNELL, CAPTAIN JOSEPH, JR.

1922–1954

The top-scoring fighter pilot in the Korean war was McConnell. He flew Sabres with the 51st Fighter Wing. Although shot down once himself, he brought down sixteen MiGs over the course of 106 missions. After the war he was posted as a test pilot at Edwards AFB but was killed on 26 August 1954 when his F-86H crashed.

McCUDDEN, MAJOR
JAMES THOMAS BYFORD, VC

1895–1918

McCudden was born in Kent and joined the Royal Engineers as a bugler in 1910. In 1913 he transferred to the RFC where he trained as a

mechanic. After moving up to become an observer and an air gunner, he became a pilot in 1916.

McCudden was a natural leader. He was promoted commander of No. 56 Squadron where he taught his men that properly maintained equipment and discretion in combat were the keys to success. His own victories were gained after a careful study of fighter tactics. Only twelve of these victories were against scout planes, the rest being two-seaters which were actually of more strategic value than scouts.

During the summer of 1918 McCudden was given command of No. 60 Squadron. In taking-off to join his new command, his SE-5A's engine failed. He made the classic error of trying to return to base with a dead engine. In turning, he stalled and crashed to his death.

His final credit stood at variously fifty-four or fifty-seven. His brother, John A. McCudden was credited with variously nine or eleven.

McCURDY, JOHN A. DOUGLAS

1886–1961

McCurdy was studying engineering at the University of Toronto when Graham Bell (qv) invited him to become a founding member of the A.E.A. in September, 1907. McCurdy's father was Graham Bell's secretary, thus the connection. Young McCurdy had been chosen to give the association expertise on structures.

Each member of the group was to design one aeroplane. McCurdy's was the last built, being completed in late 1908. Named the *Silver Dart*, it took-off from an ice covered lake at Baddeck, Nova Scotia on 23 February 1909 with McCurdy at the controls. It was the first aeroplane flight in Canada.

After the A.E.A. disbanded later that year, McCurdy founded the Canadian Aerodrome Company to build his own designs. It produced two planes before closing down. McCurdy continued in aviation though. He transmitted radio signals from an aeroplane over Sheepshead Bay, New York in August, 1910. These were the first aerial broadcasts. In January of the next year he attempted to fly the ninety-six miles from Key West, Florida to Havana. The flight ended ten miles short in shark-infested waters when the fuel ran out. McCurdy was rescued by a Navy destroyer. Despite the ditching, President Gomez of Cuba presented him with the intended $8,000 prize money. It was the effort that counted.

During World War I McCurdy directed the Curtiss factory in Canada which produced JN-3 trainers. He gave up flying altogether in 1916 because of bad eyesight. Later he entered politics and became a respected Lieutenant Governor of Nova Scotia.

On 23 February 1959, fifty years to the day after McCurdy's first flight, the RCAF flew a replica *Silver Dart* off the same frozen lake at Baddeck. McCurdy himself was the guest of honour.

McDONNELL, JAMES SMITH, JR.
1899–1980
McDonnell was born in Denver and attended Princeton. He earned an MSc from MIT, subsequently becoming an Army pilot. He took a job with Huff-Daland in 1924 but by the next year had moved on to Consolidated. He stayed there for several months before joining Stout where he helped to design the original version of what would become the Ford Tri-motor. His experience with metal aircraft landed him a job with Hamilton and he designed that company's Metalplane. While with Hamilton, he designed and built the Doodlebug, a competitor in the Guggenheim Safe Aircraft Contest. With leading edge slats and generous flaps it was a technical success, but failed to be placed because of an engine failure.

Subsequently, McDonnell spent the next three years with the Airtransport and Great Lakes companies before joining Martin in 1933 as the chief engineer in charge of landplanes. He held that post for five years. He left in late 1938 and founded his own company, finally, the next year.

During the war, his St. Louis-based firm built only sub-assemblies, though in 1943 it was awarded a contract to design the first Navy jet. The outcome of its work was the FH-1 Phantom I. Over the years, the corporation grew by leaps and bounds until 1967, when it acquired Douglas, and became the second largest military supplier in the United States. McDonnell, whose early career could certainly be described as nomadic, remained the head of the company until July, 1980. The head of the company for forty-one years, he died a month later.

McGUIRE, MAJOR THOMAS BUCHANAN, JR.
1920–1945
McGuire was born in New Jersey and upon graduating from Georgia Tech in 1941, joined the Air Corps. After an uneventful posting in Alaska, he was sent to the front lines in the South Pacific. Finally, in the thick of the fighting as he had always wanted, he began to build up an impressive kill record. He was noted for his aggressive attitude, not only to the enemy but to his fellow pilots. Their personal dislike for him didn't prevent him from risking his life to save one of theirs in combat. It was while trying to do this on 7 January 1945 that he stalled his P-38 and crashed into the sea.

He had thirty-eight kills to his credit and was thus the second highest scoring US ace of the war. In tribute to his bravery, an air base in New Jersey was named after him.

MERMOZ, JEAN
1901–1936
One of France's courageous inter-war flyers, Mermoz typified the serious pioneering pilot.

He joined the Linges Aériennes Latécoère in the mid-1920s soon rising to be their star pilot. On one flight in 1926 over the Sahara desert, his plane was forced down with engine problems. The only inhabitants of that part of the desert were Arab nomads. A group of these captured Mermoz and held him as a hostage. It was standard practice for the Arabs to kill Westerners at the time, but these decided to ransom their catch. Mermoz was exchanged for 50,000 francs.

Regaining his freedom, Mermoz continued to fly with Latécoère, helping that company pioneer many South American routes including one across the Andes into Chile. Mermoz's greatest flights were his trans-South Atlantic voyages which began in 1930. On 12 May 1930 he flew the first mail across the South Atlantic from Senegal to Brazil. In 1933 he flew the same route with six passengers in the Couzinet Arc-en-Ciel. It was the first trans-Atlantic airplane passenger flight.

This great flyer's career came to a premature conclusion when he disappeared during a South Atlantic flight in 1936. In memoriam, Saint-Exupéry (qv) wrote *Wind, Sand and Stars*, one of aviation literature's classics.

MERRIAM, FREDERICK WARREN
1880–1956

In his early twenties, Merriam was a successful antiquarian book dealer, but upon his wife's death turned to flying and received his brevet in February, 1912. He became an instructor for the Bristol flying school at Brooklands, Surrey, and in that role taught hundreds of men to fly. During World War I he continued to instruct, but after joining the RNAS, and later the RFC, he also conducted coastal patrol sorties.

Following the war he tested new aircraft, including the Saunders Kittiwake and a glider of his own design. An attempt to run a flying-boat sight-seeing business failed to earn him a steady income so he opened the aviation industry's first employment bureau.

During World War II he re-enlisted, joining the Fleet Air Arm, but bad health forced his retirement in 1944.

MESSERSCHMITT, PROFESSOR WILLY EMIL
1898–1978

Messerschmitt was born at Frankfurt am Main the son of a wine merchant. In 1910 he began to experiment with model aeroplanes, but three years later, at only fifteen, joined forces with a professional architect and together they began building full-size gliders.

During World War I Messerschmitt was exempted from military service because of bad health, so he took the opportunity to get an education at the Munich Institute of Technology. In 1923 he founded his own company. The firm's first product was a sophisticated monoplane glider built in his father's restaurant. The smells of dope and fine wine didn't mix well though and he was forced to move his 'factory'. Settling in an unused brewery in Bamberg, the company continued to build advanced gliders, but in 1924 constructed its first powered plane.

Messerschmitt slowly gained a name for himself as an innovative commercial aeroplane manufacturer. In 1927 he entered into an unusual business relationship whereby his company would only design aircraft while another company, BFW, would build them. This confusing situation evolved during the following years.

In 1934 the Bf-108 was introduced. A low wing, single-engine cabin plane, it was a remarkable advance over most sport planes of the day. It set the stage for Messerschmitt's next plane, the Bf-109 fighter, one of the most widely produced planes in history and the workhorse of the Luftwaffe in World War II.

During the war Messerschmitt endured a running battle with the German Air Ministry. Goering (qv) favoured him but Milch (qv) didn't. The company's success was predictably schizophrenic, ranging from the great Me-262 to the disastrous Me-110.

After the war, he went to Argentina where he helped to found that country's aviation industry. He returned to Germany in the early fifties, settling in Munich, where he re-established his company and even branched into automobile manufacturing.

MEUSNIER de la PLACE, LIEUTENANT JEAN-BAPTISTE MARIE
1754–1793

Meusnier was a lieutenant in the French Corps of Engineers, and widely regarded as one of the most brilliant scientific minds in Paris when, in 1784, he proposed the world's first streamlined airship. The craft was to be powered by a man-operated propeller, featured a well designed suspended nacelle, and an internal ballonet. This airship was never built, though had it been, it might have been housed in another Meusnier proposal, the aircraft hangar.

With the Revolution, Meusnier rose quickly in rank and, when killed in battle at Mainz, had attained the rank of General.

MIGNET, HENRI
1893–1965
Mignet is one of the most undeservedly maligned names in aviation history. Rather than be ridiculed, his accomplishments and goals should be lauded.

He was born the son of a provincial artist and shared with his father a fascination with nature. As a child, he carefully studied bird flight. After reading accounts of Wilbur Wright's (qv) 1908 triumphs in France, Mignet began to build gliders, writing to Gustavus Lilienthal, the brother of the dead German glider pioneer, for advice.

For his higher education, he was sent to the Bordeaux School of Electricity where he demonstrated a quick grasp of electronics. With the advent of war, he was posted to the Signal Corps, but because his unit was located near an airfield, he had an opportunity to study aircraft at close range. He spent his spare time helping the mechanics and received some plane rides in return. Once, he was allowed to taxi a Spad but in his enthusiasm gathered too much speed and flipped the fighter.

After the war, he made a career of inventing and marketing electronics components. Though he didn't become wealthy in this venture, it provided him with enough cash and time to do what he really wanted, to fly. He started in 1919 building gliders and went through a succession of failed powered designs until he developed the HM-8 in 1928. This clever, easy-to-build monoplane finally got Mignet airborne in a safe,

consistent manner. So thrilled was he by the experience that he wanted to share his joy. He contributed articles to a French flying magazine *Les Ailes* which explained how simple it was to construct the HM-8. In 1931 he published a book on constructing this plane and soon amateurs across Europe were building, and flying it.

Mignet continued to develop aircraft, always searching for a simpler design. He stated that he wasn't a pilot and couldn't make co-ordinated turns thus he was forced to find a solution. His solution came in 1934 with the advent of the 'Pou du Ciel' or 'Sky Louse'.

The Pou was a tandem wing machine with a pivoting forward wing. Its layout seemed to defy the laws of aerodynamics. It used only a stick for control, having no rudder pedals. Like many low-time pilots, Mignet couldn't co-ordinate stick and rudder so eliminated the need for them by providing a large enough tail to skid the machine into turns. The much touted 'Ercoupe' later used no rudder pedals, though it had ailerons tied into the rudder.

When Mignet published the plans for the 'Pou', he created a sensation in Europe. Even non-aeronautical journals couldn't resist the appeal of the small 'everyman's flyer' and published stories for their readers about the cute flying machine. Hundreds were started in continental garages and sheds. Though there are no exact figures as to how many were completed, a few hundred seems likely. For a year the Pou reigned supreme and offered financially limited Europeans a chance to have wings. Pou meets were organized and were always well attended. In 1935 Mignet crossed the Channel to attend a meet in England. Several companies were set up in England to market Pou kits and when word of the plane reached America, many more were built.

The joy created by Mignet ended quickly in the autumn of 1935. As more Poux became airborne, crashes occurred. The crashes were unusual in that they weren't caused by engine-outs, or structural failure, but by insidious, sudden dives from straight and level flight. Across Europe Poux were grounded until the design could be wind tunnel tested. In France and England tunnel tests showed that the plane would suddenly dive if the front wing lost its pitching moment and the rear wing continued to generate lift. Not quite understanding this phenomenon, most Poux were broken up by disappointed builders or put into storage. The indefatigable Mignet fixed the problem with a few simple modifications that made the plane safe once again, primarily moving the CG forward. But the enchanting spell had been broken and the world turned back to conventional aircraft.

Mignet continued designing planes but France listened no more. He moved to America in 1937 to build aircraft near Chicago, but returned to his homeland in 1939. During the war his wife was brutally murdered by a faction of the Resistance. In sorrow, Mignet left the country after the war and again tried to establish manufacturing companies, this time in Argentina, Brazil and Japan. Eventually he returned to France where, even though in advanced years, he continued to work in aviation. When he died, he had forty designs to his credit, and had given many people the thrill of 'Le Sport de L'Air'.

Mignet has been attacked for his lack of engineering training, poor construction methods, and, in general, silly aeroplanes. These are unfounded accusations. His training was similar to that of most of the great aviation pioneers – empirical. Many of these crashed their first designs, and most had little formal training. His construction techniques were respectable for his day, and the boxed, monospar design of the Pou wings was, in fact, a large technical advancement over most homebuilt aircraft of the 1930s which used simple planks. Tandem wing aircraft have proven to be safe and often simpler to build than conventional aircraft. The 1970s saw a resurgence of this type of planform.

Perhaps Mignet's biggest problem was that he loved aeroplanes so much and wanted to share his experience so willingly that a cynical world, not used to charity, wasn't able to receive, or appreciate, his gift. It was their loss.

MIKOYAN, ARTEM I.
1905–1970

Born in Armenia, Mikoyan attended the prestigious Zhukovsky Air Academy in Moscow from which he graduated in 1936. His first assignments entailed designing transport planes for the ZAGI Bureau. Able and aggressive, he received his own bureau shortly before World War II and collaborated with Gurevich (qv) in designing the MiG-1 fighter.

In 1944 the Red Army captured secret German designs for advanced rocket and jet fighters. These plans were given to Mikoyan who studied and adapted them to create the MiG-KB rocket fighter. In 1947 the MiG-15 appeared, the first of a long line of well designed, effective MiG jet fighters to fight against Western forces.

Mikoyan remained the head of his design bureau until his death in 1970.

MIL, MIKHAIL LEONTYEVICH
1909–1970

Mil had just graduated from school when he became involved in gyrocopter design in the early 1930s. He spent almost twenty years working for the obscure Soviet vertical flight program before finally convincing his superiors in 1947 to grant him his own design bureau. Only a year later, in 1948, the first Mil helicopter flew. The GM-1 was a simple, stress-skinned machine. In 1951 it entered production as the Mi-1 and launched Mil on a career that was to see him become the leading figure in Soviet helicopter technology. In 1952 he introduced the Mi-4, a medium size passenger and cargo helicopter of which many thousands were built.

In 1969 Mil received the Lenin Medal for his work.

MILCH, ERHARD
1892–1971

Born in Wilhelmshaven, Milch rose to become the key figure in the development of German aviation between the wars.

During World War I he served as an observer with the air service. He did not take pilot's training but a keen sense of organization earned him the command of a squadron. After the conflict, he helped Junkers (qv) organize his small airline, and this eventually brought him to the attention of the German government, which made him the director of Lufthansa in 1929. As the Nazis struggled to come to power in the early 1930s, Milch provided Hitler and other party members with free aerial transportation. The Nazi's returned the favour in 1933 when they assigned Milch the task of rebuilding the Luftwaffe, a job he was well prepared to do. One of his first tasks was to gain control of the country's aviation industry. This he did by threats and bullying. Even his old friend Junkers had to bow to his will. He forced the aging industrialist into signing over his factories to the government. Six months later the elderly pioneer died.

Milch went on despite this. He channelled millions of Reichmarks into modern airports, sophisticated communication networks, and advanced research and development programmes. In 1935, when the forbidden Luftwaffe came out of the closet, Milch could be proud of his work.

During the war he guided the production of military aircraft and was instrumental in providing funds for the Me-262 programme. It was this programme which ended his career though. Late in the war when Hitler discovered that the plane was to be used as a fighter and not a bomber, he berated Milch for disobeying orders. Milch, furious at the Führer's ignorance, shouted, 'Any child can see the plane was meant to be a fighter!' He was lucky his outburst only cost him his job.

MILES, FREDERICK GEORGE
1903–1976
MILES, GEORGE HERBERT
1911-
MILES, MAXINE FRANCES MARY
1901–1984
Frederick and George Miles were the sons of a British launderer. Frederick left school while his

father was away fighting in World War I and started a motorcycle rental business. After the war, he and some friends built a small biplane and founded a flying school. His brother George joined him at this point and over the years the company grew to own several aircraft and have a steady clientèle.

In 1932 Frederick married Lady Maxine 'Blossom' Forbes-Robertson. She was an aviation enthusiast and persuaded her husband to design an aeroplane. She, in fact, performed the stress analysis for what became the first of many Miles aircraft, the Hawk. Because they didn't have adequate facilities to build the Hawk, they made an agreement with Phillips and Powis Aircraft to put it in production. The Hawk was a great success, being faster, more modern, and more comfortable than the de Havilland Moth – and it was cheaper.

Their company built speedy racing planes along with cabin monoplanes before earning military contracts. Both Frederick and George were designers and their style tended towards innovative simplicity. At its peak, their company employed 6,000 people and seemed set for a promising future after the war. However, in 1947 the economy of Britain was in dismal shape and Miles had few orders. The company went bankrupt and its assets were sold. George joined Airspeed while Frederick started another design office. George rejoined him in 1951. Their later efforts produced few aeroplanes though they struggled on into the early 1960s.

MILLER, JESSIE MAUDE
1902–1965
In 1928, Australian 'Chubbie' Miller was the first woman to fly from England to Australia. She did this as a passenger with Bill Lancaster, a man with whom she lived though both were married to other people. Fame brought the pair to Hollywood and it was there that Miller became a pilot in her own right.

In 1929 she won a speed event at the National Air Races which earned her a contract with Fairchild. The next year she set a transcontinental speed record in an Alexander Bullet.

Her relationship with Lancaster took a strange turn when she became involved with an American writer. When the American's dead body was found with a spurious suicide note, Lancaster was indicted, though later cleared. He and Miller fled to England where they continued to live together.

In 1933 Lancaster disappeared during a flight over the Sahara and in grief, Miller gave up flying. In 1962 Lancaster's decayed body was found next to his Avro biplane.

MITCHELL, REGINALD JOSEPH

1895–1937

Mitchell was perhaps the first British casualty of World War II. Born in Stoke-on-Trent, he never received a formal aeronautical education. He was apprenticed to a locomotive factory before being hired by Supermarine in 1916. In only three years he had risen to become the firm's chief engineer and was put in charge of designing high-speed flying-boats. His efforts attracted world-wide notice in the late twenties with the thrilling Schneider Trophy victories of his S5, S6 and finally the S6B. The latter plane, which captured the trophy outright for the British, was capable of a stunning 407 mph.

In 1933 Mitchell learned that he had cancer of the rectum. A colostomy was recommended and its execution left Mitchell with an extremely uncomfortable disability. Nevertheless, he continued to design aeroplanes. A trip to Austria in the winter of 1934-35, during which he met boastful German pilots, led him to believe that war was on the horizon. He rushed home convinced that the aircraft he was already designing, a fighter, had to be a masterpiece, and had to be finished quickly.

Though suffering from his condition, Mitchell threw himself into his work, staying long hours at his office. Whether or not his condition was exasercbated by his drive to complete the project is not clear. What it certain is that he made a heroic effort for a cause that few in Britain at the time understood. His self-sacrifice in a climate of political appeasement stands as a monument for all who believe in sacrificing themselves for their country. Though Mitchell died in June 1937 the product of his gigantic effort had first flown a year earlier. The Spitfire was his great gift to a free world which could have asked for nothing more.

MITCHELL, BRIGADIER-GENERAL WILLIAM ('BILLY')

1879–1936

Mitchell exemplified the classic American warrior; tough, shrewd, and unorthodox – but to a fault.

He was born into a wealthy, influential family and counted among his youngest playmates Douglas MacArthur. The two young men decided upon military careers and while MacArthur went the traditional route to West Point and up through the ranks, Mitchell, after an education at Columbian College (now George Washington University), characteristically found his own path using his family's influence to secure himself a combat assignment to the Phillipines. In the years leading up to World War I, he toured the world from Alaska to China looking for, finding, and revelling in adventure.

In 1915 he learned to fly and the same year went to Congress demanding money for military aviation. Somehow he won his argument and the funds were provided to build an American Air Force. When the Air Service was sent to France in 1917, Mitchell went as one of its commanders. He was a fighting man above all else and led the first American air patrol over the lines in May, 1917. He then planned and led bombing missions deep behind enemy lines and even organized the first 1,000 plane raid. He also laid plans for the world's first paratrooper units, though the war's end precluded their use.

After the war, Mitchell continued to press for more military aviation, but his continual haranguing grated on the nerves of his commanding officers. He was often asked to tone down his fiery rhetoric but he ignored the warnings. In 1921 he caused his superiors much embarrassment when he sank a captured

German battleship with only a few bombs from a small formation of aeroplanes, thus disproving their belief that no capital ship could ever be sunk from the air.

He went too far in 1925 when he accused the War Department of criminal negligence in the *Shenandoah* airship tragedy. For this insubordination, he was court-martialled. He went down singing though and used the trial as a platform to cry out against the narrow-mindedness of military leaders. Mitchell only received one vote against conviction and it was probably cast by MacArthur.

Of all of Mitchell's neglected prophecies, none is more tragic than his prediction made in the *early 1920s* that the Japanese would attack Pearl Harbor, as a surprise, from the north, using carriers, and on a Sunday morning.

MOELDERS, OBERST WERNER
1913–1941

Flying did not come naturally to Moelders. The first time he flew as an Army officer he was sick – the same thing happened the second time, and frequently thereafter. He didn't give up though and eventually conquered the problem, learning to become a competent pilot.

He went with the Condor Legion to Spain in 1938 and within four months had collected fourteen kills. This tally brought him into the good graces of Goering (qv) who showered him with honours. Moelders was mature enough to accept the praise in his stride and used his new powers to bring German fighter tactics out of the First World War and into the second.

Moelders was a gifted leader who taught his junior pilots how to realize the full potential of a modern fighter plane. He abandoned the large formation flights of World War I in favour of the small 'rotte', or leader/wingman team.

When Germany invaded France in May, 1940, Moelders led Gruppe III./JG53 into battle. His victory score mounted higher as the Battle of Britain raged and in that winter he became the first pilot to surpass von Richthofen's total. He was also the first to pierce the 100 kill mark. His

tactical brilliance showed itself as Germany led the world in fighter technique, a technique that many other air forces were to follow.

He had just shot down his 115th enemy plane, a Russian, in November, 1941, when he was called back to Germany to attend Udet's (qv) funeral. En route, his plane ran out of fuel while searching for a place to land during a heavy storm. He was killed.

MOISANT, JOHN B.
1868–1910

Moisant was born in the United States to French-Canadian parents. Though trained as an architect, he sought his fortune in the jungles of Central America, moving with his brothers to El Salvador in 1896. There they acquired extensive sugar-producing properties and became involved in political intrigue. When his brothers were arrested by the dictator of that country, Moisant gathered a group of mercenaries in Nicaragua with which he hoped to secure their release. His 'army' turned tail at the first sounds of gunfire in El Salvador leaving Moisant to try again. His next attempt also failed, but eventually his brothers were released.

By now, Moisant was on good terms with Nicaragua's dictator whom he had helped to reach power. This dictator, Zelaya, in 1910 requested that he go to France to purchase an aircraft. Moisant lost no time in going to Paris where he learned to fly on Blériots after fruitlessly attempting to build two aircraft of his own design.

Not long after learning to fly he became the first to fly a passenger from London to Paris. He then left for America to participate in the Gordon-Bennett Belmont Park Meet. He achieved fame in this meet when he impulsively purchased Leblanc's (qv) Blériot to participate in the Statue of Liberty race. His own machine had been damaged and Leblanc was too injured to fly. He paid the Frenchman $10,000, twice the machine's worth. His entry technically broke the rules, but he was allowed to fly anyway and came in first, beating Grahame-White (qv).

Later, he was judged disqualified after numerous aviators cried foul.

At the meet, Moisant got together a band of aviators from France and the United States and took them on a raucous, wild tour of America with an interesting side trip to Mexico.

The 'Moisant International Aviators' was a well-planned travelling circus that brought aviation thrills to many of the big cities across the southern states. While in Texas, the Mexican President asked them to conduct reconnaissance flights over insurgent positions near the border. Moisant, perhaps nostalgic for his mercenary days, agreed. His flyers were thus the first to fly airplanes over a battlefield.

When the troupe hit New Orleans in December, Moisant's career came to a sudden end. While coming in for a landing, his plane overturned, whereupon he was thrown out. He broke his neck.

His brother, Alfred, opened a flying school at Garden City, Long Island the next year and his sister, Matilde, was briefly an exhibition pilot.

MOLLISON, JAMES ALLAN
1905–1959
Born in Lanark, Scotland, Mollison was commissioned in the RAF in 1923. For several years he flew mail routes for Australian National Airways but then embarked on a career as a competitive pilot in 1931. That year he lowered the Australia to England record to eight days twenty-one hours. Other flights included London to Capetown in four days seventeen-and-a-half-hours, and Lympne to Rio to 3·5 days – the first flight from England to South America. Mollison worked hard for his achievements and several times collapsed from exhaustion at the end of a long flight. After setting a speed record of nineteen hours fifty-nine minutes from New York to London in 1936, a reporter asked Mollison what he felt like. Climbing wearily out of his Bellanca he replied, 'A scotch and soda'.

Married for a time to Amy Johnson (qv), Mollison served with distinction in Ferry Command during World War II.

Étienne and Joseph Montgolfier who turned paper bags into flying machines.

de MONTGOLFIER, JOSEPH-MICHEL
1740–1810
de MONTGOLFIER, JACQUES-ÉTIENNE
1745–1799
The first of the many brother teams in aviation history, the Montgolfiers owned a paper manufacturing business near Lyon, France. Both were fertile inventors who introduced many improvements in the manufacture of paper and it was while experimenting with paper bags that they noticed how when hot air was collected in a bag, the bag tended to become buoyant. They then built large paper balloons which they filled with steam, but soon changed to smoke because as the steam cooled its residual water weighed down the bags. With the smoke, the bags rose easily and they realized that their discovery was of great importance.

They were invited to display their balloons to the Académie des Sciences in Paris which they did. A successful demonstration of an unmanned, full-scale balloon to this group led to an invitation from the king to show their novelty at Versailles. They built a new balloon for this important demonstration and painted it blue and gold in honour of the king.

On 19 September 1783 this balloon was launched with three animals as cargo. The first manned flight came on 21 November of that year.

Only Joseph ever flew in a balloon and then only once. In 1784 he ascended in *Le Flesseles*, a mammoth balloon, at Lyon.

MOORE-BRABAZON, JOHN THEODORE CUTHBERT
1884–1964

Moore-Brabazon was certainly *the* classic Edwardian aviator. He began his career in aviation during the balloon days, and died during the Space Race.

Born into a wealthy, aristocratic family, in late 1908 he became the first Englishman to fly – in a Voisin biplane in France (see footnote). The next spring he purchased a Voisin which he entitled *The Bird of Passage*. He brought it to England where he made what was considered at the time the first flight by an Englishman in England. This distinction has also been claimed for Roe (qv). On 30 October 1909 he won the *Daily Mail* £1,000 prize for the first circular mile (1.61km) flight in Britain on an all-British machine. The next year, ever ready to advance aeronautics, he took a pig aloft. This stunt was intended to end the ancient retort, 'Pigs might fly!'

During World War I he turned to more serious matters and led the development of photographic reconnaissance techniques for the RFC. Attached to the 1st Wing in France, Brabazon and his crews laid the foundation for this crucial aspect of military aviation.

After the war, he fulfilled many governmental duties including acting as secretary to the Secretary of State for Air, secretary to the

Minister of Transport, Chairman of the Airmails Committee, and assessor at the R101 inquiry. He was also a Member of Parliament. During World War II he was Minister of Transport and later Minister of Aircraft Production. In 1942 he was created a peer, taking the title Lord Brabazon of Tara. He also made an important survey of post-war civil aviation.

Well liked and a friend to many, Brabazon was a long-time member of the Royal Aeronautical Society whose chair he held for a number of years. He also held the Aero Club of Great Britain's Aviator Certificate No. 1.

Note: Though English by birth, Henry Farman, who flew before Brabazon, lived most of his life in France and later changed his nationality.

Brothers in aviation Léon and Robert Morane.

MORANE, LÉON
1885–1918
MORANE, ROBERT CHARLES
1886-1968

Léon Morane was the competition manager for Blériot (qv) before turning to aircraft manufacturing in association with his brother Robert, and Gabriel Borel (qv) in 1911. With Borel, they built one monoplane but design philosophy differences caused the team to disband in October of that year. The Moranes then took on another partner, Raymond Saulnier (qv) who had designed the Blériot XI.

The three Frenchmen formed Morane-Saulnier, a company which soon became synonymous with speedy monoplanes. One of their factory fliers was Roland Garros (qv). The company survived for many years as one of France's best known aviation firms, but political pressures forced it out of business in the late 1966.

MOSS, DR SANFORD A.

1872–1949

Moss was a native San Franciscan who went east to earn a Ph.D. in engineering at Cornell University. Upon graduation, he went to work for General Electric with the task of developing highly efficient turbines. At GE, he began to experiment with gas driven turbines. Though quite near to inventing the turbojet engine, his only goal was to develop a turbo-supercharger for conventional piston engines. During World War I he built a turbo-supercharger that was tested by the military with excellent results. Taken to the top of Pike's Peak, it enabled a Liberty engine to continuously sustain combustion in the rarefied air of 14,109 feet (4,300m).

The war's end almost killed the development of this device but enough money was found to equip a Le Pere biplane with a turbo-supercharged Liberty engine. This aeroplane then set an altitude record of 38,180 feet (11,637m).

Moss's work wasn't fully appreciated until 1939 when its installation on B-17 bombers dramatically improved their performance.

MOZHAISKI, ALEXANDER FEODOROVITCH

1825–1890

For many years the Soviet Union claimed that Mozhaiski invented the airplane. This assertion is utterly false, but Mozhaiski, a naval officer, nevertheless did build an interesting flying-machine in 1883.

Somewhat similar to the Henson (qv) design, his aircraft used two British steam engines to generate thirty horsepower (22kw). This power was transmitted to three large propellers, one fore and two aft, of its large, square wing. There

was a cockpit, of sorts, in the centre of the wing and the whole aeroplane with would-be pilot was launched down a ramp. In 1884 this machine was tested near St. Petersburg, and managed to hop into the air. The lift was mostly generated by the speed built up after its downhill run, and not by the pulling power of the propellers. Unable to sustain itself, without controls, overweight and under-powered, Mozhaiski's machine was a valiant try, but certainly not the first aeroplane to fly.

MUNK, MAX MICHAEL

1890–1986

Munk was born in Hamburg and despite his family's wishes that he become a rabbi, selected a scientific career. He was educated at the Hanover Technische Hochschule and later at the University of Göttingen where he received an excellent education in theoretical aerodynamics. During World War I he performed research for the German aviation industry, but in 1920 was persuaded to emigrate to America. On his arrival he joined NACA in Washington.

While with NACA, Munk explained why predictions made from wind tunnel data were so often divergent from actual full-scale test results. He said that airflow over a wing in a wind tunnel is at a different density than total airflow over a full-scale wing. He suggested factoring-in the Reynold's Number to scale results and to test aerofoils in variable density tunnels. A VDT was built at Langley and soon tunnel testing became a reliable development tool.

Munk left NACA in 1927 and spent the rest of his career at various, often minor, teaching posts.

NAVARRE, SOUS-LIEUTENANT JEAN MARIE DOMINIQUE

1895–1919

Navarre was the son of a wealthy manufacturer and was engaged in civilian flying lessons when World War I started. He finished his lessons in September and joined a Maurice Farman unit,

MF 8. Life as a reconnaissance pilot bored the energetic young pilot so he requested a transfer to a Morane fighter squadron. Navarre had a poor discipline record so the request was denied. Constant badgering finally prompted his superiors to let him switch which he did in early 1915. On 1 April of that year he scored France's third aerial victory when he shot down an Aviatik. For this action he received the Médaille Militaire.

Navarre was indeed a maverick. When not hunting Germans he would hunt ducks – by air in his Morane armed with a shotgun! In early 1916 when he transferred to a Nieuport squadron he painted his plane a challenging bright red. He hoped to entice the enemy into battle, which he did, and by June, 1916 had twelve confirmed victories. That month he was shot down himself and severely injured. It took him two years to recover. He returned to duty in the summer of 1918 but friends, knowing his recovery wasn't complete, managed to keep him from returning to the front where they knew he would be killed.

After the war, Navarre was practicing for a victory display during which he planned, unannounced, to fly under the Arc de Triomphe, when he was killed striking a telephone pole at 100 mph (161km/hr).

NESTEROV, LIEUTENANT PETR NIKOLAEVICH
1887–1914

On 9 September 1913 Lieutenant Nesterov, of the Russian Air Service, was placed under house arrest for ten days when his commanding officer learned that he had endangered government property. His crime was that he had performed the first loop in history. When word of Nesterov's action in his Nieuport reached Western Europe, it created such an uproar that he was not only released, but promoted to Captain!

Less than a year later, Nesterov was commanding the XI Corps Air Squadron when Germany and Austria invaded Russia. On 26 August 1914 he took off in an unarmed Morane-

Saulnier to intercept a flight of Austrian planes that had just bombed his airfield. Singling out the lead plane, he rammed straight into it. Both planes fell, killing their pilots.

NEWMAN, LARRY
1947–

If Newman had been born fifty years earlier, it would be easy to imagine him as an exhibition pilot making his living flying town-to-town amazing the locals.

Newman was born in Los Angeles the son of an entrepreneur. His father taught him to fly when still in his teens, and later sent him to a flight school to earn advanced licences. Newman hated school but went to college for two years anyway. This failed to hold his interest so he became a cargo pilot. He had built up 4,000 hours flying time when still in his midtwenties. In 1974 he learned to hang glide after moving to Albuquerque. In Albuquerque, he met Ben Abruzzo (qv) who helped him to start a hang glider manufacturing business that in three years became the largest in the world. In 1978 Abruzzo invited him to participate in the *Double Eagle II* crossing of the Atlantic. Newman went along, intent on hang gliding down to earth upon reaching France. He had to abandon this plan, though, and release the glider from the balloon to save weight during the final stage of the voyage.

After the flight, Newman returned to commercial aviation, but later founded an ultralight company that built an advanced composite machine. Few were sold due to its high price. He also participated in the first balloon crossing of the Pacific with Aoki (qv). In 1986 he hoped to fly a balloon around the world but this project was never realized.

de NIÉ PORT (NIEUPORT), ÉDOUARD
1875–1911

Nieuport, who changed the spelling of his name for business purposes, was born in French Algiers. He trained as an engineer before founding his own company in 1909 at Issy. His first monoplane appeared in 1910, causing an immediate sensation. Its diminutive size and careful attention to streamlining earned its builder a reputation as a force to be reckoned with. In 1911, Nieuport set a speed record in another of his monoplanes, flying a brisk 82.73 mph (134.72km/hr). On 15 September of that year, he was killed when the aircraft he was demonstrating crashed in front of a French military audience. His brother Charles continued his work but in 1913 he too died in a crash.

Arctic explorer, Umberto Nobile.

NOBILE, GENERAL UMBERTO
1885–1978

Nobile was born near Salerno and studied engineering. He became an airship designer for the Italian government, and when it sold an airship to the Norwegian explorer R. Amundsen (qv), Nobile was appointed as the captain. Amundsen planned to use the airship, the *Norge,* to become the first to fly over the North Pole, but was beaten in the attempt by Richard Byrd (qv). Amundsen and

Nobile then decided to make the first trans-Polar flight. They left Spitzbergen, north of Norway, on 11 May 1926 and three days later landed at Teller, Alaska. Nobile was hailed as a hero in the American press while Amundsen was nearly forgotten. The two became bitter rivals.

With his new found fame, Nobile organized another Polar flight in 1928. On 23 May of that year he commanded the *Italia* dirigible on an exploration flight across the Polar ice cap. The severe Arctic conditions hampered progress and finally on 25 May it crashed into the ground. A distress call was heard by a Russian farmer on a crude radio. His report launched a world-wide rescue effort with ships and aircraft from many nations participating. Amundsen joined the effort but his flying-boat disappeared without trace.

On 23 June a Swedish rescue plane landed at the crash site. The pilot was under orders to carry off Nobile, as other rescue planes were on their way. Nobile protested, saying that another member of the crew should go first, but eventually he gave in. It was nearly two months before the rest of the crew was rescued, and one had died during that time.

Back in Italy, Nobile was charged with dereliction of duty and was in danger of being shot. Anti-airship forces in the Air Force were conspiring against him. He was convicted but spared capital punishment. He emigrated to the Soviet Union where he designed airships, and in 1939 moved to the United States where he taught in an aeronautics school. After World War II he returned to Italy to clear his name, which he successfully did.

NOORDUIJN, ROBERT B. CORNELIUS
1893–

Noorduijn was the son of a Dutch father and English mother. He studied in Holland and Germany before moving to England in 1913. There, he worked for Sopwith before switching to Armstrong-Whitworth around the outbreak of the war. At Armstrong-Whitworth he served under Koolhoven (qv) who then brought him to BAT in 1917.

Glad to have an opportunity to return to Holland, Noorduijn joined Fokker (qv) in 1920. In 1924 he was sent to America to establish a Fokker factory which he did in New Jersey, but under the name Netherlands Aircraft Manufacturing Company. Noorduijn's first design in the US was the Universal, though he had previously recommended fitting three engines onto a Fokker F VII, thus creating the great Fokker Tri-motor.

In 1929 he left Fokker to work for Bellanca, changing again in 1931 to work for Pitcairn. In 1934 Noorduijn, now using the spelling Noorduyn, opened his own factory in Montreal to build robust single-engined cargo planes. His Universal had earlier received many Canadian orders and he was familiar with the harsh flying conditions of Canada's upper regions. In 1935 the first Noorduyn Norseman flew and it became an immediate success. Ultimately, 919 examples were built.

NORTHCLIFFE, LORD
(*see* Alfred Harmsworth)

NORTHROP, JOHN KNUDSON
1895–1981

Northrop was born in Newark, New Jersey and went with his parents to California in 1904. In 1916 he joined the Loughead brothers (qv) and helped design the F-1 flying-boat. He served briefly in the Signal Corps during 1917–18 but immediately returned to Loughead. When this company folded he moved on to Douglas (qv) and there participated in the design of the World Cruisers. In 1926 he returned to his friends, the Loughead brothers who had reformed the company and offered him the chance to design a stressed skin fuselage aircraft. The beautiful Vega was the product of his effort. In 1928 he left again, this time to found his own company which he called Avion. Avion was soon purchased by United Aircraft and Transport which ran it as Northrop Aircraft. Under this arrangement, Northrop designed the highly advanced Alpha and Beta monoplanes.

UA&T merged Northrop Aircraft with Stearman and moved the operation to Kansas. Northrop refused to leave California and managed to get Douglas (qv) to back him in establishing his own company as a subsidiary of Douglas. The new Northrop Corporation continued its founder's tradition of building advanced stressed skin aluminium aircraft. Its products included the Gamma, Delta, and XBT-1. The latter was to become the famous Dauntless dive-bomber.

In 1937 Northrop was plagued by union problems and the only solution was to be completely absorbed by Douglas. In 1939 Northrop tried yet again to launch a company. This time he concentrated on flying-wings and during the 1940s produced a series of truly amazing flying-wing bombers.

NORWAY, NEVIL SHUTE
1899–1960

Better known by his pen name 'Nevil Shute', Norway was born in Ealing, London. During World War I he attempted to join, but was not accepted into, the RFC. A stammer precluded this so instead he joined the infantry.

After the war he earned a degree at Oxford and then, in 1923, became a stress calculator for de Havilland. That year he also learned to fly. In 1924 he joined Vickers where he was assigned to work with Barnes Wallis (qv) on the R-100 project. In 1926 he published the first of twenty-five books. Entitled *Marazan* it was about a young pilot involved with murder and smuggling.

In 1931 Norway and several partners founded Airspeed Ltd. This company produced several designs which were used to good effect in World War II including the Oxford and the Horsa glider. In 1948 the company was merged with de Havilland. Norway had already left in 1938 to devote himself to writing.

After the war he settled in Australia and all his later novels were set there. His most famous work is *On the Beach*, a novel concerning the horrors of a nuclear war.

NOWOTNY, MAJOR WALTER
1920–1944

Nowotny was an Austrian pilot whose combat career didn't begin until February, 1941. Stationed on the Eastern Front, at first he only gradually gained kills. His first, in fact, only came after five months. During 1942, as a member of the fighter unit JG54, his score rose more quickly and by the end of the year he had over fifty. The year 1943 saw him shoot down in excess of 100 planes, a phenomenal tally.

In July, 1944 Galland (qv) chose him to organize the world's first jet fighter unit. This unit, Kommando Nowotny, named in his honour, pioneered jet fighter tactics. Nowotny was killed in a dogfight in November, 1944. He had 258 confirmed kills to his credit.

NUNGESSER, SOUS-LIEUTENANT CHARLES EUGENE JULES MARIE
1892–1927

Born in Paris, Nungesser drifted around the world during the first decade of the century seeking adventure. When the war started, he was working as a rancher in Argentina, but immediately returned to France. Back in his homeland he joined the cavalry. In 1915 he transferred to the air corps and flew Voisin bombers in the Verdun sector. In November he joined Escadrille N. 65 where he began his career as a fighter pilot.

Nungesser was a capable fighter but was several times shot and wounded himself. He was involved in an unlikely string of accidents that frequently kept him grounded. If he wasn't in a hospital recovering from bullet wounds, he'd be grounded to recover from broken bones sustained in a landing accident, or a car crash. His wounds crippled him so much that when he insisted that he be returned to active duty, the only way for him to get to and from his plane was to be carried by his mechanics in a chair!

His victories continued, though, and he ended the war with forty-five kills, making him the third ranking French ace.

After the war he returned to his drifting ways, becoming a wandering barnstormer in America.

A popular celebrity, Nungesser married the wealthy Miss Consuelo Hatmaker, the heiress to the original Sutter's Mill 1849 gold rush fortune.

In a final effort to relive the glories of World War I, he planned a trans-Atlantic flight in 1927 with his co-pilot Coli (qv). Together they took off from Paris on 9 May 1927 in the Levavasseur biplane, *L'Oiseau Blanc*, headed for New York. They were never seen again.

OBERTH, HERMANN JULIUS
1894–1989

Several people have been given the title of 'Father of Modern Rocketry', but few deserve this more than Hermann Oberth.

Oberth was born in Transylvania (today part of Romania) and was studying medicine in Munich when World War I started. He joined the infantry, but after being wounded transferred to the ambulance corps. As an ambulance driver he had plenty of time to ponder the emerging sciences of the new century and it was at this time that he devised a proposal for a liquid fuel rocket. His ideas were put before military experts who dismissed them as ridiculous.

After the war he continued his education in Germany, but now he studied physics, chemistry and mathematics. He had decided to devote his life to the development of interplanetary travel. His doctoral thesis, on this subject, was rejected at Heidelberg. Undeterred, Oberth had it privately printed and to his surprise it sold briskly.

In 1928 the great German film director, Fritz Lang, decided to capitalize on the enthusiasm generated by the book by making a film based on space flight. For the film *The Girl in the Moon*, Lang hired Oberth as technical director. Oberth's job was twofold. He had to design the rocket ship and launching facilities that would be built as props for the film and also quite incredibly, he was asked to build an actual liquid fuel rocket which could be launched on the day the film premièred, as a publicity stunt.

Oberth accepted both tasks but naturally found the second very difficult. With only minimum funds he still managed to build and test several combustion chambers though a working rocket was beyond his skill. The film premiered without the rocket stunt and still became a big hit.

Oberth retired from rocketry to teach, but in 1930 the German government asked him to accept a research grant for rocketry experimentation. He agreed and proceeded to establish laboratories in Berlin. By then he was already a 'cult' figure to young German engineering students, several of whom volunteered to assist him without pay. One of these students was von Braun (qv). Oberth and his assistants achieved a measure of success by developing a combustion chamber that produced supersonic exhaust speeds.

By the mid-thirties, other German rocket research groups had been formed whose achievements surpassed Oberth's. During the war he worked at Peenemünde with the unusual arrangement that his former assistant, von Braun, now became his boss. After the war he emigrated to the United States as a missile adviser, and in the mid-eighties witnessed the launch of a Space Shuttle.

von OHAIN, DR HANS
1911–

Von Ohain was only twenty-two years old in 1933 when he first conceived the idea of a continuous cycle combustion engine. A brilliant student who earned his doctorate in four years, instead of the usual seven, he discussed his idea for a jet engine with a supportive college professor. This man encouraged his student to patent the ideas and then try to build a working model. With limited funds, the young engineer went to a small machine shop where he and a mechanic built a working prototype. The crudely made engine didn't work very well, but it encouraged von Ohain to seek the financial support of Ernst Heinkel (qv) who was then known to be a patron of radical concepts – especially those which would lead to higher speeds.

Heinkel enthusiastically received von Ohain and offered him, in April, 1936, the unrestricted use of his vast facilities. Within a year a small test engine using a centrifugal compressor had been built. It used hydrogen as fuel and worked well enough to impress Heinkel as to its enormous potential. He ordered a full-scale engine.

Von Ohain and a team of engineers bent to the task of developing a truly airworthy powerplant. Heinkel wanted one as soon as possible. In the short time of two years an engine and airframe had been built and on 27 August 1939 it made the world's first true jet powered flight.

The jet engine, which could have drastically changed the fortunes of war for Germany in World War II, became a political football that was tossed between various Nazi factions. By the war's end, jet engined aircraft saw only limited action.

During the war, von Ohain continued to develop his powerplant. He helped to introduce the axial flow compressor, a type which eventually became used on almost all modern jet engines.

OLDS, BRIGADIER-GENERAL ROBIN
1922–

Despite many heroic actions few individual combatants stand out as heroes of the Vietnam War in the American national memory. Robin Olds became one of the few.

Olds was an Army child born in Honolulu to an Air Corps general. A gifted athlete, he was an All-American tackle for the West Point football team in 1942. Within two years he was competing on a different field, this time in the cockpit of a Lightning over Europe. Flying P-38s and later Mustangs, Olds shot down 13 enemy aircraft during the course of 107 combat missions. He destroyed a further 11·5 on the ground.

After the war he joined the first squadron to be equipped with P-80s and in 1946 came second in the Jet Division of the Thompson Trophy Race in Cleveland. Subsequent assignments took him to England where, as part of an officer exchange programme between the US and Britain, he commanded No. 1 Fighter Squadron at RAF Tangmere, and later Germany, Libya and Thailand.

In 1966, with the Vietnam War heating up, Olds became the Commander of the 8th Tactical Fighter Wing at Ubon, Thailand. At the relatively advanced age of 44 he was back in combat, this time flying Phantoms, a jet which could fly four times faster than his old P-38. Flying over enemy territory 105 times, he downed two MiG-17s and two MiG-21s. In total he flew 152 combat missions before permanently giving up his combat career. He returned to the US in 1967 to serve as Commandant of Cadets at the Air Force Academy.

von OPEL, FRITZ
1899–1971

Von Opel was the heir to the huge Opel manufacturing empire. In the late 1920s he decided to combine his two interests, automobiles and aeroplanes, and gain some publicity for the family firm. To this end, he enlisted the aid of F. W. Sander, a rocket expert. Sander designed a cluster of rockets which in turn were installed in a gutted race car. When tested on 15 March 1928, this became the first rocket-propelled car.

The first-rocket propelled aircraft was built by Lippisch (qv). When this craft, a canard, was tested on 11 June 1928, it succeeded in making the first rocket-propelled flight in history (pilot Fritz Stamer). This aircraft was very unstable and later crashed.

Von Opel became the second pilot to fly a rocket-powered craft (sustained flight). This flight occurred on 30 September 1929 when he piloted the *RAK 1*, a rocket-powered Hatry glider.

These episodes gained the desired publicity for von Opel, but they were of no practical significance.

OSBORN, EARL DODGE
1893–1988

Osborn was educated at Princeton and upon graduating went to Europe as an ambulance driver during World War I. On his return to the United States, he helped to organize Aero Marine Airways, a small concern which quickly folded. From this experience, he recognized the need for modern flying-boats. In 1924 he became the editor of *Aviation* magazine, a post he held for five years.

In 1925 he formed a company, EDO, (after his initials), to build a flying-boat. Though it flew, Osborn decided to concentrate on building quality floats as an after-market product. In 1926 the first set of EDO floats was fitted to a Waco 9. They proved completely satisfactory and a new industry was born.

OSTERKAMP, OBERLEUTNANT ZURSEE THEODORE
1892-1975

Osterkamp was too weak to be accepted into the German Army at the outbreak of World War I. By luck, he managed to get into the Volunteer Naval Flying Corps where he became a pilot. After flying with No. 2 Marine Fliegerabteilung for most of 1916 in observation planes, in the spring of 1917 he switched to fighters.

On 14 April Osterkamp had the chance to go on his first patrol. On take-off, he cracked-up his machine and was grounded by his commander. After all his comrades had taken off, Osterkamp jumped in another machine and followed them. On this maiden patrol flight he shot down an SE-5. This was the start of a headstrong career.

In a little over one year, Osterkamp claimed thirty-two victories, though he was shot down once. Following peace in the West, he and other German pilots were sent to fight the Bolsheviks in Eastern Europe. During World War II he scored six more victories before being taken off combat duties. He was then in command of various fighter units.

OVINGTON, EARLE L.
1879–1936

Ovington was an intelligent young man who was an assistant to Thomas Edison even before he had finished his education. In 1911 he learned to fly at the Pau Blériot school, returning home that year with a Type XI.

On 14 September 1911 he used a Queen monoplane (a copied Type XI) to carry the first official airmail in the United States. This flight occurred during the International Aviation Tournament at Garden City, NY, and he had to be specially sworn in by the Postmaster-General to carry mail. The mail was collected at the Meet and flown in sacks lying on Ovington's lap three miles to Mineola where they were dropped near a temporary post office.

Ovington won the Boston Globe Prize in 1911 for an air race in New England but soon faded from the aviation scene. He was a Lieutenant-Commander in the US Navy during World War I and later entered the consulting field. He also owned an air terminal in Santa Barbara, California.

PAGE, SIR FREDERICK HANDLEY
1885–1962

Page was born in Cheltenham and studied electrical engineering at Finsbury Technical College. An industrious scholar, at only twenty-one he became the chief product designer at Johnson and Phillips, a large electrical manufacturing company. Like so many other young electrical engineers of the time, Page was really more interested in aviation.

Initially he experimented on some models with Jose Weiss (qv) but started his own company in 1909. That same year he built his first plane, the *Blue Bird*. The next year he introduced the *Yellow Peril*. Its main feature was a crescent-shaped wing which Page hoped would provide more control and safety, attributes he was to strive for all his career.

Early in World War I, the Admiralty's Commodore Murray Sueter asked Page to produce 'a bloody paralyser of an aeroplane to stop the Hun in his tracks.' Less than a year later the designer responded with the HP 0/100, the company's first of many large bombers and transports.

In 1920 Page introduced leading edge slots which lowered landing speeds. All RAF planes were subsequently required to have these. He was especially proud of the HP 42 commercial airliner of 1930 which after ten years of service had caused no fatalities.

As Britain struggled economically during the 1950–70s, Page faced one last battle – to keep his company independent. Not willing to lock step with 'central planners', his company lost government orders. Page died in 1962. His company, one of the first to be formed to build airplanes in Britain, died eight years later.

PARK, AIR CHIEF MARSHAL SIR KEITH RODNEY
1892-1975

Born in Thames, New Zealand, Park entered the Army in 1911, transferring to the RFC in 1917. He gained 20 victories. During the inter-war years, he rose up through successive RAF staff positions to become the able commander of No. 11 Fighter Group during the Battle of Britain. Park's group protected the aerial gateway to London and he often flew with his men, piloting a Hurricane.

Later war commands included Air Officer Commanding Egypt, later Malta, and Allied Air Commander in Chief of South-East Asia. After retiring from service, Park returned to New Zealand where he represented Hawker-Siddeley.

von PARSEVAL, MAJOR AUGUST
1861–1942

Von Parseval was a German military officer who in 1897 invented the Drachenballon (kite balloon). This type of balloon was a major improvement over spherical observation balloons because it was much steadier in flight, thus allowing more accurate reconnaissance. This type of observation platform was extensively used by both the Germans and the Allies during World War I.

Von Parseval next introduced a flexible airship, in 1906, that could be quickly deployed or taken down. When not in use, it was easily rolled up into a small area which made it ideal for transporting behind a mobile army. His dirigibles attracted buyers from other countries including Russia, Austria, Britain and Japan.

Later in his career he became a professor at the Technical Academy in Berlin.

PATTERSON, WILLIAM ALLAN
1899–1980

Patterson was born in Hawaii where his father worked as the manager of a sugar plantation. After his father died his mother put him in a military academy and moved to San Francisco. Patterson hated the school and ran away. He got to San Francisco at the age of fifteen and went to work in a Wells Fargo bank. He worked his way up and after about ten years had the authority to make substantial loans. One of his loans was made to Pacific Air Transport which was operating a line along the west coast. Patterson became more and more involved with the airlines operating in that region and formally joined Boeing Air Transport in 1929.

BAT acquired more routes and became known as United Airlines. Patterson became the President of United in 1934 when it was forcibly parted from Boeing under the Black-McKellar Act. Patterson was to hold that post until 1963. His career was notable for the introduction of stewardesses, and for making United the first US company to commit itself to buying commercial jets.

PATTLE, SQUADRON LEADER MARMADUKE THOMAS ST. JOHN
1914–1941

Largely unsung in his short lifetime, post-war analysis shows that Pattle, a South African, was probably the highest scoring RAF pilot of the war, with fifty-one victories. Pattle claimed his first victory while flying with No. 80 Squadron in North Africa in 1940. Late in that year, he was sent to Greece and from November of that year until April, 1941 consistently scored victories. The problem in computing Pattle's true score was the remoteness of the locales in which he fought. Many of his combats were flown over water with a consequent lack of evidence left to prove a claim. With twenty-eight confirmed kills to his credit, Pattle was shot down in April, 1941 over Athens while diving to the rescue of a comrade under attack.

Marmaduke Pattle, fighter ace from South Africa.

PAULHAN, LOUIS
1883–1963

Paulhan's first connection with aviation was when he served in the French balloon corps shortly after the turn of the century. Upon discharge he went to work as a mechanic for the Astra Balloon works near Paris, but when Santos-Dumont (qv) made his historic flight in November 1906, Paulhan decided to switch from aerostats to aeroplanes. In 1908 he won a model aeroplane contest that offered the astonishing prize of a Voisin biplane (sans engine)! Friends helped him purchase a Gnome engine which, when installed, became the first of its kind used in an aircraft. He taught himself to fly on this machine at Douai in July 1909.

In August, 1909 he participated in the Rheims Meet, coming third in the Grand Prix contest. In early 1910 he went to the United States where he won a $10,000 prize for a long distance flight in California. His greatest aerial conquest also took place that year when he defeated Grahame-White (qv) in the epic London to Manchester *Daily Mail* race.

During World War I he attempted to supply aircraft to the French government, but had little success. From 1916 until 1918 he served as a fighter pilot.

PAULY, SAMUEL JOHANNES
1766–1819
EGG, URS CHRISTIAN (DURS)
1748-1831

Little is known of Pauly and Egg, though their joint balloon project in Regency England was quite remarkable.

Pauly, like his future partner Egg, was Swiss. He was a professional engineer living in France during 1804-5 when he received the backing of Marshall Ney to construct a dirigible. An oblong craft with fins and rotating blades was constructed but wasn't navigable when tested.

Pauly moved to London to capitalise on the booming armaments trade during the Napoleonic wars, and it was there in 1812 that he patented the first centre-fire brass cartridge, the forerunner of nearly all modern bullets. He was hired by the gun-maker Durs Egg, whose workshops in Pall Mall had produced some of the finest weapons of the day, to build another dirigible. Egg, who had made guns for George III, personally financed the project.

Pauly's design was as delightful to look at as it was technically advanced. The gas bag was moulded over a wooden frame from very expensive goldbeater's skin, (70,000 cow stomachs) in the shape of a huge fish. Named the *Dolphin* for its shape, it was to be propelled by large oars. Its most interesting feature was a provision for trim control via a sandbox suspended on a rope running from the nacelle to the tail. It was built in Brompton, not far from Buckingham Palace, in a large shed that was the world's first aircraft hangar.

Egg's goal was to run an air passenger service between London and Paris. He projected that the trip would take ten hours. A contemporary London newspaper lauded the project because: 'This scheme bids defiance to the usual exactions of inn-keepers, the customary search for custom-house officers, and all the ordinary impediments which so frequently annoy sensitive travellers.'

Unfortunately, sensitive travellers would have to wait another hundred years for air travel between the two capitals because Pauly died leaving an unfinished project. Egg lost his entire investment and suffered the embarrassment of hearing the project ridiculed as 'Egg's Folly'.

Part of the dirigible did fly however. P. T. Barnum later purchased the inner ballonet which, when inflated, had enough bouyancy to lift Tom Thumb as part of his circus act.

PEARSE, RICHARD WILLIAM
1877–1953

Pearse was a New Zealand farmer and engineer who attempted to fly an aircraft in March, 1904. His machine was a monoplane powered by an engine of his own design. His test hops later led to claims by others that he had flown before the Wright brothers (qv). Pearse wrote in 1915 that his trials had not been successful and confirmed their dates as the spring of 1904. A cursory inspection of his 1906 patent application shows that the plane could not have flown.

Despite its naïve crudity, the plane had a number of features that confirm the fact that Pearse was an intelligent designer. These included a tricycle landing-gear, a steerable nose-wheel, and a type of aileron.

In 1925 he began the construction of a second aeroplane. This one was to be a STOL machine. It featured a tilt engine, variable pitch prop, and an anti-torque rear rotor. In construction it was as crude as the first plane and, like it, it never flew.

Perhaps the most interesting facet of Pearse's history is that in later years his followers persisted in claims that even *he* said weren't true.

During the war he was a combat pilot but was shot down and died from a bullet wound to the neck.

PEMBERTON-BILLING, NOEL
1881–1948

Pemberton-Billing had made his fortune as a yacht salesman and gun-runner in the early years of the century. In 1908 he built three monoplanes. The last of the trio, with tricycle landing gear, managed to hop. So proud of the hop was Billing that he dragged a *Flight* magazine reporter to the site who, after looking at the wheel tracks under a magnifying glass, confirmed the lift-off. Billing later wrote that he knew this wasn't really a flight. In 1912 he founded Pemberton-Billing Ltd to build racing hulls, and aircraft in Southampton. When Britain went to war he contacted Admiral Murray Sueter inquiring as to the aircraft needs of the Navy. So informed, he set his factory to work building a biplane, the design of which he had chalked on the factory walls. According to Billing's account no one was allowed to leave the shop until the plane was completed. In six days and ten hours the PB IX was rolled out.

Billing briefly joined the RNVR and organized an attack against Zeppelin sheds near Lake Constance. He then left the confines of the military to run for Parliament. His noisy platform included vicious attacks against the government which he claimed was not providing adequate protection against Zeppelin attacks on London. He also decried the government's involvement in aircraft manufacturing. His calls were answered when more squadrons were assigned to protect the capital and the Royal Aircraft Factory was forced to end aircraft production. During one of his speeches he used the term 'Fokker Fodder' to describe the inferior quality of British combat planes.

His company's telegram address was Supermarine, and in 1916 that became its formal name.

Billing's most unusual flying experience was the day that he earned his brevet. He had bet Handley Page (qv) £500 that 'Any man who has

Adolphe Pégoud right side up.

PÉGOUD, CELESTIN-ADOLPHE
1889–1915

Pégoud began his career in aviation as a mechanic for the pre-war French Air Service. In early 1913 he took a similar position with the Blériot company. Not content just to fix planes, he wanted to fly them. As soon as he learned to fly he began stunt flying. His three most spectacular feats took place before the end of 1913.

On 20 August 1913 he ascended in a well-used Blériot and baled out at 2,000 feet in a parachute that had been sewn together by a friend. This was the first time a pilot had baled out of his aeroplane in France. Eager to follow upon this success, Pégoud flew another Blériot inverted for several seconds on 1 September 1913. The flight confounded experts who said aeroplanes could not be flown upside down.

His third stunt was the most spectacular of all. On 21 September he climbed to 10,000 feet (3,48m) and looped the loop. This was the first loop in Western Europe. Nesterov (qv) had done it earlier in Russia.

enough sense to come in out of the rain' could learn to fly in one day. Handley Page took the bet and lost. Billing, after half an hour of instruction, took off in a Farman, completed the required manoeuvres, barely managed to recover from a whip stall, and landed safely.

PÉNAUD, ALPHONSE
1850–1880

Pénaud was prevented from joining the French Navy by a crippling hip disease. Denied this profession, he turned to aeronautics and made several significant contributions to that field before tragically ending his own life at the age of thirty.

In 1870 he built the world's first practical model helicopter, powered by a twisted rubber band. The next year he applied rubber power to a light model aeroplane which flew very well. It became the prototype of all powered model aeroplanes. The significance of this model was that it firmly established the general arrangement of the aeroplane, i.e. cambered wings, stabilizing empennage, and propeller propulsion.

In 1876 he designed a highly advanced monoplane that included such advanced features as braced wings, enclosed canopy, wheeled undercarriage, streamlining, waterproof hull, and amphibious capability. It also anticipated the 'cloche' control. Pénaud showed remarkable clarity of thought in all his designs. The public, however, didn't appreciate his designs, and so in a fit of depression he committed suicide.

PERCIVAL, EDGAR WIKNER
1897–1984

Percival was a trained engineer from New South Wales, Australia. In 1915 he joined the Australian Light Horse. After being sent to the Middle East he was able to transfer to the Royal Flying Corps. After less than half an hour's flight training, he soloed. He served with No. 60 Squadron and often went on patrol with Billy Bishop (qv). While in Egypt with No. 111

Squadron in 1918, he modified a standard Bristol F.2B Fighter. This exercise in aircraft design set him on his future course.

At the war's end he returned to Australia where he operated a small commercial aircraft business. He won a government sponsored aircraft design contest in 1926 but couldn't find proper backing to build it. Frustrated, he moved to England in 1929. By 1932 he had built and introduced the Gull, a low wing monoplane. It was noted for its remarkable efficiency and soon many of the big aviation figures of the day had set records in them. From the Gull evolved the Mew Gull and Vega Gull. During World War II his company built nearly 3,000 Proctor trainers.

Percival resigned from the company in 1944, but by 1954 was ready to re-enter the aircraft business. He introduced the EP-9, a Cessna-like five seater. Percival resigned once again in 1958 having had his fill of union problems. He continued to design aircraft, though, and in 1962 proposed building a business jet. None were ever built. In the late 1960s he was engaged in STOL designs, but these too were just proposals.

PHAM, LIEUTENANT-COLONEL TUAN
1947–

In the late 1970s the Soviet Union embarked on a programme to launch cosmonauts from their client states into orbit as a way of harvesting publicity benefits. The Vietnamese cosmonaut was Pham, who was launched in Soyuz 37 in July, 1980.

An elaborate history was given to Pham by his sponsors. The Russians claimed that as a fighter pilot during the Vietnam war he returned from a mission only to find his home runway heavily bombed. He landed anyway, with the result that his fighter flipped over on its back, skidded 1,000 feet (305m), and then flipped again, righting itself. The stalwart flier escaped unharmed. Another episode of his 'official' history is a claim that he was the first Vietnamese pilot to shoot down a B-52. In fact, no B-52 was ever shot down by an enemy aircraft, though seventeen were brought down by SAMs.

On his return from space, Pham was promoted to a Lieutenant-Colonel and made a Hero of the Soviet Union. The People of South Vietnam called him the Monkey of the Soviet Union, a reference to the monkeys that were blasted into orbit in the late 1950s, but did not control their own fate.

PHILLIPS, HORATIO FREDERICK
1845–1926
Phillips was the son of a London gunsmith. While still in his teens, he became interested in aeronautics. After building a fan-driven wind tunnel, he designed a steam injector type which improved the accuracy of his aerofoil research. Present-day supersonic tunnels use an injector system directly descended from his work.

Phillips' greatest contributions to aeronautics were the aerodynamic discoveries which he patented in 1884 and 1891. He had discovered that double surface aerofoils were more efficient than a single surface type. He found also that the majority of lift comes from the small area of suction along the top of a wing. His third discovery was that a thicker leading edge not only provides greater lift but less drag.

In 1893 he built a full-scale test bed to prove the validity of his research. The unmanned aircraft had no less that forty-two wing slots, which earned it the name *Venetian Blind*. Powered by a steam engine, it managed to lift itself off the ground for a few seconds, but since it was tethered to a circular track, and its nose-wheel never left the ground, the effort can only be considered a powered hop.

Phillips built several other 'Venetian blinds' but no true flights were made. His work nevertheless contributed to the advancement of aerodynamic research.

PIASECKI, FRANK NICHOLAS
1919–
Piasecki was born in Philadelphia, the son of an immigrant Polish tailor. While still attending the University of Pennsylvania, he worked as a mechanic for Kellet Autogiro. In 1940 he earned a B.Sc. in aeronautical engineering from New York University. While earning this degree, he also worked for Platt-LaPage Aircraft. Upon graduation, he worked as an aerodynamicist for Budd, the promoters of stainless steel technology. Concurrent with his studies and work, he brought together a group of aviation enthusiasts who styled themselves the 'PV Engineering Forum'. This group's goal was to build a helicopter. By scrounging for parts in junkyards and making what they couldn't find, they succeeded in their plan. Piasecki was appointed test pilot because he had fourteen hours of Piper Cub training. Their helicopter, the PV-2 was an instant success. Piasecki earned the first helicopter licence in the United States.

The 'Forum' was incorporated as Piasecki Helicopters. In 1944 the company won a contract to design a larger helicopter. The result was the PV-3 Flying Banana, a tandem rotor machine that was very stable. In 1946 the company underwent a major expansion when Wall Street financiers invested in it. By 1955 Piasecki had been removed from the board and the company renamed Vertol.

Piasecki started another company to undertake experimental work. In the mid-eighties he built a dirigible-helicopter composite that he hoped would revolutionize cargo haulage. It crashed during an early test.

PICCARD, PROFESSOR AUGUSTE
1884–1962
Piccard was born in Basle, Switzerland and earned degrees in both mechanical engineering and natural science. He became interested in the upper atmosphere and in 1913 made a balloon ascent that reached 10,000 feet (3,050m). By 1930 he had built an aluminium gondola that could be pressurized, thus enabling flights to extreme altitudes. The first attempt to launch it in September 1930 failed because the equipment was too heavy. Finally, in 1931 it rose with Piccard and an assistant to an altitude of 52,500 feet (17,224m). Piccard used the flight to conduct ionization and cosmic ray experiments.

His later career included building bathyscaphes to explore ocean depths as deep as 10,000 feet (3,050m). He also lectured world-wide on both ballooning and oceanography.

Piccard served as the model for Hergé's 'Professor Calculus'.

Patriarch of a ballooning family Auguste Piccard.

PIETENPOL, BERNARD H.
1901–1984

'Bernie' Pietenpol was born in Cherry Grove, Minnesota where he lived most of his life. In 1922 he learned to fly in a Curtiss Jenny and then decided to build his own aeroplane. His first plane flew the next year and was powered by a Ford Model T car engine. He was familiar with Ford engines as he operated an auto repair and sales business. He next built a Gnome-powered biplane, but returned to auto engines for his subsequent aircraft. In May, 1929 he flew an aeroplane powered by a Ford Model A engine, the first of several he built powered by that engine.

In 1930 he read an article in *Modern Mechanix* magazine which said that aeroplanes powered by auto engines could never fly as they'd be too heavy. He wrote to the Editor of the magazine to say that he owned aircraft powered by Ford engines. The doubtful editor wrote back asking Pietenpol for some proof. Pietenpol said he would bring an aircraft to St Paul, Minnesota so that it might be examined. In the event Pietenpol flew in with two aircraft, to the amazement of the Editor. A deal was made where Pietenpol would draw up plans for his two-seat aeroplane, which the Editor named the Air Camper. The magazine published the plans of the aircraft in 1932 and for the first time in America a person of moderate means could fly. The Air Camper design was a miracle of simplicity and required no special tools to build. The plans to convert a Model A engine were included and they too were simple.

In 1933 the plans for a single-seater, the Sky Scout, were published, though the Air Camper remained the more popular. The Sky Scout used a Model T engine which at the time was more plentiful and dirt cheap.

During World War II Pietenpol served as a flight instructor, after which he went into the television repair business. Many years after its plans were first published, the Air Camper remained a popular homebuild and Pietenpol was honoured as the grand old man of homebuilt aviation.

PILÂTRE de ROZIER, JEAN-FRANCOIS
1757–1785

Pilâtre was born into a life of genteel poverty at Metz. He was a poor student but his father eventually secured for him an apprenticeship with an apothecary. He studied chemistry and biology under his employer until he felt qualified enough to strike out on his own. He ran away to Paris to seek fame at the Academy of Science. In Paris, he befriended a doctor who introduced him to the capital's scientific notables.

He then began to experiment in different fields in the pseudo-scientific way prevalent in the eighteenth century. His researches investigated sewer gas, electricity, and dyes. His only

Pilâtre de Rozier, the first man to fly, and the first to die in a flying accident.

potentially important accomplishment was the invention of a primitive type of scuba gear.

By 1780 Pilâtre had dropped all his provincial mannerisms and established a coterie of admirers. He founded the city's first government-approved science museum and held regular semi-scientific lectures and demonstrations there. His audience comprised wealthy, young aristocrats who found his programmes diverting entertainment.

In August, 1783, upon hearing of Montgolfier's (qv) planned balloon demonstrations, Pilâtre suggested to the Academy of Science that he become the first aeronaut. They rejected his offer. Undeterred, Pilâtre made himself known to Joseph Montgolfier and secured a promise of priority.

On 15 October he made his first tethered ascent in the Montgolfiere. At least two others followed until on 21 November 1783 he made the first balloon voyage in the company of Francois Laurent (qv), the Marquis d'Arlandes.

In 1784 Pilâtre tried to crown this achievement by becoming the first man to cross the English Channel in a balloon. His effort developed into a race with Blanchard (qv) which anticipated the Blériot-Latham (qqv) contest 125 years later. Pilâtre was delayed until 1785 but when ready, introduced a balloon that was a dangerous composite of a hot air and hydrogen balloon. It was a bomb waiting to explode – and explode it did when the contraption reached 5,000 feet (1,524m) over the French side of the Channel after being launched on 15 June 1785. Pilâtre and a passenger, Pierre Romain, the balloon's builder, plummeted to their deaths in front of a crowd of spectators that included Pilâtre's fiancé, an Englishwoman named Susan Dyer. Dyer, shocked at the horrific sight of her mangled lover, died shortly thereafter – it was said of a broken heart, though it may have been suicide.

PILCHER, PERCY SINCLAIR
1867–1899

Born in Bath, Pilcher joined the Royal Navy when he was thirteen. Six years later he resigned to study engineering. He was a talented, hard worker and was offered a job as a consultant to Maxim's (qv) aeronautical project in 1896 having a year earlier begun gliding experiments and consulted with Lilienthal (qv).

Pilcher did design several good gliders, the most notable of which was the Hawk. The Hawk's main advantage over the Lilienthal gliders was its introduction of the world's first sprung undercarriage. He also introduced the practice of tow launching, a method still used.

Pilcher's clear-sighted vision as to what he wanted to achieve – powered flight – led him to move through a logical programme of experimentation. He thought that he had conquered all the problems of flight control and was about to add a power unit. Before he could do this, though, he was mortally injured when his Hawk broke up in mid-air on 31 September 1899. He died two days later.

PIPER, WILLIAM THOMAS
1881–1970

Piper was born in New York. He took time out from his college education to fight in the Spanish American War but at its conclusion attended Harvard. He trained as an engineer and in that capacity worked for US Steel. During World War I he served in an engineering unit. Piper eventually earned a small fortune as an oilman after the war.

In 1931 he was living in Pennsylvania when he bought a local company, that had gone bankrupt, for $761. The company built aeroplanes and was named Taylor. Piper managed the finances of the company and soon it was selling a moderate amount of small civilian aircraft named E-2 Cubs. The firm's designer, C. G. Taylor (qv) left in 1936 so Walter Jamouneau was hired as a replacement. After a fire destroyed the factory in 1937, the company moved to Lock Haven. Jamouneau revised the E-2 and the new design was sold as the J-2 Cub. This Cub made Piper's second fortune.

de PISCHOFF, ALFRED
1882–1922

De Pischoff was an Austro-Hungarian emigré in France who, during the years preceeding World War I, developed several innovative aeroplanes. His first full-scale aeroplane of note was built in 1905 in partnership with a man named Koechlin. This was a curious box-kite affair of low aspect ratio with dihedral on the lower wings and anhedral on the top wings. The pilot was to fly lying flat on his stomach which would have made for a painful landing as there was no suspension. This machine was a failure, but in 1907 de Pischoff built the world's first tractor biplane in Lucien Chauvière's factory. Though barely qualifying as a success, this machine managed to hop several times in late 1907 and early 1908 piloted by de Pischoff. The aircraft also introduced the Anzani engine and Chauvière propeller to the aviation community. By 1909 the two men had started their own factory at Billancourt where they produced aircraft to a customer's own design, or sold a

client an in-house-designed craft. In 1909 they produced a successful monoplane.

Fokker's right hand man, Reinhold Platz.

PLATZ, RHEINHOLD
1886–1966

The great success of Rheinhold Platz's aircraft adds credence to the assumption that where there is simplicity there is success.

Platz was a welder in 1912 when he went to work for Fokker (qv). An expert in his field, he persuaded Fokker to adopt the steel tube fuselage, a type which provided for ease of construction, strength, and lightness. During the next few years, he became a close associate of his employer and together they developed the great Fokker fighters of World War I. Platz, to be historically correct, deserves most of the credit for the design work. A pragmatic, rule-of-thumb designer, he developed the all-wood cantilever wings that made the Fokker D VII, D VIII, and the airliners of the 1920s such great aircraft. One of the enduring questions in aviation history is whether Fokker ordered Platz to build these wings of whether he did it on his own.

Platz's instinctive talents earned him his fortune. Fokker paid him well, but never allowed him to share the limelight. In 1931 Platz left Fokker. The time had come for scientists to replace woodworkers and welders as aircraft designers.

POCOCK, GEORGE
*–1846

Pocock, an Englishman, was an inspired school headmaster, having achieved that post at the age of twenty-two, whose true love was flying kites.

Starting around the early 1820s, Pocock began to experiment with man-lifting kites. He used his children as passengers, strapping them into armchairs that were attached by ropes to large kites. The kites were well designed, easily lifting the children, and were so rigged as to act as parachutes should the kite's restraining ropes break. He launched one daughter aloft as high as 300 feet (91m) and sent a son flying out over the sea off the coast of Bristol.

In 1822 he invented the 'Char-volant', a carriage which was pulled by kites. This astounding vehicle was so easy to steer and so reliable that Pocock often took friends on long trips in it – once travelling the 115 miles (185km) from Bristol to London. The Charvolant's speed was as high as 20 mph (32km/hr), which made it the fastest thing on wheels at the time. In 1828 he demonstrated it before George IV at the Ascot Races.

So enthralled was Pocock by his novel invention that he published a self-congratulatory book about in 1827, and even wrote hymns in praise of its glory.

POKRYSHKIN, ALEKSANDR IVANOVICH
1913(?)–1985

Pokryshkin was, for most of World War II, Russia's highest scoring ace. Only in 1945 was he pushed back into second place. A talented flier and natural leader, he scored his first victory on 23 June 1941 – a Bf-109. His score rose steadily thereafter and he was often called on to instruct other fighter pilots in modern combat techniques. Over thirty of his pupils

went on to become aces.

His war total was fifty-nine kills, forty-eight of which were scored in an ex-RAF Bell Airacobra – no mean task considering the opposition. After the war he rose through the ranks serving from 1968-71 as a Deputy Commander of the Soviet Air Defence Forces and from 1972-81 he headed Dosaaf, a civil defence organization.

POLIKARPOV, NIKOLAI
1892–1944

Polikarpov's first ambition was to become a Russian Orthodox priest. After attending technical school in St Petersburg, he changed his mind and enrolled in an aeronautics course at the Department for Naval Architecture.

In 1916 the Russo-Baltic Wagon Factory hired him to help put the Sikorsky S-16 into production.

In 1918 Polikarpov was given the task of starting the production of an aircraft. This time the Red Army ordered him to build licenced copies of the Spad VII. This directive placed him in a powerful position as the head of State Aircraft Factory No. 1. In the early 1920s he began to produce aircraft of his own design. His basic design impetus was to equal Western aircraft as quickly as possible. In effect, he was trying to run before he could walk, and this impatience led to several disastrous designs. In 1929 Stalin, a self-styled aeroplane expert, like Hitler, accused Polikarpov of sabotaging the aviation programme and threatened to execute him if a suitable fighter was not produced. For the next eighteen months Polikarpov and his staff were placed under house arrest, *en masse*, at their design office. It was produce or die.

The result of their struggles was the I-5 biplane fighter. It was successful enough for Polikarpov and his team to win their relative freedom.

In 1933 he introduced the I-16 fighter, a revolutionary aircraft that incorporated a low-wing monoplane planform with retractable gear and a licence-built Jupiter engine.

Under intense political pressure it is little wonder Polikarpov died before he was fifty-three.

PORTE, COMMANDER JOHN CYRIL
1884–1919

Porte established a fine tradition of service for British naval aviators. He first came to prominence in 1912 as a pilot for the British Deperdussin Company having been invalided out of the Royal Navy the previous year. After a brief association with Pemberton-Billing (qv), and the White & Thompson Co Ltd, he joined Curtiss (qv) in the United States with the intent of developing flying-boats.

While at Curtiss, he became a close associate of its founder and helped him to design the *America* flying-boat. It was to be used to cross the Atlantic with Porte as pilot, but with the outbreak of war these plans were scrapped. Porte returned to England bringing with him permission from Curtiss to build Curtiss flying-boats. To that end he established a factory at Felixstowe. Porte wasn't content simply to build these planes, he often led anti-submarine patrols in them.

Late in the war this patriotic aviator was maliciously accused of taking licence fee kick-backs from Curtiss. A long trial ensued which ultimately exonerated him. In recognition of his true service, he received the Order of St Michael and St George from King George V.

Porte didn't live long after the scandal though. In the autumn of 1919 he died of tuberculosis.

POST, WILEY
1898–1935

Post was born in Texas but grew up in Oklahoma. The son of a farmer, he despised life in the dusty flatlands of Oklahoma and dreamed of becoming a pilot. When he was sixteen his father gave him a small cotton field to work, promising him all the profits from a year's work. Young Post worked hard, and used the money he earned to learn mechanics at a school in Kansas City.

Following his studies, he became an oilfield hand but lost an eye in a drilling accident. With the $1,600 of insurance compensation he received, he bought an old aeroplane and learned to fly. By 1928 he had become the personal pilot of a wealthy oilman, F. C. Hall. In 1931 Hall offered Post backing for an attempt to fly around the world. Post accepted the offer and on 23 June, 1931 he took-off with Harold Gatty, who served as navigator. They departed from Roosevelt Field, Long Island in a Lockheed Vega, named *Winnie Mae* after Hall's daughter. The fliers circled the globe in eight days, fifteen hours and fifty-one minutes.

Post was dissatisfied with his accomplishment, though, because he really wanted to fly the journey solo. He did just that two years later in the same plane, bettering his time by twenty-one hours.

In 1934 he began to experiment with high altitude pressure suits and supercharged aircraft engines. This research ended when he was killed in Alaska in 1935 in a plane crash. Will Rogers, the famous humorist, was a passenger in the plane and was also killed. They had been vacationing together and were en route to Russia.

POTEZ, HENRY CHARLES ALEXANDRE
1891–1981

Potez was born in Meaulte, France and educated at L'École Supérieure de L'Aéronautique. At L'École, he met Marcel Bloch (qv) and at the outbreak of World War I both were assigned to research work at Chalais-Meudon. Potez was then seconded to work for the Caudrons (qv). Bloch, in the meantime, had developed a more efficient propeller than those generally in use and he approached Potez inviting him to join in setting up a factory. In 1916 Hélices-Éclair was founded and the propellers were built in a former furniture factory. The next year the pair found financial backing to form SEA, a company to build observation planes.

The war's end saw the dissolution of the business. In 1919 Potez started his own firm to continue building military observation planes. It was a success but in 1937 was nationalized. In 1953, having been idle since the war, the company was rejuvenated. In 1958 it purchased Air Fouga but itself was absorbed in the early 1960s into Sud Aviation.

PRANDTL, PROFESSOR LUDWIG
1875–1953

More than any other scientist, Prandtl established aerodynamics as a scholarly discipline, and in the process personally trained many of the world's greatest aerodynamicists.

Born in Bavaria, he was taught the value of observing nature by his father. Prandtl studied engineering at a technical school in Munich before taking an advanced degree from the University of Munich. As an industrial engineer, he came into his own, being afforded the chance to solve many practical problems through scientific means. This method of applied science characterized all his later work.

In 1901 he became a professor of mechanics at the University of Hanover, but left in 1904 to establish an aerodynamics curriculum at the University of Göttingen. His work soon made Göttingen the greatest name in aerodynamic research in the world. Through his own investigations, he discovered the nature of boundary layer flow, also establishing the mathematics to make it understandable and predictable. He also explained the phenomenon of induced drag and tip vortices.

In 1906 he was hired to design the shape of a Parseval (qv) dirigible. He insisted that first a wind tunnel be built at Göttingen so that the flow could be visualized. The Parseval concern paid for the construction and it became the first of Göttingen's great tunnels.

Prandtl taught many of the scientists who would shape aviation's future, but perhaps his most important student was von Karman (qv).

QUIMBY, HARRIET
1875–1912

Harriet Quimby was America's first licenced aviatrix, and possibly the most intriguing. She was born in Michigan to a poor farming family. Her parents moved to California when she was still a child and eventually settled in San Francisco. There, her parents ran, among other things, a patent medicine business. Her mother was determined that Harriet and her sister would rise above the low social standing of the family. To this end she fabricated vague stories of the family's origins which, in combination with her daughter's beauty, served to open doors for them into polite society.

The connections Harriet made helped her land a job as a drama critic for *Dramatic Review*, a San Francisco arts journal. Ambitious for greater things, she travelled to New York city in 1903 where she got a job with *Leslie's Weekly*. While in New York, she met the Moisants (qv). With a wink and a smile she convinced them to teach her how to fly. In 1911 she took instruction at their school in Garden City, earning her brevet in August.

After touring the southern states and Mexico with the Moisant International Aviators she travelled to Europe determined to be the first female to pilot an aircraft across the English Channel. In Paris she purchased a Blériot which she had sent to England. There, she hired Gustav Hamel (qv) as an advisor. The gallant aviator's advice was that he should pilot the plane across dressed in women's clothes, and upon landing, he would switch position with Quimby who would wait in hiding on a deserted French shore. Quimby refused this and made the flight herself on 16 April 1912. She took off from Dover intent on landing at Calais. Instead, unfamiliar with the French coast, she drifted twenty-five miles west and landed on the Normandy coast.

The flight was certainly historic, but an unexpected news story of tremendous importance wiped her feat off the newspaper headlines. The *Titanic* had sunk the night before, overwhelming all other stories. Quimby returned to America where she received some notice, but not as much as she had planned. Looking to make up for lost accolades, she entered the Harvard-Boston Meet in late June. On 1 July she took a passenger up in her Blériot two-seater to test the machine in anticipation of a speed record attempt. Over Boston Harbour the machine was seen to make a sudden plunge. Her passenger was thrown out but she managed to return to straight and level. No sooner had she done so than it dipped again and she too was thrown. The two flyers struck the water 200 feet (60m) out from shore. Quickly, would-be rescuers retrieved the bodies only to find them lifeless.

Earle Ovington (qv), who was officiating at the meet, investigated the wrecked Blériot and found that it didn't use the standard 'cloche' controls and that the rudder and warping wires had become tangled. He said that in addition to plunging, the plane had also pulled to one side, and that the turn itself had induced the sudden nose-down attitudes.

Harriet Quimby, whose beautiful smile died when she failed to use a seat belt.

RAYNHAM, FREDERICK PHILLIP
1892–1954

Raynham was born in Suffolk, the son of a farmer. In 1911 he met A. V. Roe (qv) who taught him to fly. Thereafter he became Roe's test pilot prior to the war. During the war he went over to Martinsyde for whom he was also a test pilot. Martinsyde built a trans-Atlantic plane to compete for the *Daily Mail* prize in 1919 and chose Raynham to fly it.

Raynham took this machine to Newfoundland in the spring of that year in hopes of defeating

both Hawker (qv) and Alcock (qv) and Brown. His first attempt to take off on 18 May ended in a crash that seriously injured his navigator. The latter, in fact, had glass shards driven into his skull when his head struck the compass on the instrument panel. Raynham sent him home and proceeded to rebuild the aircraft under spartan conditions. On 17 June he tried to take off again, with a different navigator, but this flight also ended in a crash.

He returned to England, picked up a Martinsyde Semiquaver and journeyed to the Iberian penninsula. He demonstrated the fighter to the Spanish and Portuguese, picking up a half-dozen orders for his company. In 1920 he competed in the Gordon-Bennett race in a Semiquaver, but bowed out with a blown oil pump.

Raynham joined Sydney Camm (qv) and Camm's former boss, G. Handasyde (qv) to build a glider to compete for the Britannia Trophy contest. The glider flew but led to nothing further. He, along with Camm, joined Hawkers in 1924. Raynham test flew the Cygnet lightplane. The following year he joined the Air Survey Company for whom he helped map New Guinea and Sarawak.

READ, LIEUTENANT-COMMANDER ALBERT CUSHING
1887–1967

'Putty' Read was born in New Hampshire and graduated from Annapolis in 1906. He served initially on ships, but in 1916 learned to fly at Pensacola. By 1917 he had been promoted to Commander of a Naval air station and while so engaged, went on anti-submarine patrols.

In 1919 he was chosen to pilot a NC flying-boat across the Atlantic. On 8 May three 'Nancies' lifted off from Rockaway, Long Island. En route to Europe two of them were eliminated, but NC-4, commanded by Read, persevered. It stopped along the way at the Azores before finally reaching Lisbon on 27 Ma.

The flight had not been a complete success because even the NC-4 had spent more time down for repair than had been anticipated. It even changed an engine in Newfoundland. The flight progressed in fits and jerks that did little to make the public think that one day trans-oceanic flights could be done routinely.

Read's leadership was duly rewarded with a promotion to Commander. The rest of his Naval career was also distinguished. At various times he commanded aircraft carriers, taught at the Naval War College, and served at the Bureau of Aeronautics.

One of the greatest pilots of all time Hanna Reitsch.

REITSCH, HANNA
1912–1979

One of the most admirable and best skillful pilots of all time was Hanna Reitsch, a diminutive Silesian woman who began her flying career in the late 1920s. She had originally planned to become a doctor, like her father, but gave that up after learning to fly gliders at a school operated by Wolf Hirth. Her reputation as a pilot grew quickly as she demonstrated her mastery of many types in competitions, sometimes flying during terrible weather.

Reitsch progressed to powered planes and continually proved that she could fly aircraft that many men couldn't. She joined the German Institute for Glider Research as a test pilot, went on promotional tours to South America and Africa, and in 1938 reached the pinnacle of her career when she flew the Fa-61 helicopter inside the Deutschland-Halle, an auditorium in Berlin.

With licences to fly gliders, propeller planes, and helicopters under her belt, there seemed to be little more that she could do, especially now that World War II had started – but there was much more. For a time, the five foot (1.52m) tall eighty-eight pound (40kg) flier was Hitler's personal pilot. She test piloted the mammoth Me- 321 Gigant glider.

In late 1942 she was chosen to perform flight acceptance trials on the Me-163. The next year during a tow-launching of a Komet, she noticed that the jettisonable landing gear had stayed attached. She tried to side-slip into a safe landing but the plane crashed. The impact broke her skull in six places.

In only five months she recovered sufficiently to tackle the challenge of sorting out a piloted version of the V-1, an aircraft which had already killed several pilots. She succeeded in isolating the problem and went on to propose a suicide squadron of V-1s, which she offered to lead. The idea was eventually rejected.

In late April, 1945, she embarked on the most bizarre adventure of her career. Hitler had commanded General von Greim to report to his bunker in Berlin, which at that time was completely encircled by Russians. A desperate plan was formulated whereby von Greim would be flown to Gatow airport in a two-seat FW-190. From Gatow, Reitsch would help him fly to a street near the bunker. A Luftwaffe pilot knew a safe route to Gatow so he would fly the 190. Von Greim took the rear seat while Reitsch was stuffed into the fuselage via the radio compartment door! If the plane was shot down, there was no means of escape.

En route to Gatow the plane was attacked by Russian fighters but escorting Luftwaffe aircraft drove them away. At Gatow von Greim took control of a waiting Fieseler Storch and took off for central Berlin. The Russians below threw up a terrific barrage of anti-aircraft fire and a shell shattered one of von Greim's feet. Reitsch took over the craft which had now been riddled with bullets and was streaming fuel. She brought the plane through the gauntlet and made it to Berlin. Reaching Hitler's bunker, she was given a vial of poison and a personal letter by the Führer. He promoted von Greim to head the Luftwaffe and dismissed the pair. They left Berlin in an Arado 96 flown by the pilot who had got them to Gatow. Hitler committed suicide the next day.

Reitsch was captured by the Allies but released later. Her father shot her mother, sister, her sister's children, and the family maid, before killing himself to avoid capture by the Russians.

RENARD, CAPTAIN CHARLES
1847–1905

In 1884 Captain Renard of the French Engineering Corps conceived the idea of an electric powered dirigible. He enlisted the help of his comrade A. C. Krebs (qv) and together they persuaded the French Ministry of the Interior to allocate funds for its construction. The minister, Léon Gambetta, had been airlifted out of Paris by balloon during the siege of 1870, so was willing to further the cause of aeronautics and approved the money.

Renard and Krebs built their airship in the remarkably short time of two months. Powered by a relatively light electric motor, it made its maiden flight on 9 August 1884. The eight kilometre flight from Chalais-Meudon to Villacoublay and back was the first fully controlled flight in history. Although their airship, *La France*, was not completely practical, it was a major step towards true dirigibility.

RENTSCHLER, FREDERICK BRANT
1887–1956

Rentschler was born in Ohio, the son of a German immigrant who owned a foundry. He attended Princeton, and during World War I inspected engine castings for Wright-Martin in Jersey. Rentschler stayed with the company after

the war, it had been renamed Wright, and pushed for the production of advanced air-cooled engines. The company's board refused his suggestions and so in 1924 he left on sick leave to have an 'operation'. In truth, he did have an operation, but really he spent his time seeking financial backing to start his own company. Finding it, he resigned from Wright and at the end of 1924 and snatched two of their best designers, George Mead and Andy Wilgoos. These two men designed the new company's first engine, the Wasp, in a garage in Montclair, New Jersey. Rentschler bought a defunct Connecticut tool and die company in 1925 called Pratt & Whitney. The new product line would include some of the world's greatest aero-engines.

In 1929 Rentschler merged with Boeing to form United Aircraft and Transport Corporation. From his original investment of $253 in Pratt & Whitney, Rentschler, by 1929, was worth over $35 million!

REYNOLDS, OSBORNE
1842–1912

Reynolds was born in Belfast, Ireland. He studied mechanical engineering at Cambridge where he graduated in 1867. The next year he became the professor of engineering at Owens College in Manchester.

His interests were wide ranging, encompassing everything from magnetism to tidal motion. He made important discoveries relating to heat transfer which led to the improvement of boilers and condensers. His most noted work, though, was in fluid dynamics. In this field, he discovered the relationship between fluid density and streamlined flow. This relationship was expressed as the Reynolds Number, and the use of this number allowed later researchers to scale the results of wind tunnel model tests to full-scale aircraft.

RIABOUCHINSKY, DIMITRI PAVLOVITCH
1882–1962

Riabouchinsky was the son of a prominent Moscow merchant. He embarked at first on a business education, but abandoned that to travel to Heidelberg to study science. He returned to Moscow in 1904 and used his family's wealth to open a private research institute which he named the Aerodynamic Institute of Koutchino.

For fourteen years his institute, staffed by a number of Russia's brightest scholars, discovered many of the fundamental laws of aerodynamics. The institute first experimented with model aircraft by dropping them from towers. Later they converted to wind tunnel testing.

Riabouchinsky fled to Paris after the Bolshevik revolution.

Sporting a killer smile, Manfred von Richthofen in the early days.

von RICHTHOFEN, RITTMEISTER MANFRED

1892–1918

Possibly the only combatant of World War I whose *nom de guerre* is still a household word was the Red Baron – Manfred von Richthofen.

This great fighter hero of fact and fiction began his flying career under less than auspicious circumstances. Having transferred from the 1st Uhlan Regiment to an infantry unit, then into the air service, he was terrified of flying during his first flights as an observer. He gradually conquered his fear and requested pilot training. He was not a natural pilot and crashed several of his first training aircraft. Through perseverance he overcame his initial lack of co-ordination, but was then baffled by the next step, navigation. During his first combat mission, on the Western Front, he lost his bearings and had to land to ask directions! He next transferred to a bomber still on the Eastern Front but found fighting the Russians 'tedious' so he requested a transfer back to the Western Front. When Boelcke (qv) visited his unit, von Richthofen almost begged the great master to take him back west. Upon reviewing von Richthofen's dismal flying record, Boelcke refused his request. The young flier didn't relent and Boelcke finally gave in, allowing him to join Jagdstaffel 2, his own unit.

Under Boelcke's personal supervision von Richthofen began to improve his flying skills. On 17 September 1916 he shot down a FE 2b, his first confirmed kill. As his score climbed, his confidence increased and this allowed his natural leadership ability to surface. Upon Boelcke's death, he took command of the squadron. His men revered him as much as their former leader. Von Richthofen's style was that of a calculating predator. He never played at heroics, but rather planned each kill so that there would be minimum risk to himself, and yet a maximum result achieved for the German war effort. To this end, he concentrated on two-seaters, which ultimately accounted for over half of his eighty victories.

With fifty-seven kills already to his credit, he was shot down and wounded on 16 July 1917 by a British rear gunner who scored a tricky deflection shot at over 200 yards. A bullet glanced off von Richthofen's skull and he fought unconsciousness to make a landing behind German lines. He was taken to hospital where he spent a month recovering. When he returned to his unit, something about him had changed. No longer did he assume that every flight would bring a kill, or that he was invincible. He had lost some of his fighting spirit, though not the desire to keep trying. Month after month his victory tally continued to climb, reaching the seventy mark on 26 March 1918. Three weeks later on 20 April he got his eightieth kill (seventy-nine British and one Belgian). It seemed to everyone, on both sides of the conflict, that the Red Baron was invincible. On 21 April they were proved wrong.

During a patrol on that day von Richthofen broke one of his cardinal rules when he followed an intended victim down to trench level. On his tail there appeared a Camel flown by a Canadian, Roy Brown. Shots rang out from Brown's guns, but they also came up from an Australian ground unit. Whose bullets struck the Red Baron is unknown to this day. His plane smashed into the ground at high speed behind British lines. Souvenir hunters quickly stripped his aircraft before an exact determination could be made as to how he was brought down. He was buried with full military honours. His mother wrote, thirty-five years later, that after his death she received several hundred thousand letters and telegrams from all over Germany. The country mourned the passing of its last chivalrous knight, and braced itself for a less heroic future.

RICKENBACKER, CAPTAIN EDWARD VERNON

1890–1973

One of the most thrilling rags to riches stories in American history is that of 'Captain Eddie' Rickenbacker's rise from immigrant poverty in Columbus, Ohio to wealth and world fame.

Born to Swiss immigrants in Columbus, young Rickenbacher (changed during World War I to Rickenbacker) went to work in a factory at the age of thirteen upon the death of his father. Hard work agreed with him and soon he had secured a job in a small car factory. When this factory organized a racing team, Rickenbacker was taken to the competitions as the team's 'grease monkey'. A few years later he began racing cars himself and during the intervals between races sold cars. He wasn't yet twenty.

He overcame grinding poverty to become a great pilot and industrialist, Eddie Rickenbacker.

In 1911 he entered the first Indy 500 race, finishing eleventh. In the years prior to the war he was rated as the third best race driver in America, receiving along with this distinction national acclaim.

In 1917 he went to France as a driver for General Pershing's staff. One day he happened to spot a stalled Mercedes car on the side of the road. He repaired the car's engine and as a reward from its owner, Billy Mitchell (qv), was allowed into flight school. Rickenbacker was a natural flier who kept his aircraft in perfect tune. With the 94th 'Hat in the Ring' Squadron he shot down twenty-six German planes, making him the top American ace.

After the war he started his own company to build advanced automobiles. His cars featured brakes on all wheels, unlike his competitors. So nervous were other car companies about the Rickenbacker car that they spread false rumours that four-wheel brakes led to accidents when applied in a turn. Quickly, the Rickenbacker car sales shrivelled to nothing.

Heavily in debt, Rickenbacker went to work

for La Salle, a division of Cadillac. In 1928 he joined Fokker's organisation in the US which was soon purchased by General Motors. He spent a few years with American Airlines before joining North American Aviation in 1933. Two years later, when the company divested itself of Eastern Airlines, Rickenbacker became that company's chairman. All the while he had been paying off the debt from the Rickenbacker car days, and eventually he paid back every penny. From 1927 to 1945 he owned the Indianapolis Speedway.

During World War II he went on two special missions for the US government; one to Russia, and the other to US Pacific bases. En route to one base, the B-17 in which he was a passenger ditched in the ocean. The crew took to life rafts and spent twenty-two days adrift (not twenty-one as Rickenbacker himself originally wrote). Finally, they were picked up, returning to America amid great acclaim.

After the war, Rickenbacker continued to guide Eastern Airlines and he is credited with making it for many years one of the most profitable American carriers.

ROCKWELL, KIFFIN YATES
1892–1916

From a wealthy Tennessee family, Rockwell tried to fulfill his parent's wishes that he should get a good education. He found it hard to settle down to a student's life though he tried at three colleges, including Annapolis. He finally gave up and journeyed west to San Francisco in 1912. Two years later he returned east and was about to settle in Atlanta when World War I started. He changed his plans and joined the Foreign Legion.

Sent quickly into combat, Rockwell saw more ground battle than he bargained for. He sought a transfer to the air service. He joined the Escadrille Américaine in April, 1916. On 18 May he shot down his first enemy plane – the first brought down by an American. Four months later he was killed when he was shot down over Luxeuil, France. In January, 1917

Rockwell's Escadrille Américaine became officially known as the Escadrille Lafayette.

RODGERS, CALBRAITH PERRY
1879–1912

Rodgers was born into a prominent American military family. His ancestors included Oliver Perry, the Naval hero of the War of 1812, and Matthew Perry, the man who opened Japan's closed doors to America. Rodger's father had been killed while on Indian patrol in the West, not by an arrow, but by a bolt of lightning.

Rodgers himself had become determined on a Naval career, but an attack of scarlet fever left him partially deaf, thus excluding him from Annapolis. He went instead to Columbia University where he was a star football hero. He later raced yachts and automobiles. In June, 1911 he learned to fly at the Wrights' school, but didn't receive his licence until 7 August. He soloed after only ninety minutes of dual instruction! In August, he entered the Chicago International Meet where he won an endurance prize. On the basis of this type of victory, he approached J. Ogden Armour proposing that the latter sponsor his attempt to be the first to fly across the country. He hoped also to win the Hearst $50,000 prize offered to anyone who could do it before 10 October. Armour agreed to pay Rodgers $5 per mile if he would allow the plane to be painted with the logo of a new grape soda Armour was marketing. Thus Rodger's cross-country machine bore the name *Vin Fiz*.

Rodgers departed from Sheepshead Bay, near New York city on 17 September. His journey to the west coast included no less than fifteen accidents, six in-flight engine failures, numerous broken bones, and a brain concussion. After eighty-four gruelling days, on 10 December he landed on the Californian coast. He had spent most of the money Armour paid him, and had not met the time restriction placed on the Hearst prize. In April, 1912 he recklessly drove into a flock of seagulls flying near where he had earlier touched down at the end of his historic flight. One of the gulls jammed his rudder, causing the

Wright biplane to dive out of control. Rodgers died of a broken back and neck.

ROE, SIR EDWIN ALLIOT VERDON
1877–1958

Roe was the son of a Manchester doctor. At the age of fourteen he left home and journeyed to Canada where he worked as a surveyor, tree-planter, fisherman, etc. He returned to England after about a year and became an apprentice at the Lancashire and Yorkshire Railway Locomotive Works. During his years there, he was also a winning cycle racer. He next worked as a fitter at a boat yard, after which he studied marine engineering at London University.

As a ship's engineer, he was at sea from 1899 through to 1902, during which time he began to study the movements of birds wheeling above his vessel. On his return to England, he started to experiment with models. In 1906 he went to America to assist in the construction of an experimental helicopter designed by a Mr. Davidson. He was back in England in 1907, this time to stay.

In that year, he won the £75 prize of the *Daily Mail's* model aeroplane contest. With this money, he began construction of a full-size biplane. Completed in September, 1907, it was taken to Brooklands for testing. Conditions at Brooklands were made difficult by the niggardly track manager. Roe was forced to live surreptitiously in a small hangar he had built for the aeroplane. He could only afford five shillings a week for food.

Despite repeated crashes and failures he made his first hop in this machine on 8 June 1908. This hop preceded the flight of Moore-Brabazon (qv), but it was not officially recognized as a true flight. Roe struggled on and next built a triplane with the help of a partner. This unfinished machine was later auctioned off when the brief partnership ended, but was followed by yet another triplane in 1909. Because of his acute poverty, this aircraft was built under the railway arches near Lea Marshes. The wings were covered in packing paper because Roe couldn't afford cloth. Finally, it was tested at Lea Marshes where he made good flights.

Roe steadily progressed to building reliable aircraft and founded A. V. Roe and Co. in 1910. His best known plane was indisputably the dependable 504 of which 8,340 were built. In 1928 Roe sold all of his shares in his company AVRO. He bought into the S. E. Saunders Company, thus forming Saunders-Roe (SARO). If any Briton deserved to make the first flight in Britain it was certainly Roe – and maybe he did.

ROGALLO, FRANCIS M.
1912–

Rogallo went to work for NACA in 1936. He was working at Langley Center in Hampton, Virginia in the late 1940s when he first began to consider the concept of simplified flight. In 1948 he travelled to California where he interviewed dozens of aeronautical engineers, seeking ideas for simpler aircraft. In July of that year he began to make paper models in his kitchen which he 'flew' in front of a fan. Gradually he formulated the layout of the Rogallo wing. His wife sewed the prototype from material scavenged from the kitchen draperies. They tested the cloth wing and it worked!

He and his wife, Gertrude, were granted a patent on the design, and over the next eleven years attempted to interest NACA in its possibilities. It wasn't until Wernher von Braun (qv) realized that it might be used to recover spacecraft that it gained any real notice. Prior to this, it had been marketed as an advanced kite in toy stores.

In 1961 Ryan built the Flexwing, a minimal aircraft using a Rogallo wing, but it led to nothing. Rogallo wings seemed to be an interesting oddity with no real use until, in 1971, two hang gliders were built in the Rogallo configuration and appeared at the world's first hang glider meet in Los Angeles. As a hang glider, the Rogallo wing found a home, and thousands were built. Interestingly, a young Czechoslovakian student escaped from that country in the early eighties under a power driven Rogallo wing.

Adolph Rohrbach, the developer of smooth metal skinned construction.

ROHRBACH, ADOLPH

1889–1939

Rohrbach was an extremely ambitious and gifted engineer. After graduating from the Technical High School of Darmstadt, where he earned a diploma in shipbuilding, he went to work for Blohm und Voss. Tiring of ships, he joined Zeppelin to build aircraft.

During World War I he designed the Zeppelin-Staaken bombers. These huge aircraft taught him much about multi-engined aircraft structures, so after the war he was well prepared to embark on his own manufacturing venture. Rohrbach's plan was to exploit the new concept of all-metal construction but not in the way Junkers (qv) built his planes. Instead, Rohrbach would use smooth stressed skins. Most engineers then doubted this type of construction could work.

Since the Versailles Treaty prevented him from building aircraft in Germany, he set up a factory in Denmark. There he built several successful all-metal aircraft. In 1929 his company was such a success that he opened a plant in the US. By this time, other manufacturers were beginning to build similar aircraft and consequently Rohrbach received no orders from the US government.

A hard driving man, he died from a heart attack at only fifty.

ROLLS, THE HON. CHARLES STEWART

1877–1910

The son of a wealthy British peer, Rolls might have led the carefree life often associated with the young Edwardian aristocracy. Instead, he combined an adventurous spirit with an education and thus made a useful contribution to his nation.

Rolls went to Cambridge University where he earned a BA, and later MA in engineering. His love for speed led him to become a racing cyclist. Later he turned to racing automobiles along with his friend Moore-Brabazon (qv). In 1896 Rolls joined with other auto enthusiasts to break a law which forbade automobile travel at over 4 mph (6.4km/hr). Their defiance lead to a new speed limit which was 200% faster than the previous – 12 mph (19.3km/hr).

In 1901 Rolls, having become an aeronaut, helped found the Aero Club. Two years later he entered an automobile sales venture in London selling expensive French cars. One day a friend introduced him to F. H. Royce (qv) who was just beginning to build quality automobiles. Royce, who had worked hard his entire life, had little in common with Rolls yet they became friends. In 1904 they agreed that Royce would build cars and Rolls would sell them. Rolls-Royce was born.

Rolls continued to fly balloons when he wasn't demonstrating his soon-to-be-famous products. His balloon flying led to aeroplane flying and in 1910 he received certificate number 2 from the Royal Aero Club (Royal as of that year). Later in the same year he became the first man to fly non-stop across the English Channel both ways, but his triumph was short-lived. In July, 1910 he was killed when his French-built Wright biplane broke up in mid-air.

Though he came down from only 20 feet, he cracked his skull. He had become Britain's first aircraft fatality.

ROYCE, SIR (FREDERICK) HENRY
1863–1933

Although he was to rise and become the producer of some of the most luxurious cars in the world, Royce began life in abysmal poverty. Born in Alwalton, England, he was orphaned at nine. He struggled through a variety of jobs before being apprenticed to a locomotive works. There, he became an expert machinist noted for his dedication to unequalled precision. At seventeen he left a subsequent job with a train ticket that had taken him several months to save for, and travelled to London. By day he worked at an electricity generating station while at night he went to school. Three years went by before he decided to go to Manchester to open his own shop to produce dynamos and motors. Noted for their high quality, the Royce products sold well and his company grew. In 1902 he bought a second-hand Decauville automobile hoping to enjoy leisurely weekends in the countryside. Instead, the car produced an endless series of breakdowns. He decided he could build a better one. In less that a year he had. The car was so good that he decided to market it. Not long after this he entered into a partnership with Rolls (qv) to sell the automobiles.

In 1906 Royce introduced the Silver Ghost, a car which was to become known as the greatest car in the world. Royce's reputation as a leading engineer led the Royal Navy to contact him during World War I with an order to build Renault-designed aero-engines. Royce scoffed at what he considered an inferior design, and said he would come up with a better one. The result was the Eagle, a twenty-litre brute which produced 225hp. This engine, and its derivatives the Falcon and the Hawk, were so successful that by the war's end Rolls-Royce supplied fully 60 per cent of all British-built engines.

Royce stayed actively involved with the design of his company's engines up until his death in 1933. Before he died, he dictated what

was to become known as the Rolls-Royce Bible. It was a set of guidelines for future generations of Rolls-Royce engineers to follow. Even today, it is a closely guarded industrial secret.

RUDEL, OBERST HANS-ULRICH
1916-1982

'Only he is lost who gives himself up for lost!' This was the motto of the highest-decorated German serviceman in World War II – Hans Rudel. Rudel was born the son of a minister and as a child was quite timid. His only goal in life was to become a pilot, so through intense athletic training he built up his body enough to pass the Luftwaffe physical exam. Early flight training did not go well, but remembering his motto, he persevered. He finally earned his wings but when the war started he had been posted to an observation squadron. It wasn't until the campaign against Russia started that he joined a Stuka squadron.

As a Stuka pilot Rudel went to war with a passion. At first, his fellow pilots thought his iron courage was just foolhardiness. He would always press home each sortie as if the war depended on it. He was the pilot who flew on every mission; he was the pilot who always dived lower; and it was he who scored the most kills. What his comrades had perceived as foolhardiness was actually a new ground-attack technique being pioneered by Rudel. Soon, they were to follow his example, though none ever achieved his skill.

Rudel was like a one-man army. He destroyed no less than 519 Russian tanks, over 2,000 vehicles, countless gun positions, and most astounding of all – one Soviet Navy battleship, the *Marat,* in Kronstatt harbour on 23 September 1941. The Pentagon concept of cost effectiveness must have been born with Rudel! So feared and despised was he by Stalin that the Soviet leader put a price on his head – contrary to all precepts of the Geneva Convention.

When the 'tank buster' version of the Stuka was introduced in 1943, during the battle of Kursk, Rudel's squadron was the first to test it – with devastating results. Rudel had become a well known national hero. Hitler showered him with honours and by 1945 he had received every medal possible. Hitler then ordered that a new medal be struck, the Golden Oakleaves to the Knight's Cross. Rudel was the only person ever to attain this.

Shortly before the war's end, Rudel lost a leg to anti-aircraft fire. The leg was amputated below the knee, but before the wound had healed he was back in combat. He didn't stop flying missions until the very last day of the war. In total, he had flown 2,530 combat missions.

At the war's end, he was taken prisoner but eventually moved to Argentina.

Around the time of Rudel's death, a startling claim was made by one of Hitler's former advisors. He stated that the reason Rudel had received such fine medical care after his leg wound, and at a time when medical care was at a premium in the Reich, was that Hitler had already chosen Rudel to succeed him as Führer! The former advisor made the point that Hitler was a great admirer of men of action, especially aviators. There is certainly merit in this assertion as witnessed by the fact that Hitler had previously put Goering (qv), another aviator/war hero, in a position of enormous power. Hitler's discontent with Goering and his other chiefs by the war's end is well documented, so, had the war lasted a while longer, Rudel may well have been the last Führer of the Third Reich.

RUTAN, ELBERT LEANDER
1943–

Every once in a while in aviation history there appears a person or company that so radically changes the concept of what an aircraft can be that technology seems to jump ahead by ten or twenty years. First there was the monocoque Deperdussin that broke the 100 mph mark, then in the 1930s came the Gee Bee racers, in the 1940s the Me-262 – the 1970s also saw a quantum leap in design philosophy led by an unknown aeronautical engineer from California, 'Bert' Rutan.

Rutan was the son of a doctor and trained as an engineer at the California Polytechnic Institute. He then went to work at Edwards AFB as a flight technician. In the later 1960s he began experimenting with a small delta shaped aeroplane model which grew into his first full-scale aircraft, the Vari-Viggen. This craft was built mostly of wood and introduced Rutan's use of the canard. It was an interesting aeroplane, but it wasn't until he displayed, in 1975, the VariEze canard, made from foam and fibreglass, that he started a revolution in homebuilt aircraft. The VariEze was a canard pusher capable of 16Gs and 200 mph (322km/hr) on only 100hp (75kW)! The construction technique was equally remarkable with most components made by simply cutting foam slabs with a taut length of wire connected to a DC power source. Over the foam was then wrapped fibreglass. In 1977 the Quickie was introduced. This single-seater achieved 125 mph (201km/hr) on a mere 18hp (13.4kW) – nothing like it existed anywhere, and only the Moeller Stromo of the 1930s ever approached its efficiency.

Hundreds of Quickies and VariEzes were built after Rutan started a company to market parts and plans. During all of this, Rutan had begun building foam and fibreglass prototypes for the military and NASA. The first of these was the NASA AD-1 pivoting wing jet, based on a World War II German idea that for thirty years had waited to be tested. More incredible than its wing was the fact that the craft was built *under* budget!

Rutan's greatest glory came in 1986, when on 23 December his brother, Dick, and Jeanna Yeager, landed the *Voyager* aircraft at Edwards AFB, completing the first ever unrefuelled circumnavigation of the globe. The *Voyager* project had begun in 1982 with Bert designing the large canard, twin-engined aircraft. The story of its construction and funding, completely from private sources, is an epic in aviation history. The success would not have been possible without Rutan's able assistant John Roncz, who designed the aerofoil profiles for the wings and propellers.

Rutan's place in history is assured. To many aviation enthusiasts, his work stood as a symbol of what the individual could accomplish in a world of stifling bureaucracy. At a time when the homebuilt movement had stagnated under forty-year-old designs, Rutan arrived on the scene to give the lead in aviation technology back to the homebuilders, taking it away from the factories. 'Granny' Granville (qv) would have appreciated that.

RYAN, TUBAL CLAUDE
1898–1982
Ryan was born in Kansas and saw his first aeroplane in 1911. It was Cal Rodgers (qv) on his cross-country flight. After attending Oregon State College, he flew for two years in the Air Corps. In 1922 he started his own flying school in San Diego, expanding this three years later into an airline with a route between San Diego and Los Angeles. For his airline he used Standards that he had converted into cabin passenger planes. These successful modifications led Ryan to enter aircraft production in 1926. The first Ryan plane was the M 1, a high-wing monoplane. Just after entering aircraft production, Ryan and his partner, B. F. Mahoney, clashed on future policy with the result that Ryan sold out and left. Just a few months later his former company became world renowned when, almost by default, it built Lindbergh's (qv) *The Spirit of St Louis*.

Ryan then became an engine salesman until 1931 when he founded another company, Ryan Aeronautical Company. This firm never became one of the giant American manufacturers, though it did build interesting aircraft including the ST trainers of the thirties, the Fireball combination jet-piston-engined fighter of 1945, and the X-13 VTOL jet of 1957.

SADLER, JAMES
1751–1828
Sadler's family owned a profitable confectionary business in Oxford. In his spare time he enjoyed studying engineering and science publications. The first balloon flights of 1783 intrigued him greatly. With only sketchy accounts of these flights, he decided to build and fly his own balloon. His first was a small test vehicle, but the success of this encouraged him to build a full-size sixty-three-foot diameter version. On 4 October 1784 he ascended from Oxford, making a short six-mile flight. The flight was the first by an Englishman in an English balloon. Sadler then toured the country drawing enormous crowds. In 1812 he attempted to cross the Irish Sea, but failed due to poor handling of the balloon.

His son, Windham Sadler (1796–1824), was the first aeronaut to cross that body of water, on 22 July 1817. Young Sadler's life ended in a balloon accident, though, when his basket crashed into the side of a house. He was thrown out and fell to his death.

de SAINT-EXUPÉRY, ANTOINE-MARIE-ROGER
1900–1944
Saint-Exupéry was born into an aristocratic family in Lyon that had lost its fortune. He was a poor student and consequently failed to pass the exam to enter the French Naval College. Instead, he joined the air service in 1921. He was a gifted pilot who made friends easily, so after his military service he joined Compagnie Latécoère as an airmail pilot.

He flew along the company's routes from France across Spain to Africa. He later spent time in South America flying in Brazil and Argentina. These were dangerous routes and he suffered numerous crashes. He returned to France in the 1930s where he tested aircraft before working as a publicity agent for Air France.

Saint-Exupéry gained fame primarily as a writer of haunting studies of human courage in the face of twentieth century challenges. His first book, *Southern Mail*, appeared in 1929. It was the first of the seven books that would establish him as France's most famous pre-war writer. Often his subject matter was the fated lives of fliers, but *The Little Prince* was a child's fable of hope.

At the outset of World War II, though at an age normally too advanced to be involved in combat flying, Saint-Exupéry rejoined the Armée de l'Air and flew on reconnaissance missions. When France fell, he escaped to the United States where he joined the Air Corps. In 1944 while flying a photo mission in a P-38, he disappeared over the Mediterranean between France and Corsica. Post-war evidence suggests that he was shot down by an FW-190.

SAKAI, SABURO

1916–

As a student, Sakai was a troublemaker who eventually dropped out of high school. He joined the Japanese Imperial Navy in 1933, receiving flight training in 1937. He flew over 200 combat missions during World War II, continuing to fly even after losing an eye. This wound he received over Guadalcanal in August, 1942 while 600 miles (965km) from his home base. He managed to fly back to base despite his terrible injury. By the war's end he had become Japan's highest scoring ace with sixty-seven kills.

After the war he found it difficult to get a job in Japan, so he opened his own print shop in Tokyo.

A fit Saburo Sakai in front of his usual mount, a Zero.

SAMSON, CHARLES RUMNEY

1883–1931

Samson was a colourful original whose mixture of military genius and personal charisma inspired both superiors and subordinates in much the same way that Orde Wingate was to do twenty-five years later.

Born in Lancashire, he joined the Royal Navy at fifteen. Sent to sea, he participated in the 1903 Pomone campaign. In 1911, in competition with 200 other applicants, Samson and three others were chosen by the Admiralty for flight training. Samson breezed through the course, proving himself such a competent aviator and natural leader that the Admiralty gave him command of their first flying school at Eastchurch. At only twenty-eight, he was the youngest commander of a RN installation. Samson, with characteristic single-mindedness – bordering on insubordination – began to press his superiors for modern flying equipment, and a larger budget to continue exploring the growing capabilities of naval aviation. Time after time only the intervention of such far-sighted, powerful individuals as Winston Churchill saved Samson from losing his command. In January, 1912 Samson upset those in the Royal Navy who thought the aeroplane was a toy for stuntmen when he took off from the deck of a warship. His aim was to show the potential of the aeroplane as a far ranging scout for naval fleets. What the flight actually foreshadowed was the development of the aircraft carrier.

When war broke out in 1914, Samson led the first Royal Navy air unit to the Continent. Their base was near Ostend, Belgium. The ensuing exploits of his maverick squadron earned them the title 'Samson's Aeroplane Party'. When ordered to return his squadron to England after only a few days, Samson managed to side-step the command by intentionally 'losing his bearings' and flying to Dunkirk. From there he wired that continual bad weather prevented his return across the Channel. Eventually the original order was forgotten. Dunkirk was very close to the crumbling Front and soon German units reached the area. Samson's aeroplanes, without bombs, had little effect in halting the enemy ground troops, so he set about devising a new method of attack. What he developed was an entirely new weapon – the armoured car. Commandeering some sturdy civilian vehicles, he instructed his men to weld boiler plate boxes onto their chassis. Thus equipped, Samson commanded the world's first mechanized cavalry troop, personally leading them on forays against the enemy. One such expedition to Douai pinned down German forces long enough for a battalion of grateful French troops to evacuate the town.

The next year his unit was sent to Gallipoli. There they flew photo-reconnaissance missions, spotted for artillery batteries, and carried out ground attack raids. Samson himself, on one mission, chanced upon the staff car of Mustapha Kemal Ataturk (the Turkish Army Commander). Loaded with a few small bombs, he swooped down to attack the moving vehicle. Unfortunately, the bombs fell wide and Ataturk lived to become Turkey's first President, with dictatorial prowess surpassed only by Hitler and Stalin.

Samson next commanded the first carrier task force in history – three elderly vessels with wooden planks laid across their tops to serve as flight decks. These primitive carriers roamed the southern Mediterranean Sea sending their aeroplanes out to attack Turkish shipping. He produced yet another technical breakthrough when he ordered a small barge to be fitted with a forty-foot deck across its top. This craft, when towed into the wind behind a destroyer could actually launch a scout plane – surely the world's first baby flat top. With the war almost over, Samson transferred into the newly formed RAF, obtaining the rank of Colonel before the armistice.

Long hours of gruelling work had taken their toll on Samson's health. Though he had a weak heart, he continued his hectic pace after the war, and not surprisingly, died of a heart attack before he was fifty.

SANGER, DR EUGEN ALBERT
1905–1964
Sanger was born in the Czech section of the

Austro-Hungarian Empire. In 1931 he received a doctorate in engineering and physics at Vienna's Technical University. He then moved to Germany to experiment with rockets. In 1936 the Nazi government asked Sanger to head their research establishment at Trauen. There he pioneered the concepts of liquid hydrogen fuel and metal powders mixed with other rocket fuels to promote better burning. In the early forties, he and his colleague, later wife, Irene Bredt, developed the idea of an antipodal bomber. This bomber-cum-spacecraft was to be launched into orbit, and then during its return voyage circle the globe by 'skipping' along the earth's atmosphere. On its way back to base, it would be able to bomb any target on earth.

This concept was later developed into the Space Shuttle. After the war Sanger continued his research, first in France and then in Germany. In the early sixties he was recruited by the Egyptians to run their aborted ballistic missile programme. Sanger was also a leading exponent of photon propulsion.

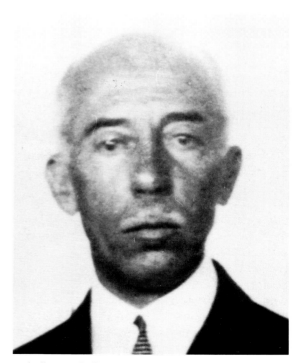

A disillusioned Alberto Santos-Dumont distressed over the airplane's military evolvement.

SANTOS-DUMONT, ALBERTO
1873–1932

No other figure holds such a place in the hearts of aviation enthusiasts as does Santos-Dumont. His life was a blend of the serious, comical, and ultimately tragic elements that surround a classical hero.

He was born the son of an extremely wealthy Brazilian coffee planter whose estate was so large that it had its own railway system. Santos-Dumont learned mechanics by helping to keep the system's locomotive in running order. Like so many others, his first notion of human flight came from reading Jules Verne's (qv) stories. On a family trip to Paris in 1891, he saw several gas balloons in flight, immediately deciding to make aviation his career.

He made his first balloon flight in 1897, after which he had a small balloon constructed to his own specifications. This balloon, *Brazil,* was at the time the smallest hydrogen balloon ever to carry a human passenger. In 1898 he changed to dirigible construction, and again he designed his own craft. His first dirigibles were generally unsuccessful because of low-powered engines and weak gas bags. In 1901 he achieved a major victory when in his airship No. 6 he made a round trip flight from Saint Cloud to the Eiffel Tower as a winning effort for the Deutsch (qv) prize. This victory made Santos-Dumont a hero across all of France and inspired other French aeronauts to build dirigibles. The Lebaudys and Archdeacon (qqv) were among these.

Though he continued to build dirigibles, Santos-Dumont began to think about aeroplanes after hearing Chanute's (qv) report of the Wright brothers (qv). In 1906 he took his plans for an aircraft to Voisin (qv), instructing him to build the machine. It was huge, ungainly canard that was first tested in September, 1906. With a twenty-four horsepower (17.9kw) engine it couldn't fly. On 12 November now equipped with a fifty horsepower (37.3kw) Antoinette, it made the first flight in Europe. Santos-Dumont was hailed as the first ever to fly as few Europeans believed the reports about the Wright brothers. When Wilbur arrived in France in 1908 and proceeded to fly with complete ease, the doubters changed their minds and Santos-Dumont's accomplishments seemed less bright.

With wounded pride he set out to recapture his earlier glory and to this end designed a miniature aircraft whose rights he freely gave to the public. This aeroplane later was named the *Demoiselle* and was without question the grandfather of all light planes ever built. It first achieved real success in 1909 and many copies were made. Santos-Dumont seemed to be back on track, but in 1910 he suffered a serious blow.

That year he learned that he had multiple sclerosis, which meant that his muscle control would progressively deteriorate. He gave up flying and eventually returned to Brazil. For many years he was not heard from, living a life of secrecy. He had become depressed at how man had come to use the aeroplane as an instrument of war. Each year seemed to bring new reports of air bombings. Finally, Santos-Dumont could stand it no longer. He hanged himself with his own necktie in his bathroom. A tragic end for a sensitive man who had done so much to popularize aviation.

SARABIA, D. A. FRANCISCO
1900–1939

Sarabia owned a small Mexican airline and was the personal pilot to President Cardenas of that country. In an attempt to bring glory to Mexico, he purchased the Gee Bee racer *QED* to set a record for a flight between Mexico City and New York. The plane was formerly owned by Jacqueline Cochran. On 24 May 1939 he flew the 2,350 miles (3,781km) between the two cities in the record time of ten hours and thirty-seven minutes.

Mexico exploded with delight and pride. Sarabia was dubbed 'Mexico's Lindbergh'. He was fêted in New York, and then Washington, where he met President Roosevelt. On 7 June he boarded his plane at Bolling Field, in the District of Columbia, intent on flying non-stop to his mother's home in Lerdo, Durango. With his wife and dignitaries on hand to bid him farewell, he fired up the 1,000 horsepower (746kw) plane and took-off. He rose 100 feet

(30m) in the air but suddenly the engine stopped. He pushed the nose down to land in the Potomac. Had he been wearing a shoulder harness he would have survived the impact, but as he wasn't his face smashed into the instrument panel and he was knocked out. Unconscious as the plane sank, he drowned.

Vicious anti-American rumours of sabotage were spread in Mexico and, as was to happen so often in later years, students rioted. Not surprisingly, the students were wrong. It was soon found that a rag had been ingested into the carburettor inlet. Had it been sabotage the rag would have clogged the duct while the engine was still warming up. At it was, chance killed a fine pilot. The *QED* was salvaged and placed in a private museum in Mexico.

Mexico's aerial conquistador Francisco Sarabia.

SAULNIER, RAYMOND
1881–*

Saulnier trained as an engineer at the École Centrale. In 1908 he joined Blériot (qv), soon proving his worth when he designed the Type XI, a plane whose success was proved by the many companies who paid to build licenced versions of it.

In late 1911 the Morane brothers (qv) asked him to join their new manufacturing venture. With his new partners, Saulnier continued to design advanced monoplanes. The outbreak of the war ensured the company's success and Morane-Saulnier scouts proved popular among military pilots. Saulnier's most important war work was the invention of a device that allowed machines to fire through a propeller arc. In April, 1914 he sought a patent for a synchroniser gear. The mechanism wasn't refined enough for practical use, so when he was approached by Garros (qv) for a means of affixing a forward-firing machine-gun, he simply mounted steel deflector plates to the blades of the propellers. These blades were inadequate for the job, but when further developed by Garros's mechanic, Jules Hue, they worked perfectly. Air combat was born.

SCHNAUFER, HEINZ-WOLFGANG
1922–1950

Schnaufer was an excellent student whose college plans were interrupted when the war began in 1939. He immediately joined the Luftwaffe, requesting night fighter training which he received. A handsome, likeable young man, he was also a born predator whose patience and cunning made him immensely suitable for the nerve-racking task of night fighting.

Soon after beginning his combat career in the spring of 1942, Schnaufer rose to public prominence in Germany, and Britain, as the 'Night Ghost of St. Trond', (his usual base in Belgium). Three out of every four missions brought kills. His choice of weapon was the Bf-110 equipped with Schrage Musik upward-firing machine-guns.

Schnaufer flew often and in any type of weather. Never one for showmanship, he managed to survive to the end of the war, chalking up 121 victories. He was the most successful night ace of the war.

Ironically, having survived the air war, he was killed in France in a bizarre automobile accident. A truck pulled out of a side street striking his car. Schnaufer was thrown clear only to have heavy oxygen bottles from the truck's bed spill out onto him, killing him.

SCHNEIDER, JACQUES
1879–1928

Jacques Schneider was an heir to a large steel and armaments empire. In fact, his family-owned business built France's first tank. Schneider was less inclined to take part in running the business than he was to indulge in sports such as motorboat racing and flying. He was taught to fly in 1909 by Blériot (qv).

When a boating accident left him with a crippled arm, thus incapable of piloting an airplane, he decided to at least promote the development of aviation. To this end he established an annual race for seaplanes. He was inspired to choose this type of plane when he witnessed Conneau (qv) land in Italy during the 1911 Paris-Rome-Turin race. Schneider found it strange that a Naval officer should fly a landplane.

The first race took place in Monaco, where it was a huge success. Maurice Prévost won it flying a Deperdussin. Schneider added a stipulation that any country that won the trophy on three successive occasions would own it. He died three years before the British accomplished that feat.

SCHWARTZ, DAVID
1845–1897

Schwartz was an Austro-Hungarian citizen who experimented in Germany. During the 1890s he designed and built two all-metal airships. The first of these was structurally unsound. The second was made in the shape of an artillery shell from aluminium sheet; although, strictly speaking it had an ovoid cross-section. A twelve horsepower (8.9kw) Daimler engine provided power to three propellers. Schwartz died suddenly before his invention was completed so his wife, Melanie, took over the project.

On 3 November 1897 the ship was prepared for its first flight at Templehof field near Berlin. One spectator with more than a passing interest was Count von Zeppelin (qv). No one had any experience in flying the ship so the officials selected a volunteer from amongst those on the launch site. This volunteer was either an engineer, a mechanic who had worked on the craft or a soldier. His name may have been either Jaegels or Platz, contemporary accounts varied. Whoever he was, he managed to get the craft into the air and moving, but several minutes later the aluminium hulk was out of control. In desperation, he accidentally released too much of the hydrogen and the ship smashed into the ground. He leaped out at the last second and was saved.

SCOTT, CHARLES W. A.
1903-1946

Scott, a Briton, learned to fly after he joined the RAF in 1922. He was a popular pilot who often won amateur boxing exhibitions, but the RAF in those years wasn't exciting enough for him so he resigned. In 1927 he moved to Australia and found work with Qantas. He craved attention though, and this yearning led him to undertake record flights. In 1931 he broke the England to Australia record and the same year broke the record going the other way.

In 1934 he achieved his greatest fame as one of the pilots of the DH 88 Comet racer that won the MacRobertson trophy. After this victory, he went into the airshow business in Britain. He purchased and operated Cobham's (qv) former Flying Circus.

As the years went by, Scott's name was forgotten and he lost the fame he loved so much. He committed suicide in Germany.

SCOTT, MAJOR GEORGE HERBERT
1888–1930

Educated at the Royal Naval Engineering College, Scott joined the RNAS in 1914 where he was assigned to fly airships. In 1915 he commanded the Parseval P 4, two years later taking command of the R-9 rigid airship.

In 1919 he commanded the R-34 on a flight from Scotland to New York and back. This incredible flight came only two months after the Curtiss NC flying-boat flights, but was more impressive because of the seeming ease with which it was conducted. Much of the credit for the success of the flight was due to Scott, who firmly guided his crew through severe North Atlantic storms and high winds. He even had to deal with a stowaway found on board after the flight started! This man, William Ballantyne, had helped to fit out the R-34 for the flight, but the day before the lift-off was told he would have to stay behind to save weight. Several of his friends helped to hide him on board shortly before the flight left.

In 1930 Scott commanded the 'Capitalist airship' R-100 on a successful round-trip voyage to Canada, though Booth (qv) was the actual captain in charge of operating the craft during the voyage. Unfortunately, his next command was the government-built 'Socialist airship' R-101, whose crash in October 1930 killed not only Scott, but most of the crew.

SCOTT, ROBERT LEE
1908–
Scott was born in Macon, Georgia. His high school grades were low because he spent too much time dreaming of aeroplanes. He went to two small colleges before leaving in 1927 to join the Army. Army life improved his work habits and he eventually received an appointment to West Point. In 1933 he became an Air Corps pilot and was assigned the next year to fly mail routes.

In the years prior to America's involvement in World War II, Scott was serving in training units though he longed to be involved in combat. The American Volunteer Group provided that opportunity, so he signed up with them and went to Asia. His adventures as a member of the Flying Tigers are vividly chronicled in *God is My Co-pilot*. As a member of that group he often flew on dangerous solo missions against the Japanese over China and the Burmese mountains. Ultimately he shot down thirteen

enemy aircraft. His greatest value to the American war effort may have been the publication of his stirring book during the war. A film version of it was released in early 1945.

After the war Scott stayed with the Air Force in various capacities, including commanding a fighter wing in Germany during the Korean War. In the 1980s he revisited China and hiked the length of the Great Wall – he was nearly eighty!

SCOTT, SHEILA
1927–1988
Sheila Scott was an English actress who took to flying in 1959. Early in her flying career she rallied and raced Tiger Moths, but in the mid-sixties she turned to serious record breaking with more powerful aircraft.

Piloting a Piper Commanche she departed Heathrow Airport on 18 May 1966 on a round-the-world attempt. Thirty-three days later she returned having set a record for the longest solo flight in a single-engine airplane (28,656 miles) (46,106km). Following this she set solo records for London to Cape Town and Cape Town to London. Her most notable flight was a 1971 round-the-world flight which took her across the North Pole. It was during this trip that she claimed to have one of her occasional ESP experiences. With her radio broken, she had been unable to contact an American tracking station that had arranged to send her flight vectoring information. Without this, she would not know when to turn her aircraft to locate an airbase to refuel. Just then, she later stated, she clearly heard an inner voice instructing her to turn. She did and soon spotted the refueling stop.

Scott was very much a product of the swinging 1960s and her candid views on a variety of subjects often appeared in British papers.

von SEECKT, HANS
1866–1936
During World War I von Seeckt served as Chief of Staff to Field Marshal Mackensen. An able

staff officer, he was chosen to reduce the German services to 100,000 men after the Treaty of Versailles. Apparently the numbers were reduced, but von Seeckt had secretly established bases outside Germany where soldiers could receive types of training that had been banned in Germany, i.e. naval, armoured, and air training.

Von Seeckt was responsible for protecting the seed of the Air Force after World War I, and it was he who ordered Milch (qv) to rebuild the Luftwaffe in the early thirties. Had it not been for von Seeckt, Germany would have had no military base at the time Hitler rose to power, and history might have been radically different.

SEGUIN, LAURENT
1883–1944
SEGUIN, LOUIS
1869–1918

When he was only twenty-six years old, Louis Seguin founded his own engine manufacturing company. Ten years later in 1905 he was joined by his half-brother Laurent, and together they reorganized the company as the Société des Moteurs Gnôme to build small automobile engines.

In 1907 the two well-educated engineers decided to enter the blossoming aviation industry by introducing a radically new aircraft engine. European aviators were in desperate need of a light, reliable powerplant. Laurent thought that a rotary engine might suit this need. The rotary engine had been adapted to aviation use by Hargrave (qv). The Seguin's production engine had seven cylinders (the prototype had five) arranged around a lightweight circular crankcase. The entire engine weighed only 165 pounds (75kg) and produced a consistent fifty horsepower (37.3kw). For 1907 this power-to-weight ratio was a considerable achievement. The engine, named the Gnôme, was evolved into larger versions, and companies around the world built copies of them. The rotary engine was the most used type of aircraft engine during World War I.

Interestingly, the Seguins were closely related

to the Montgolfier brothers (qv), though removed by several generations.

SELFRIDGE, LIEUTENANT THOMAS E.
1882–1908

Selfridge was from San Francisco and after attending West Point became a lieutenant in the Army. In early 1907 he introduced himself to Alexander Graham Bell (qv), who was visiting Washington, and told the famous scientist that he had read about the latter's kite experiments and was himself interested in aviation. Bell immediately invited him to join the Aerial Experiment Association which he was then forming. He went so far as to write to his friend President Roosevelt who promptly ordered Selfridge to be seconded as an observer to Bell.

Selfridge was indeed well acquainted with various aeronautical experiments then being conducted around the world. He related what he knew to Bell's group and was appointed to guide the construction of the group's first aircraft. When finished, this craft was named the *Red Wing*. On 12 March 1908 it made the first publicly announced flight in America. Casey Baldwin (qv) was the pilot.

Selfridge did not design the airplane completely on his own, though he did hold the power of veto over any suggestion. However, he never flew in the *Red Wing*; his turn to fly came on 19 May 1908 in the AEA's next design, the *White Wing*. He made two short flights that day.

In the summer of 1908 he was summoned to Washington to serve on the Signal Corps' Aeronautical Board, which was then engaged in performance trials of the Baldwin-Curtiss dirigible, the Wright military aeroplane, and other flying machines. In Washington he met Orville Wright (qv) who distrusted him because of his association with the AEA. Wright wrote that Selfridge was an intelligent young man who knew much about aircraft and continually pumped Wright for more information.

Because of Selfridge's position on the Aeronautical Board, Wright found it impossible to turn down his request to fly in the plane during its trials. On 17 September 1908 the pair went up for a flight. Shortly after getting airborne, they heard a tapping sound from the rear. Suddenly, the plane pitched downwards and crashed. Selfridge's head struck a strut and he was knocked unconscious. He later died, the world's first aeroplane fatality.

de SEVERSKY, ALEXANDER PROKOFIEFF
1894–1974

When he was ten years old, Seversky was sent to a military school. He next attended the Russian Naval Academy from which he graduated in 1914. He saw sea duty during the winter of 1914–15 but then transferred to the Imperial Naval Air Service. It was natural that he should become an aviator as his father was the first private Russian citizen to own and pilot a plane in that country.

Seversky was posted to a bombing squadron and on 2 July 1915 went off on a mission to bomb targets on the Gulf of Riga. His plane was shot down and upon hitting the water its bomb exploded. Seversky's leg was blown off. During his recovery he inspected aircraft in production. Seeing aircraft every day rekindled his enthusiasm for combat flying. With an artificial leg fitted he returned to flying in the summer of 1916. By the time he had finished combat flying the next summer, he had scored thirteen kills.

In the summer of 1917 he was sent to the US as part of the Russian Naval Air Mission. With Russia's withdrawal from the war, he was free to offer his services to America. His most noted contribution was advising Billy Mitchell (qv) on the bombing trials of 1921. In 1922 he started a company which produced the first automatic bombsight. He sold this invention to the US for $50,000. In 1931 he founded his next company, Seversky Aircraft Corporation, with the intention of building advanced military planes. The company's most successful plane was the P-35, predecessor to the Thunderbolt. In 1939 the company was reformed as Republic.

During his long career, Seversky was appointed to many governmental and industrial committees. His book *Victory Through Air Power*, published in 1942, explained how America could use aeroplanes to win the war.

Alan Shepard, the first free man in space.

SHEPARD, COMMANDER ALAN BARTLETT, JR.
1923-

A native of New Hampshire, Shepard graduated from Annapolis in 1944. After serving on a destroyer in the Pacific, he entered a flight training programme, earning his wings in 1947. There followed two years of duty in a fighter squadron before entering the test pilot training programme in Maryland.

In April, 1959 he was one of seven outstanding pilots chosen to be trained in America's first class of astronauts. During the next two years he underwent intensive training which prepared him for America's first space shots in 1961. Shepard was chosen to make the first flight, aboard the Mercury capsule *Freedom 7*.

On 1 May 1961 he was launched into outer space for a fifteen minute sub-orbital flight. This space shot, although of no important scientific value, at least showed Americans that they too were capable of putting a man in space. From that day on, Americans were in a neck-and-neck Space Race to the Moon with the Russians.

After this first flight, Shepard lost his active astronaut status when an ear disorder affected his equilibrium. Following surgery, he returned to duty in 1969 and two years later commanded the Apollo XIV mission to the Moon. Besides having the distinction of being the first American in space, he also became the first golfer on the Moon when he made a few lunar putts with a collapsible club and golf ball during the Apollo XIV mission.

Following his retirement from the Navy in 1974, Shepard went into the private sector where he became involved in real estate sales.

SHORT, HORACE LEONARD
1872–1917
SHORT, ALBERT EUSTACE
1875–1932
SHORT, HUGH OSWALD
1883–1969

Eustace and Oswald Short, brothers, purchased a used balloon in 1897 and taught themselves to fly it. After learning how to build balloons at Edouard Surcouf's factory in Paris in 1900, they returned to England and began to build their own balloons. In 1904 they won a contract to build balloons for the British Army, and soon were building them for private citizens. Amongst their first clients were C. R. Rolls and J. T. C. Moore-Brabazon (qqv). In 1908 their brother, Horace, joined them to establish the first company in Britain incorporated to build aeroplanes. Their first two projects were aircraft built for Rolls and Frank McClean. Neither of these was a success. In 1909 Horace, having an order from Wilbur Wright (qv), went to France to make drawings of a Wright biplane. The Shorts produced six examples of this plane and the experience taught them enough to design their own successfully.

Biplane No. 2, built for Moore-Brabazon, was their first successful design. It was designed by Horace who soon gained a reputation as one of the country's best engineers. Despite an enlarged head and disfigured face, Horace had become an expert engineer and was knowledgeable on many subjects. As a young man, he had voyaged to Buenos Aires and then hiked to Mexico, a remarkable walk! During the trek he was stricken with an illness and nursed back to health by natives who mistook him for a god because of his unusually large head!

In 1913 the brothers developed an excellent seaplane with folding wings for storage on ships. That type, and subsequent models, saw extensive use throughout the war. When Horace died during the war, Hugh took over the responsibility of design. He pushed for aluminium construction during the inter-war years. During that time the Short flying-boats in service as airliners helped to bring the British Empire closer together.

SIEGERT, WILHELM
1872–1929

Siegert learned to fly in 1910 and during World War I organized some of Germany's first bomber squadrons. His primary goal during the winter of 1914 was to bomb London. He hand-picked some thirty crews and equipped them with lumbering Aviatiks. On Christmas Eve he led them on a raid over Dover. The raid was a morale boost more than an strategic success as Aviatiks could carry only small bomb loads. The London raids were postponed. Siegert rose through the ranks and ended the war as the Inspector of Fighter Pilots.

SIGRIST, FREDERICK
1880–1956

In 1909 T. O. M. Sopwith (qv) needed a mechanic to tend his yacht and found one in Sigrist. When his employer went into aviation the next year, Sigrist followed. He was put in charge of keeping all of Sopwith's planes in flying condition. When Sopwith began to build his own planes, he promoted Sigrist to shop manager.

Sigrist demonstrated a flair for aircraft design, but his speciality was construction. In fact, he received a commission on every fuselage sold. During World War I he became a manager of the company and continued as one when Sopwith became Hawker.

A hard working, loyal companion to Sopwith, Sigrist, the former mechanic, died a millionaire in Bermuda.

SIKORSKY, IGOR IVANOVITCH
1889–1972
Sikorsky was born in Kiev to a doctor. His mother was college educated, which was a rare accomplishment in those days for a Russian woman. She taught young Sikorsky about da Vinci's (qv) aviation experiments and this sparked his interest in flying. To learn more about aircraft, he went to Paris in 1908 where he met many of the early aircraft constructors. When he returned to Russia he built two helicopters but they failed to fly. He then built aeroplanes, but it wasn't until his fifth design that he had a real aeroplane capable of sustained flight. His next plane, the S-6 of 1912, won a large cash prize at a 1912 military competition. He then took a job at the Russian-Baltic Railroad Car Company. For this company he designed the first four-engined aeroplane, the *Grand*. This plane stunned the world when it first flew in 1913. It featured an enclosed cabin, a wash room, and was even equipped with an observation platform with searchlight!

In 1917, with the advent of the Revolution, Sikorsky fled to Paris. The next year he emigrated to the United States with less than $100 in his pocket. Four years of effort later he had founded his own manufacturing company, with the help of other Russian emigrés. In only a few years the company had become known world-wide for its excellent commercial flying-boats.

Sikorsky's greatest achievement was the development of the VS-300 of 1939. It is recognized as the world's first practical single-rotor helicopter and gave the world a revolutionary new method of aerial transport.

SKALSKI, STANISLAW
1915–
Skalski was an excellent and brave pilot; flying an antiquated PZL P.11 fighter, he managed to shoot down six German aircraft in September, 1939. When Poland collapsed, Skalski escaped and joined the RAF in England. During the summer of 1940, he flew with No. 501 Squadron, and later with No. 303 Polish Squadron. As the war progressed, he fought in North Africa, Italy, France, and Germany. He shot down 22·5 enemy aircraft, making him Poland's highest scoring ace of the war.

Upon returning to Poland after the war, he was imprisoned by the Communists for protesting against his country's occupation by the Russians.

SMIRNOFF, IVAN WASSILIWITSJ
1895–1956
On the outbreak of World War I, Smirnoff, born in Vladimir, Russia, entered the infantry. He was wounded in combat and received a medal for bravery. When he returned to duty it was as a trainee pilot. He soon demonstrated his earlier bravery as he pressed home attack after attack against German aircraft. He was not afraid to fight single-handedly against numerous opponents and even under such circumstances he gained kills.

In November, 1917 he finally had to flee when outnumbered. In this case, he learned of a plot by Bolshevik sympathizers to kill the officers of his squadron. He escaped to England where he joined the RAF. He returned to Russia briefly during the civil war, but spent the rest of his flying career as a pilot for KLM. His war kills totalled twelve.

SMITH, SIR ROSS MACPHERSON
1892–1922
Smith's flying career, though brief, couldn't have been any more varied or exciting. He was born in Semaphore, Australia and as a teenager was a popular school sports figure. In 1914 he joined the Australian cavalry and was sent to Gallipoli. In 1916 he joined the Australian Flying Corps, receiving a posting to the Middle East. There, his

adventures are the stuff of legend. He was involved in aerial combat against the Germans and Turks, ultimately claiming nine kills, piloted Lawrence of Arabia on secret missions behind enemy lines, and once landed behind the lines to rescue a downed comrade. During this exploit, he had to fight off attacking Turks with a pistol while the stranded pilot sprinted to Smith's plane. He was wounded during one dogfight when a bullet grazed his cheek and another whizzed across the top of his skull. Bleeding heavily, he still managed to bring his plane back to base.

Following the war he embarked on several record-setting flights which brought his name finally to the headlines in Britain and Australia. His greatest triumph occurred during November and December, 1919 when he, his brother Keith, and two others made the first flight from England to Australia. The flight covered 11,300 miles (18,172km) and was accomplished in twenty-eight days. For the British and Australians, the two ends of the Empire were psychologically drawn together. Australia would seem less and less like a distant colony as other fliers followed in Smith's slipstream.

Smith's promising life was cut short when on 13 April 1922 the Vickers Viking aircraft he was testing crashed.

SOMMER, ROGER
1877–1965
Sommer was the son of a rich felt manufacturer from Mouzon, France. In 1908, having become intensely interested in flying, he built an aeroplane, but it failed to fly. He then approached Henry Farman (qv) and purchased a machine from him in 1909. Sommer learned to fly on this machine in July of that year. He next embarked on an exhibition career during which he set numerous records for altitude, passenger carrying, and more. In 1909 he took Gertrude Bacon on a flight thus making her the first Englishwoman to fly in an airplane. That year he again attempted to build aircraft and this time was successful. He founded a factory in

Mouzon and a flying school at Douzy, Mouremelon.

SOPWITH, SIR THOMAS OCTAVE MURDOCH
1888–1989
Sopwith's career in aviation spanned the years from the inception of powered flight to the age of jump jets. He was born into a wealthy family and trained as a civil engineer. Much of his time at university was spent in the company of ballooning or motoring friends, among them C. S. Rolls (qv). In 1910 he purchased his first aeroplane, a Howard Wright monoplane. Without instruction Sopwith tried to fly this aeroplane but, predictably, crashed. Unhurt, he tried again two weeks later with happier results. Soon he earned his aviator's certificate and became an exhibition pilot. His success was startling. In December, 1910 he won a long distance flight from Eastchurch to Thirlmont, Belgium. The next year he toured America, winning several prizes and earning a reputation as one of England's best pilots. In 1912 he began to manufacture airplanes.

Much of Sopwith's ultimate success as a manufacturer was due to his ability to pick the right people to work for him, notably H. Sigrist. Another of his selection was Harry Hawker (qv), who became his test pilot. During World War I the company built some of the world's best combat aircraft including the Camel and the Snipe. It was re-organized after the war via a voluntary bankruptcy and became known as Hawker.

Sopwith relinquished the chairmanship of his company in 1963 at the age of seventy-five. Even when he reached his hundredth birthday in 1988 his mind was active, clear, and able to recall the wondrous events of a youth long before.

SPERRLE, GENERAL HUGO
1885-1953
Sperrle, a veteran of the German Air Force in World War I, was a capable, if uninspired,

Luftwaffe General during World War II. His first combat command under the Nazi régime came in 1936 when he led the Condor Legion in Spain. During the Battle of Britain he commanded Luftflotte III, the Luftwaffe fleet closest to British soil. If Sperrle is to be remembered for anything, other than his uncanny resemblance to Hermann Goering (qv), it should be for his correct assessment on 3 September 1940 that the RAF had not been beaten and that the main task of the Luftwaffe should be to attack fighter bases, and not London. Goering overruled him, perhaps losing the war because of it.

SPERRY, DR ELMER AMBROSE
1860–1930

More than anyone else, Sperry made all-weather, long distance flying possible. He was born in New York where he received a typical public school education. In his late teens he enrolled in special day courses at Cornell University to study electricity. He quickly mastered that new science and had soon invented a new type of dynamo and arc lamp. These were put into production and sold well. After developing numerous other devices, including mining equipment and an electric car, he began to investigate the possibilities of gyroscopes around 1896.

Inventions derived from gyroscopes are what Sperry is most remembered for. In 1910 the US Navy adopted his accurate marine gyro compass. In 1912 he approached Glenn Curtiss (qv) to help him develop an automatic stabilizer for aircraft. This early auto-pilot was demonstrated the next year in a Curtiss flying boat. In 1914, in Paris, his son Lawrence (qv) flew the plane 'hands off' in front of a stunned Parisian audience while his mechanic climbed out on to the wing. Even the mechanic's off-centre weight didn't unbalance the craft.

Elmer Sperry went on to invent many other valuable flying aids including the directional gyro, the gyro horizon, and the drift indicator. These devices enabled James Doolittle (qv) to make the world's first completely blind flight in 1929.

SPERRY, LAWRENCE BURST
1892–1923

Lawrence Sperry was born with all the ambition and inventiveness that made his father, Elmer Sperry (qv), such a gigantic success in American industry. His first job was as a newspaper boy, but he soon gave that up to open a bicycle repair business. From this business he saved enough to purchase his own car at the age of sixteen. In those days that was an extremely rare purchase for such a young man. About this time, he became interested in aviation and built a glider in the family's home. It didn't fly well so he built a powered biplane in which he made a few halting flights in 1910. In 1913 his father told him that he should learn to fly a plane properly and sent him to the Curtiss school. The elder Sperry also assigned his son as project engineer on the installation of the first auto-pilot system in an aeroplane. Lawrence successfully supervised the work and that year a plane was flown completely under the control of an auto-pilot.

Sperry entered into a formal business relationship with his father to further develop aircraft instruments. He pursued his own inventions too and these included the first retractable landing gear aircraft in 1915, and the flying bomb. After the war, he built the delightful Messenger biplane that had been designed by the Army Engineering Division. It was hoped the plane would become a military liaison aircraft. Sperry embarked on a sales tour to Europe in 1923 but disappeared on a flight over the English Channel. Though his plane was recovered intact, he was not in it.

SPRINGS, CAPTAIN ELLIOT WHITE
1896–1959

Springs' father owned a large textile mill near Fort Mill, South Carolina. He wanted his son to achieve great things so he sent him to military academies and finally to Princeton University. At Princeton, young Springs joined a pre-military aviation group in which he received some flight training. From there he was sent in September, 1917 to England to complete his flight training as a fighter pilot.

Springs' easy-going manners and Southern graces made him a popular flier. Amongst his friends and advisors were Billy Bishop and Edward Mannock (qqv), both of whom guided his early combat training. He was seconded to the RFC and shot down his first enemy aircraft on 5 June, 1918. He scored his first four victories flying an S.E.-5a, but was then shot down and wounded. On recovery, he joined a Camel squadron and proceeded to score eight more victories.

At the war's end he returned to South Carolina to work in his father's mill. The hum of weaving machines seemed somewhat mundane to Springs compared to the whirl of rotary engines, and he often found himself day-dreaming. Finally, his father grew tired of his son's drifting off and fired him. Undaunted, Springs moved to Paris along with other fashionable American ex-patriates where he embarked on a writing career. His first book was a phenomenal success entitled *WAR BIRDS, Diary of an Unknown Aviator*. It is supposedly an account of the life of one of Springs' comrades who died in battle. It is a bittersweet tale of young people caught in the emotional highs and lows of war-time flying. The story's success relies on its truthful retelling of a pilot's world during the war, a world where raucous parties were punctuated with frequent funerals.

Springs wrote other books and eventually returned in glory to his father's business. He took over that business on his father's death and built it into a huge textile empire of a size his father never could have imagined.

STEINHOFF, JOHANNES
1913–

As incredible as it may seem, Steinhoff, with 176 victories, ranks only twenty-third on the German World War II ace list. Steinhoff was an especially talented flyer, capable of fighting in any theatre and with any type of machine. He began the war in JG 26, which in the summer of 1940 was based at Abbeville. Later he helped to organize the famous NJG 1 nightfighter unit and later still the JV 44 jet fighter unit. It was while

beginning a mission with this unit on 18 April, 1945 that he crashed in an Me-262 and suffered severe burns.

Following the war, he began a commercial advertising agency but gave that up in 1955 to rejoin the Luftwaffe as Deputy Chief of Staff. He retired from active duty in 1972.

Flying sisters Marjorie and Katherine Stinson.

STINSON, EDDIE
1894–1932
STINSON, KATHERINE
1896–1977
STINSON, MARJORIE CLAIRE
189*–1975

There were many famous 'brother teams' in aviation history, but only one 'sister team' ever became famous. The sisters were Katherine and Marjorie Stinson. They were from a liberal-minded family living in Jackson, Mississippi. One of their grandparents was a Cherokee Indian. Katherine had a great admiration for her piano teacher whose career she wanted to emulate. Because this teacher had studied abroad, Katherine knew she would need a lot of money to fulfil her goal. At that time, exhibition flying was making newspaper headlines daily and much of the talk was about the high fees commanded by the pilots. With a youthful brand of logic, Katherine decided that if she became an exhibition pilot she'd soon earn enough to train to be a great pianist. Her mother, surprisingly, supported her idea and paid for her to take flying lessons at Cicero Field, Chicago in July, 1912. The lessons were exorbitantly expensive – $150 per hour, but Katherine soloed after only 3·5 hours dual. She became only the fourth American woman to earn her certificate.

Her mother next bought for her a used Wright Model B and Katherine went on to the next phase of her plan – earning a lot of money as a barnstormer. She was an instant smash hit, earning $500 per show. In September, 1913 she became the first woman to fly official airmail, this on a route between the fairgrounds near Helena, Montana, and the government office in the city. In 1916 she travelled to the Orient where she dazzled the Chinese and Japanese with her flying skills – and the fact that a woman, a small woman at that, could fly.

In 1914 her sister Marjorie had learned to fly at the Wright school after which she too became an exhibition flyer. In 1915 they joined their mother to start a flying school near San Antonio where during the war hundreds of military pilots would take training.

Eddie Stinson, a brother, learned to fly in 1915 at the Wright school and then helped establish the family's flying school in Texas. During the war he shared in the training duties, but afterwards hit the exhibition circuit as a daredevil flyer. One of his specialities was to race an automobile around fairground circuits, and for this he earned $1,500 per show! Unfortunately he developed a drinking problem which resulted in his squandering money season after season. He thought that if he could raise his fee by an additional $500 he might be able to save some of his money. To this end, he fitted some motorcycle brakes to his aircraft's wheels and announced that in addition to his normal routine, from now on he would also land on any

race track's infield – a sure crowd pleaser. His promoter was able to squeeze another $500 from each show's organizing committee for this, raising Stinson's fee to $2,000. Stinson's spendthrift ways had led to the development of the first practical landing brakes.

In 1925 he founded his own aircraft company in a warehouse in Detroit. The Stinson Company built commercial planes in its early years, but later switched to general aviation aircraft. Eddie was killed when an aeroplane he was flying ran out of fuel and crashed. In 1940 his company was absorbed by Vultee.

STOUT, WILLIAM BUSHNELL
1880–1956

Stout was one of America's most inventive engineers, though he is best remembered for one design – the Ford Tri-motor, a plane he didn't design! He was born in Quincy, Illinois and attended both Hamline University and the University of Minnesota where he studied mechanical engineering. In 1912 he went to work at the *Chicago Tribune* as its aviation editor, before leaving to found his own publication, *Aerial Age*. Nicknamed 'Jack-knife' because of his sharp personality and cutting comments, he served briefly at Packard as an engineer, then during the war as a consultant for the Aircraft Production Board.

In 1918 he built the Batwing cantilever monoplane. Though a believer in the future of metal aircraft, he built this Gothic-looking craft of wood to save money. A limousine version of this followed which attracted the attention of the US Navy who ordered a cantilever torpedo plane from him. This became the ST-1. It was an all aluminium twin-Packard powered monoplane.

Ever the bold salesman of grandiose plans, Stout then sent 100 wealthy industrialists mimeographed letters asking for $1,000 each in order for him to start his own business. He warned they might never see their money again. About twenty cheques came back, including one each from Henry and Edsel Ford. Thus was formed The Stout Metal Plane Company, the first product of which was the 1923 Air Sedan. This clean, practical design used corrugated aluminium skin. It was followed by the equally practical 2-AT, basically a single-engined version of what would become the famous Tri-motor. Stout's string of successes so impressed Henry Ford that he purchased Stout's company outright in August, 1925. Later that year, the 3-AT Tri-motor appeared. It was an ugly brute whose abilities matched its looks. A mysterious hangar fire destroyed this airplane and it was not long before Stout and Ford, men of enormous talents and egos, parted company. The Ford Tri-motor was thus designed by Howard Hicks, Thomas Towle, and other Ford men.

In 1926 Stout founded an airline with routes between Detroit, Cleveland, Grand Rapids, and Chicago. This company was absorbed by United Aircraft and Transport in 1929. Stout, during these years, also built several prototype aircraft including the Sky Car and the Stout Amphibian, both small aircraft built of corrugated skin. In addition to designing motorcycles, buses and trains; he penned, and built, the Scarab automobile. This was a futuristic rear engined art-deco dream machine of which about five were built.

Stout's famous design credo is as true today as when he first said it. It applies not only to aircraft design, but to politics and government. He said: 'Simplicate. Add lightness'.

STRINGFELLOW, JOHN
1799–1883
Stringfellow, an English lace manufacturer, was the partner of Samuel Henson (qv). His true talent lay in his ability to design light steam engines. After his partner had fled to America, Stringfellow continued to design model aeroplanes although none ever flew. In 1868 he became a member of the Aeronautical Society where he valiantly predicted that heavier-than-air flight would be a reality in a matter of years. Twenty years later, almost to the day, after Stringfellow died, the Wright brothers (qv) confirmed his faith.

STUDENT, GENERALLEUTNANT KURT
1890–1978
A pilot in World War I, Student flew over Tannenberg during the first battle in history whose outcome was affected by aircraft. Before the war had ended, he had become a Group Commander, leading Jagdgruppe III. During the 1920s he was the Weimar government's 'aviation advisor', a title which disguised the fact that he was clandestinely organizing secret Luftwaffe training bases. When the Luftwaffe came out into the open, Student was assigned the task of organizing its paratroop battalion.

During the battle for Holland, he personally led his élite troops in the first airborne assault in history. The attack was a complete success. Student's next mission was the invasion of Crete in May, 1941. This bloody invasion showed that without ground or naval support, an airborne army could be only partially successful.

For the rest of the war his paratroops were grounded. Student continued to be a valued commander though and played a major role in the Battle of the Bulge and the Arnhem offensive.

SUKHOI, PAVEL OSIPOVICH
1895–1975
Upon graduating from the Zhukovski Air Academy, Sukhoi went to work as a designer with the Tupolev (qv) design bureau. His first product was the ANT-5 (I-4) fighter. This became the standard Russian fighter in the late 1920s and early 1930s. His most notable prewar success was the ANT-25 long range monoplane that flew non-stop from Moscow to San Francisco via the North Pole in 1937. The tremendous publicity value of this flight, which greatly enhanced the image of Russia, prompted Stalin to give Sukoi his own design bureau.

However, Sukhoi's war record was to be uneven. His only successful military plane was the Su-2 attack bomber. Shortly after the war he lost Stalin's favour and was stripped of his bureau.

In 1952, with the death of Stalin, he was 'rehabilitated'. He made the most of the opportunity and designed capable attack jets. When he died in 1975 he had earned the Order of Lenin and was accepted as one of the Soviet Union's greatest designers.

Scientist, religious philosopher Emanuel Swedenborg.

SWEDENBORG, EMANUEL
1688–1772

Swedenborg was an unprecedented figure in the annals of aviation. It would not be facetious to say that his life combined elements of Roger Bacon, Leonardo da Vinci (qqv) and Buddha!

He was born in Stockholm and educated at the University of Uppsala. Between 1710 and 1715 he travelled throughout northern Europe where he came into contact with most of the eminent scientists of the age. During this period, he developed theories of navigation, mathematics, religion, government and even flight. On his return to Sweden he began to publish his ideas and after a few years he had won a European reputation. His income was derived mostly from his government-appointed post with the Board of Mines. In conjunction with this job, he established new mining techniques and pushed Sweden to develop both copper and iron industries. In addition, he called for the establishment of a system of coinage based on the decimal system, but was ignored.

In 1714 he proposed that manned flight was possible in a craft with a fixed main wing and flapping wings for propulsion. For the first time in history the value of a fixed wing for lift had been recognized. Swedenborg was the first to separate wings used for lift from wings used for propulsion. It was a titanic breakthrough, but of course completely ignored at the time. In fact, it wasn't until the end of the nineteenth century that his ideas were rediscovered and this only after the experiments of Cayley, Le Bris (qqv) and others. Swedenborg influenced no one, he just arrived at the right conclusion first. His work was unknown to Chanute (qv) in the 1890s, thus the Wrights (qv) had no knowledge of it.

Swedenborg, however, was not completely forgotten. In his later career, he devoted himself to religious philosophy and wrote many books on the subject. His philosophy was a mixture of pragmatism, populism, and mysticism. After his death, it attracted more and more followers and became an established religion. Its followers became known as Swedenborgians. Today it has many thousands of followers, including at least one former American astronaut.

TALLMAN, FRANK
1919–1978

Tallman was born into a well-off family and made a deal with his father that if he kept good grades in school his father would pay for his flying lessons. Both sides did their part and Tallman soloed on his sixteenth birthday. During World War II he was a Navy instructor in Florida. After the war he moved to California to become a stunt pilot in films. He used his large collection of different types of aircraft to get film jobs and in just a few years he was Paul Mantz's (qv) biggest competitor. In 1961 the two merged their companies to create Tallmantz Aviation.

Tallman personally flew the stunts in many

films including *It's a Mad, Mad, Mad, World, Murphy's War, Catch-22,* and *The Great Waldo Pepper*. He was scouting locations for a new project when, flying a Piper Aztec, he crashed into mountains in California and was killed.

TANK, PROFESSOR KURT WALDEMAR
1898-1983

Kurt Tank designed some of Germany's greatest combat aeroplanes and it was under his direction that Focke-Wulf rose from obscurity to become one of the largest aircraft manufacturers in the world in 1945.

Tank's first engineering job was with the Rohrbach-Metallflugzeugbau. There he gained valuable experience in the fabrication of all-metal aircraft. In 1930 when this company folded, he joined BFW, but that company's continuing financial woes caused him to leave and join Focke-Wulf in 1931. Tank brought with him seven years of experience in all phases of aircraft construction and the professional drive that until then Focke-Wulf had been lacking.

His first design for them was the FW-56 Stösser, a beautiful parasol trainer whose clean lines were well ahead of their time in 1933. Following this came the FW-58 Weihe and then the stunningly graceful FW-200 Condor passenger plane. His masterpiece, however, was the FW-190 fighter.

By 1942, Tank had become the leader of the company, Focke (qv) having left to explore helicopters, and Wulf (qv) having died in a crash. When the war ended Tank emigrated to Argentina, and later moved to India where he helped to design the Hindustan HF-25 Marut.

TATIN, VICTOR
1843–1913

Tatin was a French watchmaker and mechanic who assisted Marey (qv) in his studies of bird flight. In 1876 he built a mechanical flap-wing model that flew, but gave up ornithopters in favour of fixed-wing models. In 1879 he built a model monoplane driven by a compressed air motor. The motor turned twin propellers and the streamlined craft was fitted with three wheels for landing gear. It flew about 100 feet while tethered to a pole.

After his model work Tatin receded from the aviation scene until the turn of the century. He helped Santos-Dumont (qv) to design his dirigibles, consulted with Blériot (qv) on his aeroplanes, and designed the Clement-Bayard dirigible *Ville de Paris*, later designing that company's 1909 monoplane. He also collaborated with de la Vaulx (qv) on a 1907 monoplane project, and with Paulhan (qv) on the 1911 Aéro-Torpille.

TAYLOR, CHARLES E.
1867(?)–1956

Taylor was a machinist for the Dayton Electric Company and lived just a short distance from the Wright brothers' (qv) bicycle shop. In 1901 the brothers asked him to work for them, offering him a twenty per cent increase in pay. He accepted the offer and took over the management of their bicycle business while they were away at Kittyhawk.

Because of his excellent machining skills, the Wrights asked him to fabricate their first engine in early 1903. The result of his work was the famous engine that powered the *Flyer*. He also built most of the metal parts for the aeroplane.

Taylor was a faithful employee to the Wrights. He followed Wilbur to France, supported the brothers' exhibition flights in the US, and even followed Cal Rodgers' (qv) trip across the country, repairing his aircraft after each crash.

As the Wright company went through business evolutions after the war, Taylor drifted off. When Henry Ford bought the Wright brothers' shop to install in Greenfield Village, he wanted to find Taylor to help to restore it to its original condition. A nationwide search found Taylor in California operating a lathe for North American Aviation. No one in the plant knew his history as he was as modest as his famous previous employers. Though the Wrights had left him an annuity, he died impoverished.

TAYLOR, CLARENCE GILBERT
1898–1988

Taylor and his brother, Gordon, started an aircraft company in the early 1920s. The company sold an aircraft called the Chummy, building each one only after an order was received. In 1928 Gordon was killed in the crash of a Chummy but Taylor soldiered on until 1929, by which time only five aircraft had been sold. That year he received an offer from the city of Bradford, Pennsylvania to relocate his factory there in exchange for financial backing.

Upon moving to Bradford he met William Piper (qv) a shareholder in the reorganized Taylor firm. Piper pressed Taylor to redesign the Chummy so that it was lighter, and used a less expensive engine. In 1930 the E-2 appeared. Those were rough times for aircraft sales and the company folded in early 1931. Piper bought out the assets and reconstituted the company again under the name Taylor, retaining Taylor himself as half partner and chief engineer. The E-2 was continued in production and that year twenty-four were sold. By 1935 the planes were selling very well but Taylor's relationship with Piper had worsened. Piper permitted another engineer to round off the E-2 wings and tails in an attempt to give it more sales appeal. The modification was a visual success but Taylor considered the change a personal insult. He allowed Piper to buy out his share of the company and left to found Taylorcraft.

For Taylorcraft, Taylor designed another small monoplane, but this one had side-by-side seating, unlike the E-2's which was in tandem. Ironically, it also had rounded surfaces. The Taylorcraft company was never anywhere near as successful as Piper's company, although it did spawn an English subsidiary in 1938. This company changed its name to Auster Aircraft Ltd in 1946.

Taylor continued to design aircraft right into the 1970s.

TEDDER, MARSHAL OF THE ROYAL AIR FORCE LORD (ARTHUR WILLIAM)
1890–1967

An officer in the RAF since World War I, Tedder commanded the Desert Air Force during much of the Battle of North Africa. He was an innovative tactician and his ability to co-ordinate air and ground forces helped to win the Battle of El Alamein.

After serving in 1943 as Allied Air Commander in the Mediterranean, he became Eisenhower's deputy in command, earning distinction as one of the war's finest Allied leaders.

Back on earth, cosmonaut Valentina Tereshkova hugs her child Yelena.

TERESHKOVA, LIEUTENANT VALENTINA VLADIMIROVNA
1937–

Tereshkova became the first woman to be launched into space. Her historic flight occurred on 16 June 1963 when she was launched in the *Vostok 6*. She spent seventy hours, fifty minutes in space, during which time she orbited the Earth forty-eight times. The fact that she was only twenty-six at the time raised questions as to how well trained a cosmonaut she really was, and therefore of what real value, other than propaganda, her flight demonstrated.

Following her flight Tereshkova became an official of the Soviet government with the task of promoting the role of women in Russian society. In early 1987 she lost her job during Gorbachev's efficiency drive.

THADEN, LOUISE McPHETRIDGE
1905–1979

Louise McPhetridge was born in Arkansas. She grew up something of a tomboy and in 1927 learned to fly in San Francisco. She persuaded Walter Beech (qv) to allow her to fly one of his Travel Air Speedwings in the first Women's Air Derby. She won this hotly-contested, and deadly, race from Santa Monica to Cleveland with ease. Three years later she set an aircraft re-fuelling record of 196 hours in the air along with Frances Marsalis. Her crowning glory came in 1936 when she beat a largely male line-up of pilots in the Bendix cross-country race. She did this by emphasizing endurance and consistency over sheer speed. Her Beech Staggerwing, flown at only sixty-five per cent throttle, nevertheless won.

She continued to fly after this success but also sold aeroplanes and managed a flying school. She married Herb von Thaden in the late 1920s.

THOMAS, GEORGE HOLT
1869–1929

Thomas was a business entrepreneur and newspaper publisher whose first experience with aviation was a balloon flight in 1906. In 1909 he hired Louis Paulhan (qv) to give exhibition flights at Brooklands. In 1911 he began to produce licenced versions of Farmans in Britain at Hendon. His company, the Aircraft Manufacturing Company, grew slowly but in 1912 he hired Geoffrey de Havilland (qv) whose design talent soon won a deluge of military orders. Their aircraft were built as Aircos DH 1, 2, 3 etc.

During the war Thomas incorporated Britain's first airline, Aircraft Transport and Travel Ltd. This company started operations after the war, running a successful London to Paris service.

AT&T was later incorporated into Imperial Airways. Not long after the war Thomas retired due to an illness and took up farming.

THULIN, DR ENOCH LEONARD
1881–1919

After learning to fly in France, Thulin returned to his native Sweden where he began construction of his first aeroplane in 1913. In 1914 he formed A. B. Enoch-Thulins Aeroplanfabrik, a company founded to build licence version Blériots. Within a few years, the company had expanded sufficiently to build a variety of airframes and engines, mostly of foreign design, but some from Thulin's own design pen. In 1917 he designed a monoplane fighter, the Thulin Type K, two examples of which were sold to the Swedish Army.

Thulin's promising career was cut short in 1919 when he was killed in an air crash. The company he founded continued to prosper though, eventually becoming one of the principle members of the SAAB organization.

TISSANDIER, ALBERT
1839–1906
TISSANDIER, GASTON
1843–1899

In 1875 Gaston Tissandier, a balloon pilot during the Franco-Prussian war of 1870, attempted to break Glaisher's (qv) altitude record. Soaring high into the rarefied air his two assistants on the flight died while Tissandier returned to Earth barely alive, having just failed to break Glaisher's record.

In 1881 he and his brother began to experiment with electrically-powered airship models. These proved successful so they built a full-size example. Powered by a Siemens 1.5 horsepower electric motor (1.1kw), it flew in 1883. The best speed it achieved was 3 mph (4.8km/hr) though it was virtually unsteerable. The brothers' efforts served to inspire later builders.

TOURNACHON, GASPARD-FÉLIX

1820–1910

Popularly known as Nadar, Tournachon had become a photographer after failing at several other careers. He was a flamboyant self-publicist who sought any opportunity to draw attention to his portrait studio. In 1874 he hosted the first exhibition of Impressionist paintings at his studio, which itself was painted a bright red. The show caused a great sensation and confirmed his position as a leader of the Parisian avant-garde.

In 1855 he patented a system of aerial cartography through photography, but it wasn't until a year or so later that he took the world's first aerial photograph from a balloon. Tournachon fell in love with ballooning and built a huge balloon of 212,000 cubic feet (6,000cu m)! Named *Le Géant*, it could carry no less than fourteen passengers, and was equipped with a bunk, toilet, studio and dark room!

During the Franco-Prussian War of 1870-71 he prepared the microfilm messages that were flown out of besieged Paris by balloon.

TRANUM, JOHN

1900–1935

Often forgotten are the European aerial performers and barnstormers of the inter-war years. One of the most thrilling was John Tranum of Denmark. A veteran of almost 1,500 parachute jumps by 1931, he specialized in wing-walking, jumping from one plane to another, parachuting from a plane with a woman in his arms, setting his plane on fire in flight before jumping, and much more.

Tranum also performed high altitude delayed jumps. Intent on setting a new record for such a jump in 1935, he was flown to an altitude of 33,000 feet (10,058m). When he failed to jump from the plane, the pilot landed and discovered Tranum dead in the seat. He had died from a heart attack.

TRENCHARD, MARSHAL OF THE ROYAL AIR FORCE VISCOUNT (HUGH MONTAGUE)

1873–1956

Trenchard seems to have stumbled into history by complete accident. Mediocre scholastically, he barely managed to join a militia regiment after failing to enter either the Naval or engineering academies. For twenty years he soldiered around the world, never gaining any distinction except for being wounded in South Africa. In 1912 a friend convinced him to take flying lessons as a sport and as a possible way of gaining faster promotion. Trenchard agreed and was taught to fly by Sopwith (qv) at Brooklands.

At that point in time the newly formed RFC was looking for experienced officers to organize its ranks. Trenchard happened to be in the right place at the right time and was chosen to establish the programme at the Central Flying School, Upavon. In 1915 he was appointed Commander of all RFC units in France. Such an important post as this would, for him, have been unimaginable only three years earlier.

Trenchard never looked back though and set out to get the job done. His men called him 'Boom' because of his deep voice, and they admired him. He was a firm believer in the role of aeroplanes as strategic weapons and continually pressed for more bombing units. He also believed that the RFC and RNAS should be combined as one service. On 1 April 1918 he got his way and the RAF was born – with Trenchard as its head.

After the war, he continued to shape RAF policy, establishing an Air Force college at Cranwell, setting up a permanent Air Force staff, and pressing for larger bombers. From 1931-35 he served as the Commissioner of the London Metropolitan Police. In this position, he established a police training school at Hendon.

Trenchard became regarded as the 'Father of the RAF'. When he died in 1956 he was afforded full military honours, and buried in Westminster Abbey.

TRIPPE, JUAN TERRY

1899–1981

Juan Trippe was certainly the greatest of America's airline tycoons. With regard to the vast political and financial power he wielded, some have even referred to him as a robber baron.

important international route granted by the US government.

One of Trippe's greatest successes was the spanning of the Atlantic and Pacific oceans shortly before World War II. These routes were pioneered in mighty Boeing and Martin clippers. The one plum that had been denied to Trippe for over fifty years was finally granted to Pan Am in 1979. That year they purchased National Airlines, thus acquiring its domestic routes and, the eighty-year-old tycoon was alive to see it.

Juan Trippe, always at home with politicians, discusses business with New York's greatest mayor, Fiorello La Guardia.

His aviation career began in 1917 when he left Yale to join the Navy as a bomber pilot. In 1919 he returned to Yale from which he graduated in 1922. He spent a year working in his deceased father's bank, but with aviation in his veins he soon left that business and in 1923 organized his first airline – Long Island Airways. When the US Post Office Department offered airmail contracts, Trippe abandoned this venture and organized Colonial Air Transport which received an early government airmail contract. Trippe's partners at Colonial weren't ambitious enough for the young businessman so he left to start an airline on his own and Pan American Airways was born.

The company's first route was a ninety-mile flight between Key West and Havana. Trippe quickly expanded the service deep into South America. Under his skilful leadership the company grew rapidly. Many of his routes were won through political intrigue and shadowy dealings with foreign governments. His airline became the flag carrier of the US as it won every

The greatest figure in space flight history, schoolteacher Konstantin Tsiolkovsky.

TSIOLKOVSKY, KONSTANTIN EDUARDOVITCH
1857–1935

Tsiolkovsky was to astronautics what Cayley (qv) was to aeronautics – the founding father. He was born to a middle class family at Izhevshoye, Russia. Poor hearing prevented him from attending school, so his father educated him from his own library. Young Tsiolkovsky loved mathematics and science, and grew to make his living by teaching them. His true passion though was flight. With a scientist's approach, he considered everything from dirigibles, to aeroplanes, to rocketships.

In 1892 he wrote a paper which theoretically described the building of an all-metal airship. Three years later he designed an all-metal aeroplane, the aerofoils for which he tested in a wind tunnel of his own construction.

His greatest work was with rockets however. In 1898 he was the first ever to propose, and theoretically demonstrate, the liquid fuel rocket. He followed this by designing such a rocket and then space-support systems for it, including a rotating space station.

This far-sighted genius often presented his papers to the Imperial Technical Society, but they were almost always rejected. His ideas did not reach the Western world until after the Bolshevik revolution. When he died at seventy-eight in 1935, he had earned the world-wide recognition he deserved. Subsequent Soviet claims that he invented the turbojet and turboprop engines were untrue, and only served to degrade his name.

TUCK, WING COMMANDER ROBERT ROLAND STANFORD
1916–1987

Tuck was just nineteen when he transferred from the Merchant Navy into the RAF in 1935. As natural a pilot as he was a leader, he rose steadily through the ranks and by May, 1940 had become a Flight Commander with No. 92 Squadron. He loved aerial combat and during one three-day period shortly before the Battle of Britain he took credit for downing six enemy aircraft.

He was no lucky beginner though. Prior to the war he had studied air combat tactics which convinced him that the traditional, tightly packed fighter formations were of little value. He advocated a wider spread of fighters which, he theorized, would be able to patrol effectively a large area of sky in a shorter period of time. When this tactic was tested during September, 1940, it proved to be well founded. Tuck's idea helped to equalize the disparity between the RAF and Luftwaffe.

Tuck always seemed to be where the action was. He survived the Battle of Britain and during most of 1941 led the fighter wing at Duxford. In December he took command of a Spitfire wing at Biggin Hill, but only a month later was shot down near Boulogne. While attempting a dead stick landing in his flaming plane he happened to choose the very field in which the AA gun that had brought him down was located. Just before smashing into the ground he pulled the trigger and blasted the AA gun's crew. They all died while Tuck survived the landing. He became a prisoner of war for three years, until 1945 when he escaped from prison and made his way back to England.

At the war's end he had twenty-nine kills to his credit. He retired to mushroom farming.

TUPOLEV, ANDREI NIKOLAEVICH
1888–1972

Throughout his entire adult life Tupolev was in the vanguard of Russian aircraft design and by the time of his death he had justly earned the title of 'the grand old man' of Soviet aviation.

Tupolev first studied aeronautics under Zhukovski (qv) himself at the Moscow Technical High School beginning around 1908. Three years later he was arrested for the first time, accused of anti-Czarist activity. Released later, he found work at the Dux aircraft factory in Moscow. With the Bolshevik revolution of 1917 Tupolev rose to power at a young age. Lenin rewarded him for his pre-war activities by making him Chairman of the Special Committee for Heavy Aviation. His first major task was to set up a proper advanced research centre. He did this by persuading Lenin to allocate funds for the Central Aerodynamics and Hydrodynamics Research Institute (TsAGI) located in Moscow. Tupolev, along with his former professor Zhukovski, were the guiding forces behind the great institute that eventually produced every leading Russian aircraft designer.

While Tupolev was setting up TsAGI he had been designing his first aeroplane. It was a single-seat monoplane which made its first flight in 1922. The plane resembled a Junkers K-16 and in fact had been built in Junkers' (qv) surreptitious Moscow plant. Tupolev was to learn a lot from Junkers' factory which had been established in Russia to sidestep the Versailles Treaty prohibitions. One of the important techniques he learned was the use of aluminium sheeting, the mastery of which he proved with the ANT-2 monoplane, Russia's first all-metal aeroplane.

As Russia's leading aircraft designer, Tupolev nurtured a whole generation of young designers including Ilyushin, Petlyakov, Sukhoi, and Yakovlev (qqv). Tupolev was arrested for the second time in his life in 1936 during the opening stages of Stalin's purges. Stalin, a self-styled aviation expert, tried to blame Tupolev for the combat failure of Russian aircraft used in the Spanish Civil War. Whether it was dedication to his ideology or dedication to his profession that kept Tupolev designing aircraft while in prison is unknown, but fortunately for the Russians in World War II, he did. From behind bars he designed the TB-7 strategic bomber (known for political reasons as the PE-8), and the Tu-2 twin-engine bomber.

In 1942, when Stalin was in desperate need of someone to revitalize the aviation industry, he pardoned Tupolev, 'generously' awarding him the Stalin Prize. Soon Tupolev's design bureau had engaged in the design of several large transports and bombers. These planes, among them the Tu-14 jet bomber, Tu-95 turboprop bomber, the Tu-104, 124 and 134 transport planes, all helped to elevate his reputation to one of world stature.

His son Alexis also became a designer and was responsible for the ill-fated Tu-144 supersonic transport, the design of which was largely based on plans stolen from the British and French.

TURNER, ROSCOE
1895–1970
Born in Mississippi, Turner joined the Army in 1917. He was posted to an observation balloon unit where he learned how to parachute. After

A champion air racer, Roscoe Turner.

the war he entered show business as a lion tamer but thought he could make more money as a stunt flier. Since, in 1919, he wasn't yet a pilot, he invested in a one-man flying circus owned by Harry Rusner who, having just broken the wings off his aeroplane, needed a partner to help pay for the repairs. The Rusner-Turner partnership worked very well. Their most popular stunt was to stage a mock in-flight aircraft fire during which Turner would leap from the plane in his parachute while Rusner would land at some distant spot to simulate a real crash. In 1921 Rusner taught Turner to fly after which Turner set his sights on record flying, though in 1929 he briefly ran the Nevada Air Line.

While Turner had been a barnstormer, he had sported a waxed moustache and a pseudo-military uniform. He also adopted the title 'Colonel' and was often in the company of a pet lion, Gilmore. Other fliers saw him as a 'dude' flier looking for cheap publicity with little chance of doing anything really important. Over the course of the next ten years they were to be proven completely wrong.

In 1929 he set a speed record between Los Angeles and New York, while carrying passenger, of twenty hours and twenty minutes. Over the next few years he continued to beat his own record, though his most important victories came in the highly competitive Thompson Trophy races. He won in 1934, 1938 and 1939 – the only person to win three times. He also took a hand in designing and building his own racing plane. His most famous mounts were the Wedell-Williams and Laird-Turner racers. In 1933 he won the Bendix transcontinental race. In 1934 he and Clyde Pangborn came in third in the gruelling MacRobertson England to Australia race, this while flying a Boeing 247. Turner often flew between races in a Lockheed Vega with his lion as co-pilot!

Turner was indeed a showman – but at a time when the world was gripped in a bleak depression and threatened by dark political forces and war, Turner brought colour and style to the headlines. He was a glamorous flier, but he was also an extremely competent one.

TWISS, PETER
1921–

Twiss was one of Britain's most successful post-war test pilots. He joined the Fleet Air Arm in 1939, learning to fly the next year in a Tiger Moth. His war record included flying torpedo bombers in the Mediterranean, catapult launched Hurricanes and Seafires off North Africa, and night interdiction in Mosquitoes. As a Ferry Command pilot he logged hours on a wide variety of machines, thus putting himself in a position to apply to the Empire Test Pilot School after the war.

In 1946 he joined Fairey Aviation as a test pilot and in that capacity on 10 March 1956 flew the FD-2 to over 1,000 mph to achieve a new world speed record (1,132 mph) (1,822km/hr). He remained with Fairey until 1960 when that company was swallowed into a larger national corporation.

TYTLER, JAMES
1747–1804

Tytler was an eccentric and impoverished Edinburgh ship's surgeon, and editor of the *Encyclopedia Britannica's* second edition, before becoming involved in aviation. In 1784 he successfully raised, by public subscription, the funds to build a balloon. Within a short time his balloon was built, but unlike most balloons which were spherical, Tytler's looked like a large beer barrel. His problems began at the balloon's first inflation. The fire used to inflate the bag grew too large and burned part of the bag. Repairs were made, but after a failed second attempt to launch it the next night due to high winds, the crowd that has assembled to witness the proposed flight rioted and wrecked the balloon and its launching equipment. Tytler courageously made repairs, and a few weeks later, on 25 August 1784, he finally managed to get the balloon aloft. Because of earlier difficulties, he dispensed with the balloon's furnace and full-size basket, simply heating the bag over a fire prior to launch. The amount of success he achieved that day is disputable, but he undoubtedly did float freely.

Tytler made several more mediocre ascents, but was often the object of ridicule because of his poorly constructed balloon. When the balloon was completely destroyed in a storm in July, 1785 Tytler's aviation career ended.

In 1792 he was accused of sedition because of his radical political views. He fled at first to Ireland, but later to America where he settled in Massachusetts and became a newspaper editor. A hard life of unfulfilled expectations led him to become a drunk, a lifestyle that eventually killed him. Drunk, he fell into a salt pan and was killed.

His first flight was the first in Britain made in an indigenous balloon. Why was Tytler considered eccentric by his peers? For one thing, he believed in aeronautics, and for another, he espoused republican politics – in fact the basis of his indictment for sedition.

UDET, ERNST
1896–1941

A native of Frankfurt am Main, Udet served in the infantry before paying for private flying lessons in 1915 so that he could become a military pilot. His World War I flying exploits are legendary. They include a dogfight with Guynemer (qv), a combat in which his guns jammed and the Frenchman very chivalrously spared his life. He was the first pilot ever to knock out a tank, doing this through very accurate gun fire which so frightened the tank's driver that he drove into a ditch and overturned his machine. Twice during the war his life was saved by a parachute. He was one of the few fliers in the war to have one, a thoughtful gift from his father. His war tally was sixty-two, making him second only to von Richthofen (qv) on the German list.

During the war, Udet's airplanes were distinguishable by the legend 'LO!' painted on their sides. This word was a shortened version of his girlfriend's name, Eleonore. They were later married, but shortly after the war they divorced because she didn't like his sporting habits. After they parted, Udet became a barnstormer in Germany where he drew large audiences. He then set up his own aircraft factory to produce his 'ideal' aeroplane, the Flamingo. He toured the world with his products and won several speed contests in South America. Later, he sold his factory and journeyed to Hollywood where he became a stunt pilot.

By the early 1930s Udet had received overtures from the Nazi government asking him to help recast the air service. He resisted joining the military for as long as he could, although he did offer some far-sighted technical suggestions, one being that Germany should develop a dive bomber. The fruit of this idea was the Ju 87 Stuka.

Udet was always a man of romantic temperament which perhaps explains why when Messerschmitt (qv) first showed him the Bf 109 in 1935 he exclaimed, 'This will never be a fighting aeroplane!' He went on to explain that a real fighter needed an open cockpit and two wings! He finally did join the Luftwaffe in 1935 although he never liked life in the Nazi régime. Appointed head of technical development, he felt incompetent in the job. In 1941 the pressures of duty became too much for him and he committed suicide.

Ernst Udet glares defiance during WWI.

VALIER, MAX
1885–1930

As the world journeys from age to age it needs ushers to introduce it to new ideas. Often these ushers are scorned in their lifetimes, but eventually their roles are appreciated. One such usher was Max Valier, an Austrian pseudo-scientist.

Around 1924 Valier became extremely interested in the possibilities of space flight. Following on the heels of Oberth (qv) he published a book about rocket flight that became a best seller. In 1927 he and a friend formed the Verein fur Raumschiffahrt (VfR) in Breslau. This Society for Space Travel galvanized German interest in rockets and attracted over 500 members, many of whom would later lead the world into the space age. The society published a bi-annual journal called *Die Rakete* which served as a clearing house for new concepts regarding rocket flight.

Valier wasn't content to be just a writer. He wanted to build working rockets. As a way of gaining publicity for rocket experimentation, he persuaded Fritz von Opel (qv) to finance rocket car and rocket plane experiments. These were conducted in 1928 and had no real value other than to heighten public interest in rockets, which they did. Valier believed in the future of liquid rockets, not the solid type as used in the von Opel machines. In January, 1930 he began to build a liquid fuel rocket with funds he had received from the Heylandwerke Company. He tested this rocket in the Rak-7 automobile in April, 1930. He seemed to be on his way to a practical rocket but, unfortunately while testing the combustion chamber of a liquid fuel rocket in May, the device exploded and he was killed when a metal fragment pierced one of his lungs.

Dornberger (qv) was later to call Valier nothing but a dreamer. Though it is true he was unqualified to lead the world technically into space flight, it is unquestionable that he, along with Oberth (qv), was a spiritual leader of those who did.

VÉDRINES, JULES
1881–1919

Védrines was a working-class factory hand at the Gnôme works when he first came into contact with aeroplanes. He was one of the plant's best mechanics and by 1910 had joined Farman (qv) as the chief mechanic at his flying school. That year he learned to fly, earning his brevet in December.

In the spring of 1911 he began to make headlines as a great racing pilot. In May he was the only finisher in the difficult Paris–Madrid race. When he arrived in Madrid, none of the expected crowds were waiting because they had given up and gone home. Védrines took this as an insult and a snobbish snub against his social background. He blasted the reception committee with a torrent of abuse that was soon to become his hallmark, along with the permanently etched scowl on his face. He was finally placated by an introduction to King Alphonso who graciously ignored Védrines' earlier personal insults against him. The king in fact invited the pilot to a bull fight.

A rivalry grew between Védrines and Jean Conneau (qv) that came to symbolize the class

struggle of the early part of the twentieth century. Conneau was a cool, unflappable flier, while Védrines was known for his vitriolics. Their constant battles sold a lot of newspapers and they were known as the best race pilots in Europe. Conneau beat Védrines in the 1911 Great Circuit of England Air Race by flying the course in just under 22·5 hours. When Védrines finished an hour later and found that he had lost, he burst into tears.

In early 1912 Védrines broke the 100 mph barrier by winning the Gordon-Bennett race at an average speed of 108 mph. The next year he made a remarkable flight from Paris to Cairo with a passenger.

During World War I he volunteered to join the air service and flew with a Morane squadron. He became a specialist in landing spies behind enemy lines at night. He survived the war only to be killed on a flight between Paris and Rome.

VERNE, JULES
1828–1905

No one advanced the cause of technology in the nineteenth century more than Jules Verne. Untold thousands of young people were inspired by his stories and these people grew to build the wondrous machines of a new age. Nearly every autobiography of an aviation pioneer contains some reference to an early exposure to Verne. The machines he created as fiction, his readers turned into fact.

Verne was born in Nantes and sent to Paris to study law. Literature was more to his liking and he became associated with the art circle led by Alexandre Dumas. His earliest works were plays that appeared in Dumas' theatre but he soon turned to prose fiction. In 1863 he wrote *Five Weeks in A Balloon*, his first science-fiction novel. Its tremendous popularity decided Verne on sticking to the adventure genre. The next year he wrote *Voyage to the Centre of the Earth* and *From Earth to the Moon*. In 1870 appeared his classic *Twenty Thousand Leagues Under the Sea*. In all his works Verne strove for an authenticity that bordered on scientific intuition. He accurately predicted that a vehicle launched to the Moon would take three days to get there. He also said that such a launch would take place in Florida. Even more astounding was the prediction in his 1886 novel *Clipper of the Clouds* that an aircraft capable of flying around the world would be made from composite materials in a pressure mould. The *Voyager*, which made its globe-girdling flight in 1986, was indeed made of moulded composites that were cured in an autoclave – a pressure oven!

A review of the propellers and machinery used by the pioneers at the turn of the century shows that they borrowed heavily from the illustrations in Verne's books. Life imitated art? It is often said that art and science are closely related and Verne, like da Vinci (qv), proved that to be true.

VERVILLE, ALFRED VICTOR
1890–1970
Verville was an engineer with Hudson in 1914 when he witnessed an exhibition flight by a Curtiss (qv) pilot. He left his job and moved to Hammondsport where he went to work for Curtiss. His earliest jobs included design work on the *America* flying-boat and the 'Jenny' trainer. He left Curtiss to work for Fisher Body but in 1918 was loaned to the Air Service Engineering Division at McCook Field. That year he was sent to France to study trends in aircraft production. A French speaker, he spent much of his time there with Béchereau (qv) at Spad, with whom he became friends.

When Verville returned to the United States he began the design of a high-speed biplane with a monocoque fuselage, like the latest Spads. The aeroplane he designed was the VCP-1. A version of it competed in the 1920 Pulitzer speed race. In 1921 he returned to Europe with Billy Mitchell (qv) to study further European development and this time when he returned he designed the outstanding Verville-Sperry R-3. The R-3 was purely a Verville design though it was built in the Sperry factory. It featured a welded tube fuselage mounted on a cantilever wooden wing which also housed inward-retracting landing gear. This plane, which won

the 1924 Pulitzer Speed Trophy, served as an inspiration to future warplane designs though those planes were fifteen years away.

Verville continued in government service for the remainder of his career, working at times for the Bureau of Air Commerce, the Navy and others.

da VINCI, LEONARDO
1452–1519
It is a curious reversal of history that the world today thinks of da Vinci firstly as a great artist, and next as an innovative engineer, whereas his contemporaries thought just the opposite. They prized his engineering talents more highly than his artistic ones.

Da Vinci wasn't the first to consider the possibilities of heavier-than-air flight, nor was he the first to design a helicopter-like device, submarine, parachute, or automobile, as is commonly reported. He probably never built a full-scale flying machine, and if he had built one based on his own designs, it couldn't have flown. So what did he contribute to aviation?

His brilliant contribution was his legacy of reducing to a scientific problem that which often seemed impossible. Through reason, he said, a person of imagination could create almost anything. He clearly demonstrated and represented the unique tie between art and science.

Where others had merely speculated on mobile vehicles, Leonardo was the first to try to devise ways to make them work. His sketches of artificial bird wings suggested what Lilienthal (qv) was later to make functional. Late in life, he became obsessed with flight and his notebooks were jammed with designs for ornithopters, wings and even an airscrew.

VODOPYANOV, MIKHAIL V.
1900(?)–1980
Vodopyanov began his aviation career as a pilot of early Soviet airliners in the 1920s. During the 1930s he gained world attention as the pilot of several Soviet Polar expeditions. In 1934 he was

part of a fleet of aeroplanes that rescued the crew of the ship *Chelyuskin* that had become stuck in the ice off the coast of Siberia. Pilots of this rescue fleet were the first recipients of the title 'Hero of the Soviet Union'. In 1937 Vodopyanov flew a team of scientists over the North Pole and landed thirteen miles away from it where a base camp was established.

During World War II Stalin ordered him to form a bomber unit with the express purpose of bombing Berlin. The crew members that Vodopyanov gathered all knew that if necessary their mission would be a suicide run. The TB-7 bombers that were used didn't have enough range for a full return run to Soviet soil, so after the bomb run, Vodopyanov landed his plane behind German lines. He and his crew, according to official Soviet accounts, miraculously worked their way back to Russian territory.

VOISIN, GABRIEL
1880–1973
VOISIN, CHARLES
1888–1912

Gabriel Voisin played a key role in the development of European aviation, though his later statements regarding that contribution were exaggerated. Since Voisin's claims about his life were so often wilfully false, it is impossible to know the exact details of his earliest experiences with flight, but it seems probable that even before the turn of the century he had experimented with kites with an eye to producing man-lifters. These tests were probably conducted with the aid of his brother Charles, who served in a minor role. There is evidence that he sought out Ader(qv) in 1900 which supports the theory that he had a prior interest in flight.

In 1904 Voisin was a student of architecture in Paris, but on a visit to Lyon he stopped to hear a lecture given by Ferber (qv). After the lecture Voisin introduced himself and described his interest in flight whereupon Ferber suggested that he contact Archdeacon (qv). Archdeacon at that time was testing a Wright-type glider and hired

Voisin immediately as a pilot. In 1905 the two formed the Syndicat d'Aviation to build aircraft. This company was the first established for that purpose. During the first half of that year Voisin built two gliders which were tested behind speedboats on the Seine. The first glider had been built for Archdeacon and the second for Blériot (qv). In July Blériot proposed that he and Voisin join to form an aircraft business. Voisin agreed and thus was formed the Bleriot-Voisin Company, establishing itself in a shop Blériot purchased from the balloon builder Surcouf.

Their collaboration produced a glider and a powered plane. Neither was successful. During this time, Voisin was also working for Santos-Dumont (qv) building the 14bis. It is not recorded how Blériot felt about this extra-partnership affair, or if he even knew about it. Voisin built the 14bis in Santos-Dumont's hangar in Neuilly St James. Double-dealing was not unusual for Voisin. After the success of the 14bis in November, 1906, the Blériot-Voisin partnership broke up. Voisin retained the factory and invited his brother to join him, thus forming Voisin Frères.

In 1907 Voisin finally achieved flight. His first powered plane was built for Henry Kapferer but did not fly. The next plane was built for Léon Delagrange (qv) and successfully test flown by Voisin in March at Bagatelle.

After building another airplane for Delagrange, he built one for Henry Farman (qv) which became the first to fly a circular kilometre in Europe. A second machine built for Farman was deviously sold by Voisin to Moore-Brabazon (qv). Infuriated, Farman set out to establish his own company to compete with Voisin. Charles assisted Gabriel during these times, but played a far smaller part. He was killed in a car crash in 1912.

Voisin built bombers during World War I but they were not very advanced types. Nevertheless, his company prospered and he became rich.

Following the war, he began production of the world's first prefabricated houses but, fearing reprisals from envious building constructors, he gave up this business. His building interests had led him to sketch, with his friend Le Corbusier, a vision of what Paris would look like in the future. The drawings show great motorways, and high-rises and are remarkably accurate predictions of what did occur.

He then turned to automobiles in 1919. From then until 1937 he produced some of the most advanced automobiles in the world. He used sleeve-valve engines of gigantic dimensions housed in underslung chassis. Cost was no object because his clientèle were the wealthiest buyers of the time. The Voisin automobile was a rolling work of futuristic art purchased in great numbers by the great celebrities of France. Even though sales were good, Voisin expended vast sums in the development of new concepts, most of which never paid off. Nearly broke, he lost control of his company in 1929 but regained it for a short time four years later. His cars were so advanced that Rolls-Royce sent engineers to his plant in 1934 to learn from a master.

During World War II the German-owned Gnôme Rhône Company took over Voisin's factory and required that he remain to supervise operations. After the war he was accused of aiding the Nazis and the French government, then in a frenzy of nationalization, seized the chance to swallow the company. Voisin, later exonerated, continued to develop new autos and designed a micro-car called the Biscuter of which 18,000 were built in Spain. Despite the sales success of this car he received virtually nothing.

By the 1950s Voisin was almost bankrupt. Fortune again smiled on him when a former girlfriend, to whom he had once given a cottage, reappeared after having become wealthy. She gave the cottage back to Voisin and he lived there for the rest of his life.

VOSS, LEUTNANT WERNER
1897–1917

Voss began World War I on horseback. As a cavalry hussar, he earned the Iron Cross before transferring to the Air Force in 1915. His first flights were made as an observer, but eventually he received pilot training, after which he joined von Richthofen's (qv) Jasta Boelcke in 1916. His

natural flying talents expressed themselves as month by month his score rose with remarkable rapidity. In only ten months he shot down forty-eight enemy planes, often while flying on lone patrols. On 23 September 1917, while flying on such a patrol, he was intercepted by 'B' flight of No. 56 Squadron. What ensued became *the* epic dogfight of the war.

Six of the seven British planes were flown by veteran aces. The British were in fact led by McCudden (qv). Voss was cornered, but fought off the attacking British single-handedly. Voss's plane was hit several times, but more often he scored hits on the enemy. Finally, he began to tire and one of the British planes slid under him unnoticed. Its pilot fired a long burst from a flexible Lewis gun into the belly of Voss's plane. His aircraft crashed behind British lines and he was afforded a burial with full military honours.

VUIA, TRAJAN
1872–1950

Vuia was from Transylvania, now a part of Romania, and studied law in Budapest but also qualified as an engineer. After his education he moved to Paris where he became interested in flight. He was associated with members of the Aéro-Club and from Tatin's (qv) suggestion designed a monoplane in 1905. Early the next year he attempted to fly this machine, powered by a Serpollet twenty-five horsepower carbonic acid gas engine. It hopped several times but, despite Vuia's claim, it never really flew. He had constructed another monoplane the next year, which was powered by an Antoinette engine, but this one also only hopped.

Having failed with both these machines, Vuia gave up aircraft. His contribution to aviation was important though. His tractor monoplanes, the first of their type since Du Temple (qv), influenced Blériot (qv) to give up on biplanes, and introduced pneumatic tyres to aircraft.

WALLIS, SIR BARNES NEVILLE
1887–1979

Wallis was a ubiquitous figure in British aviation

who seemed to be involved in everything. Born in Derbyshire, he received only a minimal mathematics and science education. In fact, his early education wasn't enough to get him into a university. He took a job at a shipyard where he befriended an engineer named H B Pratt. When Pratt was hired by Vickers, in 1913, to initiate their airship programme, he took young Wallis along with him. Within two years Wallis had become an airship designer in his own right. During World War I he designed the R-80, considered by some the most beautiful craft ever to fly. After the war he stayed with Vickers and, having been appointed chief designer, developed the immensely successful R-100 airship.

When the British airship programme ended in the early 1930s, the versatile Wallis turned to aeroplane design and brilliantly adapted his geodetic structures to that field. The first Wallis aeroplane was the Wellesley bomber. It was quickly followed by the Wellington which was to be affectionately known by its crews as the 'Wimpy'. Its unorthodox geodetic structure made it one of the most rugged war planes of World War II.

The war brought out another of Wallis' talents – bomb design. He was responsible for reviving the old concept of skip bombing. He invented a special spinning bomb that, when dropped from an aeroplane, 'skipped' to its target so as to strike it broadside. The first, and only, use of this weapon was the 1943 raid on the Mohne, Eder, and Sorpe dams. The action became known as the 'Dambuster Raid'. Other bombs designed by Wallis included the Grand Slam, and the Tallboy – two huge bombs that could level a city block.

After the war Wallis became the champion of swing-wing supersonic aircraft. Rejected in Wallis' own country, the idea was first put into production in the US with the F-111. His final engineering efforts went into developing hydrogen-powered aircraft. This type of propulsion has been considered by many post-war experts to be fanciful – but no one thought much of geodetic structures or skip bombs when they were first introduced either.

WARREN, EDWARD
1771–*

In June, 1784 a lawyer from Maryland named Peter Carnes built a hot-air balloon, probably the first of its type in the United States. He attempted to fly in the craft but his weight was too great. A thirteen-year-old boy volunteered to go up in the balloon and Carnes allowed him to. Thus Edward Warren seemingly became the first aeronaut in America. The only authority for this account is a short, contemporaneous newspaper article, but it is considered authentic. Warren made an ascent only, and probably not a voyage. Carnes later attempted a flight in Philadelphia but crashed into a wall as his balloon rose.

WATSON-WATT, ROBERT ALEXANDER
1892–1973

Watson-Watt was born in Brechin, Scotland and received an engineer's education at University College, Dundee. In 1915 he joined the London Meteorological Office, which gave him the difficult task of developing a long-range electronic method of detecting thunderstorms. He failed to discover such a method, but experience in the field led him in the 1920s to develop radio-beacon navigation aids for aircraft.

In 1934 he was again asked the impossible when a committee from the Air Ministry proposed that he try to develop an anti-aircraft 'ray-gun'. He refused this assignment but suggested that the time was right, technologically, for a long-range detecting beam – radar. With Air Ministry money he set up a crude experiment where, with a cathode ray tube and a radio receiver, he tried to detect the short waves of a BBC broadcast bouncing off an RAF Heyford bomber. The test was an unexpected success and radar was born.

Watson-Watt eventually developed a radar beam powerful enough to detect aircraft over fifty-five miles away. A series of these machines were placed along the southern coast of England in 1938 and played a vital role in saving Britain during 1940.

WEICK, FRED ERNEST
1899-1993
Weick was largely responsible for making general aviation a safe, recreational sport that could be enjoyed by people of just average skills. He was born in Chicago and educated at the Armour Institute of Technology and at the University of Illinois. His first job was as a draughtsman for the US Air Mail Service. After a stint with the Yackey Aircraft Company he went to work for the Bureau of Aeronautics. In 1925 he joined NACA where he discovered how to improve the cooling of radial engines while reducing their drag. To do this, he invented what became known as the NACA cowl which was announced in 1929. The cowl was so shaped as to be a round aerofoil. As the propeller blast struck it, it actually created a forward pull. So effective was it that early examples of the cowl were known to pull themselves into the propeller disk!

In the early 1930s he began to develop methods to make aircraft much safer. He was an early advocate of tricycle landing gear and tested this layout with the W-1 light plane. This plane's success earned him an offer from ERCO in 1936 to develop a marketable light plane. This plane again featured tricycle gear, in addition to interconnected rudder and ailerons. It was all-metal with a very simple wing structure. The plane, named the Ercoupe, was in fact the first modern general aviation aeroplane and it foretold the end of the Piper Cub tube and cloth domination of the light plane market.

Fifty years after the Ercoupe first appeared many are still flying, cherished by proud owners. Weick later joined Piper for whom he developed crop-dusters and designed the Cherokee.

WEISS, JOSE
1859-1919
Weiss was born in France and as a child read accounts of the balloon flights out of besieged Paris during the Franco-Prussian war. He became interested in technical matters and so studied science and engineering at Lille. Upon graduating he entered the business world but found it distasteful. With support from his wealthy father he became an artist and settled in England. There he mass-produced landscape paintings that sold well in America.

With a steady income from his art, Weiss began to build model gliders. He built over 200 during the early years of the century before building a full-size glider in 1909. The glider was based on theories of stability that he had formed in the preceding year. In 1907 and 1908 he had presented these ideas to the Aeronautical Society through papers he read there. His main concept was that wings should be curved along their forward edge, and swept back.

His glider flew well near Arundel Castle, Sussex and attracted the attention of Handley Page (qv). Handley Page and Weiss entered into a short-lived partnership to market powered planes, but none were sold. Though their partnership dissolved, Handley Page based his early aircraft on Weiss's wing design.

WELLMAN, WALTER
1858–1934
Wellman was a journalist for several Chicago newspapers. For a time, he covered the Washington beat for the *Times-Herald*. He decided to try to make his own news in 1907 by becoming the first to fly over the North Pole. That year he left Smeerenberg, Spitzbergen, in a semi-rigid dirigible named *America*. The *America* was a good design except for its leather drag ropes, one of which broke thirty-five miles into the trip. Without it, Wellman had to abandon the voyage. A 1909 attempt ended in much the same way.

In 1910 Wellman set his sights on crossing the Atlantic in the *America*. The ship and crew departed Atlantic City on 15 October. Just eighty miles out one of the engines died and the *America* became unmanageable. Wellman refused to turn back despite the protests of his crew. He preferred death to a third failure. Finally, a radio distress call was made. It was the first ever from an aircraft. They were rescued on 17 October by a steamer which spotted them by chance. They had drifted far off course yet their flight actually set, for a while, an airship distance record of 1,008 miles (1,622km).

Wellman's career began to sink and near the end of his life he was thrown in jail for a bad debt of $280. H. Murray Jacoby, a banker and admirer, bailed him out.

WELLS, EDMUND CURTIS
1910–1986
Wells was born in Boise, Idaho, and as a young man enjoyed building model aeroplanes and automobiles. In 1930 he took a summer job with Boeing while still attending Stanford University. Upon graduation he joined Boeing full-time where he was given engineering work on biplanes. Very soon he was made a project engineer and in 1934 he joined a team to develop the Model 299. Wells played a major role in creating this plane which was to evolve as the famous B-17 bomber.

Following this project, he led the work on designing the B-29, the Stratocruiser, the B-47 and the B-52. His last major project was the 747 commercial transport.

WENHAM, FRANCIS HERBERT
1824–1908
Wenham was born in Kensington, London and studied engineering. While on a trip to Cairo in 1858 he began to study bird flight. He closely examined the structure of a bird's wing, correctly determining that cambered surfaces provide the greatest lift. He also reasoned that most lift is generated at the front of an aerofoil, therefore long wings are the most efficient.

He announced his discoveries in 1866 in a paper he read before the newly formed Aeronautical Society, of which he was a charter member. His paper *Aerial Locomotion* was well received and exerted a great influence on the subsequent development of aerodynamics.

In association with John Browning, Wenham designed and built the world's first wind tunnel in 1871-72. In addition to aeronautics, Wenham experimented in such diverse fields as optics, engines, and photography.

Richard Whitcomb who gave the world routine supersonic flight.

WHITCOMB, RICHARD TRAVIS
1921–
Whitcomb was by far the most significant of post-war aerodynamicists. His discoveries led to the development of supersonic combat planes and, later, to fuel-efficient commercial jet liners.

Although he was born in Illinois, he grew up in Massachusetts where he attended the Worcester Polytechnic Institute. In 1943, upon his graduation, NACA hired him to work on problems related to supersonic flight. In the early 1950s he formed the Area Rule concept of transonic drag. In this concept, the total profile area of any section of an aircraft is used to calculate drag and thus streamlining. Whitcomb's Area Rule was first applied to the F-102 Delta Dagger and it transformed the plane from a failure into a supersonic success. Simply put, the concept requires that a fuselage be pinched where it joins the wing – thus forming a 'Coke bottle' shape.

In the 1960s he scored another breakthrough with the development of the NASA super-critical wing. This advanced wing concept allows high-speed subsonic aircraft to fly faster while using less fuel. Super-critical wings feature a flattened top which delays air flow separation. He went on to develop and promote the addition of 'winglets' on the ends of aircraft wings. These are used to turn ordinarily-wasted vortex energy into thrust.

WHITEHEAD, GUSTAVE
1874–1927

Gustave Weisskopf was born in Leutherhausen, Germany and as a young boy demonstrated a keen interest in flight. He built small parachutes, and even trapped birds so that he could examine their wings. After grammar school he found work in a machine shop in Augsburg. He gave that up to become a sailor and was shipwrecked in the Gulf of Mexico in 1894. He decided to settle in America, moving to Bridgeport, Connecticut in 1900. By then, he had anglicized his name to Whitehead.

In 1901 claims were made by Whitehead and others that he flew a powered machine on 14 August at Fairfield, Connecticut. The machine featured a Lilienthal (qv)-type wing mounted on a fabric covered body. It was driven by a ten horsepower (7.5kw) acetylene engine that Whitehead had built. Gustave later claimed that he had also flown in 1899 in Pittsburg, but that his machine had crashed. A further claim was made that, in 1902, he flew seven miles (11.3km) out over the Long Island Sound.

An examination of Whitehead's 1901 machine shows that he was no crank. The craft was carefully built and demonstrated an understanding of lift, balance and, to some extent, control. The machine probably could have flown had its engine and propeller combination been effective. This seems to be the weak link in the Whitehead claim. A ten horsepower engine is unlikely to have been able to sustain flight, especially when driving Whitehead's inefficient twin propellers. It is possible that in 1901 he succeeded in generating enough ground speed to hop along a given course, which his followers seemed to think qualified as flights. The clearest reason to

doubt the Whitehead story is that he couldn't duplicate the results. Had he been able to, why did he give up aviation when he seemed to be the most successful aeronaut in the world, and enter the concrete business?

WHITEHOUSE, ARTHUR G. J.
1895–1979

Whitehouse was a prolific aviation author who based much of his writings on his own experiences. He was born in Northampton, England, but, as a child, emigrated to the United States with his parents. With the advent of World War I he returned to England to enlist in the infantry. In 1916 he answered the call for volunteers to become air gunners. He was that day taken to an airfield and sent up to fire at dummy ground targets. Later, the same day, he flew on his first combat mission and shot down a German plane. All this in less than six hours!

At the war's end he hurried back to the United States to marry his grammar school girlfriend. He never attended high school, but managed to become a sports writer for a newspaper in New Jersey. In 1928 he began to write aviation novels, dipping into his wartime experience for subject matter.

At the outbreak of World War II he served as a correspondent attached to the RCAF. With them, he flew over the Atlantic on anti-submarine patrols. He went to work for the US Writer's Board after America entered the war.

He published hundreds of stories, including over forty novels, though not all of his works were fiction.

WHITTLE, AIR COMMODORE SIR FRANK
1907–

Other than von Ohain (qv), the only real effort to produce a jet engine during the 1930s was the work of a young RAF officer whose government would provide him with neither the funds nor the encouragement to get the job done. Whittle was that officer.

He had joined the RAF in 1923 and while a

Frank Whittle and Hans von Ohain who, as young men, invented the jet engine.

cadet at Cranwell speculated on the possibilities of gas turbine propulsion. In 1928 he wrote his graduating thesis *The Future Developments in Aircraft Design* in which he described how a turbine engine might be built. The paper formed the basis for his first patent which was filed in 1930.

Whittle was now a regular RAF officer whose duties included test piloting many types of aircraft. Therefore, it proved difficult for him to find the time to develop his jet engine idea. Few of his senior officers would listen to him and the Air Ministry considered the idea theoretically impossible. Whittle persevered and in 1932 received some financial backing from private investors and a leave of absence from the RAF. He thought he could have a practical device in just a few years.

Breaking new ground was harder than he had first thought and the first test model was not finished until 1937. Whittle and his investors, now incorporated as Power Jets Ltd, finally achieved success in 1939 with the running of the WU engine. The problems of combustion, metallurgy, and bearing resilience had all been solved. In May, 1941 a Whittle engine powered a Gloster aircraft on the first ever British jet flight.

For several years Whittle continued to refine his engines, but in 1944 left Power Jets when the company was nationalized. Having received

the jet engine from Whittle, Britain abruptly pushed him aside. He left the RAF in 1948 and later emigrated to America where he was an advisor to the oil industry before becoming a professor at the US Naval Academy.

WILKINS, GEORGE HUBERT, MC
1888–1958

Wilkins' life was so full of adventure and action that it seems more like the stuff of a boy's pulp novel than of fact, but it really happened.

Wilkins was born in South Australia, and in the loneliness of the Outback fed his imagination with stories of travel and heroism. At 16 he enrolled in the Adelaide School of Mines and it was here that he began to learn about photography. His passion to become a professional cinematographer drove him to stow away on a ship bound for Africa. He later got to England where he became a professional newsreel man.

He was swept up in the flying craze and in 1910 learned to fly. To out-do his rivals, he would climb atop an aircraft wing and shoot footage as the aircraft performed stunts. This bit of daring caused him to be sent to the Balkan wars as a photographer where he narrowly avoided being shot as a spy. In fact, he was in a line of captives who were being shot one by one, and only at the last moment was he reprieved.

With the advent of the Great War he attempted to join the Australian Flying Corps, but was turned down due to poor eyesight. Undaunted, he got to the Front as a photographer with the Australian Imperial Force in France and while serving in this capacity earned a Military Cross when he took battlefield command of a troop whose officer had been killed.

Prior to the war Wilkins had several experiences exploring Polar regions, and at the war's end redirected his attention to these areas. After two unsuccessful attempts to fly in an aeroplane across the North Pole he triumphed in 1928 with a two-stage flight from Point Barrow, Alaska to Spitzbergen. Close to their goal,

Wilkins' Lockheed Vega was forced down in a snow storm. With his pilot Carl Eielson, Wilkins had to wait five long days for the storm to abate. Even then, his troubles were not over for the Vega was found to be unable to taxi in the snow.

Wilkins got out and began to push while Eielson manned the left seat. Twice, frozen and nearly exhausted, Wilkins managed to assist the Vega enough so that it could taxi. Both times Eielson took off thinking Wilkins had jumped in through the cargo door. Running low on fuel a third attempt was made to free the Vega and get Wilkins on board. The third time was the charm and the two aviators arrived at Point Barrow quickly thereafter.

In 1931 Wilkins attempted his most daring, and prophetic feat. With the token sum of $1 he purchased a surplus US Navy submarine and christened it *Nautilus*. He proposed sailing it under the North Pole. Several attempts to penetrate through the drifting ice were fruitless, and when the rudder gear malfunctioned the mission was called off. It was not until 1958 that the North Pole was crossed by a submarine. In that year, the year of Wilkins' death, a nuclear-powered submarine completed the trans-Polar voyage. It too had been named *Nautilus*.

WILLARD, CHARLES K.
1883–1977
Willard first experimented with engines and aeronautics around the turn of the century. He was a member of the Aeronautical Society, based in New York, when that group purchased a Curtiss aeroplane in 1909. This was the first aircraft purchase in the United States and was made with the stipulation that Curtiss (qv) would teach two of the group's members to fly. Willard became the first person taught to fly by Glenn Curtiss.

Immediately upon learning to fly, and under the auspices of the Aeronautical Society, Willard embarked on a career as a barnstormer – the first in the United States. During one flight he was shot down by a squirrel gun – thus becoming the first pilot in history to be brought down by hostile fire. His credits also include being the first to fly over Los Angeles, and the first to make an exhibition flight in Canada.

Willard was more than just a stunt pilot. He was a serious engineer who led Glenn Martin's (qv) design staff during 1913 and 1914. He spent 1915 with Curtiss as an engineer helping to design flying-boats before joining with partners to found LWF Engineering in 1916. LWF stood for two things. Firstly it was the initials of the founders – Lowe, Willard and Fowler. Secondly, it meant 'laminated wood fuselages', which were the type the company built. In 1916 Willard also joined Aeromarine where he served as Chief Engineer.

WILLIAMS, ALFORD JOSEPH, JR.
1896–1958
Williams was an intensely motivated New Yorker who, after attending Fordham University, became a Major League pitcher for the New York Giants from 1916-17. He left baseball to join the Navy where he learned to fly, becoming an instructor at Pensacola. He went next to Hampton Roads, Virginia to become a test pilot, a role he was born to play. He not only tested planes, he innovated new tactics and manoeuvres in them, including vertical dive-bombing. In 1923, besides winning the Pulitzer Trophy, he set several speed records. He earned a law degree from Georgetown University in 1925, but continued flying for the Navy.

In 1930 he resigned from the Navy to fly promotional aircraft for the Gulf Oil Company. During the 1930s he and his bright orange Curtiss Gulfhawks were well-known aerobatic attractions at airshows all across America. When he had resigned from the Navy, he had taken the rank of a reserve officer in the Marines. In 1940, when he advocated a separate Air Force, he was forced to resign from the Marines. During World War II he performed flying displays as part of a recruiting and morale campaign. After the war Williams retired to farming in North Carolina.

WISE, JOHN
1808–1879

Wise was America's greatest aeronaut. He was born in Pennsylvania where he received only a rudimentary education. In his twenties he began to experiment with balloons, making his first flight in 1835 in Philadelphia. He designed and built his own balloons, even making the rubberizing solution with which he coated the fabric.

After his first balloon ascent, Wise embarked on a career as a professional showman during which he made 440 ascents! As part of his act he would cut away the bottom of his balloon and descend as with a parachute. He invented the rip panel and also was the first to predict that there was a steady easterly current above the United States. In 1843 he tried unsuccessfully to get funding from Congress for a trans-Atlantic balloon voyage. Three years later he proposed to the same body that balloons be used to attack Mexican forces during the siege of Vera Cruz.

Wise's greatest flight was made as a warm-up to a proposed trans-Atlantic flight scheduled for 1859. In July of that year he flew from St Louis to Hendersonville, New York, covering a ground track of an astounding 1,193 miles (1,920km)! It was forty-one years before de La Vaulx (qv) broke the record. The trans-Atlantic flight was never made as it was thought that the balloon would not endure the journey.

Wise promoted himself as a 'Professor', and indeed he had taught himself enough to earn the title. He was much more than a mere showman. His classic book of 1850 entitled *A System of Aeronautics* clearly marks him as a scientist, an historian, and a man of letters. In 1879, while attempting to cross Lake Michigan with a companion, his balloon *Pathfinder* disappeared.

WITTMAN, S. J.
1904–

'Steve' Wittman was born in Byron, Wisconsin and learned to fly in Fond du Lac during 1924. He operated a small flying service until 1927 but also flew as a test pilot for the Pheasant Aircraft Company. In 1931 he moved to Oshkosh to manage that city's airport. That same year he built his first aeroplane, a racer named *Chief Oshkosh*. As this aircraft evolved over the next thirteen years, it was a perennial race winner. It won the Glenn Curtiss Trophy in 1932, the 1933 National Air Race for 350 cubic inch (5.75 litres) engines, and the 1947 and 1949 Goodyear races, by which time its name had been changed to *Buster*.

Wittman's most important aviation accomplishment was the invention of spring steel landing gear, for which he held a patent. Also known as 'Cessna gear', this type of undercarriage greatly simplified construction and allowed training craft to suffer extreme abuse from ham-fisted students. His sleek, yet simple, Tailwind aircraft set new standards in speed for homebuilt aircraft and many were built. During World War II he trained military pilots and after the war was long associated with the Experimental Aircraft Association.

Wilbur Wright, an American hero of classical proportions.

WRIGHT, WILBUR
1867–1912
WRIGHT, ORVILLE
1871–1948

Orville Wright, dressed properly for flight in the pioneering years.

The distinction of being the first men in history to fly a heavier-than-air craft could not have been won by a more deserving team that the brothers Wright. Unlike so many before them, the Wrights had little formal education. Their only financial resource was their bicycle business in Dayton, Ohio. Yet they quietly risked all they owned on the conviction that through patient, hard work they could solve the problem that had eluded some of the greatest minds in history – and they did.

Wilbur first became interested in flight when he read accounts of Lilienthal's (qv) death in 1896. Three years later he wrote to the Smithsonian Institute requesting a bibliography of aeronautical books. One recommendation sent to him was to contact Octave Chanute (qv) which he did. The engineer's advice was crucial to their success. In 1899 they built a biplane kite which they used to test their early theories. For three more years they experimented with gliders, bit by bit piecing together the parts that were necessary for a controllable aircraft. Their 1902 glider was the breakthrough machine. With it they proved their mastery of balance, control and scale. All their gliders had been tested at Kitty Hawk, North Carolina as they had

learned that the site offered that steadiest winds in all of the Untied States.

During 1903 they designed an engine which their loyal mechanic Charley Taylor (qv) built. As important as the engine were the two highly efficient propellers that they also built. These were fitted to a biplane. The whole aircraft was not the result of rule-of-thumb engineering, but of a carefully executed plan that incorporated scientific investigations into aerodynamics, aerofoil shapes, and centre of pressure movements, concepts that were often far beyond most would-be aircraft builders of the day. They even made their own wind tunnel which used bent hack-saw blades for a balance!

In November they shipped the 1903 aircraft to Kitty Hawk by train. Unhurried, without press coverage, without government support of any kind, they assembled the machine and waited for good weather. After a false start on 14 December in which Wilbur caused some slight damage, the machine was made ready again by the 17th. It was Orville's turn to pilot the *Flyer* and with the help of the crew from a nearby life-saving station all was made ready. At 10.35am the *Flyer* lifted off for the first powered, controlled, and sustained flight in history. It lasted a full twelve seconds (twelve seconds is not as brief as might be casually imagined – count it!). Three more flights were made that day, the longest covering 852 feet (260m).

When they announced their success to the world, few listened. Professor Langley's (qv) failures had so jaded public thinking that the Wrights' efforts were seen as yet another farce. For the next several years the Wrights tried to sell their plane to the Army. The Army refused to believe that an actual flight had been made, thinking instead that the Wrights simply wanted grant money. Doubted, weary, and depressed, the brothers abandoned flying in 1905 after building new planes capable of long flights.

In 1908 they tried again, this time taking the world by storm with public flights in both America and Europe. In Europe, Wilbur showed the French that America was indeed the home of the first flight. His flights near Le Mans stunned the Europeans present. Finally, he and his brother began to receive the credit they rightfully deserved.

Their influence on aviation was, of course, profound. Even Santos-Dumont's (qv) 14bis was shaped by the Wright *Flyer's* layout – via Chanute and Ferber (qv). Voisin (qv) came into contact with the Wrights' ideas through the Archdeacon (qv) Wright-type glider of 1904.

Wilbur died of typhoid fever in 1912, and Orville sold his manufacturing and patent rights in 1915. The most remarkable aspect of their accomplishment was that they did it mostly on their own, with no government support, succeeding through hard work and dedication.

YAKOVLEV, ALEXANDER SERGEYEVICH
1906–1989

Born in Moscow, Yakovlev was an ambitious young man who found the funds to build his first glider in 1923 when he raised a public subscription amongst school children. Eight years later he graduated from the Zhukovski Air Academy as one of Tupolev's (qv) star pupils. His career really took off during the mid-1930s when Stalin considered him one of the few designers he could 'trust'. The Yak-1 fighter established his design bureau as one of the leaders while the Yak-9 became the most produced fighter in Soviet history.

Following the war Yakovlev and his team designed many types of aircraft including helicopters, jet fighters, transports, and VTOL aircraft.

YEAGER, MAJOR CHARLES ELWOOD
1923–

Born in West Virginia, 'Chuck' Yeager joined the Air Corps after graduating from high school in 1941. In November, 1943 he was assigned to the 357th Fighter Group in England. While flying a Mustang he shot down thirteen German aircraft including one Me-262. He was himself shot down once, but evaded capture with the help of the French underground.

In 1947, while serving as a test pilot, he volunteered to join the X-1 sonic aircraft project

Chuck Yeager, who wouldn't let broken ribs keep him from breaking the sound barrier.

located at Rogers Dry Lake in California. On 14 October, 1947 he made history when he flew the X-1 rocket plane through the sound barrier, achieving a speed of Mach 1.15. It was the world's first supersonic flight. In 1953 he set another speed record, 1650 mph (2,655km/hr), while flying the X-1A.

He continued in service with the military after this flight, and later commanded fighter units. He was also associated with the astronaut training programme.

YOST, PAUL EDWARD
1919–

Ed Yost was at various times an inventor, airline pilot and scientist. He began to fly airplanes in 1939, but in the 1950s designed a way to reheat the bag of a hot air balloon using a propane burner. His invention sparked the hot air balloon renaissance of the next two decades.

Having established himself as a balloon manufacturer in Sioux Falls, South Dakota, he attempted in 1976 to make a trans-Atlantic flight in a helium balloon. Lifting off from Maine he drifted 2,500 miles (4,023km), setting a world's record, before he force-landed just 750 miles (1,207km) short of his goal.

It was in a Yost balloon that Abruzzo, Anderson and Newman (qqv) finally conquered the Atlantic in 1978.

ZAHM, DR ALBERT FRANCIS
1862–1954

Zahm was one of the best educated of America's early aeroplane experimenters. Born in Ohio, he received degrees from Notre Dame, Cornell, and Johns Hopkins Universities. During his college career he had experimented with models and full-size craft, and upon becoming a professor at Catholic University he built a wind tunnel to test aerodynamic resistance on different shapes.

In 1898 he witnessed Herring's (qv) experiments with a powered craft in Michigan, and that same year proposed the use of ailerons in a paper delivered to the Third International Conference on Aerial Navigation. In 1911 he published *Aerial Navigation*, a serious look at the history of aeronautics and the science underlying its development. The next year he proposed the formation of a national aeronautics laboratory. This suggestion eventually led to the creation of NACA in 1915.

Zahm at different times served as the director of the Navy's aerodynamic laboratory at the Washington Navy Yard, as an advisor to Glenn Curtiss (qv), and as holder of the Guggenheim Chair of Aeronautics at the Library of Congress. In that capacity he brought several important aviation history collections to the Library including the famous Tissandier (qv) collection of aerostatic memorabilia.

von ZEPPELIN, COUNT FERDINAND ADOLF AUGUST HEINRICH
1838–1917

Born into a wealthy, aristocratic family in Württemberg, Germany, von Zeppelin chose a career in the Army. Not long after becoming an officer he travelled to the United States to observe the Civil War. There he met a balloonist who described Thaddeus Lowe's (qv) work with military balloons. This discussion began von Zeppelin's interest in aeronautics. During his time in America, von Zeppelin met President Lincoln in the White House and later journeyed up through Minnesota and Wisconsin by canoe.

After serving with distinction in the Franco-Prussian War, he turned his thoughts to solving the problems of dirigibility, fearing that the French were pulling ahead in this field. By 1893 he had designed his first airship which he built after collecting funds through a public subscription. It was built mainly of zinc and aluminium girders and equipped with two fifteen horsepower (11kw) engines. Though huge, 420 feet (128m) long, it was well designed. Its first flight on 2 July 1900 was less than the grand success hoped for, but over the next fourteen years Zeppelin dirigibles were progressively refined until they became an instrument of war.

Von Zeppelin himself was an able airship pilot, even into his seventies. After a Zeppelin exploded killing twenty-eight men in 1915, he became embroiled in a policy dispute with the Naval Office which resulted in him turning his back on his own creation.

Ferdinand von Zeppelin, who was inspired by witnessing American aeronauts in the Civil War.